WHERE TO RIDE

—1999—

A Guide to BHS-Approved Establishments

BHS
08701 202244

BSJA

(024) 7669 6685

0247669 8 800

Shelley Ashman Int

0044 1884 849 008

Sheila

KENILWORTH PRESS

in association with The British Horse Society

Produced for the British Horse Society by
The Kenilworth Press Ltd
Addington, Buckingham, MK18 2JR

ISBN 1-872119-10-7
British Library Cataloguing in Publication Data
A catalogue record for this book is available
from the British Library

Design by Sandie Boccacci
Set in 9/9.5 Helvetica
Typeset by Kenilworth Press
Printed and bound in Great Britain by
Hillman Printers (Frome) Ltd

CONTENTS

BHS-APPROVED
ESTABLISHMENTS

RIDING IN THE NORTH 19

RIDING IN YORKSHIRE 26

RIDING IN THE
NORTH WEST 37

RIDING IN THE
EAST MIDLANDS 45

5

What is the British Horse Society?

The British Horse Society is a charity to promote the welfare, care and use of the horse and pony; to encourage horsemastership and the improvement of horse management and breeding; to represent all equine interests.

The Society is internationally recognised as the premier equestrian riding, training and examination organisation in the United Kingdom, and operates an Approvals scheme for all types of equestrian establishment. It incorporates some 395 Riding Clubs and works closely with the Pony Club. The Society is also the governing national body for recreational riding and fully supports the independent sporting disciplines within the British Equestrian Federation.

The BHS plays a major role in equine welfare, safety, provision of access to the countryside, and protection of riding and driving Rights of Way. It represents riders to Government and to the EU in Brussels in all matters, especially those concerning taxation, rates, planning and the law.

Membership benefits include £5 million public liability insurance, personal accident insurance, a yearbook, magazines, special facilities and discounts at BHS functions, and access to BHS advice and support.

On the 30th September 1998 the BHS had approximately 40,000 members. In addition, Affiliated Riding Clubs represented approximately 40,000 members.

By joining the Society you are helping all who ride. For further information and membership details write to: The British Horse Society, Stoneleigh Deer Park, Kenilworth, Warwickshire, CV8 2XZ, phone 01926 707 700.

The BHS Approval Scheme and How it Works

For over thirty years the British Horse Society has been running a scheme for the approval of riding schools and other equine establishments throughout the British Isles. The BHS Approval Scheme is also now available outside the UK.

The basis on which approval is granted is that the establishment offers sound instruction in riding and horsemastership, and its premises, facilities, safety equipment, and animals are properly looked after.

Any riding establishment in Britain that offers instruction in riding, at whatever level, or provides riding on horses and/or ponies that are its property, requires a Local Authority Licence. This is required by the Riding Establishments Acts of 1964 and 1970, the Welfare of Animals Act (N.I.) 1972 (in Northern Ireland), and the Isle of Man Riding Establishment (Inspection) Acts 1968-1986. No BHS Approval can be granted unless such a licence is held. The only exception to this rule is in the case of training establishments which offer sound instruction and facilities, but which do not have horses for hire. The BHS is the only national organisation operating throughout the UK that regularly inspects its schools on an unannounced basis.

The BHS Approval Scheme has over 700 Approved Establishments. Each application for inclusion in the scheme is formally considered by the Riding Schools and Recreational Riding Committee of the British Horse Society after an initial visit by one of the Society's inspectors. Thereafter, it is re-considered after periodic visiting or after the investigation of a complaint.

Approval is withheld from establishments which allow clients to ride without hats or which provide hats which are not of a current standard as recommended by BHS policy.

The aims of the scheme

Through the administration of this Approval Scheme, the BHS hopes to provide members of the public with reliable information as to where, in the opinion of the Society, good riding can be obtained, together with an accurate description of the facilities on offer at any Approved centre.

By visiting and inspecting riding establishments, and providing an advisory service for their proprietors, the Society hopes to assist in raising the standard of riding instruction, horsemastership and horsemanship.

For their part, the proprietors are given publicity for their business through the medium of *Where to Ride* and the equestrian press, plus advantageous rates for public liability insurance.

Where to Train

Those Approved Establishments which are approved to train career students and competition riders are also shown in *Where to Train* and are classified in one of the following groups:

Instruction in riding and jumping, students to BHSAI
Instruction in riding and jumping, students to BHSII
Instruction in riding and jumping, students to BHSI
Instruction in riding and jumping, students to all BHS exams including FBHS Specialist, e.g. competition riding

Why Choose a BHS-Approved Establishment?

Whatever your reason for seeking out a riding centre – be it for a pleasant hour's hacking, or training up to advanced level – you will want to choose an establishment that is both reputable and well run.

By selecting one of the establishments listed in *Where to Ride* and *Where to Train*, you will not only be able to satisfy yourself on that point, but you will also be able to discover a good deal about the centre before you pick up the telephone to discuss your ride.

Each of the establishments listed in *Where to Ride* and *Where to Train* has been inspected by a fully qualified representative of the British Horse Society, who will have looked carefully at the level of instruction available to clients, the on-site facilities and equipment, and the standards of safety, horse care and management.

A riding centre will not be approved by the BHS unless it has a Local Authority Licence. As a general rule, *every* riding establishment is supposed to have a Local Authority Licence; without this licence it will not have proper third party insurance cover. To hold such a licence, granted annually, the establishment will have been inspected by a council representative who will have been concerned primarily with riders' safety and the welfare of the animals being used. Unlike the BHS inspector, the council inspector will *not* have assessed the standard of the instructors or whether the horses are well-schooled and forward-going.

It is also reassuring to know that at an Approved establishment you will not be allowed to ride without the correct protective head gear. An Approved centre will be able to supply you with an appropriate hard hat if you do not already possess one of the correct standard. And newcomers to riding can expect to be offered helpful advice on what to wear so that their first lessons are safe and enjoyable.

Another advantage is that many BHS-Approved establishments run the BHS Progressive Riding Tests, a scheme of instruction and assessment designed for riders of all ages and abilities. Further details of these tests – which can be administered only by an Approved centre – will be available from your chosen BHS Approved centre.

The staff at the **RIDING SCHOOLS OFFICE** are available to answer any queries during normal working hours, whether you want to know more about the Society's system of approving riding establishments, about an individual Approved Establishment or just have a general enquiry about finding your nearest Approved Centre. The staff at Stoneleigh are:

Robert Jones – Executive Officer for Riding Schools and Recreational Riding
Janet Lovick – Approvals Assistant
Christine Doran – Approvals Assistant

We are always pleased to deal with any enquiries. Please do not hesitate to contact us on 01926 707 700.)

Riding Holidays

The establishments listed in *Where to Ride* include many which offer a variety of activities for those wishing to spend their holidays riding or learning more about horses.

Riding Courses give riders the chance for more rapid learning, with the opportunity to ride more than once a day under the skillful eye of a qualified instructor. By choosing a BHS-Approved establishment offering specialised courses it is possible to feel confident that the level of tuition will be appropriate and that the horses will be well schooled. Some centres will allow you to take your own horse for training, which means that you can learn and improve together.

An afternoon's **trekking** in beautiful countryside or along the coastline is the dream of many weekend and urban riders. This sort of ride can be easily arranged – and possibly fitted into a weekend break or as part of a longer holiday. The regional organisation of the entries in *Where to Ride* enables you to identify quickly the centres in your chosen location and for a dream to become a reality.

Trekking ponies are usually sure-footed animals that are sturdy and safe, but be sure to tell the riding centre about your own level of riding so that you can be matched to an appropriate horse or pony. Treks can vary in length from an hour or two up to a full day's ride, and are a marvellous way to explore the more scenic areas of Britain.

Trail riding holidays, often covering quite long distances with organised stopping points for picnics and overnight rests, can give the more adventurous and experienced rider an exhilarating holiday that will be hard to beat.

Trail riding horses are usually pretty fit and capable of maintaining a fast pace over a variety of terrain. In order to enjoy this type of riding, you will need to be fairly experienced and reasonably fit yourself, so never be tempted to exaggerate your riding ability when booking such a holiday. Day trails, weekend trails and five-day trails are all options for consideration.

Some centres offer the pony-mad youngster a chance to **'own a pony'** for a week. Here, a child can be given responsibility, under supervision, for a pony's grooming, mucking-out, feeding and exercise, and thereby can experience the joys – and hard work – that pony ownership entails. Many of these holidays are for unaccompanied children, giving parents and children an enjoyable break. As stated elsewhere, all the centres included in *Where to Ride* have been inspected and approved by the British Horse Society, but it makes sense to discuss at length your child's requirements and the amount of supervision that will be on hand. The proprietors of all the riding holiday establishments listed here will be happy to talk to you about such matters and show you around the centre if you prefer to visit.

BHS Riding Schools Competition

The **BHS Riding Schools Competition** was launched in the Autumn of 1997, thanks to the support of a major educational trust, with sponsorship for an initial three-year period.

The competition is aimed at young clients at BHS Approved riding schools, who are often either denied the chance to compete, or are put at a disadvantage, because they are not horse owners. Competitors must be under 17 years (there are at present three classes: 16 years & under, 13 years & under, and 10 years & under), and they compete on bona fide riding school horses and ponies.

The purpose of the competition is to broaden the base of effective and confident young riders, to encourage quality professional instruction, to offfer non-horse owners competition experience, and to benefit the welfare of the horse by encouraging correct riding.

The competition is run in two parts. A flat or dressage test is ridden first with a commander, followed by a simple jumping test. The competitor is judged on style and effectiveness in dealing with the particular horse or pony they ride, and the competition is based on the very successful equitation competitions run in South Africa and the USA.

Very generous prizes are available at both regional competitions and at the national finals, for competitors and their instructors.

'TREC'

For the past 25 years a competitive discipline linked to equestrian tourism has been growing in popularity on the Continent. The discipline has its roots in France, and began as a means to help professional equestrian guides develop their skills. Equestrian tourists soon demanded to join in and the sport of TREC (Techniques de Randonnée Equestre de Competition) was born.

In 1996, the 12th Annual European Championships was held in Barcelona, run under the auspices of the international governing body, the Fédération International de Tourism Equestre (FITE). In 1997, the first World Championships took place at St Pierre d'Albigny in the French Alps, with teams from three continents taking part.

A team of 6 riders represented Great Britain at these Championships, finishing in a very creditable seventh place. One of the team took the individual World title in one of the three phases of the competition, an outstanding achievement on horses borrowed from the French organisers only three days before the competition began.

The competition is designed to test an individual's ability to deal with anything they may encounter as an equestrian tourist whilst riding alone in the countryside. The first and most important phase involves map-reading on horseback (very much along the lines of competitive orienteering), the second phase is a simple test demonstrating the rider's ability to influence the horse in canter and walk, and the final phase takes place around a cross-country course which includes tests involving jumping, crossing water, opening gates and dealing with some problems whilst dismounted. Great emphasis is placed on safety, care of the horse and the flexibility of both horse and rider throughout the competition.

The BHS are looking to encourage the develpoment of this sport in Great Britain during 1998 through the network of BHS-Approved Riding Establishments. The sport is designed to appeal directly to those for whom riding is an enjoyable and relaxing recreation, and is just as accessible to non-horse owners as it is to those who have their own horses.

More information can be obtained from the BHS RS&RR Office.

An Outline of the BHS Examinations and Professional Instructors' Services

The British Horse society administers an examination system designed to meet the requirements of the riding instructor, yard management, riding holiday sector, and those who wish to further their knowledge in riding, stable management and horse care. It holds these examinations – aimed primarily at career students – at BHS-Approved centres throughout the British Isles and overseas.

Before embarking on a career with horses it is important to select carefully the place of training. Whilst it is not obligatory for candidates to receive their training at a BHS-Approved centre, it is certainly advisable to do so. Details of approved BHS Training Centres can be found in the publication **Where to Train** available from the RS&RR Office, British Horse Society, Stoneleigh Deer Park, Kenilworth, Warwickshire, CV8 2XZ – price £5.50 including p&p.

Examinations are taken at officially appointed BHS Approved centres throughout the UK and overseas.

Candidates for all examinations must be **Gold** members of the BHS **at time of application** and **on the day of their examination**.

FIRST STAGE: The minimum age for entry is 16 years. The candidate must understand the basic principles of horse care and, working under supervision, must show some knowledge and practice of looking after a well-mannered horse in the stable or at grass. He/she must be capable of riding a quiet, experienced horse or pony in an enclosed space.

SECOND STAGE: Before entering the Riding section of this examination the candidate must have passed the **BHS RIDING AND ROAD SAFETY TEST**. The candidate must understand the general management and requirement of horses for their health and well being. Working under regular but not constant supervision, the candidates should be able to carry out the care of a stabled and grass kept horse during all seasons of the year. The candidate must be capable of riding a quiet, experienced horse or pony in the countryside and on the public highway, as well as in a manege.

THIRD STAGE: The minimum age for entry is 17 years. The candidate must show an ability to look after up to 4 horses under a variety of circumstances. He/she should be tactful, yet effective, understanding the reasons for his/her actions, both in horse care and while riding. A written test is also included in the examination. A candidate taking just the H K & Care section (Groom's Certificate) at this stage is expected to be a competent enough rider to be able to take horses on ride-and-lead exercises.

THE BHS PRELIMINARY TEACHING TEST: The minimum age for entry is 17 $^1/_2$ years. Candidates under the age of 18 years are required to hold four GCSEs, Grades A, B or C, one subject of which must be English Language or Literature. Candidates are examined in their ability to give instruction in basic subjects. In order to enter the Preliminary Teaching Test a candidate must have passed the H K & R Stage II examination.

BHS PRELIMINARY TEACHER (BHSPTC): This is the first certificate on the instructor's ladder and is awarded to those passing the Horse Knowledge and Riding Stage III and the Preliminary Teaching Test. This certificate qualifies the holder at a 'Trainee Teacher' level. The candidate then needs to log 500 hours of teaching experience (25% of which may be Stable Management teaching). Once the 500 hours have been completed the Log Book (which is despatched with the BHSPT Certificate from the office) is returned to the BHS, together with a copy of a current Health & Safety Executive First Aid at Work certificate, where random checks are made. Mature candidates (over 25 years) with extensive experience of teaching in the industry may apply for exemption from the requirement of 500 hours (information sheet available from the Examinations Office). The candidate is then awarded a BHSAI certificate.

BHS ASSISTANT INSTRUCTOR'S CERTIFICATE (BHSAI): Candidates holding the Certificate of Horsemastership (pre-1986) and passing the Preliminary Teaching Test will become BHSPTC (unless they can prove extensive experience – see BHSPTC).

FOURTH STAGE: The minimum age for entry is 20 years. The candidate must be capable of taking sole charge of a group of horses of various types in stables and at grass. He/she must be an educated rider capable of training and improving horses in their work on the flat and over fences. Candidates passing the H K & Care section will be awarded the Intermediate Stable Manager's Certificate.

THE BHS INTERMEDIATE TEACHING EXAMINATION: The minimum age for entry is 20 years. This is open to candidates who hold the Assistant Instructor's Certificate. Candidates are examined on their general teaching abilities relating to class rides; individual dressage and jumping lessons; lunge lessons and general discussion, talks and short lectures.

THE INTERMEDIATE INSTRUCTOR'S CERTIFICATE: This is achieved by passing the Intermediate Teaching Examination and the complete H K & R Stage IV examination. Candidates are also required to hold a full Health & Safety Executive First Aid at Work certificate.

THE BHS INSTRUCTOR'S CERTIFICATE: The minimum age for entry is 22 years. Candidates must hold the Intermediate Instructor's Certificate. The Instructor's Certificate is obtained by passing the two following two examinations:

a) **THE BHS STABLE MANAGER'S EXAMINATION:** This is also an examination in its own right and candidates need not necessarily go on to complete the full Instructor's Examination by taking b) below. The entry requirement for this examination is the Intermediate Stable Manager's Certificate (H K & C Stage IV). The minimum age for entry is 22 years.

b) **THE BHS EQUITATION AND TEACHING EXAMINATION:** On passing this examination, the candidate completes the full BHS Instructor's Certificate. The entry requirements are the Intermediate Instructor's Certificate and the BHS Stable Manager's Certificate.

THE BHS FELLOWSHIP EXAMINATION: The BHS Fellowship Certificate is the senior qualification. **The minimum age for entry is 25 years.** The candidate must show a depth of knowledge and effectiveness in all aspects of equitation and horsemanship; proving themselves to be persons to whom others can turn for advice in the various spheres of equestrian activities. The Fellowship is available in five formats to assist those who have followed specific discipline routes or those who have reached a high overall level of ability.

In addition, the British Horse Society is an awarding body for **Scottish and National Vocational Qualifications (S/NVQs)** in the Horse Industry. Full details on request.

The present structure of the BHS examination system is shown below. If you wish to find out more about the syllabi and requirements of the different exams, you should contact the Examinations Office, The British Horse Society, Stoneleigh Deer Park, Kenilworth, Warwickshire, CV8 2XZ, phone 01926 707 700.

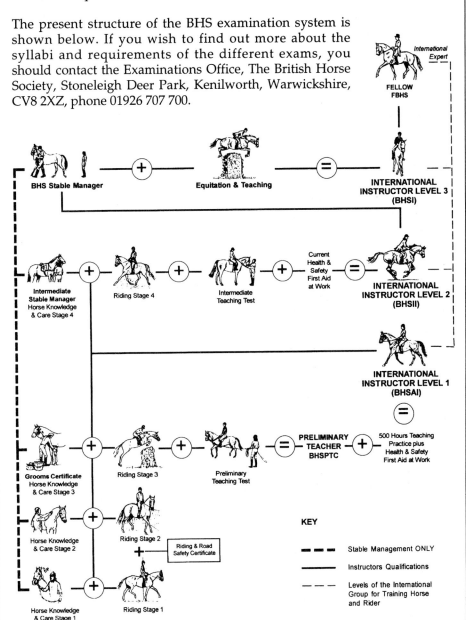

13

The BHS Register of Instructors

The BHS, as the governing body of recreational riding in the UK, maintains a register of those qualified to teach riding, both competitively and in the leisure industry.

There is a two-fold need to register. The Single European Market is evolving a compilation of national registers, and the BHS has set up this Register before there is a legal requirement to do so. You will also be aware that there is an increasing number of unqualified people who are professing to hold BHS qualifications. The level of inquiries to the Examinations Office regarding this problem necessitated the formation of the Register. It is patently unfair to those who hold genuine qualifications and the general public that this situation should be allowed to continue. The Register also includes those top level trainers who wish to be included and have been recommended by their discipline committee. From 1st January 1994 all registered instructors have been required to hold a full **Health & Safety Executive First Aid at Work Certificate** (or equivalent for overseas). All First Aid Certificates and BHS membership must be kept up to date. (If you are unsure of the First Aid Certificate required, please contact us.)

The Society is urging the public not to use instructors who profess to hold BHS qualification but who are not registered. The minimum qualification required for application to the Register of Instructors is the BHS Preliminary Teacher. Those listed under this heading are working towards the required 500 hours in order to gain the BHSAI Certificate. The BHS will support those on the Register, copies of which are circulated to County/District Councils and to Main Libraries throughout the country. County or Regional lists are available to the general public, who can be confident that:

a) The Instructor is qualified to the level stated

b) The Instructor holds a current First Aid Certificate

c) The Instructor is up-to-date in teaching method and content

d) The Instructor holds Public Liability insurance to teach anywhere in the UK or Ireland, for a minimum of £5,000,000. Those Instructors <u>who live and work outside the UK and Republic of Ireland</u> are exempted from the isurance requirement. However, we would strongly recommend those Instructors overseas to ensure they carry adequate liability insurance cover.

All other registered instructors will be part of the Group Insurance scheme. This is a Group Insurance Policy negotiated by the BHS and arranged by NASC (National Association of Sports Coaches). Details and joining forms from: The Examinations Office, The British Horse Society, Stoneleigh Deer Park, Kenilworth, Warwickshire, CV8 2XZ, phone 01926 707 700.

BHS Examination Centres

The North
Houghall College, Durham
New Moors Training Centre, Bishop Auckland

Yorkshire
Acrecliffe Riding School, Otley
Bishop Burton College of Agriculture, Beverley
Longfield Equestrian Centre, Todmorden
Snainton Riding Centre, Scarborough
Yorkshire Riding Centre, Markington

The North West
Bold Heath Equestrian Centre, Widnes
Eccleston Equestrian Centre, Chorley
Longacres Riding School, Lydiate
Myerscough College, Bilsborrow, Preston
Wrea Green Equitation Centre, Wrea Green

The East Midlands
Birchwood Riding Centre, Somercotes, Derby
Brackenhurst College of Agriculture, Southwell
Brampton Stables, Northampton
Brooksby College, Melton Mowbray
De Montfort University, Caythorpe, Grantham
Elvaston Castle Riding Centre, Derby
Hill House Riding School, Market Rasen
Moulton College, Northampton
Thorpe Grange Equestrian Centre, Lincoln
Wellow Park Stables, Newark

The West Midlands
Berriewood Farm, Shrewsbury
Endon Riding School, Stoke-on-Trent
Ingestre Stables, Ingestre
Pittern Hill Stables, Kineton
Prescott Riding Centre, Shrewsbury
The Mounts Equitation Centre, Kidderminster
Tong Riding Centre, Tong, Shifnal
Warwickshire College of Agriculture, Warwick
Waverley Riding School, Leamington Spa
Walford College, Baschurch

Eastern
The College of West Anglia, Milton
Newton Hall Equitation Centre, Ipswich
Patchetts Equestrian Centre, Watford

Poplar Park Equestrian Centre, Woodbridge
Rayne Riding Centre, Braintree
Writtle College, Chelmsford

Greater London
Lee Valley Riding School, Leyton
Suzanne's Riding School, Harrow Weald
Trent Park Equestrian Centre, Southgate

The South East
Bedgebury Park Riding Centre, Cranbrook
Berkshire College, Maidenhead
Brinsbury College of Agriculture, Pulborough
Ditchling Common Stud, Burgess Hill
Kingston Riding Centre, Kingston-on-Thames
Limes Farm Equestrian Centre, Hawkinge
Nelson Park Riding Centre, Birchington
Orchard Cottage Riding Stables, Tadworth
Plumpton Agricultural College, Lewes
Wildwoods Riding Centre, Tadworth
Wishanger Equestrian Centre, Churt

The South
Loughton Manor Equestrian Centre, Milton Keynes
Naval Riding Centre, Fareham
Rycroft School of Equitation, Eversley
Wellington Riding Ltd, Basingstoke

The South West
Bicton College of Agriculture, Budleigh Salterton
Cannington College, Bridgwater
Duchy College of Agriculture, Callington
Fortune Centre, Christchurch
Hartpury College, Hartpury
Huntley School of Equitation, Huntley
Lackham College, Chippenham
RAC Saddle Club, Dorset
Stonar School, Melksham
Summerhouse Equitation Centre, Hardwicke
Talland School of Equitation, Cirencester
Urchinwood Manor Equitation Centre, Bristol

Scotland
Gleneagles Mark Phillips Equestrian Centre, Perth
Hayfield Eequestrian Centre, Aberdeen
Oatridge Agricultural College, Broxburn

Wales
Bowling Riding School, Haverfordwest, Pembroke
Clyn-Du Riding Centre, Llanelli
The Equestrian Centre, Hope, Wrexham
Pencoed College, Bridgend
South Wales Equestrian Centre, Bridgend

Ireland
Brennanstown Riding School, Co Wicklow
Calliaghstown Riding School, Rathcoole, Co Dublin
Grennan College, Co Kilkenny

Overseas
Grand Cypress Equestrian Center, Orlando, USA
Millbrook Equestrian Center, Millbrook, NY, USA
The Hong Kong Jockey Club, Hong Hong
Centro Ecuestre Epona, Sevilla, Spain
Manas de la Hoz, Cantabria, Spain

British Equestrian Tourism Examination Centres
Ayrshire Equitation Centre, Ayr
Rhiwiau Riding Centre, Gwinedd
Wynlass Beck Stables, Windermere, Cumbria

Key to Abbreviations

Adv	Advanced	GR	Grade
CC	Cross-Country	HT	Horse Trials
Chng	Changing	Inst	Instruction
CT	Combined training	Int	Intermediate
Db	Double	Lec Rm	Lecture Room
Dor	Dormitory	Med	Medium
DRESS	Dressage	S	Single
DIY	'Do it Yourself'	SC	Self-catering
El	Elementary	SJ	Show jumper/ Show-jumping
Ev	Evening		
FB	Full board	Tw	Twin
fl lt	Floodlit	Vis Aids	Visual aids
gly	Gallery	WP	Working pupils

17

Using the Listings

The list of Approved establishments which follows is divided into regional areas for easy reference, and provides a detailed profile of each of the centres featured. Simply by studying the listings, you can find out, for example:

◆ How many horses or ponies a centre has
◆ The level of instruction on offer
◆ How many qualified staff are employed
◆ The type of riding it specialises in – e.g. hacking, dressage, show jumping, cross-country etc.
◆ What facilities the centre has
◆ Whether evening classes are available

In addition to the full address and telephone number, basic directions to the location are given.

Standard of Horses

Levels of Schooling for Horse Trials, Dressage and Show Jumping are:

Advanced (A), Grade A (A)
Intermediate (I), Grade B (B)
Elementary (E)
Novice (N), Grade C (C)

General-purpose riding school horses and ponies are animals which are trained to a sufficient standard to enable instruction to be given in riding and jumping and are safe and tractable mounts for hacking out and pleasure riding.

Definitions used in *Where to Ride*

Riding Establishment

A Riding School which offers instruction in riding and horsemastership, at what ever level, on horses and ponies that are the property of that Establishment.

Training Centre

This covers centres which offer the full range of vocational training. It also covers an establishment without horses or ponies of its own for hire, that is fully equipped and capable of giving specialist instruction and training in equitation.

Livery Yard

An Establishment which offers adequate facilities for the accommodation and care of horses and ponies. Such service can be on Full, Part or DIY basis.

Trekking Centre

An Establishment which offers for hire, horses, and/or ponies for conducted tours. Such centres are normally situated in area of Outstanding Natural Beauty.

Stud

An Establishment specialising in the breeding of horses and/or ponies and training students in the branch of husbandry.

Riding in the North

CLEVELAND ◆ CUMBRIA ◆ DURHAM
NORTHUMBERLAND

CLEVELAND

ESTON EQUITATION CENTRE
Jubilee Road, Eston,
Cleveland, TS6 9HA
Tel 01642 452260
Contact Mr & Mrs J & E Thomson
Riding School Inst Riding & Jumping
Staff Chief Instructor Mrs E Thomson
(BHSII)
Plus 1 full time instructor
Ave No 14 Horses, 11 Ponies
inc 2 El Dress
Courses WP, YT, Short, Hol
Facilities
Covered School 20 x 40
Outdoor Manege 20 x 40
SJ: Nov, 1 Paddock
Hacking
Livery Full, Break, School
Schooling General, to Nov Dress, to
El Dress
Accom Dor
Exclusions Wt Limit, 14st, Age Limit, 7
Location Off A174, 1/2 mile south of
Eston

FORD CLOSE RIDING CENTRE
Brass Castle Lane, Marton,
Middlesborough,
Cleveland, TS8 9EE
Tel 01642 300257
Contact Miss S Ritchie
Riding School, Training Centre Inst
to BHSI
Specialities Career training
Staff Chief Instructor Miss S Ritchie
(BHSI)
Plus 1 full time instructor
Ave No 6 Horses, 6 Ponies
inc 2 El Dress, 2 Med Dress, 1 Adv
Dress, 2 SJ GR C, 1 HT Adv
Courses WP, Short, P/T
Facilities
Covered School 20 x 40

Outdoor Manege 21 x 50 fl lt
SJ: Nov, Grade C, 1 Paddock
CC: Course, Basic, Nov, Banks, Water,
Natural
Lec Rm, Vis Aids, Chng Rm, Wait Rm
Schooling General, to Nov Dress, to
Adv Dress, to SJ GR C, to HT Adv
Exclusions Wt Limit, 12st, Age Limit, 5
Location East of A172, 5 miles south of
Middlesborough

KIRKLEVINGTON RIDING SCHOOL
Town End Farm, Forest Lane,
Kirklevington, Yarm,
Cleveland, TS15 9LX
Tel 01642 780756
Contact Mrs & Miss Tate
Riding School Inst Riding & Jumping
Staff Chief Instructor Miss J Tate
(BHSAI)
Plus 1 full time instructor
Ave No 4 Horses, 11 Ponies
Courses WP
Facilities
Outdoor Manege 50 x 40 fl lt
SJ: Nov
CC: Course, Nov, Gallops
Lec Rm, Vis Aids, Wait Rm
Hacking
Livery Full, P/T, Break, School, Hunt
Schooling General, Break, to Nov
Dress, to SJ GR C, to HT Nov
Exclusions Wt Limit, 12st, Age Limit, 3,
No unaccompanied hacks/rides
Location Kirklevington village, off A67 2
miles south of Yarm,1 mile north of A19

STAINSBY GRANGE RIDING CENTRE
Thornaby, Cleveland,
TS17 9AB
Tel 01642 762233
Contact Mr & Mrs P Allen
Riding School, Facility Centre Inst
Basic
Specialities Specialise in Show Jumping

for riders with own horses
3 full time instructors
Ave No 4 Horses, 14 Ponies
inc 4 SJ GR C, 1 SJ GR B
Courses YT, Short, Ev, Hol
Facilities
Covered School 55 x 24 gly
Covered School 20 x 60
SJ: Grade A, 1 Paddock
CC: Banks
Lec Rm, Vis Aids, Showers, Wait Rm
Livery Full, P/T, DIY, Break, School,
Grass
Schooling General, Break, to SJ GR
C, to SJ GR B, to SJ GR A, to HT Nov
Accom FB
Exclusions Wt Limit, 15st, Age Limit, 5
Location At Jn of A19/A1130, 3 miles
west of Middlesborough

CUMBRIA

ARMATHWAITE HALL
EQUESTRIAN CENTRE
Coalbeck Farm, Bassenthwaite,
Keswick, Cumbria, CA12 4RD
Tel 01768 776949
Contact Mr Charles J Graves
Riding School, Facility Centre Inst
Riding & Jumping
Staff Chief Instructor Mr Frank Hewett-
Smith
Plus 3 full time instructors
Ave No 22 Horses, 7 Ponies
inc 1 El Dress, 4 Horse Trials Novice
Facilities
Outdoor Manege 60 x 40 fl lt
SJ: Grade C, Grade B, Grade A
CC: Course, Basic, Nov
Lec Rm, Vis Aids, Chng Rm, Wait Rm,
Tack Shop
Hacking
Livery Full, P/T, Break, School, Grass
Schooling General, Break, to Nov
Dress
Accom S, Tw, Db, F, FB, SC
Exclusions Wt Limit, 17st, Age Limit, 4
Location 1/2 mile west of A591 at
Castle Inn

BIRKBY COTTAGE STABLES
Birkby Hall Cottage, Cartmel,
Grange Over Sands,
Cumbria, LA11 7NP
Tel 015395 36319
Contact Mrs J Rogers BHSI
**Riding School, Training Centre, Side
Saddle/Driving Instruction - comp
Dressage** Inst Riding & Jumping

Specialities Pony club, Road safety
centre
Staff Chief Instructor Mrs J Rogers
(BHSI)
Ave No 10 Horses, 6 Ponies
inc 2 El Dress, 1 SJ GR C
Courses WP, YT, Short, Ev, P/T, Hol
Facilities
Covered School 36 x 24
Hacking
Livery Full, School
Schooling General, to El Dress, to
Med Dress, to SJ GR C
Exclusions Age Limit, 5
Location 1 1/2 miles south of Cartmel

BLACKDYKE FARM RIDING CENTRE
Blackford, Carlisle,
Cumbria, CA6 4EY
Tel 01228 74633
Contact Mr & Mrs J I Collier
Riding School, Facility Centre Inst
Riding & Jumping
Staff Chief Instructor Mrs A Collier
(BHSII)
Plus 5 full time instructors
Ave No 15 Horses, 15 Ponies
inc 4 El Dress, 2 SJ GR C
Courses WP, YT, Short
Facilities
Covered School 51 x 24 gly
Covered School 37 x 24
SJ: Nov, Grade C, Grade B, 1 Paddock
CC: Course, Basic, Nov, Banks, Water,
Natural
Lec Rm, Vis Aids, Chng Rm, Tack Shop
Hacking
Livery Full
Schooling General, to Med Dress, to
SJ GR C, to HT Nov, to HT Int
Exclusions Age Limit, 7
Location M6 Jnc 44, take A7 to
Longtown. 2 miles turn left at Blackford
Church signposted Newtown. 1 mile to
T-junction, turn right, immediately left

CALVERT TRUST RIDING CENTRE
Old Windebrow,
Keswick,
Cumbria, CA12 4QD
Tel 01768 774395
Contact Calvert Trust
Riding School, RDA Centre Inst Basic
3 full time instructors
Ave No 5 Horses, 5 Ponies
Courses YT
Facilities
Covered School 17 x 35 gly
Outdoor Manege 20 x 40 fl lt
Accom Dor, SC
Exclusions Wt Limit, 14st

CARGO RIDING CENTRE
Cargo, Carlisle,
Cumbria, CA6 4AW
Tel 01228 74300
Contact Miss J Weedall
Riding School, Training Centre Inst
Riding & Jumping
Staff Chief Instructor Miss J Weedall
(BHSAI)
Plus 2 full time instructors
Ave No 7 Horses, 12 Ponies
Courses WP, YT, Short, P/T, Hol
Facilities
Outdoor Manege 26 x 44 fl lt
Outdoor Manege 20 x 40 fl lt
SJ: Nov, Grade C, 1 Paddock
CC: Course, Nov, Banks, Water,
Natural, 53 Schooling
Chng Rm, Showers, Wait Rm
Hacking
Livery Full, P/T, Break, School, Grass
Schooling General, Break, to Nov
Dress, to SJ GR C, to HT Nov
Exclusions Wt Limit, 16st, Age Limit, 5
Location 4 miles north west of Carlisle
on Rockcliffe Road

GREENLANDS
Wreay, Carlisle,
Cumbria, CA4 0RR
Tel 01697 473374
Contact Mr & Mrs S W Wilson
Livery
Facilities
Covered School 84 x 33 gly
Outdoor Manege 20 x 45 fl lt
SJ: Nov, Grade A, 4 Paddock
CC: Natural, 15 Schooling
Wait Rm
Livery Full, DIY, School, Hunt, Grass
Location 5 miles south of Carlisle

HOLMESCALES RIDING CENTRE
Holmescales, Old Hutton,
Kendal, Cumbria, LA8 0NB
Tel 01539 729388
Contact Mr P M Jones
Riding School Inst Riding & Jumping
Staff Chief Instructor Mrs E G Jones
(BHSII)
Plus 1 full time instructor
Ave No 12 Horses, 13 Ponies
Courses WP, YT
Facilities
Covered School 20 x 40
Outdoor Manege 30 x 30 fl lt
SJ: Nov, 1 Paddock
CC: Basic, Banks, Water, Natural,
Gallops, 8 Schooling
Chng Rm
Hacking

Livery Full, Break, School
Schooling Break, to Nov Dress
Exclusions Age Limit, 5

LAKELAND RIDING CENTRE
Lakeland Leisure Park,
Flookburgh,
Cumbria, LA11 7LP
Tel 015395 58131
Contact Mrs S Myers
Specialities Horse Riding Activity Days
Ave No 15 Horses, 15 Ponies
Courses YT, Short, Ev, P/T, Hol
Facilities
Outdoor Manege 50 x 30
SJ: Nov
Lec Rm, Vis Aids, Wait Rm
Hacking
Livery Full, P/T, Break, School, Hunt
Accom Caravan, SC
Exclusions No unescorted hacking

LARKRIGG RIDING SCHOOL
Natland, Nr Kendal,
Cumbria, LA9 7QS
Tel 015395 60245
Contact Miss A R Wilson
Riding School Inst Riding & Jumping
Specialities Children aged between
6-12; complete beginners and novices
Staff Chief Instructor Ms Anne Wilson
Plus 1 full time instructor
Ave No 10 Horses, 15 Ponies
Courses WP, YT, Short, Ev, P/T
Facilities
Outdoor Manege 20 x 40
SJ: Nov, 1 Paddock
Hacking
Livery Full, P/T
Exclusions Age Limit, 5, No unescorted
hacking
Location Off A6 2 miles south of Kendal
in Natland village

NEWTON RIGG COLLEGE
EQUESTRIAN CENTRE
Newton Rigg, Penrith,
Cumbria, CA11 0AH
Tel 01768 863791
Contact Miss G Griffin
Riding School Inst Riding & Jumping
Specialities Career training
2 full time instructors
Ave No 13 Horses
inc 2 El Dress, 2 SJ GR C, Horse Trials
Novice 2
Courses WP, Ev, P/T
Facilities
Covered School 24 x 43
Outdoor Manege 20 x 60 fl lt

SJ: Nov
Lec Rm, Vis Aids, Chng Rm, Showers
Schooling General
Exclusions Wt Limit, 14st
Location 1 mile north of Penrith

STONERIGG RIDING CENTRE
Great Orton, Carlisle,
Cumbria, CA5 6NA
Tel 01228 576232
Contact Mrs J M Johnstone
Riding School, RDA Inst Riding &
Jumping
Staff Chief Instructor Miss D Johnstone
(BHSAI)
Ave No 4 Horses, 10 Ponies
inc 1 SJ GR C
Courses WP, YT
Facilities
Covered School 18 x 37
SJ: Nov, Grade C, 1 Paddock
Chng Rm, Wait Rm
Hacking
Livery Full, P/T, Break, School, Grass
Schooling General, Break, to SJ GR C,
to HT Nov
Exclusions Wt Limit, 12st, Age Limit, 5
Location 5 miles west of Carlisle

WYNLASS BECK STABLES
Wynlass Beck, Windermere,
Cumbria, LA23 1EU
Tel 01539 443811
Contact Lakeland Equestrian
**Riding School, Training Centre,
Trekking Centre, Post trail rides** Inst
Riding & Jumping
Specialities Individual clinics for event
riders, taken by Francis Hay Smith.
Post trail rides around Lake
Windermere. Weekend breaks - adults
only, transport from Manchester airport
3 full time instructors
Ave No 9 Horses, 7 Ponies
Courses WP, YT, Short, Hol
Lec Rm, Vis Aids, Chng Rm
Hacking
Livery Full, P/T, DIY, Break, School,
Grass
Schooling General, Break, to Med
Dress, to HT Adv
Exclusions Wt Limit, 18st

DURHAM

HOUGHALL COLLEGE
Houghall,
Co Durham, DH1 3SG
Tel 0191 386 1351

Contact Miss W L Suddes
Training Centre, Livery Inst Riding &
Jumping
5 full time instructors
Ave No 20 Horses, 2 Ponies
inc 2 El Dress, 2 SJ GR C, 1 HT Int
Courses WP, YT, Short, Ev, P/T, Hol
Facilities
Outdoor Manege 40 x 60
SJ: Grade B, 1 Paddock
CC: Course, Basic, Nov, Banks, Water,
Natural, Gallops, 20+ Schooling
Lec Rm, Vis Aids, Chng Rm, Showers,
Wait Rm
Livery Full, P/T
Schooling General, Break, to Nov
Dress, to El Dress, to SJ GR C, to HT
Nov, to HT Int
Accom S, FB
Exclusions Wt Limit, 12st, Age Limit, 13
Location 1 mile from Durham City,
A177 Bowburn road

IVESLEY EQUESTRIAN CENTRE
Waterhouses,
Co Durham, DH7 5HB
Tel 0191 373 4324
Contact Mrs P Booth
**Riding School, Training Centre,
Facility Centre** Inst Riding & Jumping
Specialities Comfortable instructional
adult holidays & young adults
Staff Chief Instructor Miss J Rutter
(BHSAI)
Plus 3 full time instructors
Ave No 20 Horses, 7 Ponies
inc 3 El Dress, 1 Med Dress,
4 SJ GR C, 1 HT Int
Courses WP, YT, Short, Ev, P/T, Hol
Facilities
Covered School 45 x 20 gly
Outdoor Manege 45 x 25 fl lt
SJ: Grade A, 1 Paddock
CC: Course, Int, Banks, Water, Natural,
Gallops, 73 Schooling
Lec Rm, Vis Aids, Chng Rm, Wait Rm
Hacking
Livery Full, P/T, DIY, Break, School,
Hunt, Grass
Schooling General, Break, to Med
Dress, to SJ GR C, to HT Int
Accom S, Tw, Db, F, FB
Exclusions Wt Limit, 18st, Age Limit, 3
Location 6 miles west of Durham City,
adjacent to Zetland & Tyndale hunt

LOW FOLD RIDING CENTRE
Low Fold Farm, Sunnybrow,
Crook,
Co Durham, DL15 0RL
Tel 01388 747313

Contact Miss M Hedley
Riding School, Training Centre Inst
to BHSII
4 full time instructors
Ave No 20 Horses, 16 Ponies
inc 5 El Dress, 1 HT Int
Courses WP, YT, Ev, P/T, Hol
Facilities
Covered School 15 x 30 gly
Outdoor Manege 45 x 25
SJ: Nov, Grade C
CC: Course, Basic, Nov, Int, Banks,
Water, Natural
Lec Rm, Vis Aids
Livery Full, P/T, DIY, Hunt, Grass
Schooling General, to El Dress, to
Med Dress, to SJ GR C, to HT Nov, to
HT Int
Exclusions Wt Limit, 15st, Age Limit, 5
Location Between Willington and
Hunwick on B6286

NEW MOORS TRAINING AND LIVERY CENTRE
Evenwood Gate, Bishop Auckland,
Co Durham, DL14 9NN
Tel 01388 833542
Contact Dr A Lewis
**Training Centre, Facility Centre,
Livery, Welsh Cob Stud & Stud
Training** Inst Riding & Jumping
Specialities Regular unaffiliated
dressage and showjumping
competitions as well as Examination
Centre
Staff Chief Instructor Miss G Lewis
(BHSAI)
Plus 1 full time instructor
Ave No 9 Horses, 4 Ponies
inc 1 El Dress, 1 Med Dress, 1 Adv
Dress, Welsh Cobs
Courses WP, Short, Ev, P/T, Hol
Facilities
Covered School 20 x 40
Outdoor Manege 20 x 60
SJ: Nov, 1 Paddock
CC: Course, Basic, Nov, Banks, Water,
Natural, 18 Schooling
Lec Rm, Vis Aids, Wait Rm
Hacking
Livery Full, P/T, DIY, Break, School,
Grass
Schooling General, Break, to Nov
Dress, to El Dress, to Med Dress, to
Adv Dress, to HT Nov
Accom Tw, Cottage, SC
Exclusions Wt Limit, 12st7,
Age Limit, 8
Location Zetland Hunt country,
between West Auckland and Barnard
Castle, off A688

RAYGILL RIDING CENTRE
Raygill Farm Lartington,
Barnard Castle,
Co Durham, DL12 9DG
Tel 01833 690118
Contact Mrs K A Wall
**Riding School, Trekking Centre, B & B
for horses** Inst Basic
Specialities Use of good Dale ponies
1 full time instructor
Ave No 10 Horses, 7 Ponies
inc Dale show ponies & show/working
hunter
Courses Short, Ev, P/T, Hol
Facilities
Outdoor Manege 20 x 40 fl lt
SJ: Nov, 1 Paddock
CC: Course, Basic
Lec Rm, Vis Aids, Chng Rm, Showers,
Wait Rm
Hacking
Livery Full, P/T, DIY, Hunt, Grass
Schooling General
Accom Tw, F, Dor, FB
Exclusions Wt Limit, 14st

SOUTH CAUSEY EQUESTRIAN CENTRE
Beamish Burn Road, Stanley,
Co Durham, DH9 0LS
Tel 01207 281136
Contact Ms Jean Gibson
Riding School Inst Basic
Specialities Horseball & Vaulting
Staff Chief Instructor Mrs Susan Moriser
Plus 2 full time instructors
Ave No 6 Horses, 12 Ponies
Facilities
Covered School 50 x 30 gly
Outdoor Manege 60 x 40
SJ: Nov, 1 Paddock
Lec Rm, Vis Aids, Tack Shop
Hacking
Livery Full, DIY, Grass
Exclusions Age Limit, 4
Location 1/2 mile north of Stanley, on
A6076

NORTHUMBERLAND

CALVERT TRUST KIELDER
Kielder Water, Nr Hexham,
Northumberland, NE48 1BS
Tel 01434 250232
Contact Mr P J V Cockerill
Riding School Inst Basic
Staff Chief Instructor Ms Nadia
MacLucas (BHSAI)
Ave No 2 Horses, 8 Ponies
inc RDA

Courses Hol
Facilities
Covered School 20 x 40 gly
SJ: Nov
Chng Rm, Showers, Wait Rm
Hacking
Livery P/T
Schooling General
Accom Tw, FB, SC
Exclusions Wt Limit, 14st, Age Limit, 7
Location 30 miles north of Hexham

FOWBERRY FARMS
Heathery Hall, Wooler,
Northumberland, NE71 6EU
Tel 01668 281417
Contact Mrs M R Matheson
Riding School Inst Basic
Ave No 2 Horses, 5 Ponies
inc 2 HT Int
Facilities
Covered School 18 x 18 gly
SJ: Nov
CC: Course, Basic, Nov, Int, Banks,
Water, Natural, Gallops, 20 Schooling
Hacking
Livery Full, DIY, Grass
Schooling General, to HT Nov
Accom Tw, Caravan, FB, SC
Location 2.5 miles east of Wooler
(B6348)

KIMMERSTON RIDING CENTRE
Kimmerston, Near Wooler,
Northumberland, NE71 6JH
Tel 01668 216283
Contact Mr & Mrs R E Jeffreys
Riding School Inst Basic
1 full time instructor
Ave No 15 Horses, 10 Ponies
inc Hunters
Courses YT, Hol
Facilities
SJ: Nov
Hacking
Livery Full, P/T, School, Hunt, Grass
Schooling General
Accom Cottage, SC
Exclusions Wt Limit, 18st,
No unaccompanied hacking
Location 1 1/2 miles from Ford village
and 2 miles from Milfield on the A697

KIRKLEY HALL COLLEGE
(EQUINE UNIT)
Kirkley Hall College, Ponteland,
Northumberland, NE20 0AQ
Tel 01661 860808
Contact Mrs J McCowie
Riding School Inst Riding & Jumping

Specialities Career courses for
students at college
Staff Chief Instructor Mrs Judith McCowie
Plus 2 full time instructors
Ave No 12 Horses, 6 Ponies
inc 4 El Dress, 1 Med Dress,
1 SJ GR C, 3 RDA
Facilities
Outdoor Manege 60 x 30
SJ: Nov, Grade C, 2 Paddock
CC: 12 Schooling
Lec Rm, Vis Aids, Chng Rm, Showers,
Wait Rm
Livery Full
Schooling General
Location 2 miles north east of Ponteland

PENSHAW HILL
EQUESTRIAN CENTRE
Penshaw Village, Houghton-le-Spring,
Tyne & Wear, DH4 7ER
Tel 0191 584 4828
Contact Miss J & Mr M Roseberry
Riding School, Training Centre Inst
Riding & Jumping
2 full time instructors
Ave No 9 Horses, 12 Ponies
inc 1 SJ GR C, 2 SJ Jun C
Courses WP, Short, Ev, P/T, Hol
Facilities
Covered School 24 x 42
Covered School 24 x 24
SJ: Nov, 1 Paddock
Lec Rm, Vis Aids, Wait Rm
Hacking
Livery Full, Break, School
Schooling General, Break, to El Dress,
to SJ GR C
Exclusions Wt Limit, 13st, Age Limit, 5

STEPNEY BANK STABLES
Stepney Bank, Byker,
Newcastle upon Tyne, NE1 2PW
Tel 0191 233 2046
Contact Miss S Tron
Riding School Inst Basic
Staff Chief Instructor Miss Susan Tron
Ave No 3 Horses, 8 Ponies
Courses WP, Short, Ev, Hol
Facilities
Outdoor Manege 20 x 40
Lec Rm, Vis Aids
Hacking
Exclusions Wt Limit, 13st
Location Newcastle inner city

WHITEHOUSE RIDING SCHOOL
Cornhill House, Cornhill on Tweed,
Northumberland, TD12 4UD
Tel 01890 882422

Contact Ms Susan Smith
Riding School Inst Basic
Staff Chief Instructor Mrs Elizabeth Smith
Ave No 8 Horses, 5 Ponies
Courses WP
Facilities
Outdoor Manege 42 x 21
SJ: Nov
Chng Rm., Wait Rm
Hacking
Livery Full, Grass
Exclusions No unescorted riding
Location On A697 at Cornhill on Tweed. Collingwood Arms Hotel

WHITTINGTON MILL STABLES
Whittington Mill, Great Whittington, Northumberland, NE19 2HU
Tel 01434 672264
Contact Mrs J Findeisen
Riding School, Training Centre Inst Riding & Jumping
Staff Chief Instructor Mrs J Findeisen Plus 1 full time instructor
Ave No 5 Horses, 12 Ponies
Courses WP, YT, Short, P/T, Hol
Facilities
Outdoor Manege 20 x 40 fl lt
SJ: Nov, 1 Paddock

CC: Course, Basic, Water, Natural, 14 Schooling
Vis Aids, Chng Rm, Showers
Hacking
Livery Full, P/T, School, Hunt
Schooling General, to Nov Dress
Exclusions Wt Limit, 10st7, Age Limit, 5
Location 6 miles from Corbridge and 8 miles from Hexham

WINDY EDGE STABLES
Alnmouth Road, Alnwick, Northumberland, NE66 2QB
Tel 01665 602284
Contact Miss I White & Miss I Sisterson
Riding School Inst Basic
2 full time instructors
Ave No 4 Horses, 8 Ponies
Courses YT
Facilities
Outdoor Manege 37 x 37
CC: Basic, Natural, 10 Schooling
Wait Rm
Hacking
Livery Full, Hunt, Grass
Schooling General
Exclusions Age Limit, 5O, open May August only
Location 1 1/2 miles from A1, 30 miles from Berwick and 17 miles from Morpeth

Riding in Yorkshire

EAST YORKSHIRE
NORTH YORKSHIRE
SOUTH YORKSHIRE ◆ WEST YORKSHIRE

EAST YORKSHIRE

BISHOP BURTON COLLEGE
Bishop Burton, Beverley,
North Humberside, HU17 8QG
Tel 01964 553000
Contact Mr G Kerr
Riding School, Training Centre Inst to BHSI
Specialities College courses
Staff Chief Instructor Miss A Paling (BHSI)
Plus 12 full time instructors
Ave No 70 Horses, 4 Ponies
inc 4 El Dress, 6 Med Dress, 8 SJ GR C, 2 HT Int, 1 Driving
Courses YT, Short, Ev, P/T, Hol
Facilities
Covered School 60 x 20 gly
Covered School 45 x 30
Outdoor Manege 50 x 50 fl lt
SJ: Grade A, 1 Paddock
CC: Course, Basic, Nov, Int, Adv, Banks, Water, Natural, 12 Schooling
Lec Rm, Vis Aids, Chng Rm, Showers, Wait Rm
Livery Full, P/T, Break, School
Schooling General, Break, to Nov Dress, to El Dress, to Med Dress, to SJ GR C, to HT Nov, to HT Int, to HT Adv
Accom S, Tw, FB
Exclusions Wt Limit, 14st, Age Limit, 12
Location Approx 8 miles from M62 on the A1079, York to Hull road, 3 miles west of Beverley

BURTON CONSTABLE RIDING CENTRE
Burton Constable, Nr Hull, HU11 4LN
Tel 01964 562019
Contact Mr & Mrs Thompson
Riding School Inst to BHSAI
Specialities Quality instruction for the individual or small groups, of all abilities. Courses specially tailored to the level of rider
1 full time instructor
Ave No 12 Horses, 8 Ponies
Courses WP, Short, Ev, P/T
Facilities
Covered School 17 x 41 gly
Outdoor Manege 20 x 48 fl lt
SJ: Nov, Grade C, 1 Paddock
Lec Rm, Vis Aids, Wait Rm
Hacking
Livery Full, Break, School, Hunt
Schooling General, Break, to Nov Dress, to SJ GR C, to HT Nov
Exclusions No Casual Hire
Location 10 miles east of Hull, sign posted off A165 Hull to Brimlington

CARRIER HOUSE RIDING SCHOOL
Main Street, Newton upon Derwent, York, YO4 5DA
Tel 01904 608373
Contact Mr P Teasdale
Riding School Inst Basic
Staff Chief Instructor Mr P Teasdale
Plus 1 full time instructor
Ave No 9 Horses, 8 Ponies
inc Show Hunters and Racehorses
Courses YT, Ev, Hol
Facilities
Covered School 43 x 19
Outdoor Manege 37 x 14
SJ: 1 Paddock
CC: Natural, Gallops, 8 Schooling
Chng Rm, Showers, Wait Rm
Hacking
Livery Full, Break, School, Grass
Schooling General, Break
Exclusions Age Limit, 2
Location 1 mile off York/Hull road (A1079)

NORTH HUMBERSIDE RIDING CENTRE
Easington, Nr Hull,
East Yorkshire, HU12 OUA

Tel 01964 650250
Contact Mrs T Biglin
Riding School, Training Centre Inst
to BHSAI
Specialities Career training
1 full time instructor
Ave No 6 Horses, 8 Ponies
inc 2 El Dress
Courses WP, YT, Short, Ev, P/T, Hol
Facilities
Covered School 40 x 20 gly
SJ: Nov, 1 Paddock
CC: Basic, Banks, Water, Natural
Lec Rm, Vis Aids, Showers
Hacking
Livery Full, Break, School
Schooling General, Break, to El Dress,
to SJ GR C, to HT Nov
Accom Tw, Dor, Caravan, FB
Exclusions Wt Limit, 13st,
No casual hire
Location Approx 3/4 mile from
Easington Church

NORTH YORKSHIRE

BARROWBY RIDING CENTRE
Kirkby Overblow, Harrogate,
North Yorkshire, HG3 1HU
Tel 0113 2886201
Contact Mrs S J Caley
Training Centre, Livery Inst to BHSAI
Specialities Career training
Staff Chief Instructor Mrs S J Caley
(BHSAI, BHS SM)
Plus 1 full time instructor
Ave No 6 Horses
Courses WP, YT
Facilities
Outdoor Manege 21 x 42 fl lt
SJ: Nov, 1 Paddock
CC: Banks, 5 Schooling
Hacking
Livery Full, P/T, School, Hunt
Schooling General, to Nov Dress,
to El Dress, to SJ GR C, to HT Nov
Exclusions Clients on own horses only
Location 5 miles from A1 at Wetherby,
12 miles from M1 & M62

BLEACH FARM STABLES
Bridlington Road, Stamford Bridge,
York, YO4 1HA
Tel 01759 371846
Contact Mr J J Hutchinson
Riding School Inst Riding & Jumping
Staff Chief Instructor Miss S Crompton

(BHSAI)
Ave No 7 Horses, 11 Ponies
Courses YT, Short, Ev
Facilities
Outdoor Manege 40 x 24 fl lt
SJ: Nov, 1 Paddock
CC: Water, 3 Schooling
Lec Rm, Vis Aids, Showers
Hacking
Livery Full, P/T, DIY, Break, School,
Hunt
Schooling General, Break
Exclusions Wt Limit, 16st, Age Limit, 4,
No unaccompanied hacking
Location 1 mile east of Stamford Bridge
on A166

CHEQUER FARM STABLES
Main Street, Elvington,
York, YO4 5AG
Tel 01904 608618
Contact Mr J C Nicholson
Riding School Inst Riding & Jumping
Specialities Instruction in riding &
jumping
1 full time instructor
Ave No 6 Horses, 7 Ponies
Courses WP, YT, Short, Ev, P/T, Hol
Facilities
Outdoor Manege 40 x 40 fl lt
SJ: Nov, 1 Paddock
CC: Basic, Banks, Natural, 17 Schooling
Lec Rm, Vis Aids, Chng Rm, Wait Rm
Hacking
Livery Full, P/T, Break, Grass
Schooling General
Exclusions No unescorted riding
Location About 7 miles east of York on
B1228 & 7 miles from Pocklington off
1079 on C18. Located in centre of
Elvington village

COTTAGE FARM STABLES
Ruston, Scarborough,
North Yorkshire, YO13 9QE
Tel 01723 862608
Contact Mrs J Charlton
Riding School Inst Riding & Jumping
Specialities Excellent hacking country
Instruction for recreational riders,
students and competitors
2 full time instructors
Ave No 7 Horses, 9 Ponies
Courses YT
Facilities
Outdoor Manege 22 x 44
SJ: Nov, 1 Paddock
CC: Basic, Banks, Water, Natural,
6 Schooling
Wait Rm
Hacking

Livery Full, P/T, Break, School, Hunt, Grass
Schooling General, Break
Exclusions Wt Limit, 14 stone,
No unescorted riding
Location Off A170 6 miles west of Scarborough

FOLLYFOOT PARK STABLES
Pannal Road, Follifoot, Harrogate,
North Yorkshire, HG3 1DN
Tel 01423 870912/372
Contact Ms Julie Cotterill
Riding School Inst Riding & Jumping
Specialities Beginners, Novices and Nervous riders a speciality
Staff Chief Instructor Miss Julie Cotterill (BHSAI)
Plus 1 full time instructor
Ave No 8 Horses, 9 Ponies
Courses WP, Short, Ev, P/T, Hol
Facilities
Covered School 29 x 30 gly
Outdoor Manege 20 x 40 fl lt
SJ: Nov, Grade C, 1 Paddock
Showers
Hacking
Livery Full, P/T, DIY, Break, School, Grass
Exclusions Wt Limit, 14st,
No unescorted Hacking
Location Off A658 South of Harrogate between the A661 & A61 roundabouts

FRIARS' HILL RIDING STABLES
Friars' Hill, Sinnington,
Nr Pickering,
North Yorkshire, YO6 6NF
Tel 01751 432758
Contact Mrs A Brown
Riding School Inst Riding & Jumping
Specialities Hunt hires, Side Saddle and Riding & Road Safety courses
Staff Chief Instructor Mrs A Brown (BHSAI)
Plus 1 full time instructor
Ave No 8 Horses, 10 Ponies
inc Hunters for hire
Courses YT, Short, Ev, P/T, Hol
Facilities
Outdoor Manege 40 x 27 fl lt
SJ: Nov, Grade C
Lec Rm, Vis Aids
Hacking
Livery Full, P/T, Break, School, Hunt, Grass
Schooling General, Break, to Nov Dress, to SJ GR C, to HT Nov
Exclusions Wt Limit, 13st, Age Limit, 3
Location Off A170 - 5 miles from Pickering, 2 miles from Kirbymoorside

HIGH BELTHORPE LIVERY
Bishop Wilton,
York, YO4 1SB
Tel 01759 368238
Contact Ms M Abu Hamdan
Livery
Specialities All livery
Livery Full, P/T, DIY, Hunt, Grass
Accom Db, F, FB
Location Off A166 between York & Great Driffield

HOME FARM STABLES
Langton, Malton,
North Yorkshire, YO17 9QW
Tel 01653 658207/226
Contact Mr & Mrs Aitken
Riding School Inst Basic
Specialities Small friendly riding school, tuition tailored to the individuals' requirements
Staff Chief Instructor Miss Michelle Dellar (BHS PTC)
Ave No 8 Horses, 14 Ponies
inc 1 El Dress
Courses WP, YT, Short, Ev, P/T, Hol
Facilities
Outdoor Manege 15 x 30 fl lt
SJ: Nov
Wait Rm
Hacking
Livery Full, P/T, DIY, Break, School, Hunt
Schooling General, Break, to El Dress
Exclusions Wt Limit, 14st,
No unaccompanied hacking
Location Off B1248 4 miles south of Malton

LACY'S COTTAGE RIDING SCHOOL
Scrayingham, York,
North Yorkshire, YO4 1JD
Tel 01759 371586
Contact Mrs N Pimlott
Riding School Inst Basic
Specialities Riding instruction for children, residential summer camp for children & two day PRT courses
Staff Chief Instructor Mrs N Pimlott
Ave No 2 Horses, 12 Ponies
Courses YT, Hol
Facilities
Outdoor Manege 28 x 23 fl lt
SJ: Nov, 1 Paddock
CC: Gallops, 6 Schooling
Hacking
Livery Full, P/T, DIY, Break, School, Grass
Exclusions Age Limit, 3,
No unescorted rides
Location Screyingham village, approx 3 miles off A166

MOOR HOUSE RIDING CENTRE

Moor House, Wiggington, York,
North Yorkshire, YO32 2RB
Tel 01904 769029
Contact Mrs S & Miss P Kemp-Welch
**Riding School, Training Centre,
Facility Centre** Inst to BHSAI
Specialities Career training
Staff Chief Instructor Miss P Kemp-Welch (BHSII, BHS SM)
Plus 1 full time instructor
Ave No 11 Horses, 9 Ponies
inc 1 Med Dress, 1 Adv Dress,
2 Vaulting
Courses WP, YT, Short, Ev, P/T, Hol
Facilities
Covered School 20 x 40 gly
Outdoor Manege 60 x 20 fl lt
Outdoor Manege 41 x 21 fl lt
SJ: Nov, 1 Paddock
CC: Course, Basic, Nov, Banks, Water,
Natural
Lec Rm, Vis Aids, Chng Rm, Wait Rm
Schooling General, to Med Dress,
to HT Nov
Exclusions Wt Limit, 12st,
No riding on Thursdays
Location 4 miles north of York on the
B1363, on bus route

NABURN GRANGE RIDING CENTRE

Naburn, York, YO1 4RU
Tel 01904 728283
Contact Mrs D Horn
Riding School, Training Centre Inst
to BHSAI
Specialities Career Training
Staff Chief Instructor Mrs D Claydon
(BHSAI)
Plus 2 full time instructors
Ave No 12 Horses, 8 Ponies
inc 1 El Dress, 1 SJ GR C, 2 HT Int,
3 Novice HT
Courses WP, Short, Ev, P/T, Hol
Facilities
Covered School 20 x 40
Outdoor Manege 60 x 40 fl lt
SJ: Nov, Grade C
CC: Course, Basic, Banks, Natural
Lec Rm, Vis Aids, Chng Rm, Wait Rm
Hacking
Livery Full, P/T, DIY, Break, School,
Hunt, Grass
Schooling General, Break, to Nov
Dress, to El Dress, to SJ GR C, to HT
Int
Accom S, Tw, FB
Exclusions Wt Limit, 15st, Age Limit, 5,
No unaccompanied hacking
Location On B1222 off A19, 4 miles
from York

QUEEN ETHELBURGA'S COLLEGE

Thorpe Underwood Hall, Ouseburn,
York, YO5 9SZ
Tel 01423 330859
Contact Mr B R Martin
Riding School Inst to BHSAI
Specialities 8 all weather half mile
gallop track
Staff Chief Instructor Miss Kate Caborn
(BHSII)
Plus 6 full time instructors
Ave No 30 Horses, 7 Ponies
Courses Ev, Hol
Facilities
Covered School 60 x 40
Outdoor Manege 60 x 40
SJ: Nov, 1 Paddock
CC: Course, Nov, Banks, Water, Natural
Lec Rm, Vis Aids, Chng Rm, Showers,
Wait Rm
Schooling General
Exclusions Instruction for college
students only term time
Location Between Harrogate & York,
off A59 and B6265

RICHMOND EQUESTRIAN CENTRE

Brough Park, Richmond,
North Yorkshire, DL10 7PL
Tel 01748 811629
Contact Mrs C Renner
Riding School Inst Riding & Jumping
Specialities Instruction to suit all ages
and abilities. Horses produced for
competitions, breaking & schooling.
Residential courses and riding holidays
Staff Chief Instructor Mrs Christine
Renner
Ave No 14 Horses, 17 Ponies
inc 2 El Dress, 1 Med Dress
Courses WP, YT, Short, Ev, P/T, Hol
Facilities
Covered School 55 x 30 gly
Outdoor Manege 46 x 37 fl lt
SJ: Nov, Grade B, 1 Paddock
CC: Course, Nov, Banks, Natural
Lec Rm, Vis Aids, Chng Rm, Showers,
Wait Rm
Hacking
Livery Full, P/T, DIY, Break, School,
Hunt, Grass
Schooling General, Break
Accom S, Tw, Dor, Caravan, Cottage,
FB, SC
Location Between Tunstal & Colburn
2 miles from A1 at Catterick

SKERNE LEYS FARM

Driffield, East Yorkshire,
YO25 9HN
Tel 01377 253102

Contact Mr & Mrs T A Watson
Livery
Facilities
Outdoor Manege 20 x 40
Livery Full, P/T, DIY
Accom Tw, F, FB
Location 1 mile south of Great Driffield

SNAINTON RIDING CENTRE
Snainton, Scarborough,
North Yorkshire, YO13 9AP
Tel 01723 859218
Contact Mr A Lyall
Riding School Inst to BHSI
Specialities Career training
Staff Chief Instructor Mr A Lyall (BHSI)
Plus 2 full time instructors
Ave No 15 Horses, 10 Ponies
inc 3 El Dress, 2 Med Dress, 1 Adv Dress
Courses WP, YT, Short, Ev, P/T, Hol
Facilities
Covered School 25 x 42 gly
Outdoor Manege 22 x 59 fl lt
SJ: Nov, Grade A, 2 Paddock
CC: Basic, Nov, Int, Banks, Natural
Lec Rm, Vis Aids, Chng Rm, Wait Rm
Hacking
Livery Full, Break, School, Hunt
Schooling General, Break, to Adv
Dress, to SJ GR A, to HT Adv
Accom Tw, Cottage, SC
Exclusions Wt Limit, 13st, Age Limit, 3
Location Off A170, 10 miles from
Scarborough

YORK RIDING SCHOOL
Wigginton Road, York,
Yorkshire, YO3 3RH
Tel 01904 763686
Contact Mr & Mrs Holstead
Riding School, Stud. Inst to BHSI
Specialities Career training
Staff Chief Instructor Mrs L A Holstead
(BHSI)
Plus 4 full time instructors
Ave No 15 Horses, 11 Ponies
inc 4 El Dress, 2 Med Dress, 1 Adv
Dress, 4 SJ GR B, 1 SJ GR A,
6 SJ Jun A, 1 HT Int
Courses WP, YT, Short, Ev, P/T, Hol
Facilities
Covered School 60 x 20 gly
Outdoor Manege 60 x 25 fl lt
SJ: Grade C, Grade B, Grade A,
1 Paddock
CC: Course, Basic, Nov, Banks, Water,
Natural
Lec Rm, Vis Aids, Chng Rm, Wait Rm,
Tack Shop
Livery Full, P/T, DIY, Break, School,
Grass

Schooling General, Break, to Adv
Dress, to SJ GR A, to HT Adv
Exclusions No hacking
Location At Jn of A1237 and B1363

THE YORKSHIRE RIDING CENTRE
Markington, Harrogate,
North Yorkshire, HG3 3PE
Tel 01765 677207
Contact Mr C Bartle BHSI
Riding School, Training Centre,
Facility Centre, Breaking/Schooling
Inst to BHSI
Specialities Career training
Staff Chief Instructor Mrs J Bartle-
Wilson (BHSI)
Plus 11 full time instructors
Ave No 35 Horses, 10 Ponies
inc 8 El Dress, 5 Med Dress, 3 Adv
Dress, 3 SJ GR C, 5 SJ Jun C,
2 SJ Jun A
Courses WP, Short, Ev, P/T, Hol
Facilities
Covered School 20 x 50 gly
Covered School 25 x 50 gly
Outdoor Manege 30 x 60
SJ: Grade B, Grade A, 1 Paddock
CC: Course, Basic, Nov, Banks, Water,
Natural
Lec Rm, Vis Aids, Chng Rm, Showers,
Wait Rm
Livery Full, P/T, DIY, Break, School
Schooling General, Break, to Adv
Dress, to SJ GR C, to HT Adv
Accom S, Tw, F, FB, SC
Exclusions Wt Limit, 13st, Age Limit, 8
Location Off A61, 5 miles from Ripon
and 7 miles from Harrogate

SOUTH YORKSHIRE

BARNES GREEN RIDING SCHOOL
Woodseats Farm, Barnes Green,
Grenoside, Nr Sheffield, South
Yorkshire, S30 3NA
Tel 01142 402548
Contact Mrs C Walker
Riding School, Training Centre Inst
Riding & Jumping
Staff Chief Instructor Miss S Ellis
(BHSAI, BHS Int.SM)
Plus 3 full time instructors
Ave No 8 Horses, 12 Ponies
inc 1 side saddle
Courses WP, YT, Short, Ev, P/T
Facilities
Outdoor Manege 47 x 24 fl lt
SJ: Nov, 1 Paddock
CC: Nov, Natural, 15 Schooling

Lec Rm, Vis Aids
Hacking
Livery Full
Schooling General
Exclusions Wt Limit, 16st, Age Limit, 5
Location 3 miles north west of
Sheffield

BROCKHOLES FARM
RIDING CENTRE
Branton, Doncaster,
DN3 3NH
Tel 01302 535057
Contact Mrs J Humphries
Riding School, Training Centre Inst
Riding & Jumping
Specialities Career training
Staff Chief Instructor Miss D Brentnall
(BHSAI)
Plus 5 full time instructors
Ave No 30 Horses, 30 Ponies
inc 1 El Dress, 1 Med Dress, 1 SJ GR
C, 1 SJ GR B
Courses YT, Short, Ev, P/T, Hol
Facilities
Covered School 60 x 20
Outdoor Manege 40 x 20 fl lt
SJ: Grade A, 1 Paddock
CC: Course, Basic, Nov, Natural,
Gallops
Lec Rm, Vis Aids, Wait Rm
Hacking
Livery Full, P/T, Break, School, Hunt,
Grass
Schooling General, Break, to El Dress,
to SJ GR A, to HT Int
Exclusions Wt Limit, 18st,
Age Limit, 2 1/2,
No first time riders on hacks
Location 2 miles south of Doncaster

GLEBE FIELD
RIDING ESTABLISHMENT
Forecourt Park Road, Mexborough,
South Yorkshire, S64 9PE
Tel 01709 583377
Contact Miss J Hemingway
Riding School, Training Centre, RDA
Inst Riding & Jumping
Specialities Private lessons,
Side saddle, RDA, NVQ
Staff Chief Instructor Miss Jane
Hemingway (BHS SM, BHS T)
Plus 1 full time instructor
Ave No 5 Horses, 6 Ponies
inc Exam preparation, career students
& NVQ location
Courses WP, YT, Short, Ev, P/T
Facilities
Outdoor Manege 20 x 40 fl lt
Outdoor Manege 20 x 40

SJ: Nov, 1 Paddock
Lec Rm, Vis Aids, Tack Shop
Livery Full
Schooling to El Dress
Exclusions Wt Limit, 15st, Age Limit, 4
Location 1/2 mile north of Town centre

GROVE HOUSE STABLES
Grove Wood Road, Misterton,
Doncaster,
South Yorkshire, DN10 4EF
Tel 01427 890802
Contact Mr A Stennett
Riding School, Training Centre,
Facility Centre Inst to BHSAI
Specialities Career training &
Pre-school children
Staff Chief Instructor Mr A Stennett
(BHS Int.SM, BHSAI)
Plus 7 full time instructors
Ave No 20 Horses, 10 Ponies
inc 1 El Dress, 1 Med Dress
Courses WP, YT, Short, Ev, P/T, Hol
Facilities
Outdoor Manege 60 x 20 fl lt
Outdoor Manege 20 x 60 fl lt
SJ: Nov, 1 Paddock
CC: Nov
Lec Rm, Vis Aids, Chng Rm, Wait Rm
Hacking
Livery Full, P/T, Break, School, Hunt
Schooling General, Break, to El Dress
Location South of Doncaster between
Gainsborough & Bawtry

MASSARELLA RIDING CENTRE
Thurcroft Hall, Brookhouse,
Loughton, Sheffield,
South Yorkshire, S31 7YA
Tel 01909 566429
Contact Mr S Massarella &
Miss G Liggins
Training Centre, Livery Inst Riding &
Jumping
Specialities Competition training - Show
Jumping / Dressage, clients & students
with their own horses
Staff Chief Instructor Miss G Liggins
(BHS Int Teach)
Plus 2 full time instructors
Courses WP, YT
Facilities
Covered School 24 x 37
Outdoor Manege 60 x 100
SJ: Grade A, 1 Paddock
CC: Banks, Water, Natural, 5 Schooling
Lec Rm, Vis Aids, Wait Rm
Livery Full, Break, School
Schooling General, Break, to El Dress,
to SJ GR A
Location 2 miles east of M1/M18 Jn

MOORHOUSE EQUESTRIAN CENTRE
Gap Farm, Moorhouse, Doncaster,
South Yorkshire, DN6 7HA
Tel 01977 642109/642008
Contact Mr W Hobson
Riding School, BSJA shows/unaffiliated dressage Inst Riding & Jumping
3 full time instructors
Ave No 15 Horses, 12 Ponies
inc 1 El Dress, 2 SJ GR C, 1 SJ GR B
Courses WP, YT, Short, Ev, P/T
Facilities
Covered School 24 x 64 gly
Covered School 24 x 18
SJ: Grade A
CC: Basic, 10 Schooling
Lec Rm, Vis Aids, Chng Rm, Wait Rm,
Tack Shop
Hacking
Livery Full, P/T, Break, School, Hunt
Schooling General, Break, to El Dress,
to SJ GR A
Accom Tw, Dor, Caravan, SC
Exclusions Wt Limit, 16st,
No hiring of horses
Location Off A638 from A1 towards
Wakefield

NEWFIELD STABLES EQUESTRIAN TRAINING CENTRE
Newfield Lane, Dore,
Sheffield, S17 3DD
Tel 01142 621362
Contact Mrs B Lenihan
Riding School, Training Centre Inst
Riding & Jumping
Specialities Student training
Staff Chief Instructor Mrs D Clough
(BHSAI, BHS Int Teach)
Ave No 8 Horses, 2 Ponies
inc 4 El Dress, 8 SJ GR C, 2 HT Int
Courses WP, YT, Short, Ev, P/T, Hol
Facilities
Outdoor Manege 20 x 40 fl lt
SJ: Nov, Grade C, 1 Paddock
CC: Course, Basic
Lec Rm, Vis Aids, Chng Rm
Livery Full, Break, School, Hunt, Grass
Schooling General, Break, to Nov
Dress, to El Dress, to SJ GR C, to HT
Nov, to HT Int
Exclusions no unescorted riding
Location 5 miles south of Sheffield City
Centre

PARKLANDS RIDING SCHOOL
Worksop Road, Aston,
Sheffield, South Yorkshire, S31 0AD
Tel 0114 2875278/2879492
Contact Mrs R Sampson

Riding School Inst Riding & Jumping
Staff Chief Instructor Mrs R Sampson
(BHSAI)
Plus 2 full time instructors
Ave No 15 Horses, 20 Ponies
Courses YT, Ev, P/T
Facilities
Covered School 32 x 43 gly
Outdoor Manege 25 x 40 fl lt
SJ: Nov
Lec Rm, Vis Aids, Chng Rm, Wait Rm,
Tack Shop
Hacking
Livery Full, P/T, Break, School, Hunt,
Grass
Schooling General, Break, to Nov
Dress, to SJ GR C, to HT Nov
Exclusions Age Limit, 5,
Only experienced riders for hacking
Location 5 miles east of Sheffield off
A57

ROCKINGHAM HOUSE FARM
Upper Haugh, Rawmarsh, Rotherham,
South Yorkshire, S62 7DP
Tel 01709 524045
Contact Mrs J E Lindsey & Mr G C
Knight
Riding School, RDA Inst Basic
Staff Chief Instructor Mrs J E Lindsey
(BHSAI)
Ave No 6 Horses, 4 Ponies
inc 1 SJ GR C, 1 SJ GR B
Courses YT, Short, Hol
Facilities
Covered School 19 x 23 gly
SJ: Nov, 1 Paddock
Hacking
Livery Full, Break, School
Schooling General, Break, to SJ GR C
Exclusions No unaccompanied
hacking
Location 5 miles from Rotherham and
15 miles from Sheffield

SMELTINGS FARM RIDING CENTRE
Ringinglow Road, Sheffield, S11 7TD
Tel 0114 230 7661
Contact Mrs S V Stenton
Riding School Inst Riding & Jumping
Specialities Career training
Staff Chief Instructor Mrs S V Stenton
(BHSAI)
Plus 3 full time instructors
Ave No 9 Horses, 17 Ponies
Courses WP, YT, Short, Ev, P/T
Facilities
Covered School 25 x 20
Outdoor Manege 20 x 40 fl lt
SJ: Nov
CC: Natural, 14 Schooling

Lec Rm, Vis Aids, Chng Rm
Hacking
Livery Full, P/T, Break, School, Grass
Schooling General, Break, to Nov
Dress, to SJ GR C, to HT Nov
Location 4 miles from Sheffield, off the
A625

SNOWDON FARM RIDING SCHOOL
Snowdon Lane, Troway, Marsh Lane,
Nr Sheffield, Derbyshire, S21 5RT
Tel 01246 417172
Contact Mr & Mrs G R Jones
Riding School, Training Centre Inst
to BHSAI
Specialities Instruction in all three
disciplines. Individual courses for the
competition rider
Staff Chief Instructor Mr G R Jones
Plus 1 full time instructor
Ave No 12 Horses, 6 Ponies
Courses WP, Short, Ev, P/T, Hol
Facilities
Covered School 20 x 40
SJ: Nov, Grade C, Grade B, 1 Paddock
CC: Course, Basic, Nov, Int, Banks,
Water, Natural
Lec Rm, Vis Aids, Tack Shop
Livery Full, Break, School
Schooling General, Break, to Nov
Dress, to Med Dress, to SJ GR B, to
HT Int
Exclusions Age Limit, 5, Instructional
lessons only, No Hacking
Location Between Sheffield and
Chesterfield

WEST YORKSHIRE

**ACRE CLIFFE RIDING SCHOOL
& EQUESTRIAN CENTRE**
Ellar Ghyll, Bradford Road,
Otley, West Yorkshire, LS21 3DN
Tel 01943 873912
Contact Mrs A Everall
Riding School Inst to BHSAI
Specialities Training for BHS
Examinations, Evening courses, Side
saddle instruction, RDA
Staff Chief Instructor Mrs A Everall
(BHSII)
Plus 3 full time instructors
Ave No 10 Horses, 10 Ponies
inc 1 El Dress, 1 Med Dress,
3 sidesaddle
Courses WP, YT, Short, Ev, P/T, Hol
Facilities
Covered School 40 x 20
Outdoor Manege 40 x 20 fl lt
SJ: Nov, Grade C

CC: Course, Basic, Banks, Water
Lec Rm, Vis Aids, Wait Rm
Livery Full, P/T, School
Schooling General, to Nov Dress, to El
Dress
Exclusions Wt Limit, 15st, Age Limit, 6,
No Hacking
Location 1 mile SW of Otley on A6038

ASTLEY RIDING SCHOOL
Home Farm, Swillington, Leeds,
West Yorkshire, LS26 8UA
Tel 0113 287 3078
Contact Miss L Rafferty
Riding School Inst Riding & Jumping
Specialities Showjumping
Staff Chief Instructor Miss L Rafferty
(BHSAI)
Plus 3 full time instructors
Ave No 10 Horses, 10 Ponies
Courses YT, Hol
Facilities
SJ: Grade C, 1 Paddock
CC: Course, Banks, Water
Wait Rm
Hacking
Livery Break, School
Schooling General, Break
Exclusions Wt Limit, 16st

CALDER FARM
Sands Lane, Mirfield,
West Yorkshire, WF14 8HJ
Tel 01924 493359
Contact Mr A Chappelow
Livery
Facilities
Outdoor Manege 40 x 25
Livery Full, P/T, DIY, Break, School,
Hunt, Grass

CHERRY TREE LIVERY STABLES
Gill Lane, Kearby, Nr Wetherby,
West Yorkshire, LS22 4BS
Tel 0113 288 6460
Contact Miss R A Search
Training Centre Inst to BHSAI
Specialities Career training
Staff Chief Instructor Miss R A Search
(BHSAI)
Plus 1 full time instructor
Ave No 9 Horses
inc 2 Med Dress
Courses WP, YT
Facilities
Outdoor Manege 23 x 43 fl lt
SJ: Nov
CC: Basic, Banks, Natural, 13 Schooling
Lec Rm, Vis Aids
Hacking

Livery Full, Break, School
Schooling General, Break, to Med Dress, to HT Int
Accom S, Tw, FB
Exclusions No external students unless with own horse
Location 4 miles from Wetherby, 15 miles from Leeds

HOPTON HORSE CENTRE
Mount Pleasant Farm, Jackroyd Lane,
Upper Hopton, Mirfield,
West Yorkshire, WF14 8EH
Tel 01924 492020
Contact Miss K J Chambers
Livery
Facilities
SJ: 1 Paddock
CC: Course, Basic, Nov, Int, Banks, Water, Natural
Wait Rm
Livery DIY, Grass

J-SIX S.C.RIDING SCHOOL
Thorpe Lane, Tingley, Wakefield,
West Yorkshire, WF3 1QY
Tel 0113 252 0429
Contact Miss J Howarth
Riding School Inst to BHSAI
Specialities Career training
Staff Chief Instructor Miss J Howarth (BHSII, BHS SM)
Plus 2 full time instructors
Ave No 12 Horses, 10 Ponies
inc 3 El Dress, 1 SJ GR C, 2 horses & pony for side saddle
Courses Short, Ev, Hol
Facilities
Covered School 44 x 18 gly
Outdoor Manege 20 x 20 fl lt
SJ: Nov, Grade A, 1 Paddock
Lec Rm, Vis Aids, Chng Rm, Showers, Wait Rm, Tack Shop
Livery Full
Schooling General, to Nov Dress, to SJ GR C, to HT Nov
Accom Caravan, FB
Exclusions Wt Limit, 14st, Age Limit, 2
Location Near Jn 28, off M62

LEDSTON HALL EQUESTRIAN CENTRE
Ledston, Castleford,
West Yorkshire, WF10 2BB
Tel 01977 513544
Contact Mrs S A Compton
Riding School Inst Riding & Jumping
2 full time instructors
Ave No 11 Horses, 14 Ponies
Courses WP, YT, Short, Ev, Hol

Facilities
Covered School 61 x 28 gly
SJ: Nov
CC: Gallops
Lec Rm, Vis Aids, Chng Rm
Hacking
Livery Full, P/T, School
Schooling General, Break
Accom S, Tw, Db, FB
Exclusions Wt Limit, 13st
Location 3 miles north of Castleford, off A656

LONGFIELD EQUESTRIAN CENTRE
Middle Longfield Farm, Todmorden,
West Yorkshire, OL14 6JN
Tel 01706 812736
Contact Miss C Farnaby
Riding School, Training Centre Inst to BHSAI
Specialities Ridden Mountain & Moorland ponies
Staff Chief Instructor Miss C Farnaby (BHSII, BHS SM)
Plus 4 full time instructors
Ave No 10 Horses, 12 Ponies
inc 2 El Dress, 1 Med Dress, 1 SJ GR C
Courses WP, YT, Short, Ev, P/T, Hol
Facilities
Covered School 27 x 14 gly
Covered School 41 x 23 gly
Outdoor Manege 37 x 18
SJ: Nov, 1 Paddock
CC: 6 Schooling
Lec Rm, Vis Aids, Wait Rm
Hacking
Livery Full, P/T, Break, School
Schooling General, Break, to Med Dress, to SJ GR C
Accom Tw, Db, F, Cottage, FB, SC
Exclusions Wt Limit, 12st7, Age Limit, 5
No hacking or trekking for novices
Location 1 mile east of Todmorden

MIDDLETON PARK EQUESTRIAN CENTRE
Middleton Grove, Off Dewsbury Road,
Leeds, West Yorkshire, LS11 5TZ
Tel 0113 277 1962
Contact Mrs B Backhouse
Riding School, RDA centre Inst Basic
Specialities RDA instruction, Instruction for beginners & novice riders
Staff Chief Instructor Mrs B Backhouse (BHSAI)
Plus 2 full time instructors
Ave No 7 Horses, 6 Ponies
Courses WP, YT, Short, Ev, P/T
Facilities
Covered School 40 x 20 gly
Outdoor Manege 40x20

SJ: Nov, 1 Paddock
CC: Banks, Water, 6 Schooling
Lec Rm, Vis Aids, Chng Rm, Showers,
Wait Rm
Hacking
Schooling General, to Nov Dress, to
HT Nov
Exclusions Wt Limit, 13st,
No unescorted riding
Location On A653 between Jn 28
M62 - Dewsbury

MOORSIDE EQUESTRIAN CENTRE
Baildon, Shipley,
West Yorkshire, BD17 6BJ
Tel 01274 587849
Contact Mrs K Metcalfe
Riding School, Training Centre Inst
to BHSII
Specialities Career training
Staff Chief Instructor Mr T Pearson
(BHSI)
Ave No 15 Horses, 2 Ponies
inc 3 El Dress, 4 SJ GR C
Courses WP, YT, Short, Ev, P/T, Hol
Facilities
Outdoor Manege 50 x 30 fl lt
SJ: Nov, Grade B, 1 Paddock
CC: Course, Basic, Banks, Natural
Lec Rm, Vis Aids, Chng Rm, Wait Rm
Livery Full, Break, School, Hunt
Schooling General, Break, to Adv
Dress, to SJ GR B, to HT Adv
Exclusions Wt Limit, 16st,
Age Limit, 3 to 60,
No unaccompanied hacking
Location Adjacent to Baildon Moor

NORTHERN RIDING &
CARRIAGE DRIVING CENTRE
The Stables, Water Lane,
Thornhill Road, Dewsbury,
West Yorkshire, WF12 9PY
Tel 01924 466240
Contact Mr D Wray
Riding School, Training Centre,
Carriage driving lessons Inst Basic
Specialities Cariage driving lessons -
single, pairs, tandems or teams.
Instruction tailored to individual
requirements
Ave No 6 Horses, 5 Ponies
inc Carriage driving-single, pair,
tandem or team
Facilities
Outdoor Manege 37 x 21 fl lt
Outdoor Manege 37 x 21 fl lt
SJ: Nov, 3 acr Paddock
Hacking
Livery Full, P/T, Break, School
Schooling General, Break, to Nov Dress

Exclusions No unescorted riding
Location 2.5 miles from Jn 40 off M1
near to Dewsbury town centre

SHAY LANE STABLES
Ovenden, Halifax,
West Yorkshire, HY3 6RR
Tel 01422 363069
Contact Mr & Mrs S Yates
Riding School Inst Riding & Jumping
Specialities Schooling of ponies,
showing hacks, ponies & hunters, show
jumping competitions
Ave No 4 Horses, 6 Ponies
Courses YT, Short, Hol
Facilities
Covered School 74 x 19
SJ: Nov
Chng Rm
Hacking
Livery Full, Break, School
Schooling General, Break, to Nov
Dress, to SJ GR C
Exclusions Wt Limit, 13st, Age Limit, 4
Location 2 miles from Halifax, off A629

SPRINGFIELD LIVERY
Springfield Farm, Flappit, Keighley,
Yorkshire, BD21 5PT
Tel 01535 643181
Contact Mr & Mrs J Poole
Livery
1 full time instructor
Facilities
Outdoor Manege 25 x 45
SJ: Nov, 1 Paddock
Wait Rm
Livery Full, P/T, DIY, Break, School,
Grass
Location A629 Keighley to Halifax

THROSTLE NEST RIDING SCHOOL
Throstle Nest Farm, Fagley Lane,
Bradford, West Yorkshire, BD2 3NU
Tel 01274 639390
Contact Mrs B Howorth & Mrs J
Wheeler
Riding School Inst Riding & Jumping
Staff Chief Instructor Mrs Jeannette
Wheeler (BHSAI)
Ave No 5 Horses, 10 Ponies
Courses WP, YT, Short, Ev, P/T, Hol
Facilities
Outdoor Manege 40 x 20
SJ: Nov, 1 Paddock
CC: Course, Basic, Water
Tack Shop
Hacking
Livery Full, P/T, DIY, Break, School,
Grass

Schooling General
Exclusions Wt Limit, 14st, Age Limit, 3,
Hacking riders must be able to canter
Location On Leeds side of Bradford,
just off the A658 (Airport route)

WADLANDS HALL
EQUESTRIAN CENTRE

Priesthorde Road, Farsley,
Pudsey, LS88 5RD
Tel 0113 2363648/2570840
Contact J Driver & Partners
Riding School Inst Riding & Jumping
Specialities Instruction in Riding &
Jumping for novice, and beginners
2 full time instructors
Ave No 6 Horses, 7 Ponies
Courses WP, YT, Short, Ev, P/T, Hol
Facilities
Covered School 37 x 18
SJ: 2acr Paddock
CC: Banks, Water, Natural, 1
0 Schooling
Lec Rm, Vis Aids, Chng Rm, Wait Rm,
Tack Shop
Livery Full, P/T, DIY, Break, School
Schooling General, Break, to Nov
Dress

Exclusions no unescorted hacking
Location On A6120 between Pudsey -
Horsforth

WESTWAYS RIDING SCHOOL

The Homestead, Carr Lane, Thorner,
Leeds, West Yorkshire, LS14 3HD
Tel 01132 892598
Contact Miss Y C Beaumont
Riding School Inst Basic
Staff Chief Instructor
Miss Y C Beaumont
Plus 1 full time instructor
Ave No 5 Horses, 20 Ponies
Courses Short, P/T, Hol
Facilities
Outdoor Manege 23 x 55 fl lt
Outdoor Manege 40 x 60
Outdoor Manege 18 x 20 fl lt
SJ: Nov, 1 Paddock
CC: Course, Basic, Banks, Water,
Natural
Lec Rm, Vis Aids, Chng Rm
Hacking
Livery Full, DIY
Exclusions Wt Limit, 12st, Age Limit, 5
Location Between A58 and A64,
5 miles from the centre of Leeds

Riding in the North West

CHESHIRE ◆ GREATER MANCHESTER
MERSEYSIDE ◆ LANCASHIRE ◆ ISLE OF MAN

CHESHIRE

**BOLD HEATH
EQUESTRIAN CENTRE**
Heath House Farm, Bold Heath,
Widnes, Cheshire, WA8 3XT
Tel 0151 424 5151
Contact Mrs J E Baker
**Riding School, Training Centre,
Facility Centre** Inst Riding & Jumping
Staff Chief Instructor Mrs J E Baker
(BHSII)
Plus 5 full time instructors
Ave No 16 Horses, 21 Ponies
inc 3 El Dress, 1 Med Dress, 2 SJ GR
C, 1 SJ Jun C
Courses WP, YT, Short, Ev, P/T, Hol
Facilities
Covered School 27 x 64 gly
Covered School 24 x 43
Outdoor Manege 27 x 61 fl lt
SJ: Nov, Grade A, 1 Paddock
CC: Course, Basic, Nov, Banks, Water,
Natural, Gallops, 34 Schooling
Lec Rm, Vis Aids, Chng Rm, Wait Rm,
Tack Shop
Livery DIY, Break, School
Schooling General, Break, to Nov
Dress, to El Dress, to Med Dress, to SJ
GR C, to HT Nov
Exclusions Wt Limit, 15st, Age Limit, 2,
No casual hiring
Location 2 miles from Jn 7 on M62.
Situated on A57

CLOVERFIELD RIDING SCHOOL
Fairy Lane, Sale,
Cheshire, M33 2JT
Tel 0161 969 0701
Contact P E Long
Riding School Inst Riding & Jumping
Specialities Instruction for clients of all
ages, children, nervous riders,
beginners, novices. For the more serious
rider courses for BHS exams can be
provided for individual needs
Staff Chief Instructor Miss Nicola
Hudson (BHSAI)
Plus 1 full time instructor
Ave No 6 Horses, 6 Ponies
inc 5 SJ GR C
Courses WP, Short, Ev, P/T, Hol
Facilities
Covered School 25 x 25 gly
Outdoor Manege 20 x 40 fl lt
SJ: Nov, Grade C, 1 Paddock
Lec Rm, Vis Aids, Wait Rm
Livery Full, P/T, DIY, Break, School
Exclusions Age Limit, 5,
No hacking
Location About 2 miles Jn 8 off M63

CROFT RIDING CENTRE
Spring Lane, Croft, Warrington,
Cheshire, WA3 7AS
Tel 01925 763715
Contact Mrs J Daniels
Riding School Inst Basic
2 full time instructors
Ave No 8 Horses, 12 Ponies
Courses YT, Short, Ev, P/T
Facilities
Covered School 20 x 40 gly
Covered School 15 x 30
SJ: Nov, 1 Paddock
CC: Course, Int, Banks, Water, Natural,
Gallops
Lec Rm, Vis Aids, Chng Rm, Wait Rm
Hacking
Livery DIY
Schooling General, to Nov Dress, to HT
Nov
Exclusions Wt Limit, 15st, Age Limit, 3
Location On A357 in the centre of
village. 2 miles from Jn 22 on M6

FOXES RIDING SCHOOL
Badgers Rake Lane, Ledsham,
South Wirral, Cheshire, L66 8PF
Tel 0151 339 6797
Contact Mrs J E Davey
Riding School, Training Centre,
Facility Centre Inst to BHSAI
Staff Chief Instructor Mrs S Hinchliffe
(BHSII)
Plus 11 full time instructors
Ave No 20 Horses, 15 Ponies
inc 2 El Dress
Courses WP, YT, Short
Facilities
Covered School 42 x 22 gly
Covered School 15 x 37 gly
Outdoor Manege 24 x 43 fl lt
SJ: Nov, Grade C
Lec Rm, Vis Aids, Chng Rm, Wait Rm,
Tack Shop
Livery Full, P/T, DIY, Break, School
Schooling General, Break, to Nov
Dress, to SJ GR C, to HT Nov
Exclusions Wt Limit, 15st, Age Limit, 3
Location 3 miles from M56, towards
Hoylake on the A540. Right at Two
Mills for 1/2 mile

MOBBERLEY RIDING SCHOOL
Oak House, Newton Hall Lane,
Mobberley, Cheshire, WA16 7LQ
Tel 01565 873123
Contact Miss P Rigby
Riding School Inst Riding & Jumping
Staff Chief Instructor Miss P Rigby
(BHSII)
Plus 3 full time instructors
Ave No 10 Horses, 24 Ponies
inc 1 El Dress, 1 Med Dress
Courses YT
Facilities
Covered School 46 x 24 gly
Covered School 24 x 14
Outdoor Manege 41 x 21 fl lt
SJ: Nov
Lec Rm, Vis Aids, Wait Rm
Schooling General
Exclusions Wt Limit, 14st, Age Limit, 6,
Hacking not available
Location B5085 between Alderley
Edge and Knutsford

POOL BANK FARM STABLES
Pool Bank Farm, Bow Lane, Bowdon,
Cheshire, WA14 3BY
Tel 0161 929 9713
Contact Mr N P Kennerley
Livery
Facilities
Outdoor Manege 20 x 44 fl lt
SJ: Nov
Chng Rm

Hacking
Livery DIY
Exclusions No instruction given
Location 2 miles from Tatton Park

PUMP HOUSE FARM STABLES
Chance Hall Lane, Scholar Green,
Cheshire, ST7 3ST
Tel 01270 873072
Contact Mr & Mrs F A Baskerville
Livery
Specialities The provision of a livery
facility
Facilities
Outdoor Manege 40 x 30
Chng Rm
Livery Full, P/T, DIY, Hunt
Location Off A34 between Stoke-on-
Trent and Congleton

REASEHEATH COLLEGE
Reaseheath, Nantwich,
Cheshire, CW5 6DF
Tel 01270 625131
Contact Ms Caroline Booth
Inst Riding & Jumping
Specialities Student training, equine
courses
4 full time instructors
Ave No 25 Horses, 3 Ponies
Courses WP
Facilities
Outdoor Manege 60 x 30
SJ: Nov, 2 Paddock
CC: 5 Schooling
Lec Rm, Vis Aids, Chng Rm
Exclusions Age Limit, 16,
College students only
Location Near the centre of Nantwich
close to Jns 16, 17 & 18 off M6

WILLINGTON HALL RIDING CENTRE
Willington, Nr Tarporley,
Cheshire, CW6 0NA
Tel 01829 751920
Contact Mr & Mrs K Hassett
Riding School Inst to BHSAI
Specialities Adult instruction in riding
and stable management. preparation
for BHS exams
5 full time instructors
Ave No 21 Horses, 5 Ponies
Courses WP, Short, Ev, P/T
Facilities
Covered School 23 x 40
SJ: Nov
Hacking
Livery Full, P/T, Break, School
Schooling General
Exclusions No unescorted hacking

GREATER MANCHESTER

CARRINGTON RIDING CENTRE
Nursery Farm, Isherwood Road,
Carrington, Urmston,
Manchester, M31 4BH
Tel 0161 969 5853
Contact Mr B Groos
**Riding School, Training Centre,
Facility Centre** Inst Riding & Jumping
Specialities Show jumping, Student courses
1 full time instructor
Ave No 12 Horses, 10 Ponies
Courses WP, YT, Short, Ev, P/T, Hol
Facilities
Covered School 40 x 15
Outdoor Manege 20 x 40
Outdoor Manege 20 x 40
Outdoor Manege 40 x 60
Lec Rm, Vis Aids, Chng Rm, Showers,
Wait Rm, Tack Shop
Hacking
Livery Full, P/T, DIY, Break, School
Schooling General
Accom Caravan, SC
Exclusions Wt Limit, 13st
Location Off A6144 7 miles east of
Warrington M63-62-61-M6

DEANDANE RIDING STABLES
397 Gathurst Road, Shevington,
Wigan, WN6 8JB
Tel 01257 253086
Contact Mr M Whalley
Riding School Inst Riding & Jumping
2 full time instructors
Ave No 8 Horses, 10 Ponies
Courses YT, P/T, Hol
Facilities
Covered School 20 x 32
Outdoor Manege 30 x 15
SJ: Nov, 1 Paddock
CC: Course, Basic
Lec Rm, Vis Aids, Chng Rm, Wait Rm
Hacking
Livery Break, School
Schooling General, Break
Exclusions No unaccompanied hacking
Location 2 miles from M6 Jn 26 and 27

MOSS BROOK STUD
Lower Green Lane, Astley,
Manchester, M29 7JZ
Tel 01942 888287
Contact Mr A Fazakerley & Ms P Clark
Livery

Specialities "Livery" to produce
competition horses and to hold Show
Jumping clinics for the competitive rider
Courses WP, Short, Ev, P/T
Facilities
SJ: Grade A, 1 Paddock
Chng Rm
Livery Full, P/T, Break, School
Schooling General, Break, to SJ GR A
Location Off A580 at Astley between
Jn 14 M62 and Jn 23 M6

**RYDERS FARM
EQUESTRIAN CENTRE**
Manchester Road, Kearsley,
Bolton, BL4 8RU
Tel 0161 794 0058/1446
Contact Mr P C A Reading
Riding School Inst Riding & Jumping
Specialities Individual or small group
courses which can be full or part-time.
Private tuition is an accepted ingredient
of all courses
Staff Chief Instructor Mrs Sarah Fitton
(BHS Int.SM)
Plus 2 full time instructors
Ave No 7 Horses, 8 Ponies
Courses WP, Short, Ev, P/T, Hol
Facilities
Covered School 20 x 40
Outdoor Manege 20 x 30 fl lt
SJ: Nov, 1 Paddock
Lec Rm, Vis Aids, Wait Rm, Tack Shop
Hacking
Livery Full, P/T, DIY, Break, School
Schooling General, Break, to Nov
Dress, to SJ GR C, to HT Nov
Exclusions Age Limit, 3, Hacking and
escorted rides only
Location On the main A666 Bolton -
Manchester Rd, 1 1/4 miles from Jn 15
of the M62 & Jn 3 of the M61

MERSEYSIDE

BARNSTON RIDING CENTRE
Gills Lane Farm, Barnston, Wirral,
Merseyside, L61 1AH
Tel 0151 648 2911
Contact Mr A Wlodarski
**Riding School, Training Centre, Road
safety training and test centre** Inst
Basic
Staff Chief Instructor Mr K Richards
(BHSII, BHS SM)
Plus 1 full time instructor
Ave No 10 Horses, 14 Ponies
Courses WP, YT, Short, Ev, P/T, Hol
Facilities
Covered School 49 x 21 gly

Outdoor Manege 20 x 60 fl lt
SJ: Nov, Grade C, 1 Paddock
CC: 8 Schooling
Lec Rm, Vis Aids, Chng Rm, Wait Rm,
Tack Shop
Hacking
Livery DIY, Break, School
Schooling Break, to El Dress, to SJ
GR C, to HT Nov
Exclusions Wt Limit, 13st, No casual
hacking
Location Leave A540 near Heswell.
Gills Lane is off A551 through Barnston

BEECHLEY STABLES
Riding for the Disabled, Harthill Road,
Allerton, Liverpool, L18 3HU
Tel 0151 724 4490
Contact Ms Lynne Williams
Riding School Inst Basic
3 full time instructors
Ave No 6 Horses, 4 Ponies
Courses WP, Short, Ev, P/T, Hol
Facilities
Covered School 20 x 40 gly
Outdoor Manege 20 x 40
SJ: Nov
Lec Rm, Vis Aids, Showers
Hacking
Exclusions Age Limit, 8,
Escorted riding only
Location Allerton, next to Calderstones
Park, opposite Calderstone School

CROXTETH PARK RIDING CENTRE
Croxteth Country Park,
Liverpool, L12 0HA
Tel 0151 220 9177
Contact Mr & Mrs Stephen
Riding School Inst Basic
Specialities General instruction
Staff Chief Instructor Mrs Vivienne
Stephen
Ave No 9 Horses, 21 Ponies
Courses WP, Short, Ev, P/T, Hol
Facilities
Outdoor Manege 45 x 35
SJ: Nov
Hacking
Exclusions Wt Limit, 12st7, Age Limit, 5,
No unescorted hacking
Location Croxteth Country Park, 4
miles from M57 Jn 2

LONGACRES RIDING SCHOOL
290 Southport Road, Lydiate,
Merseyside, L31 4EQ
Tel 0151 526 0327
Contact Mr J E Kirkham
Riding School, Training Centre Inst

to BHSAI
Specialities Career training & RDA
classes
5 full time instructors
Ave No 10 Horses, 15 Ponies
inc 6 El Dress
Courses YT, Short, P/T
Facilities
Covered School 20 x 40 gly
SJ: Nov
CC: Basic, Nov, Natural, 22 Schooling
Lec Rm, Vis Aids, Chng Rm, Wait Rm
Hacking
Livery Full, P/T
Schooling General, to Med Dress
Exclusions Wt Limit, 11st,
Age Limit, 2 1/2,
No unaccompanied rides
Location On the A5147 at Lydiate

NORTHFIELD RIDING CENTRE
Gorsey Lane, Bold, Nr St Helens,
Merseyside, WA9 4SW
Tel 01744 816075
Contact Mr T J Cotterill
Riding School, Training Centre Inst
Riding & Jumping
Staff Chief Instructor Mrs H M Showne
(BHSII)
Plus 1 full time instructor
Ave No 11 Horses, 10 Ponies
inc 4 El Dress, 1 Med Dress, 1 SJ GR
C, 2 SJ Jun C, 1 HT Int
Courses WP, YT, Short, Ev, P/T, Hol
Facilities
Covered School 46 x 21 gly
Outdoor Manege 50 x 25 fl lt
SJ: Nov, Grade C
CC: Basic, Banks, Natural
Lec Rm, Vis Aids, Chng Rm, Showers,
Wait Rm
Livery Full, P/T, Break, School, Hunt,
Grass
Schooling General, Break, to Med
Dress, to SJ GR C, to HT Nov
Accom S, Tw, Cottage, FB
Exclusions Wt Limit, 14st, Age Limit, 3
Location 2 miles from Jn 7 on
M62/A57 & A570 & Gorsey Lane

WHEATHILL RIDING CENTRE
Naylors Road, Huyton,
Merseyside, L27 2YA
Tel 0151 487 8515
Contact Mrs H Anastasi & Mr T Danher
**Riding School, Training Centre,
Horse/pony sales** Inst Basic
Staff Chief Instructor Mr A Smith (BHSAI)
Plus 1 full time instructor
Ave No 6 Horses, 9 Ponies
Courses YT, Short, Ev

Facilities
Outdoor Manege 51 x 40 fl lt
Outdoor Manege 51x40 fl lt
SJ: Nov, 1 Paddock
CC: Banks, Water, Natural, 8 Schooling
Lec Rm, Vis Aids, Chng Rm, Wait Rm,
Tack Shop
Livery Full, P/T, DIY, Break, School
Schooling General, Break
Exclusions no hacking
Location Off A5080 from M62 Jn 6

WIRRAL RIDING CENTRE
Haddon Lane, Ness, South Wirral,
Cheshire, L64 8TA
Tel 0151 336 3638
Contact Mrs M Ward
Riding School, Training Centre Inst
Riding & Jumping
Specialities Career training
Ave No 16 Horses, 12 Ponies
inc 2 El Dress, 1 Med Dress
Courses WP, YT, Short, Ev, P/T, Hol
Facilities
Covered School 60 x 30 gly
Outdoor Manege 65 x 30 fl lt
SJ: Nov, Grade C, 1 Paddock
CC: Banks, Water, Natural
Lec Rm, Vis Aids, Chng Rm, Wait Rm
Livery Full, P/T, DIY, School
Schooling General, Break
Exclusions Wt Limit, 16st, Age Limit, 5,
No casual hire
Location 7 miles from M56, 8 miles
from Chester

LANCASHIRE

BICKERSTAFFE HALL
Hall Lane, Bickerstaffe, Ormskirk,
Lancashire, L39 0EH
Tel 01695 722023
Contact Mr M W Rimmer
Livery
Facilities
Outdoor Manege 48 x 27 fl lt
Chng Rm
Hacking
Livery DIY
Location 1 mile from Jn 3 of M58

CHARITY FARM LIVERY STABLES
Charity Farm, Wrightington, Nr Wigan,
Lancs, WN6 9PP
Tel 01257 451326
Contact Mr & Mrs F Waring
Livery, DIY Livery
Specialities DIY Livery

Facilities
Outdoor Manege 60 x 20 fl lt
SJ: Nov, 1 Paddock
CC: Course, Basic, Nov, Water, Natural,
Gallops
Chng Rm, Showers, Wait Rm
Hacking
Livery P/T, DIY, Grass
Exclusions Hacking for livery owners
only
Location 3 miles from Jn 27 on the M6

CHORLEY EQUESTRIAN CENTRE
Higher Garstang Farm, Chapel Lane,
Heapey, Chorley,
Lancs, PR6 8TB
Tel 01257 268801
Contact Mrs J Berry
Riding School, Training Centre Inst
Riding & Jumping
Specialities Individual/small group, BHS
exam courses tailored to clients needs
Staff Chief Instructor Mrs J Berry (BHSII)
Plus 1 full time instructor
Ave No 12 Horses, 14 Ponies
Courses WP, YT, Short, Ev, P/T, Hol
Facilities
Covered School 18 x 39
Outdoor Manege 20 x 40 fl lt
SJ: Nov, 1 Paddock
CC: Course, Basic, Banks, Water,
Natural, Gallops
Chng Rm
Hacking
Livery Full, P/T, Break, School, Hunt
Schooling General, Break, to Nov
Dress, to HT Nov
Exclusions Wt Limit, 16st, No beginners
hacking, No unescorted rides
Location Off the A674 near Wheelton,
2 miles from Jn 8 on the M61

EARNSDALE FARM RIDING SCHOOL
Off Duddon Avenue, Off Lynwood
Avenue, Darwen, Lancs, BB3 0LB
Tel 01254 702647
Contact Mrs J Crook
**Riding School, Training Centre,
Breaking and Schooling** Inst Basic
Staff Chief Instructor Mrs J Crook
(BHSAI)
Plus 1 full time instructor
Ave No 14 Horses, 10 Ponies
inc 2 El Dress, 2 SJ GR C, 6 RDA
ponies, 3 horses
Courses WP, YT, Ev, P/T, Hol
Facilities
Covered School 20 x 40
Outdoor Manege 20 x 40 fl lt
SJ: Nov, 1 Paddock
CC: Natural, 6 Schooling

Lec Rm, Vis Aids, Wait Rm, Tack Shop
Livery Full, P/T, Break, School
Schooling General, Break, to El Dress,
to SJ GR C, to HT Nov
Exclusions Wt Limit, 16st, Age Limit, 3,
No casual hire
Location Off A666 Bolton - Blackburn
road, between Darwen golf course and
Sunnyhurst Woods. Turn up Lynwood
Avenue

ECCLESTON EQUESTRIAN CENTRE
Ulnes Walton Lane, Leyland, Preston,
Lancs, PR5 3LT
Tel 01772 600093
Contact Miss KA Green
**Riding School, Training Centre,
Facility Centre** Inst to BHSAI
Specialities Career training
Staff Chief Instructor Mrs K Green
(BHSII)
Plus 5 full time instructors
Ave No 12 Horses, 8 Ponies
inc 2 El Dress, 3 SJ GR C
Courses WP, YT, Short, Ev, P/T
Facilities
Covered School 61 x 24 gly
Outdoor Manege 43 x 21 fl lt
SJ: Nov, Grade C, Grade B, 1 Paddock
CC: Course, Nov, Banks, Natural
Lec Rm, Vis Aids, Chng Rm, Showers,
Wait Rm, Tack Shop
Hacking
Livery Full, DIY, Break, School, Hunt,
Grass
Schooling General, Break, to El Dress,
to SJ GR C, to HT Nov
Exclusions Wt Limit, 14st, Age Limit, 3,
No casual hiring without supervision
Location Off A581 Chorley to Croston
road

FIR TREE RIDING CENTRE
Fir Tree Lane, Aughton, Ormskirk,
Lancashire, L39 7HH
Tel 01695 423655
Contact Mrs S Temme
Riding School Inst Basic
Staff Chief Instructor Miss L Temme
(BHS Int Teach, BHS Int.SM)
Ave No 10 Horses, 9 Ponies
inc 2 El Dress, 2 SJ GR C, 1 SJ Jun C
Courses WP, Short, Ev, P/T, Hol
Facilities
Covered School 21 x 42 gly
SJ: Nov, Grade C, Grade B, 1 Paddock
CC: Basic, Nov, Banks, Natural,
Gallops, 10 Schooling
Lec Rm, Vis Aids, Chng Rm, Wait Rm,
Tack Shop

Hacking
Livery Full, P/T, DIY, Break, School,
Hunt
Schooling General, Break, to Med
Dress, to SJ GR C, to HT Nov
Exclusions Wt Limit, 13st7,
Age Limit, 4, No casual hire
Location A59 from Ormskirk,
3rd turning on right, dual carriageway
and 1st right into Fir Tree Lane

HALSALL RIDING &
LIVERY CENTRE
Terra Nova, Gregory Lane,
Halsall, Nr Ormskirk,
Lancs, L39 8SP
Tel 01704 840001
Contact Mr & Mrs B Beilensohn
Riding School Inst Riding & Jumping
Staff Chief Instructor Mrs June
Beilensohn (BHSAI)
Plus 2 full time instructors
Ave No 14 Horses, 10 Ponies
inc 1 El Dress
Courses Short, P/T
Facilities
Covered School 43 x 24 gly
Outdoor Manege 41 x 21 fl lt
SJ: Nov
 Chng Rm, Wait Rm
Hacking
Livery Full, P/T, DIY, Grass
Schooling General, to El Dress
Exclusions No unaccompanied hacking
Location Off the A570 Ormskirk to
Southport Road

LANDLORDS FARM
RIDING CENTRE
Dicconson Lane, Aspull,
Wigan, Lancashire, WN2 1QD
Tel 01942 831329
Contact Mr & Mrs W J Hurst
Riding School Inst Basic
Staff Chief Instructor Miss Lesley Hurst
(BHSAI)
Plus 1 full time instructor
Ave No 6 Horses, 16 Ponies
Courses YT, Ev
Facilities
Covered School 48 x 24 gly
Covered School 24 x 12
Outdoor Manege 18 x 33 fl lt
SJ: Nov, 1 Paddock
Chng Rm, Wait Rm
Hacking
Livery Full, DIY, School
Schooling General
Exclusions Wt Limit, 16st, Age Limit, 3
Location 2 minutes from Jn 6 on M61

LORDS HOUSE FARM
RIDING THERAPY CENTRE
Wilpshire Road, Rishton,
Blackburn, Lancs, BB1 4AH
Tel 01254 877400
Contact Mrs M Walker, Centre
Administrator
Riding School Inst Basic
Specialities Riding Therapy Centre run
as a Licenced Charity
Staff Chief Instructor Miss J Kenyon
(BHSAI)
Plus 3 full time instructors
Ave No 5 Horses, 13 Ponies
Courses WP, Short, Ev, P/T, Hol
Facilities
Outdoor Manege 50 x 20 fl lt
SJ: Nov
CC: Course, Basic, Water, Natural
Lec Rm, Vis Aids, Chng Rm, Wait Rm,
Tack Shop
Livery Full, P/T, DIY, School, Grass
Exclusions No casual hire
Location Off the A6064 Great
Harwood - Rishton Road

MIDGELAND RIDING SCHOOL
460 Midgeland Road, Marton,
Blackpool, Lancashire, FY4 5EE
Tel 01253 693312
Contact Mr & Mrs P H Ellis
Riding School Inst Riding & Jumping
Staff Chief Instructor Mrs Wendy Ellis
(BHSAI)
Plus 2 full time instructors
Ave No 10 Horses, 7 Ponies
inc Novice Dressage
Courses YT, Ev
Facilities
Covered School 20 x 50 gly
Outdoor Manege 20 x 40
SJ: Nov
Lec Rm, Vis Aids
Hacking
Livery Full, P/T, DIY, Grass
Schooling General, to Nov Dress,
to SJ GR C
Exclusions Wt Limit, 15st, Age Limit, 3,
No unaccompanied riding
Location Near Jn 4 of M55, between
South Blackpool and Lytham St Annes

MYERSCOUGH COLLEGE
Myerscough Hall, Bilsborrow,
Preston, Lancashire, PR3 0RY
Tel 01995 640611
Contact Prof. John Moverley
Training Centre Inst to BHSII
Specialities Career training
Staff Chief Instructor Mrs S Pimbley
(BHSI)

Plus 10 full time instructors
Ave No 35 Horses, 2 Ponies
inc 2 El Dress, 5 SJ GR C, 2 HT Int,
1 HT Adv
Courses Short, Ev, P/T, Hol
Facilities
Covered School 62 x 22 gly
Outdoor Manege 60 x 20
SJ: Grade C, 1 Paddock
CC: Basic, Banks, Water, Gallops,
12 Schooling
Lec Rm, Vis Aids, Chng Rm, Showers,
Wait Rm
Hacking
Livery School
Schooling General, Break, to El Dress,
to SJ GR B, to HT Int
Accom S, Tw, F, FB
Exclusions No casual hire.
Only students on short courses
Location Off A6 at Bilsborrow.
College is signposted

OSBALDESTON RIDING CENTRE
Osbaldeston, Blackburn,
Lancs, BB2 7LZ
Tel 01254 813159
Contact Mr N E Bargh
Facility Centre, Livery
Staff Chief Instructor Miss J Bargh
(BHSII)
Facilities
Covered School 60 x 32 gly
Covered School 35 x 17
Outdoor Manege 61 x 26
SJ: Nov, Grade C, Grade B, Grade A,
1 Paddock
CC: Course, Nov, Banks, Water, Natural
Lec Rm, Vis Aids, Chng Rm, Showers,
Wait Rm
Livery P/T, DIY, School, Grass
Schooling General, to Med Dress, to SJ
GR C
Location Near M6 Jn 31 just off the A59

WHITEMOOR RIDING CENTRE
Whitemoor Bottom Farm, Foulridge,
Colne, Lancs, BB8 7LX
Tel 01282 861890
Contact Mrs R M Stanworth
Riding School, Training Centre Inst
Riding & Jumping
Specialities Show horses
Staff Chief Instructor Mrs R M Stanworth
(BHSAI)
Plus 1 full time instructor
Ave No 10 Horses, 9 Ponies
inc 2 El Dress, Show Hunter/Ponies
Courses WP, YT, Short, Ev, P/T, Hol
Facilities
Covered School 20 x 42

43

Outdoor Manege 20 x 40 fl lt
SJ: Nov, 1 Paddock
CC: Natural, 5 Schooling
Lec Rm, Vis Aids, Chng Rm, Wait Rm
Hacking
Livery Full, P/T, Break, School, Hunt
Schooling General, Break, to El Dress
Exclusions Wt Limit, 15st, Age Limit, 5,
No unescorted hacking
Location Back road from Barrowford to
Barnoldswick, Lancs

WREA GREEN
EQUITATION CENTRE
Bryning Lane, Wrea Green,
Lancs, PR4 1TN
Tel 01772 686576
Contact Miss C A Pollitt
**Riding School, Training Centre, RDA
& SSA** Inst to BHSAI
Specialities Career training
Staff Chief Instructor Miss C A Pollitt
(BHSAI, BHS Int Teach)
Plus 2 full time instructors
Ave No 8 Horses, 12 Ponies
inc Side Saddle, RDA
Courses WP, YT, Short, Ev, P/T, Hol
Facilities
Covered School 37 x 18 gly
SJ: 1 Paddock
Lec Rm, Vis Aids, Chng Rm, Wait Rm,
Tack Shop
Livery Full, School
Schooling General, Break, to Nov
Dress, to El Dress
Accom Db, FB
Location 4 miles from Jn 3 on M55,
10 miles Blackpool, 5 miles Preston

WRIGHTINGTON
EQUESTRIAN CENTRE
Mossey Lea Road, Wrightington,
Nr Wigan, Lancs, WN6 9RE
Tel 01257 427319

Contact Mr & Mrs K W Garner
**Riding School, Training Centre, RDA
approved** Inst Riding & Jumping
3 full time instructors
Ave No 10 Horses, 10 Ponies
inc 1 El Dress, 1 Med Dress
Courses WP, YT, Short, Ev, P/T
Facilities
Covered School 20 x 40 gly
Outdoor Manege 30 x 65 fl lt
SJ: Nov, Grade C, 1 Paddock
CC: Basic, 10 Schooling
Lec Rm, Vis Aids
Hacking
Livery Full, P/T, DIY, Break, School,
Hunt
Schooling General, Break, to Med
Dress, to SJ GR C, to HT Nov
Exclusions Wt Limit, 12st,
No unescorted rides
Location 1/2 mile from Jn 27 on M6

ISLE OF MAN

GGH EQUITATION CENTRE
Ballacallin Beg, Crosby,
Marown,
Isle of Man
Tel 01624 851574/851450
Contact Mrs C Matthews & Mrs Gilbey
Riding School Inst Riding & Jumping
Ave No 6 Horses, 12 Ponies
inc 2 Med Dress
Courses Short, Ev, P/T, Hol
Facilities
CC: Course, Banks, Water, Natural
Chng Rm
Livery Full, P/T, Break, School, Hunt,
Grass
Schooling General, Break, to Med
Dress, to HT Nov

Riding in the East Midlands

DERBYSHIRE ◆ LEICESTERSHIRE
LINCOLNSHIRE ◆ NORTHAMPTONSHIRE
NOTTINGHAMSHIRE

DERBYSHIRE

ALTON RIDING SCHOOL
Alton, Chesterfield,
Derby, S42 6AW
Tel 01246 590267
Contact Mrs J D Butler
Riding School Inst Riding & Jumping
Staff Chief Instructor Mrs J D Fisher
(BHSAI)
Plus 5 full time instructors
Ave No 9 Horses, 11 Ponies
inc 5 El Dress, 1 SJ GR C
Courses YT, Short, Ev, P/T, Hol
Facilities
Covered School 19 x 45
Outdoor Manege 20 x 40 fl lt
SJ: Nov
CC: Natural, 12 Schooling
Lec Rm, Vis Aids, Tack Shop
Hacking
Livery Full, P/T, DIY, Break, School,
Hunt, Grass
Schooling General, Break, to El Dress
Accom Db, F, FB
Exclusions Wt Limit, 20st, Age Limit, 5
Location 5 miles from Chesterfield and
5 miles from Matlock

AMBER HILLS EQUESTRIAN
Whitehouse Farm, Belper Lane,
Belper, Derbys, DE56 2UJ
Tel 01773 824080
Contact Mrs V Cooke
Livery
Staff Chief Instructor Mrs V Cooke
(BHSAI, BHS Int Teach, BHS Int.SM)
inc 2 Nov HT
Facilities
Outdoor Manege 20 x 40 fl lt
Outdoor Manege 17 x 36
SJ: Nov
CC: Banks, 8 Schooling
Livery Full, P/T, Break, School
Schooling General, Break, to El Dress,
to SJ GR C, to HT Nov
Exclusions No beginners on hacks
Location Off A517, 1 mile from the
centre of Belper

**BARLEYFIELDS
EQUESTRIAN CENTRE**
Ash Lane, Etwall,
Derby, DE65 6HT
Tel 01283 734798
Contact Mrs F Smith
Riding School, Training Centre Inst
Riding & Jumping
Specialities Providing a sound base for
riders in a safe environment, which
allows riders to progress according to
their level of ability or ambition
Staff Chief Instructor Mrs F Smith
(BHSAI)
Ave No 10 Horses, 12 Ponies
inc 1 SJ GR C, 1 HT Int
Courses WP, YT, Short, Ev, P/T, Hol
Facilities
Outdoor Manege 25 x 60 fl lt
SJ: Nov, Grade C, 1 Paddock
CC: Course, Basic, Nov, Banks, Natural
Lec Rm, Vis Aids, Wait Rm, Tack Shop
Hacking
Livery Full, P/T, School, Hunt, Grass
Schooling General, to Nov Dress
Exclusions Wt Limit, 15st, Age Limit, 5,
No unescorted hacking
Location Ash Lane off the A516 Derby
to Uttoxeter road - as the A516 becomes
the Etwall By-pass

45

BIRCHWOOD
RIDING SCHOOL & SADDLERY
Birchwood Lane, Somercotes,
Derbyshire, DE55 4NE
Tel 01773 604305
Contact Ms L J Coyle
Riding School, Training Centre Inst
to BHSAI
Specialities Career training
Staff Chief Instructor Ms L J Coyle
(BHSAI, BHS Int Teach, BHS Int.SM)
Plus 2 full time instructors
Ave No 10 Horses, 8 Ponies
inc 1 El Dress, 1 SJ GR C
Courses WP, YT, Short, Ev, P/T, Hol
Facilities
Outdoor Manege 20 x 60 fl lt
Outdoor Manege 25 x 40
SJ: Nov, Grade C, 1 Paddock
CC: Banks, Natural, 10 Schooling
Lec Rm, Vis Aids, Tack Shop
Hacking
Livery Full, Break, School
Schooling General, Break, to El Dress
Location 5 mins Jn 28 M1

BREASTON EQUESTRIAN CENTRE
Sawley Road, Breaston,
Derby, DE72 3EF
Tel 01332 872934
Contact Mrs S Colley
Riding School, Training Centre Inst
Riding & Jumping
Specialities Individual intensive
courses to BHS intermediate exam level
Staff Chief Instructor Mrs S Colley
(BHSII, BHS SM)
Plus 2 full time instructors
Ave No 10 Horses, 11 Ponies
inc 1 Med Dress, 2 SJ GR C, 1 HT Int
Courses WP, YT, Short, Ev, P/T, Hol
Facilities
Outdoor Manege 40 x 20 fl lt
Outdoor Manege 40 x 20 fl lt
SJ: Nov, Grade C, Grade B, Grade A,
1 Paddock
CC: Course, Basic, Nov
Lec Rm, Vis Aids, Wait m, Tack Shop
Livery Full, P/T, Break, School, Hunt
Schooling General, Break, to Nov
Dress, to El Dress, to Med Dress, to SJ
GR C, to SJ GR B, to SJ GR A, to HT
Nov, to HT Int, to HT Adv
Exclusions Wt Limit, 13st
Location Between Jn 24 & 25 on M1,
off A6005, 1/2 mile Breaston village centre

BRIMINGTON EQUESTRIAN CENTRE
130 Manor Road, Brimington,
Chesterfield, Derbyshire, S43 1NN
Tel 01246 235465

Contact Miss T E Priest
Riding School, Training Centre Inst
Riding & Jumping
Staff Chief Instructor Miss T E Priest
(BHSAI, BHS Int Teach, BHS SM)
Plus 1 full time instructor
Ave No 10 Horses, 5 Ponies
inc 1 El Dress, 2 Med Dress, 1 Adv Dress
Courses WP, YT, Short, Ev, P/T, Hol
Facilities
Outdoor Manege 20 x 40 fl lt
SJ: 1 Paddock
CC: 6 Schooling
Lec Rm, Vis Aids, Tack Shop
Hacking
Livery Full, P/T, DIY, Break, School,
Hunt
Schooling General, Break, to El Dress,
to Med Dress, to SJ GR C, to HT Nov
Accom Dor, FB, SC
Exclusions Wt Limit, 16st, Age Limit, 2,
No unaccompanied hacks
Location 10 minutes from Jn 29/30 M1

BUXTON RIDING SCHOOL
Fern Farm, Fern Road, Buxton,
Derbyshire, SK17
Tel 01298 72319
Contact Miss L Andrew
Riding School, Trekking Centre Inst
Riding & Jumping
Staff Chief Instructor Miss L Andrew
(BHSAI)
Plus 1 full time instructor
Ave No 1 Horses, 5 Ponies
Courses YT, Ev, Hol
Facilities
Outdoor Manege 26 x 19 fl lt
Hacking
Livery Full, P/T, DIY, Break, School,
Hunt, Grass
Schooling General, Break
Location On A515 between Buxton
and Ashbourne

E M R A FOR THE HANDICAPPED
East Midlands Riding Association for
the Handicapped,
The Riding Centre, Scropton,
Derby, DE6 5PN
Tel 01283 812753
Contact Mrs Y Austin
Riding School Inst Riding & Jumping
Staff Chief Instructor Mrs Y Austin
(BHSAI)
Plus 3 full time instructors
Ave No 6 Horses, 18 Ponies
Courses WP, YT, Short, Ev, P/T, Hol
Facilities
Covered School 35 x 40 gly
Outdoor Manege 20 x 40 fl lt

SJ: Nov
Lec Rm, Vis Aids, Chng Rm, Showers,
Wait Rm
Hacking
Livery Full, P/T, DIY
Accom S, SC
Exclusions Wt Limit, 15st, Age Limit, 3,
No YT
Location Off the A50, 5 miles from
Burton-on-Trent, between Uttoxeter &
Derby

ELVASTON CASTLE RIDING CENTRE
Thulston, Derby,
Derbyshire, DE72 3EP
Tel 01332 751927
Contact Mr P J Coe & Mr F F
Anderson
Riding School, Training Centre Inst
to BHSAI
Staff Chief Instructor Mr P J Coe
(BHSII)
Plus 4 full time instructors
Ave No 15 Horses, 15 Ponies
inc 3 El Dress, 1 Med Dress, Riding
Club Level Eventing & Dressage
Courses WP, Short, Ev, P/T, Hol
Facilities
Outdoor Manege 40 x 20 fl lt
Outdoor Manege 45 x 45 fl lt
Outdoor Manege 30 x 0
SJ: Nov, 1 Paddock
CC: Course, Basic, Nov, Int, Banks,
Water, Natural
Lec Rm, Vis Aids, Wait Rm, Tack Shop
Hacking
Schooling General, to Nov Dress, to El
Dress, to Med Dress, to HT Nov
Accom S, Tw, Db, Dor, SC
Exclusions Wt Limit, 17st, Age Limit, 3,
Hunting/hire
Location Nr Borrowash on B501,
5 miles Derby and 10 miles Nottingham

HARGATE HILL RIDING SCHOOL
Hargate Hill, Glossop,
Derbyshire, SK13 9JL
Tel 01457 865518
Contact Mr & Mrs M C Tyldesley
Riding School, RDA Inst Riding &
Jumping
4 full time instructors
Ave No 10 Horses, 10 Ponies
inc 1 Med Dress, 2 SJ GR C
Courses WP, YT, Short, Ev, P/T, Hol
Facilities
Outdoor Manege 20 x 40
Outdoor Manege 40 x 20 fl lt
SJ: Grade C
CC: Basic, 15 Schooling

Lec Rm, Vis Aids, Chng Rm, Wait Rm
Hacking
Livery Full, P/T, DIY
Schooling General, Break, to El Dress,
to SJ GR C, to HT Nov
Exclusions Wt Limit, 14st,
No unescorted hacking
Location On A626 off A57 Charlesworth
- Marple

HOLME FARM EQUESTRIAN CENTRE
Watery Lane, Scropton,
Derbyshire, DE65 5PL
Tel 01283 813284
Contact Mrs J E Freer
Riding School Inst Riding & Jumping
Staff Chief Instructor Mrs J Freer (BHSII)
Ave No 15 Horses, 15 Ponies
inc 4 SJ GR C, Show horses x 2 at
County level
Courses WP, YT, Short, Ev, P/T, Hol
Facilities
Outdoor Manege 25 x 45 fl lt
SJ: Nov, Grade C
Lec Rm, Vis Aids, Wait Rm
Hacking
Livery Full, Break, School
Schooling General, Break, to Nov
Dress, to SJ GR C
Exclusions Hacking for experienced
regular riders only
Location Scropton, off A50

KNOWLE HILL EQUESTRIAN CENTRE
Knowle Hill Farm, Ingleby Lane, Ticknall,
Derby, Derbyshire, DE73 1JQ
Tel 01332 862044
Contact Mrs H Stanton
Riding School Inst Riding & Jumping
Specialities Teaching beginners and
novice riders (mainly children at present)
in riding and jumping
Staff Chief Instructor Miss Heather
Parnham
Plus 2 full time instructors
Ave No 4 Horses, 14 Ponies
Courses WP, YT, Short, Ev, P/T, Hol
Facilities
Covered School 18 x 37 gly
SJ: Nov, 1acr Paddock
CC: Course, Basic, Nov, Banks, Water,
Natural, Gallops
Lec Rm, Vis Aids, Chng Rm, Showers,
Wait Rm
Hacking
Livery Full, P/T, DIY, Break, School,
Hunt, Grass
Schooling General, Break
Exclusions Age Limit, 6,
No unescorted hacking
Location Near centre of Ticknall village

47

MANOR FARM LIVERY
Hartshorne, Swadlincote,
Derbyshire, DE11 7ER
Tel 01283 215769
Contact Mr & Mrs D J Burchell
Livery
Facilities
SJ: Nov
CC: Course, Nov, Int, Water, Natural
Chng Rm
Hacking
Livery DIY, Grass
Exclusions All potential livery owners
interviewed
Location Off A514 5 miles from Ashby
De La Zouch

NORTHFIELD FARM RIDING & TREKKING CENTRE
Flash, Buxton,
Derby, SK17 0SW
Tel 01298 22543
Contact Mrs D C Andrews
Trekking Centre, Livery Inst Basic
1 full time instructor
Ave No 20 Horses, 15 Ponies
Courses YT
Facilities
Outdoor Manege 20 x 40
Chng Rm, Wait Rm
Hacking
Livery Full, P/T, DIY, Break, School,
Hunt, Grass
Schooling General
Accom Tw, F, Dor, Cottage, SC
Exclusions Wt Limit, 18st, Age Limit, 7
Location 1/2 mile from A53 Buxton -
Leek road, in the village of Flash

RED HOUSE STABLES
Old Road, Darley Dale,
Matlock, Derbyshire, DE4 2ER
Tel 01629 733583
Contact Mrs C Dale-Leech
**Riding School, Training Centre,
Stage coach & four in hand trips,
Driving Inst** Inst Riding & Jumping
Specialities B.D.S. courses - up to
level 4
Staff Chief Instructor Miss J Green
(BHSII)
Plus 2 full time instructors
Ave No 10 Horses, 8 Ponies
Courses WP, YT, Short, P/T, Hol
Lec Rm, Vis Aids, Chng Rm, Showers,
Wait Rm
Hacking
Livery Break, School
Schooling General, Break
Accom Tw, Db, Dor, Caravan
Exclusions Wt Limit, 16st, Age Limit, 3

Location Just off A6, 2 miles north of
Matlock. Between Matlock and
Bakewell

RINGER VILLA EQUESTRIAN CENTRE
Ringer Lane, Clowne,
Derbyshire, S43 4BX
Tel 01246 810456
Contact Mrs Y M Evans
**Riding School, RDA & Training
Agency for Special Needs** Inst Riding
& Jumping
Specialities Career training
4 full time instructors
Ave No 10 Horses, 14 Ponies
Courses WP, YT, Short, Ev, P/T, Hol
Facilities
Outdoor Manege 40 x 20
Lec Rm, Vis Aids, Chng Rm, Showers,
Wait Rm
Livery Full, P/T, DIY, Break, School,
Grass
Location 2 miles off Jn 30 M1 near
town centre

STUBLEY HOLLOW RIDING CENTRE
Stubley Hollow, Dronfield,
Derbyshire, S18 1PP
Tel 01246 419207
Contact Miss Patsy Day
Riding School, Facility Centre Inst
Riding & Jumping
Specialities Career training,
Adults only
2 full time instructors
Ave No 10 Horses
Courses WP, YT, Ev, P/T
Facilities
Covered School 20 x 40 gly
Outdoor Manege 60 x 30 fl lt
Outdoor Manege 20 x 20 fl lt
SJ: Nov, 1 Paddock
Lec Rm, Vis Aids, Chng Rm, Showers,
Wait Rm, Tack Shop
Hacking
Livery Full, P/T, DIY, Break, School
Schooling General, Break, to Nov
Dress, to Med Dress, to SJ GR C
Exclusions Wt Limit, 16st
Location Just off A61 between
Chesterfield and Sheffield

YEW TREE FARM STABLES
Hazelwood, Derbyshire, DE6 4AE
Tel 01332 841364
Contact Messrs M & H Lester
**Riding School, Training Centre,
Horse Dealer/Importer** Inst Riding &
Jumping

Specialities High peak trail rides, `Own A Pony` sessions and cobs/ponies for sale
2 full time instructors
Ave No 10 Horses, 10 Ponies
Courses WP, YT, Short
Facilities
Covered School 24 x 30
CC: Basic
Wait Rm
Hacking
Livery Full, P/T, School, Hunt, Grass
Schooling General, Break
Exclusions Wt Limit, 16st,
Age Limit, 5 1/2
Location 7 miles north of Derby off A6

LEICESTERSHIRE

BROOKSBY COLLEGE
Brooksby, Melton Mowbray,
Leicestershire, LE14 2LJ
Tel 01664 434291/424280
Contact T J Gray
Riding School, Training Centre, Facility Centre Inst to BHSII
Specialities College students
Staff Chief Instructor Mrs F Bird (BHSI)
Plus 10 full time instructors
Ave No 22 Horses, 1 Ponies
inc 4 El Dress
Courses Short, Ev, P/T, Hol
Facilities
Covered School 60 x 30 gly
Covered School 30 x 20
Outdoor Manege 20 x 40
SJ: Nov, Grade C, 1 Paddock
CC: Course, Nov, Banks, Natural, Gallops
Lec Rm, Vis Aids, Chng Rm, Wait Rm
Livery Full, Break, School, Hunt
Schooling General, Break, to Med Dress, to SJ GR B, to HT Int
Exclusions Wt Limit, 15st,
No casual hire
Location On A607 between Melton Mowbray & Leicester

CANAAN FARM RIDING SCHOOL
Loughborough Road, Costock,
Loughborough, Leics, LE12 6XB
Tel 01509 853351
Contact Mrs J Chiasserini
Riding School Inst Riding & Jumping
1 full time instructor
Ave No 4 Horses, 10 Ponies
Courses WP, YT
Facilities
SJ: Nov, 1 Paddock
CC: Natural, 6 Schooling

Hacking
Livery Full, P/T, DIY, Break, School, Hunt
Schooling General, Break, to Nov Dress, to SJ GR C
Exclusions Wt Limit, 13st7, Age Limit, 5, No casual hire
Location Off A60 between Nottingham and Loughborough

HARDWICKE LODGE FARM
Forest Road, Enderby,
Leicester, LE9 5LD
Tel 01162 863056
Contact Mr & Mrs J Smith
Riding School Inst Riding & Jumping
2 full time instructors
Ave No 12 Ponies
Facilities
Outdoor Manege 60 x 25 fl lt
SJ: Nov
Lec Rm, Vis Aids
Livery DIY
Exclusions Age Limit, 5, No horses with stable vices accepted
Location 2 miles from Jn 21 of M1-M69 interchange

IVANHOE EQUESTRIAN CENTRE
Ivanhoe House, Smisby Road,
Ashby de la Zouche, Leics, LE6 5UG
Tel 01530 413629
Contact Mr & Mrs J D Lebutt
Riding School Inst Riding & Jumping
Specialities Children, native ponies, preparation for shows and showing
1 full time instructor
Ave No 1 Horses, 18 Ponies
inc 2 SJ Jun C
Courses WP, YT, Ev, P/T
Facilities
Covered School 22 x 45
Outdoor Manege 45 x 50 fl lt
SJ: Nov, 1 Paddock
Lec Rm, Vis Aids, Chng Rm, Showers, Wait Rm
Schooling General
Exclusions Wt Limit, 12st, Age Limit, 5, Hacking for regular clients only
Location On B5006 1 mile from centre of Ashby

MARKFIELD EQUESTRIAN CENTRE
Stanton Lane Farm, Markfield,
Leics, LE6 0TT
Tel 01530 242373
Contact Mr & Mrs J Duffield
Riding School, Competition Centre for Show Jumping & Dressage Inst Riding & Jumping

3 full time instructors
Ave No 17 Horses, 21 Ponies
Courses WP, Ev
Facilities
Covered School 30 x 60 gly
Covered School 20 x 40
Outdoor Manege 30 x 60 fl lt
SJ: Grade A
Lec Rm, Vis Aids, Chng Rm
Livery Full, P/T, DIY
Exclusions Wt Limit, 15st, Age Limit, 5
Location 500 yards from A50. 1 mile
from M1 Jn 22

MEADOW SCHOOL OF RIDING
The Stables, Stanford-on-Soar,
Loughborough, Leics, LE12 5PY
Tel 01509 263782
Contact Mr D Allonby
**Riding School, Training Centre,
Facility Centre** Inst Basic
Specialities Specialise in breeding
Highland & Native ponies & RDA work
Staff Chief Instructor Miss D Whitmore
(BHSAI)
Ave No 5 Horses, 10 Ponies
inc RDA Horses/Quality native breeding
ponies
Courses WP, YT, Short, Ev, P/T
Facilities
Covered School 41 x 21
SJ: Nov, 1 Paddock
CC: 4 Schooling
Lec Rm, Vis Aids, Chng Rm
Hacking
Livery Full, P/T, Break, School, Hunt,
Grass
Schooling General, Break
Exclusions Wt Limit, 15st, Age Limit, 3
Location 1 mile from Loughborough

PARKVIEW LEICESTER
EQUESTRIAN CENTRE
Anstey Lane, Thurcaston,
Leicester, LE7 7JB
Tel 0116 236 4858
Contact Mrs McDonald
Riding School, Trekking Centre Inst
Riding & Jumping
4 full time instructors
Ave No 10 Horses, 14 Ponies
Courses YT
Facilities
Covered School 20 x 40
Outdoor Manege 20 x 40 fl lt
SJ: Nov, 1 Paddock
CC: Course, Basic, Natural
Chng Rm, Showers, Wait Rm, Tack
Shop
Hacking
Livery Full, P/T, DIY

Schooling to SJ GR A
Exclusions Age Limit, 3
Location Leave A46 bypass 5 miles
north of centre of Leicester at Ansty Jn

STRETTON RIDING CENTRE
Manor Bungalow Farm, Stretton,
Oakham, Rutland, Leics, LE15 7QZ
Tel 01780 410323
Contact Mrs J L Ward
Riding School, Training Centre Inst
Riding & Jumping
Staff Chief Instructor Miss S Dalby
(BHSAI)
Ave No 8 Horses, 20 Ponies
Courses WP, Short, Ev, P/T, Hol
Facilities
Covered School 90 x 30
Outdoor Manege 20 x 40
SJ: Nov, 1 Paddock
CC: Course, Basic, Nov, Banks, Water,
Natural
Chng Rm
Schooling General, Break, to Nov
Dress, to HT Nov
Exclusions Wt Limit, 15st, Age Limit, 5
Location Off A1 within the triangle of
Grantham/Oakham/Stamford

SWAN LODGE
EQUESTRIAN CENTRE
Station Road, Upper Broughton,
Melton Mowbray,
Leics, LE14 3BH
Tel 01664 823686
Contact Mr I R Jalland & Miss D A T
Jalland
Riding School Inst Riding & Jumping
Specialities Unaffiliated shows on a
regular basis, Progressive Riding Test
& Riding and Road Safety Courses
arranged
Staff Chief Instructor Miss Lara
Penlington (BHSAI)
Plus 3 full time instructors
Ave No 8 Horses, 18 Ponies
Courses WP, YT, Short, Ev, P/T, Hol
Facilities
Outdoor Manege 40 x 20 fl lt
Outdoor Manege 40 x 40 fl lt
SJ: Grade C, 1 Paddock
CC: Course, Basic, Nov, Banks, Water,
Natural
Lec Rm, Vis Aids, Chng Rm, Showers,
Wait Rm
Hacking
Livery Full, P/T, Break, School, Hunt,
Grass
Schooling General, Break, to El Dress,
to SJ GR C, to HT Nov
Accom Tw, Dor, Cottage, SC

Exclusions Wt Limit, 17st, Age Limit, 5,
No casual hire
Location Off A46 7 miles from Melton
Mowbray

WITHAM VILLA
Witham Villa Riding Centre,
Cosby Road, Broughton Astley,
Leicestershire, LE14 6PA
Tel 01455 282694
Contact Mrs V Saul
**Riding School, Training Centre,
Facility Centre, Trekking Centre** Inst
to BHSAI
Specialities Career training
Staff Chief Instructor Mrs V Saul
(BHSII)
Plus 2 full time instructors
Ave No 13 Horses, 13 Ponies
inc 3 El Dress, 2 SJ GR C
Courses WP, YT, Short, Ev, P/T, Hol
Facilities
Covered School 20 x 37 gly
Outdoor Manege 20 x 40 fl lt
SJ: Grade C, 1 Paddock
Lec Rm, Vis Aids, Wait Rm
Hacking
Livery School
Schooling General, to El Dress, to SJ
GR C, to HT Nov
Exclusions Wt Limit, 14st,
No casual hire
Location Off B4114 towards Broughton
Astley, 2nd on the left towards Cosby

LINCOLNSHIRE

AUSTER LODGE RIDING STABLES
Dolan Lane, Edenham, Bourne,
Lincolnshire, PE10 0LH
Tel 01778 591287
Contact Mr R F D Haddow
**Riding School, Training Centre,
Facility Centre** Inst Basic
Specialities Interesting hacking
Staff Chief Instructor Miss L Cornall
(BHSAI)
Plus 1 full time instructor
Ave No 14 Horses, 7 Ponies
inc 1 SJ GR C
Courses WP, YT, Short, Ev, P/T, Hol
Facilities
Covered School 27 x 18 gly
Outdoor Manege 30 x 15
SJ: Nov, Grade C, 1 Paddock
CC: Course, Nov, Int, Banks, Water,
Natural, Gallops
Lec Rm, Vis Aids, Chng Rm, Showers,
Wait Rm
Hacking

Livery Full, P/T, DIY, Break, School,
Hunt, Grass
Schooling General, Break, to Nov
Dress, to El Dress, to SJ GR C, to HT
Nov
Accom Db, FB
Exclusions Wt Limit, 20st, Age Limit, 3
Location 10 miles north of Stamford on
Edenham - Toft road

CAYTHORPE COURT
EQUESTRIAN CENTRE
De Montfort University, Lincoln,
Caythorpe Court, Caythorpe,
Grantham, Lincs, NG32 3EP
Tel 01400 272521
Contact Mr N Locke
**Riding School, Training Centre,
Facility Centre** Inst to BHSII
Specialities Career training
8 full time instructors
Ave No 54 Horses
inc 5 El Dress, 2 Med Dress, 3 SJ GR C,
2 HT Int, 2 HT Adv
Courses YT, Short, Ev, P/T, Hol
Facilities
Covered School 20 x 40
Outdoor Manege 40 x 60 fl lt
SJ: Nov, Grade C, 1 Paddock
CC: Natural, 15 Schooling
Lec Rm, Vis Aids, Chng Rm, Showers,
Wait Rm
Livery Full, P/T, School
Schooling General, to Med Dress, to SJ
GR C, to HT Int
Accom S, Tw, Dor, FB, SC
Exclusions Wt Limit, 13st, Age Limit, 13
Location Caythorpe Heath, off A607 or
A17

FOUR WINDS EQUESTRIAN CENTRE
Leaveslake Drove, West Pinchbeck,
Lincs, PE11 3QJ
Tel 01775 640533
Contact Mrs P V Matthews
Riding School Inst Riding & Jumping
Staff Chief Instructor Mrs P V Matthews
(BHSAI, BHS Int Teach)
Plus 1 full time instructor
Ave No 10 Horses, 7 Ponies
inc 4 El Dress, 1 SJ GR C, 2 Horse
Trials Novice
Courses WP, YT, Ev, P/T, Hol
Facilities
Covered School 20 x 43 gly
Outdoor Manege 20 x 40 fl lt
SJ: Nov, 1 Paddock
CC: Course, Basic, Banks
Lec Rm, Vis Aids, Wait Rm
Hacking
Livery Full, P/T

Schooling General
Exclusions Wt Limit, 12st
Location Off A1511, 4 miles from
Spalding and 6 miles from Bourne

HILL HOUSE EQUESTRIAN CENTRE
Sand Lane, Osgodby, Market Rasen,
Lincs, LN8 3TE
Tel 01673 843407
Contact Ms L Tither
**Riding School, Training Centre,
Facility Centre,
RDA/Competition/Hacking** Inst to
BHSAI
Specialities Sidesaddle and Driving
6 full time instructors
Ave No 26 Horses, 12 Ponies
inc 4 El Dress, 4 SJ GR C, 2 SJ Jun C
Courses WP, YT, Short, Ev, P/T, Hol
Facilities
Covered School 67 x 24 gly
Covered School 37 x 18
Outdoor Manege 30 x 55 fl lt
Outdoor Manege 40 x 20 fl lt
SJ: Grade A, 3 Paddock
CC: Basic, Nov, Banks, Water, Natural,
16 Schooling
Lec Rm, Vis Aids, Chng Rm, Wait Rm
Hacking
Livery Full, P/T, Break, School, Hunt
Schooling General, Break, to El Dress,
to SJ GR B, to HT Int
Accom S, Tw, Caravan, Cottage, FB,
SC
Exclusions Wt Limit, 14st
Location Off A46 2 1/2 miles from
Market Rasen

LAUGHTON MANOR
EQUESTRIAN CENTRE
Manor Farm, Laughton, Folkingham,
Sleaford, Lincolnshire NG34 0HB
Tel 01529 497519
Contact Mrs M J Key
**Riding School, Training Centre,
Facility Centre, Driving tuition** Inst
Riding & Jumping
Specialities Driving tuition
Staff Chief Instructor Mr Sam Twyman
Plus 2 full time instructors
Ave No 10 Horses, 13 Ponies
inc 1 El Dress, 1 Adv Dress, 1 SJ GR
C, 1 SJ GR B, 1 SJ Jun C, 2 HT Int
Courses WP, YT, Short, Ev
Facilities
Covered School 12 x 35
Covered School 60 x 24 gly
Outdoor Manege 60 x 36
SJ: Grade C, Grade A, 1 Paddock
CC: Course, Basic, Nov, Banks, Water,
Natural, Gallops, 30 Schooling

Lec Rm, Vis Aids, Chng Rm, Wait Rm
Hacking
Livery Full, P/T, DIY, Break, School,
Hunt
Schooling General, Break, to Adv
Dress, to SJ GR B, to HT Adv
Exclusions Age Limit, 2 No casual hire
Location On A15, 8 miles from Bourne
& 7 miles from Sleaford

LINESIDE RIDING STABLES
Lineside Farm, Amber Hill,
Boston, Lincs, PE20 3RA
Tel 01205 820744
Contact Miss J Key
Riding School, Training Centre Inst
Basic
Staff Chief Instructor Mrs N Betts
(BHSAI, BHS Int.SM)
Plus 2 full time instructors
Ave No 25 Horses, 40 Ponies
inc 3 El Dress, 3 SJ GR C
Courses WP, Ev, P/T, Hol
Facilities
Covered School 31 x 22 gly
Outdoor Manege 25 x 45 fl lt
SJ: Nov, 1 Paddock
CC: Banks, Natural, 5 Schooling
Lec Rm, Vis Aids, Chng Rm, Tack
Shop
Hacking
Livery Full, P/T, Break, School, Hunt
Schooling General, Break, to SJ GR C
Exclusions Wt Limit, 15st, Age Limit, 4,
No unaccompanied riding
Location On A1122, 6 miles from
Boston

REDNIL FARM
EQUESTRIAN CENTRE
Lincoln Road, Welton,
Lincoln, LN2 3JE
Tel 01673 860548
Contact Mrs A C Linder
**Riding School, Driving and Side
Saddle Instruction** Inst Riding &
Jumping
1 full time instructor
Ave No 19 Horses, 9 Ponies
inc 3 El Dress, 5 SJ GR C
Courses YT, Short, Ev, P/T, Hol
Facilities
Covered School 30 x 17 gly
Outdoor Manege 20 x 40 fl lt
Outdoor Manege 20 x 40 fl lt
SJ: Nov, 1 Paddock
CC: Course, Basic, Nov, Banks, Water,
Natural
Lec Rm, Vis Aids, Chng Rm, Showers,
Wait Rm, Tack Shop
Hacking

Livery Full, P/T, DIY, Break, School, Grass
Schooling General, Break, to El Dress, to SJ GR C
Exclusions Wt Limit, 14st7, Age Limit, 6
Location 6 miles north of Lincoln, between A15 and A45

SAXILBY RIDING SCHOOL
High Street, Saxilby,
Lincoln, LN1 2HA
Tel 01522 702240
Contact Mr & Mrs M J Scott
Riding School, RDA riding & hunter hire Inst Basic
Specialities Riding for the disabled
1 full time instructor
Ave No 10 Horses, 12 Ponies
Courses WP, YT, Ev, P/T, Hol
Facilities
SJ: Nov, 1 Paddock
Lec Rm, Vis Aids, Chng Rm, Showers, Wait Rm
Hacking
Livery Full, P/T, Break, School, Hunt, Grass
Schooling General, Break, to SJ GR B
Accom Dor, FB
Exclusions Wt Limit, 13st, Age Limit, 4, No casual hire
Location 1 mile A57 in centre of village

THORPE GRANGE EQUESTRIAN CENTRE
Newark Road, Lincoln, LN5 9EJ
Tel 01522 680159/500022
Contact Mrs E Poskitt
Riding School, Training Centre, Facility Centre Inst Riding & Jumping
Staff Chief Instructor Mr S Cruickshank (BHSII, BHS SM)
Plus 3 full time instructors
Ave No 25 Horses, 14 Ponies
inc 1 El Dress, 1 SJ GR C, Riding Club comp. horses
Courses WP, YT, Short, Ev, P/T, Hol
Facilities
Covered School 25 x 80 gly
Covered School 48 x 20
SJ: Grade A, 1 Paddock
CC: Course, Basic, Nov, Banks, Water, Natural, 21 Schooling
Lec Rm, Vis Aids, Chng Rm, Wait Rm
Hacking
Livery Full, P/T, DIY, Break, School, Hunt, Grass
Schooling General, Break, to El Dress, to SJ GR C, to HT Nov
Exclusions Wt Limit, 13st, Age Limit, 5, No unaccompanied
Location Off A46 4 miles from Lincoln

NORTHAMPTONSHIRE

BRAMPTON STABLES
Church Brampton,
Northampton, NN6 8AU
Tel 01604 842051
Contact Mr D Ward
Riding School, Training Centre Inst to BHSI
Specialities Career training
Staff Chief Instructor Mrs J Ward (BHSI)
Plus 3 full time instructors
Ave No 20 Horses, 20 Ponies
inc 4 El Dress, 4 Med Dress, 2 SJ GR C, Side-Saddle
Courses WP, YT, Short, Ev, P/T
Facilities
Covered School 20 x 40 gly
Outdoor Manege 20 x 60
Outdoor Manege 20 x 40 fl lt
SJ: Nov, Grade C, 1 Paddock
CC: Course, Nov, Banks, Water, Natural
Lec Rm, Vis Aids, Chng Rm, Wait Rm
Hacking
Schooling General, to Adv Dress, to SJ GR B, to HT Int, to HT Adv
Accom S, Tw, Db, Cottage, SC
Exclusions Wt Limit, 13st7, Age Limit, 6, No unescorted hiring
Location 5 miles north of Northampton. 12 miles from Jn 18 on M1

EAST LODGE FARM RIDING ESTABLISHMENT
East Lodge Farm,
Ecton,
Northampton, NN6 0QV
Tel 01604 810244
Contact Mr & Mrs R D White
Riding School, Training Centre Inst Basic
2 full time instructors
Ave No 8 Horses, 10 Ponies
Courses WP, YT, Short, Ev, P/T, Hol
Facilities
Covered School 20 x 14
SJ: Nov, 1 Paddock
CC: Course, Basic, Nov, Banks, Water, Natural, Gallops
Lec Rm, Vis Aids, Chng Rm, Showers
Hacking
Livery Full, P/T, DIY, School, Hunt, Grass
Schooling General, to Nov Dress
Accom Tw, Db, Dor, FB
Exclusions Wt Limit, 15st, Age Limit, 3 1/2
Location Between Northampton and Wellingborough on A4500

EVERGREEN RIDING STABLES
Gayton,
Northampton, NN7 3HD
Tel 01604 858247/832916
Contact Mr M D East
Riding School Inst Basic
1 full time instructor
Ave No 8 Horses, 12 Ponies
Courses YT, Short, Hol
Facilities
Outdoor Manege 40 x 40 fl lt
SJ: 1 Paddock
Wait Rm
Hacking
Exclusions Wt Limit, 13st, Age Limit, 4
Location Jn 15A off M1, 3 miles off
A43

FOXHILL FARM
EQUESTRIAN CENTRE
Sywell Road, Holcot,
Northampton, NN6 9SN
Tel 01604 781191
Contact Miss L Stephenson & Miss J
Giles
Riding School, Training Centre Inst
Riding & Jumping
Staff Chief Instructor Miss Laurie
Stephenson (BHSI)
Plus 1 full time instructor
Ave No 8 Horses, 9 Ponies
inc 3 El Dress, 1 Med Dress
Courses Short, Ev, P/T, Hol
Facilities
Outdoor Manege 45 x 23
Outdoor Manege 40 x 20
SJ: Nov, Grade C, 1 Paddock
CC: Basic, Banks, Natural, 15
Schooling
Lec Rm, Vis Aids, Chng Rm, Wait Rm
Hacking
Exclusions Wt Limit, 13st, Age Limit, 6,
Escorted hacks only
Location 1 mile off A43, 7 miles north
of Northampton

GREENACRES LIVERY CENTRE
Green Farm, Puxley,
Towcester, Northants, NN12 7QS
Tel 01908 566092
Contact Mrs T J Smith
Livery
Specialities Four RDA groups
Staff Chief Instructor Miss B
McLachlan (BHSAI)
Plus 1 full time instructor
Facilities
Covered School 30 x 15 gly
Covered School 25 x 65 gly
Wait Rm
Hacking

54

Livery Full, P/T, DIY, Break, School,
Grass
Exclusions Instruction available on
clients' own horses
Location Off A5, 5 miles from
Towcester, 10 miles from Milton Keynes

MANDI'S LIVERY SERVICES
Teeton Lodge Farm,
Ravensthorpe Road, Teeton,
Northamptonshire, NN6 8LP
Tel 01604 505777
Contact Miss A Gale
Livery
Ave No 2 Horses, 6 Ponies
Facilities
SJ: Nov, 1 Paddock
CC: Course, Nov, Banks, Water, Natural
Hacking
Livery Full, P/T, DIY, Hunt, Grass

MOULTON COLLEGE
West Street, Moulton,
Northants, NN3 1RR
Tel 01604 491131/492653
Contact Mr C Moody
Training Centre, Facility Centre,
Livery Inst to BHSII
Specialities Career training
5 full time instructors
Ave No 33 Horses, 3 Ponies
inc 2 El Dress, 2 Med Dress, 1 Adv
Dress, 2 SJ GR C, 1 SJ Jun C, 1 HT
Int, 1 HT Adv
Courses WP, Short, Ev, P/T, Hol
Facilities
Covered School 20 x 62 gly
Outdoor Manege 24 x 60
Outdoor Manege 20 x 40
SJ: Grade C, 1 Paddock
CC: Course, Basic, Nov, Banks, Water,
Natural
Lec Rm, Vis Aids, Chng Rm, Wait Rm
Hacking
Livery P/T, Break, School
Schooling General, Break, to Med
Dress, to SJ GR B
Accom S, Tw, FB
Exclusions Wt Limit, 12st7,
No casual hiring
Location Situated on the Pitsford -
Moulton road, between the A43 and
A508

SHUCKBURGH HOUSE
RIDING CENTRE
Naseby, Northampton, NN6 6DA
Tel 01604 740481
Contact Mrs D S Muirhead
Training Centre, Livery, NVQ Stud

Training, Levels 1 & 2 Inst Riding & Jumping
Staff Chief Instructor Miss Pauline Rich (BHSAI)
Plus 1 full time instructor
Courses WP
Facilities
Outdoor Manege 20 x 40 fl lt
SJ: Nov
CC: 8 Schooling
Lec Rm, Vis Aids, Chng Rm
Livery Full, Break, School, Hunt
Schooling General, Break, to Adv Dress, to SJ GR C, to HT Adv
Exclusions Schooling on clients' own horses only
Location On B4036 in Naseby village centre

NOTTINGHAMSHIRE

BEVERCOTES GRANGE STUD & EQUESTRIAN CENTRE
Bevercotes, Tuxford, Newark,
Nottinghamshire, NG22 0PS
Tel 01623 860305
Contact Mrs S M Goodlad
Riding School Inst Basic
Specialities Encouragement to riders to improve their riding and general knowledge of horsemanship
Staff Chief Instructor Mrs S Goodland
Ave No 10 Horses, 10 Ponies
inc 1 El Dress, 1 SJ GR C
Courses YT, Short, Ev, P/T, Hol
Facilities
Covered School 30 x 15
Outdoor Manege 38 x 23
SJ: Nov, 1 Paddock
Lec Rm, Vis Aids, Chng Rm, Wait Rm
Hacking
Livery Full, P/T, DIY, Break, School, Hunt, Grass
Schooling Break, to El Dress, to SJ GR C, to HT Nov
Accom Db, FB
Exclusions Wt Limit, 14st, Age Limit, 4
Location 1 mile from A1 & A57 Jn

BLOOMSGORSE TREKKING CENTRE
Bloomsgorse Farm, Bilsthorpe,
Nr Newark,
Nottinghamshire, NG22 8TA
Tel 01623 870276
Contact Mrs Z Grant
Trekking Centre, R.D.A.
Staff Chief Instructor Mrs R Monks (BHSAI)
Plus 2 full time instructors

Ave No 15 Horses, 15 Ponies
Facilities
Outdoor Manege 30 x 40
Chng Rm, Wait Rm
Hacking
Exclusions No children under 7 years
Location Off A614, 4 miles south of Ollerton

BRACKENHURST COLLEGE
Nottinghamshire County Council,
Southwell,
Nottinghamshire, NG25 OQF
Tel 01636 817000
Contact Mrs J Rodgerson
Riding School, Training Centre, Facility Centre Inst to BHSI
Specialities Career training
Staff Chief Instructor Miss E J Jones (BHSI)
Plus 8 full time instructors
Ave No 55 Horses
inc 8 El Dress, 4 Med Dress, 1 Adv Dress, 5 SJ GR C, 2 SJ GR B, 3 HT Int, 2 HT Adv, 2 Sidesaddle, 1 Drive, 1 Endurance
Courses YT, Short, Ev, P/T, Hol
Facilities
Covered School 60 x 40
Outdoor Manege 60 x 40
Outdoor Manege 40 x 20
SJ: Grade B, 5 Paddock
CC: Basic, Nov, Natural, 12 Schooling
Lec Rm, Vis Aids, Chng Rm, Showers, Wait Rm
Hacking
Livery Full, P/T, DIY, Break, School, Hunt
Schooling General, Break, to Adv Dress, to SJ GR B, to HT Int
Accom Dor, Caravan, FB
Exclusions Wt Limit, 14st, Age Limit, 14, College students only during term time
Location On A612 just south of Southwell

COLLEGE FARM EQUESTRIAN CENTRE
West Markham, Tuxford,
Newark, Notts, NG22 0PN
Tel 01777 870886
Contact Mrs V H G Hayton
Riding School, Training Centre, Facility Centre Inst Riding & Jumping
Specialities Competition training and courses tailored to individual needs
Staff Chief Instructor Mrs V H G Hayton (BHS SM)
Plus 4 full time instructors
Ave No 16 Horses, 12 Ponies
inc 5 El Dress, 3 Med Dress, 5 SJ GR C,

3 SJ GR B, 3 SJ Jun C, 2 HT Int,
5 Horses trained to Side-Saddle
Courses WP, YT, Short, Ev, P/T, Hol
Facilities
Covered School 20 x 40 gly
Outdoor Manege 20 x 60
Outdoor Manege 20 x 60
Outdoor Manege 20 x 40
SJ: Nov, Grade C, Grade B, 1 Paddock
CC: Course, Basic, Nov, Banks, Water,
Natural
Lec Rm, Vis Aids, Chng Rm
Hacking
Livery Full, P/T, DIY, Break, School,
Hunt
Schooling General, Break, to El Dress,
to Med Dress, to SJ GR B, to HT Int
Accom S, FB
Exclusions Wt Limit, 14st, Age Limit, 3
Location Off A1, 10 miles north of
Newark

LINGS LANE RIDING STABLES
Keyworth,
Nottinghamshire, NG12 5AF
Tel 0115 937 2527
Contact Mr & Mrs I T and J M Flint
Riding School Inst Riding & Jumping
Specialities Instruction tailored to
individual needs
Staff Chief Instructor Mr T Flint
Ave No 15 Horses, 20 Ponies
inc General hacking & Schooling
Courses YT, Short, Ev, P/T, Hol
Facilities
Outdoor Manege 20 x 40
SJ: Nov, 1 Paddock
CC: Banks, Natural, 13 Schooling
Hacking
Livery P/T, Grass
Exclusions No unescorted hacking
Location Off A60 between Nottingham
& Loughborough

MANOR FARM LIVERY YARD
Manor Farm, Moor Lane, Gotham,
Nottingham, NG11 0ZH
Tel 0115 983 0051
Contact Mr R Davey
Livery
Facilities
Outdoor Manege 60 x 20 fl lt
SJ: Nov, Grade C, 1 Paddock
CC: Course, Basic, Nov, Banks, Water,
Natural, Gallops
Chng Rm
Livery Full, P/T, DIY, Grass
Location 6 miles south of Nottingham,
7 miles from Jn 24 off the M1, 20 miles
north of Leicester and 10 miles from
Derby

SELSTON EQUESTRIAN CENTRE
Commonside, Selston,
Notts, NG16 6FJ
Tel 01773 813817
Contact Mr Eric Burr
Riding School, Training Centre Inst
to BHSII
Staff Chief Instructor Mr Eric Burr (BHSI)
Plus 1 full time instructor
Ave No 10 Horses, 12 Ponies
inc 4 El Dress, 2 SJ GR C
Courses WP, YT, Short, Ev, P/T
Facilities
Covered School 25 x 50 gly
Outdoor Manege 20 x 40 fl lt
SJ: Grade A, 2 Paddock
CC: Banks, Natural, 12 Schooling
Lec Rm, Vis Aids, Wait Rm, Tack Shop
Livery Full, Break, School, Hunt
Schooling General, Break, to Med
Dress, to SJ GR A, to HT Int
Exclusions Wt Limit, 13st7, Age Limit, 6
Location 5 minutes Jn 27 & 28 off M1

ST CLEMENTS LODGE
RIDING SCHOOL
Woods Lane, Calverton,
Nottingham, Notts, NG14 6FF
Tel 0115 965 2524
Contact Mr N Burrows
Riding School Inst Riding & Jumping
Staff Chief Instructor Mr N Burrows
(BHSII)
Plus 3 full time instructors
Ave No 12 Horses, 14 Ponies
Facilities
Covered School 21 x 60 gly
SJ: Nov, 1 Paddock
Lec Rm, Vis Aids, Wait Rm, Tack Shop
Hacking
Schooling General
Exclusions Wt Limit, 14st, Age Limit, 6,
No hiring out for hacking
Location 8 miles north of Nottingham
off A614

WELLOW PARK
STABLES & SADDLERY
Rufford Lane, Wellow, Newark,
Notts, NG22 0EQ
Tel 01623 861040
Contact Mrs M M Willett
Riding School, Training Centre,
Facility Centre, Exam
Centre/Driving/Side Saddle Inst to
BHSAI
Specialities Side Saddle & driving
2 full time instructors
Ave No 20 Horses, 10 Ponies
inc 1 HT Int, Single Driving Ponies &
Side Saddle

Courses WP, YT, Short, Ev, P/T, Hol
Facilities
Covered School 20 x 40
Outdoor Manege 20 x 60 fl lt
Outdoor Manege 20 x 20 fl lt
SJ: Nov, Grade C, 1 Paddock
CC: Course, Basic, Nov, Banks,
Natural, Gallops, 30 Schooling
Lec Rm, Vis Aids, Chng Rm, Showers,
Wait Rm, Tack Shop

Hacking
Livery Full, P/T, Break, School, Hunt,
Grass
Schooling General, Break, to El Dress,
to SJ GR C, to HT Int
Accom Tw, Db, Dor, Caravan, FB
Exclusions Age Limit, 4
Location 1 mile from Ollerton
Roundabout, 10 miles from Newark on
A616

E
A
S
T

M
I
D
L
A
N
D
S

Riding in the West Midlands

HEREFORDSHIRE ◆ WORCESTERSHIRE
STAFFORDSHIRE ◆ WARWICKSHIRE
WEST MIDLANDS ◆ SHROPSHIRE

HEREFORDSHIRE

COUNTY COMPETITION STUD & LIVERY YARD
Home Farm, Munderfield Harold,
Bromyard, Herefordshire, HR7 4SZ
Tel 01885 482062
Contact Mrs Y L Wall
Training Centre, Livery, Stud Ridden & in Hand Stallions
Courses WP, YT, Short
Facilities
Outdoor Manege 20 x 30 fl lt
SJ: Nov
CC: Banks, Water, Natural, Gallops,
10 Schooling
Vis Aids, Chng Rm, Tack Shop
Livery Full, P/T, Break, School, Hunt,
Grass
Schooling General, Break, to Nov
Dress, to SJ GR C, to HT Nov
Accom FB
Exclusions No DIY
Location Off A44 2 miles from
Bromyard, 11 miles from Leominster

COURT EQUESTRIAN
Llangarron Court, Llangarron,
Ross-on-Wye,
Herefordshire, HR9 6NP
Tel 01989 770472
Contact Mrs Sara Scudamore
Riding School Inst Riding & Jumping
Specialities Childrens riding lessons,
from complete beginner to those wish-
ing to compete
Staff Chief Instructor Mrs S Scudamore
Plus 1 full time instructor
Ave No 5 Horses, 9 Ponies
Courses Short, Ev, P/T

Facilities
Outdoor Manege 20 x 40
SJ: Nov
Wait Rm
Livery Full, Break, School
Schooling General, Break, to Nov
Dress, to HT Nov
Exclusions Hacking is part of instruc-
tional riding
Location Midway between Ross-on-Wye
& Monmouth

HOLME LACY GROUP
Riding for the Disabled Association,
Holme Lacy College of Agriculture,
Holme Lacy, Hereford, HR2 6LL
Tel 01432 870831
Contact Mrs C Baker
Riding School Inst Riding & Jumping
Staff Chief Instructor Mrs C Baker (BHSAI)
Plus 1 full time instructor
Ave No 6 Horses, 6 Ponies
Courses WP, YT
Facilities
Covered School 40 x 20 gly
SJ: Nov, 1 Paddock
Lec Rm, Vis Aids, Wait Rm
Hacking
Schooling General
Exclusions Wt Limit, 16st, Age Limit, 2
Location On B4399 between Lower
Bullingham & B4224 Jn

HOLME LACY COLLEGE
Holme Lacy, Hereford, HR2 6LL
Tel 01432 870566
Contact Mr P Savidge
Training Centre, Livery Inst Riding &
Jumping
3 full time instructors

Ave No 14 Horses, 1 Ponies
Courses YT, Short, Ev, P/T, Hol
Facilities
Outdoor Manege 40 x 36 fl lt
SJ: Nov, Grade C, 1 Paddock
CC: Course, Nov, Banks, Water,
Natural, Gallops
Lec Rm, Vis Aids, Chng Rm, Showers,
Wait Rm
Livery Full, P/T, DIY, Break, School
Schooling General, Break, to Nov
Dress, to HT Nov
Location On B4399 between Lower
Bullingham & Holme Lacy

ST RICHARDS SCHOOL
Bredenbury Court, Bromyard,
Herefordshire, HR7 4TD
Tel 01885 482491
Contact Mr R Coghlan
Prep School Inst Riding & Jumping
Staff Chief Instructor Mrs S Pearson
(BHSAI)
Ave No 4 Horses, 6 Ponies
Facilities
Outdoor Manege 20 x 40
CC: Course, Basic, Nov, Banks,
Natural
Lec Rm, Vis Aids, Chng Rm, Showers
Hacking
Accom Dor, FB
Exclusions For pupils only
Location On A44 between Leominster
and Bromyard

SUE ADAMS RIDING SCHOOL
The Ox House, Shobdon,
Leominster,
Hereford, HR6 9LT
Tel 01568 708973
Contact Ms S Adams-Wheeler
Riding School, Training Centre,
Facility Centre, RDA Inst to BHSAI
Specialities Career training
Staff Chief Instructor Ms S Adams-
Wheeler (BHSAI, BHS Int Teach)
Plus 3 full time instructors
Ave No 8 Horses, 7 Ponies
inc 1 El Dress, 1 Med Dress,
2 SJ GR C, RDA/vaulting
Courses WP, YT, Short, Ev, P/T, Hol
Facilities
Covered School 20 x 40
Outdoor Manege 20 x 40
Outdoor Manege 50 x 60
SJ: Nov, Grade C, 1 Paddock
CC: Course, Basic, Nov, Natural
Lec Rm, Vis Aids, Wait Rm
Hacking
Livery Full, P/T, Break, School, Hunt
Schooling General, Break, to Med

Dress, to SJ GR C, to HT Int
Exclusions Wt Limit, 15st7,
Hacking only for escorted riders
Location Between Leominster and
Presteigne, off B4362

WORCESTERSHIRE

BEOLEY EQUESTRIAN CENTRE
The Ranch, Icknield Street,
Beoley, Worcestershire, B98 9AL
Tel 01527 65494
Contact Ms G Edmonds
Riding School Inst Riding & Jumping
Specialities Instruction for nervous rid-
ers and confidence building for begin-
ners. Working pupils career training.
Excellent hacking facilities
Staff Chief Instructor Mrs G Edmonds
(BHSAI)
Plus 2 full time instructors
Ave No 11 Horses, 12 Ponies
Courses WP, Short, Ev, P/T
Facilities
Covered School 30 x 20 gly
Outdoor Manege 40 x 20 fl lt
Lec Rm, Vis Aids, Chng Rm, Wait Rm,
Tack Shop
Hacking
Livery Full
Schooling General
Exclusions No unescorted hacking
Location Between Jnc 3 off M42 -
Redditch Beoley is signposted off A435

COUNTRY TREKS
c/o The Old Vicarage Activity Centre,
Ginny Hole, Stottesdon,
Nr Kidderminster,
Worcestershire, DY14 8UH
Tel 01746 718436
Contact Mrs Stephanie Eddies-Davies
Trekking Centre
Specialities Complete off-road riding for
beginners; for the more experienced
rider there are bridle paths and quiet
country lanes
Ave No 6 Horses, 5 Ponies
Courses Short, Ev, P/T, Hol
Facilities
Outdoor Manege 37 x 18
SJ: Nov, 1 Paddock
Lec Rm, Vis Aids, Chng Rm, Showers
Hacking
Accom Dor, FB
Exclusions Escorted hacking only
Location Off B4363 between
Bridgenorth & Cleobury Mortimer

FAR FOREST EQUESTRIAN CENTRE
Far Forest, Kidderminster,
Worcs, DY14 9DG
Tel 01299 266438
Contact Mr & Mrs A Fitzpatrick
Riding School, Training Centre Inst to BHSAI
Specialities Career training
Staff Chief Instructor Mr A Fitzpatrick (BHSII)
Ave No 6 Horses, 3 Ponies
inc 2 El Dress, 1 Med Dress, 1 SJ GR C
Courses WP, YT, Short, Ev, P/T, Hol
Facilities
Outdoor Manege 30 x 40 fl lt
SJ: Grade C, 1 Paddock
CC: Banks, Natural, 12 Schooling
Lec Rm, Vis Aids, Chng Rm, Wait Rm
Hacking
Livery Full, P/T, Break, School, Hunt
Schooling General, Break, to Med Dress, to SJ GR C, to HT Nov
Accom S, Tw, Db, Cottage, SC
Exclusions Wt Limit, 14st, Age Limit, 7, No unaccompanied hacking
Location 4 miles west of Bewdley

HALLOW MILL EQUESTRIAN CENTRE
Hallow, Worcester,
Worcs, WR2 6PR
Tel 01905 640373
Contact Mrs R Johnson
Riding School, Training Centre Inst Riding & Jumping
Specialities Career training
Staff Chief Instructor Mrs R Johnson (BHSI)
Plus 1 full time instructor
Ave No 4 Horses, 11 Ponies
inc 1 El Dress, 1 SJ GR C
Courses WP, Short, P/T, Hol
Facilities
Outdoor Manege 49 x 31 fl lt
SJ: Grade B, 1 Paddock
CC: Banks, Natural, 4 Schooling
Lec Rm, Vis Aids, Chng Rm
Livery Full, Break, School, Hunt
Schooling General, Break, to Med Dress, to SJ GR B, to HT Int
Exclusions Wt Limit, 10st7, Age Limit, 6, No hiring for hunting
Location 2 miles from Worcester, west of the River Severn

THE MOUNTS EQUITATION CENTRE
Crumpsbrook, Cleobury Mortimer,
Kidderminster, Worcs, DY14 0HX
Tel 01746 718677
Contact Mrs M A Linington-Payne
Riding School, Training Centre,

Facility Centre, Riding Holidays Inst to BHSII
Specialities Career training
Staff Chief Instructor Mrs M A Linington-Payne (BHSI)
Plus 2 full time instructors
Ave No 12 Horses, 6 Ponies
inc 3 El Dress, 1 Med Dress, 1 Adv Dress, 3 SJ GR C, 1 HT Int, 1 HT Adv
Courses WP, Short, Ev, P/T, Hol
Facilities
Covered School 19 x 40 gly
Outdoor Manege 30 x 60
SJ: Nov, Grade C, Grade B
CC: Course, Basic, Nov, Banks, Water, Natural
Wait Rm
Hacking
Livery Full, P/T, Break, School, Hunt
Schooling General, Break, to Med Dress, to SJ GR C, to HT Nov
Accom S, F, Cottage, FB
Exclusions Wt Limit, 14st7, Age Limit, 5, No novices on hacks out, escorted only
Location Off A41175, 5 miles from Cleobury Mortimer and 8 miles Ludlow

MOYFIELD RIDING SCHOOL
South Littleton, Evesham,
Worcestershire, WR11
Tel 01386 830207
Contact Mrs J Bomford
Trekking Centre, Livery Inst Basic
Staff Chief Instructor Mrs J Bomford
Plus 4 full time instructors
Ave No 50 Horses, 50 Ponies
Courses WP, YT, Short, Ev, P/T, Hol
Facilities
Covered School 40 x 60 gly
Covered School 20 x 30 gly
Outdoor Manege 40 x 60
SJ: Nov, Grade C, 1 Paddock
CC: Course, Banks, Water, Natural, Gallops
Lec Rm, Vis Aids, Chng Rm, Tack Shop
Hacking
Livery Full, P/T, Break, School, Hunt, Grass
Accom S, Tw, Db, F, Dor, Caravan, FB, SC
Exclusions Wt Limit, 20st, Age Limit, 2 1/2, No unaccompanied rides
Location 4 miles east of Evesham, 12 miles from Stratford-on-Avon

PERSHORE & HINDLIP COLLEGE
Hindlip Equestrian Centre, Hindlip,
Worcestershire, WR3 8SS
Tel 01905 754575/451310
Contact Ms J Adams

**Training Centre, Facility Centre,
Livery** Inst to BHSII
Specialities The training of students
for equine courses
Staff Chief Instructor Ms J Adams (BHSI)
Plus 3 full time instructors
Ave No 30 Horses, 2 Ponies
inc 2 El Dress, 1 Med Dress,
2 SJ GR C, 2 HT Int
Courses WP, YT, Short, Ev, P/T
Facilities
Covered School 18 x 36
Outdoor Manege 25 x 60
SJ: Grade C, 1 Paddock
CC: Course, Banks
Lec Rm, Vis Aids, Chng Rm, Wait Rm
Livery Full, P/T, Break, School, Hunt
Schooling General, Break, to Med
Dress, to SJ GR C, to HT Int
Accom S, Cottage, SC
Exclusions Wt Limit, 13,
All riders under instruction only
Location Near exit 6 off M5, on A4538

PORTMANS FARM
Newbridge Green, Upton-on-Severn,
Worcs, WR8 0QP
Tel 01684 592873
Contact Mrs J D Challens & P Challens
Riding School, Training Centre Inst
Riding & Jumping
Staff Chief Instructor Mrs J D Challens
(BHSI)
Plus 1 full time instructor
Ave No 5 Horses, 5 Ponies
inc 2 El Dress, 1 Med Dress
Courses WP, YT, Short, Ev, P/T
Facilities
Covered School 37 x 21
SJ: Nov, 1 Paddock
CC: Basic, Banks, Water, Natural,
10 Schooling
Wait Rm
Schooling General, Break, to Med
Dress, to SJ GR C, to HT Int
Accom Caravan, SC
Exclusions Wt Limit, 13st, Age Limit, 5
Location On B4211 Upton-on-Severn
to Longdon road opposite Drum &
Monkey public house

STAFFORDSHIRE

ABBOTS BROMLEY
EQUESTRIAN CENTRE
School of St Mary & St Anne,
Abbots Bromley,
Staffordshire, WS15 3BW
Tel 01283 840203/840841

Contact Miss Carmen Smith, Director of
Equitation
**Riding School, Training Centre,
Facility Centre** Inst to BHSAI
Specialities General instruction, Career
students, Livery, Activity Holiday
Courses
Staff Chief Instructor Miss C Smith
(BHSII)
Plus 4 full time instructors
Ave No 7 Horses, 14 Ponies
inc 1 El Dress, 1 SJ GR C, 1 HT Int
Courses WP, Short, Ev, P/T, Hol
Facilities
Covered School 43 x 22 gly
Outdoor Manege 62 x 22 fl lt
SJ: Nov
CC: Course
Lec Rm, Vis Aids, Chng Rm, Showers,
Wait Rm
Hacking
Livery Full, P/T, Break, School
Schooling General, Break, to Nov
Dress, to El Dress, to Med Dress, to Adv
Dress, to SJ GR C, to HT Nov, to HT Int,
to HT Adv
Accom S, Tw, Dor, FB
Exclusions Wt Limit, 13st, Age Limit, 4+,
No riding for the general public
Location Centre of village on the B5104

BARLASTON RIDING CENTRE
Barlaston Old Road, Barlaston,
Stoke on Trent, Staffs, ST12 9EQ
Tel 01782 373638
Contact Mr J P Hirrell
Riding School, Training Centre Inst
Riding & Jumping
Ave No 12 Horses, 9 Ponies
inc 1 El Dress
Courses YT, Short, Ev
Facilities
Covered School 40 x 20
SJ: Nov, Grade C
CC: Basic, 12 Schooling
Lec Rm, Vis Aids, Chng Rm
Hacking
Livery Full, P/T, Break, School, Hunt,
Grass
Schooling General, Break, to El Dress,
to HT Nov
Location Off A34, 5 miles from Jn 15 on
M6

BUTTERLANDS FARM
EQUITATION CENTRE
Top Road, Biddulph Moor,
Stoke-on-Trent, Staffordshire, ST8 7LF
Tel 01782 522281
Contact Mr & Mrs R Attenborough
Riding School Inst Riding & Jumping

Ave No 16 Horses, 16 Ponies
Courses YT, Short, Ev, P/T, Hol
Facilities Covered School 20 x 55
Outdoor Manege 35 x 55
Outdoor Manege 20 x 40
CC: Course, Basic, Nov, Banks, Water,
Natural
Hacking
Exclusions Wt Limit, 17st, Age Limit, 3,
No novices on hacks
Location Off the A527, 3 miles south of
Congleton

COURSES FOR HORSES
Lower Stonehouse Farm, Brown Edge,
Stoke-on-Trent, Staffordshire, ST6 8TF
Tel 01782 503090
Contact Mrs Mary Stitson
Riding School Inst Riding & Jumping
Specialities Instruction and courses for
equestrian examinations tailored to the
individual. Nervous riders. Lessons in
all disciplines for all ages and abilities
Staff Chief Instructor Mrs Mary Stitson
(BHSAI, BHS Int.SM, BHS Int Teach)
Ave No 8 Horses, 1 Ponies
Courses WP, Short, Ev, P/T
Facilities Outdoor Manege 18 x 38
Outdoor Manege 44 x 22
SJ: Nov
Lec Rm, Vis Aids, Wait Rm
Livery Full, P/T, DIY, Break, School,
Grass
Schooling General, to Med Dress, to
SJ GR C, to HT Nov
Exclusions Wt Limit, 15st, Age Limit, 7,
No Hacking
Location Off A53 between Stoke on
Trent and Leek

CRAYTHORNE FARM
LIVERY STABLES
Craythorne Road, Stretton,
Burton-upon-Trent,
Staffordshire, DE13 0AZ
Tel 01283 532762
Contact Mrs P S Tullett
Livery
Ave No 10 Horses, 1 Ponies
Facilities
Outdoor Manege 20 x 40
SJ: Nov, 1 Paddock
Livery Full, P/T, DIY, Hunt
Location 1 mile from A38 on the
outskirts of Stretton village

DALE SCHOOL OF EQUITATION
White House Farm, Bradley, Stafford,
Staffs, ST18 9EA
Tel 01785 780279

Contact Miss H Kesson
Riding School, R.D.A. Inst Riding &
Jumping
Staff Chief Instructor Miss H Kesson
(BHSAI)
Plus 1 full time instructor
Ave No 7 Horses, 8 Ponies
Courses WP, YT, Short, Ev, P/T, Hol
Lec Rm, Vis Aids, Chng Rm
Hacking
Livery Full, P/T, Break, School, Grass
Schooling General, Break
Exclusions Wt Limit, 14st, Age Limit, 4,
No unescorted hacking
Location Off A449 south of Stafford

DENSTONE STUD
Hall Riddings, Denstone,
Staffordshire, ST14 5HW
Tel 01889 591472
Contact Ms P Price & Mr A Lawler
**Riding School, Training Centre,
Facility Centre** Inst Riding & Jumping
Staff Chief Instructor Ms P Price
(BHSAI)
Ave No 4 Horses, 5 Ponies
inc 2 El Dress, 1 Med Dress,
Side Saddle
Courses WP, YT, Short, Ev, P/T, Hol
Facilities
SJ: Nov
Lec Rm, Vis Aids, Chng Rm, Showers,
Wait Rm
Hacking
Livery Full, P/T, Break, School, Hunt,
Grass
Schooling General, Break, to Med
Dress, to SJ GR C
Accom Tw, Db, FB
Location Off B5032 between Uttoxeter
and Ashbourne

ENDON RIDING SCHOOL
Stanley Moss Lane, Stockton Brook,
Stoke-On-Trent, Staffs, ST9 9LR
Tel 01782 502114
Contact Mrs D K Machin
**Riding School, Training Centre,
Facility Centre** Inst Riding & Jumping
Staff Chief Instructor Mrs L Lear
(BHSAI)
Plus 2 full time instructors
Ave No 18 Horses, 12 Ponies
inc 2 SJ GR B, 2 HT Int
Courses WP, YT, Short, Ev, P/T, Hol
Facilities
Covered School 37 x 23 gly
Outdoor Manege 26 x 42
SJ: Nov, Grade C, 1 Paddock
CC: Course, Nov, Banks, Water,
Natural, 26 Schooling

Lec Rm, Vis Aids, Chng Rm, Showers,
Wait Rm
Hacking
Livery Full, P/T, DIY, Hunt, Grass
Accom Tw, F, Dor, Cottage, FB, SC
Location Off A53 midway between
Leek and Stoke-on-Trent

FIELD HOUSE
EQUESTRIAN CENTRE
Marchington, Uttoxeter,
Staffs, ST14 8NX
Tel 01283 820310
Contact Mrs M & Miss S J Snow
Riding School Inst Riding & Jumping
2 full time instructors
Ave No 15 Horses, 12 Ponies
inc 6 El Dress, 6 Med Dress, 5 SJ GR C
Courses WP
Facilities
SJ: Grade A
CC: Nov
Chng Rm, Showers, Wait Rm
Schooling General, to Med Dress, to
SJ GR C, to HT Nov
Accom S, SC
Exclusions Age Limit, 5
Location Off B5017 Uttoxeter to
Burton-on-Trent

GARTMORE RIDING SCHOOL
Hall Lane, Hammerwich,
Burntwood, Nr Walsall,
Staffs, WS7 0JT
Tel 01543 686117
Contact Miss T & M Evans

INGESTRE STABLES
Ingestre, Staffs, ST18 0RE
Tel 01889 271165
Contact Mr T Downes FBHS &
Mr R Lovatt BHSI
Riding School, Training Centre,
Facility Centre Inst to BHSI
Specialities Career training, English
lessons given to overseas visitors
Staff Chief Instructor Mr T Downes
(FBHS)
Plus 4 full time instructors
Ave No 35 Horses, 8 Ponies
inc 6 El Dress, 4 Med Dress, 4 Adv Dress,
1 SJ GR C, 2 SJ GR B, 1 SJ GR A,
2 HT Int, Side Saddle
Courses WP, YT, Short, Ev, P/T, Hol
Facilities
Covered School 18 x 44 gly
Covered School 12 x 24
Outdoor Manege 25 x 50 fl lt
Outdoor Manege 25 x 60 fl lt
SJ: Grade B

CC: Basic, Banks, Water, Natural,
20 Schooling
Lec Rm, Vis Aids, Chng Rm, Showers,
Wait Rm
Hacking
Livery Full, P/T, Break, School
Schooling General, Break, to Adv Dress,
to SJ GR C, to HT Adv
Accom Tw, Dor, FB, SC
Exclusions Wt Limit, 15st,
No unescorted hiring
Location Close to A51 between Weston
and Great Haywood, adjacent to
Cannock Chase

MIDDLETON EQUESTRIAN CENTRE
Vicarage Hill Lane, Middleton,
Nr Tamworth,
Staffordshire, B78 2AT
Tel 0121 311 1601
Contact Mr & Mrs J Everill
Riding School Inst Riding & Jumping
2 full time instructors
Ave No 12 Horses, 17 Ponies
Courses YT, Short, Ev, P/T, Hol
Facilities
Covered School 40 x 20 gly
SJ: Nov, 1 Paddock
Lec Rm, Vis Aids, Chng Rm, Wait Rm
Hacking
Exclusions Wt Limit, 15st, Age Limit, 3,
No unescorted hacking
Location Off A446, easily accessible
from Lichfield, Tamworth, Sutton
Coldfield and Birmingham

MOW COP RIDING CENTRE
Mow Lane, Mow Cop,
Stoke-on-Trent,
Staffordshire, ST7 3PP
Tel 01782 514502
Contact J & S Siddall
Riding School, Trekking Centre Inst
Basic
Ave No 9 Horses, 10 Ponies
Courses YT, Short, Ev, Hol
Facilities
Outdoor Manege 25 x 50 fl lt
Outdoor Manege 20 x 20
SJ: Nov
CC: Basic
Wait Rm
Hacking
Livery Full, DIY
Schooling General
Exclusions Wt Limit, 14st,
No unaccompanied hacking
Location Off A527, 4 miles south of
Congleton

POPLARS FARM RIDING SCHOOL
Hilderstone Road,
Meir Heath,
Stoke-on-Trent,
Staffs, ST3 7NY
Tel 01782 394686
Contact Mrs A J Smith
Riding School Inst Riding & Jumping
Specialities Instruction in riding and jumping mainly for children
Staff Chief Instructor Mrs A Smith (BHSAI)
Ave No 5 Horses, 12 Ponies
Courses YT, Ev, P/T, Hol
Facilities
Outdoor Manege 40 x 20 fl lt
Outdoor Manege 30 x 35 fl lt
Outdoor Manege 50 x 25
SJ: Nov, Grade C, 1 Paddock
Chng Rm, Wait Rm
Hacking
Livery P/T, DIY, School
Schooling General, to SJ GR C, to HT Nov
Exclusions Wt Limit, 13st, Age Limit, 3, Instructional riding only
Location Off A50 between Stoke-on-Trent & Uttoxeter

RODBASTON COLLEGE
Rodbaston, Penkridge,
Stafford,
Staffordshire, ST19 5PH
Tel 01785 712209
Contact Dr R Alcock
Training Centre, Livery Inst to BHSAI
Specialities Career training
Staff Chief Instructor Ms S Strachan (BHSI)
Plus 5 full time instructors
Ave No 24 Horses, 2 Ponies
inc 1 El Dress, 1 HT Int
Courses YT, Short, Ev, P/T
Facilities
Covered School 30 x 60
Outdoor Manege 20 x 50 fl lt
SJ: Nov, 1 Paddock
CC: Course, Basic, Nov, Water, Natural, Gallops, 20 Schooling
Lec Rm, Vis Aids, Chng Rm, Showers, Wait Rm
Livery P/T, Break, School, Hunt
Schooling General, Break, to Adv Dress, to SJ GR C, to HT Nov
Accom S, Tw, Dor, FB
Exclusions Wt Limit, 13st, Age Limit, 16
Location On the A449 between Jn 12 and 13, off the M6 (Wolverhampton to Stafford road)

WARWICKSHIRE

BAXTERLEY EQUESTRIAN & TRAINING CENTRE
Main Road, Church End, Baxterley,
Nr Atherstone,
Warwickshire, CV9 2LW
Tel 01827 872222
Contact Mrs S Smallman
Riding School, Training Centre Inst Riding & Jumping
Staff Chief Instructor Mrs S Smallman Plus 1 full time instructor
Ave No 5 Horses, 1 Ponies
inc 1 Adv Dress, 1 SJ GR C, 3 Side Saddle
Courses WP, YT, Short, Ev, P/T, Hol
Facilities
Outdoor Manege 20 x 40
SJ: Grade C, 1 Paddock
Wait Rm
Hacking
Livery Full, P/T, DIY, Break, School, Grass
Schooling General, Break, to Adv Dress, to SJ GR C, to HT Int
Exclusions Wt Limit, 14st, Age Limit, 3, No unescorted riding
Location Off A5 between Jn 10 or M42 & Atherstone

BEANIT FARM
Hob Lane, Balsall Common,
Warwickshire, CV7 7GX
Tel 01676 535115
Contact Mr Brian Charley
Livery, Competition Training
Specialities 'Livery' to produce competition horses. Showjumping a speciality
Staff Chief Instructor Mr Brian Charley Plus 1 full time instructor
Courses WP, Short, Ev, P/T, Hol
Facilities
Covered School 60 x 20
SJ: Grade A
Chng Rm, Wait Rm
Livery Full, P/T, Break, School, Hunt
Schooling General, Break, to Nov Dress, to SJ GR A, to HT Nov

BRITISH EQUESTRIAN CENTRE
Stoneleigh Park, Stoneleigh,
Kenilworth, Warwickshire, CV8 2LR
Tel 01203 696697
Contact The Training Office
Training Centre, Facility Centre
Courses Short
Facilities
Covered School 60 x 24 gly

Covered School 40 x 20 gly
Outdoor Manege 65 x 25 fl lt
Outdoor Manege 44 x 23 fl lt
SJ: Grade A
Lec Rm, Vis Aids
Exclusions Facility hire only
Location NAC Showground, on the
A444, Leamington - Coventry road

CALDECOTE RIDING SCHOOL
Anker Cottage Farm, Caldecote,
Nuneaton, Warks, CV10 0TN
Tel 01203 383103
Contact Mrs S Sandon
Riding School Inst Basic
Staff Chief Instructor Mrs S Sandon
(BHSAI)
Ave No 2 Horses, 16 Ponies
Courses YT
Facilities
Outdoor Manege 20 x 30 fl lt
SJ: Nov, 1 Paddock
CC: Banks
Lec Rm, Vis Aids, Chng Rm, Wait Rm,
Tack Shop
Hacking
Livery Full, P/T, Break, School
Schooling General, Break, to Nov
Dress
Exclusions Wt Limit, 12st,
No unaccompanied hacking
Location 1 mile from Jn of A444 and
A5 on the Nuneaton side

CASTLE HILL RIDING SCHOOL
Brandon, Coventry,
Warwickshire, CV8 3HQ
Tel 01203 542762
Contact Mrs P Potter
Riding School, Training Centre Inst
Riding & Jumping
Specialities General instruction,
Livery, Dressage, Side Saddle &
Driving. Private lessons up to PSG
level Dressage on pupils' own horses
Staff Chief Instructor Mrs P Potter
(BHSAI, BHS Int Teach)
Plus 1 full time instructor
Ave No 10 Horses, 20 Ponies
inc 4 El Dress, 1 Med Dress, 1 Adv
Dress, 1 SJ GR C, 1 SJ Jun C
Courses YT, Hol
Facilities
Covered School 44 x 18
Outdoor Manege 60 x 20
SJ: Nov, Grade C, 1 Paddock
CC: Course, Basic, Nov, Banks, Water,
Natural
Lec Rm, Vis Aids, Chng Rm, Wait Rm
Hacking
Livery Full, P/T, Break, School, Grass

Schooling General, Break, to El Dress,
to Med Dress, to Adv Dress, to SJ GR C,
to HT Nov
Exclusions Wt Limit, 13st, Age Limit, 5,
No casual hiring
Location 5 miles Coventry, 6 miles
Rugby, between Brandon and Wolston
close to A45 and M6

COTTAGE FARM STABLES
Illshaw Heath Road, Warings Green,
Earlswood, Solihull,
West Midlands, B94 6DL
Tel 01564 703314
Contact Mr V Perry
Riding School, Training Centre Inst
Basic
Staff Chief Instructor Mrs H Perry
Ave No 12 Horses, 14 Ponies
inc 1 El Dress, 1 Med Dress
Courses WP, Short, Ev, P/T, Hol
Facilities
Outdoor Manege 40 x 20 fl lt
Outdoor Manege 20 x 30
SJ: 2 Paddock
CC: Basic, Nov, Gallops, 4 Schooling
Lec Rm, Vis Aids, Chng Rm, Showers,
Wait Rm, Tack Shop
Hacking
Livery Full
Accom Caravan
Exclusions Wt Limit, 14st,
No unescorted hacking
Location Off A34 between Jn 1 off M42
& Hockley Heath

PITTERN HILL STABLES
Kineton, Warwickshire, CV35 0JF
Tel 01926 640370
Contact Mr R L Philpot
Riding School, Training Centre Inst to
BHSAI
Specialities General instruction. Siide
saddle. Career students
1 full time instructor
Ave No 18 Horses, 10 Ponies
inc 4 El Dress, Side Saddle
Courses WP, YT, Short, P/T, Hol
Facilities
Covered School 20 x 55 gly
Outdoor Manege 20 x 40 fl lt
SJ: Nov
CC: Course, Basic
Lec Rm, Vis Aids, Tack Shop
Hacking
Livery Full, P/T, Break, School, Hunt
Schooling General, Break, to El Dress,
to HT Nov
Exclusions Wt Limit, 17st, Age Limit, 5
Location On B4086 between Kineton
and Wellesbourne

UMBERSLADE EQUESTRIAN CENTRE
Blunts Green Farm, Blunts Green,
Nr Henley-in-Arden,
Warwickshire, B95 5RE
Tel 01564 794609
Contact Mr P W Pettitt & C P
Billingham
**Riding School, Training Centre,
Facility Centre, RDA & Stud.** Inst
Riding & Jumping
5 full time instructors
Ave No 15 Horses, 12 Ponies
Courses WP, YT, Short, Ev, P/T, Hol
Facilities
SJ: Grade C
CC: Basic
Lec Rm, Vis Aids, Chng Rm, Showers,
Wait Rm, Tack Shop
Hacking
Livery Full, P/T, Break, School, Hunt
Schooling General, Break
Accom Tw, Dor, FB, SC
Location Off A3400 2 miles north of
Henley-in-Arden, 8 miles from
Stratford-upon-Avon

WARWICKSHIRE COLLEGE
Moreton Morrell Centre,
Warwickshire, CV35 9BL
Tel 01926 318333
Contact Mr B Jarvis
**Training Centre, Facility Centre,
Livery** Inst to BHSI
Specialities Career courses at all
levels. Stud work, shows and events.
Also offered, home study courses for
the career student, horse owner or
leisure rider
Staff Chief Instructor Mrs P Francis
(BHSI)
Plus 12 full time instructors
Ave No 45 Horses
inc 5 El Dress, 4 Med Dress, 3 Adv
Dress, 5 SJ GR C, 1 SJ GR B, 1 SJ GR
A, 1 HT Int, 1 HT Adv, Driving Ponies,
RDA, Heavy Horse
Courses Short, Ev, P/T, Hol
Facilities
Covered School 25 x 65 gly
Outdoor Manege 65 x 25 fl lt
Outdoor Manege 20 x 40
Outdoor Manege 20 x 20
Outdoor Manege 100 x 60
SJ: Grade A, 1 Paddock
CC: Course, Basic, Nov, Banks, Water,
Natural, Gallops, 35 Schooling
Lec Rm, Vis Aids, Chng Rm, Showers,
Wait Rm
Hacking
Livery Full, P/T, DIY, Break, School,
Grass

Schooling General, Break, to Adv
Dress, to SJ GR A, to HT Adv
Accom S, Tw, Caravan, FB
Exclusions Wt Limit, 16st, Age Limit, 10,
Public lessons limited on school horses
Location Adjacent to the village of
Moreton Morrell, just off the Fosse
Way. 5 miles from Stratford, 2 miles
from Wellesbourne and 8 miles from
Warwick

WAVERLEY EQUESTRIAN TRAINING
Coventry Road, Cubbington,
Leamington Spa, Warks, CV32 7UJ
Tel 01926 422876
Contact Mr A Ruyssevelt
**Riding School, Training Centre,
Facility Centre, RDA** Inst to BHSAI
Specialities Dressage,
Breaking/Schooling
Staff Chief Instructor Mrs G Ruyssevelt
(BHS Int Teach, BHS SM)
Plus 2 full time instructors
Ave No 20 Horses, 9 Ponies
inc 3 El Dress, 1 Med Dress, 1 Adv
Dress, 4 SJ GR C, 8 horses competing
at novice HT level
Courses WP, Short, Ev, P/T, Hol
Facilities
Covered School 37 x 20 gly
Outdoor Manege 50 x 60
SJ: Nov, Grade C, 1 Paddock
CC: Basic, Nov, Banks, Natural,
12 Schooling
Lec Rm, Vis Aids, Chng Rm, Wait Rm,
Tack Shop
Livery Full, Break, School
Schooling General, Break, to Med
Dress, to SJ GR C, to HT Int
Accom S, Caravan, SC
Exclusions Wt Limit, 13st, Age Limit, 6
Location Situated on the Coventry
road, approx. 2 miles from Stoneleigh

WOODBINE STABLES
Woodbine Farm, Grandborough Fields,
Nr Rugby, Warks, CV23 8BA
Tel 01788 810349
Contact Mrs S A Ward
Riding School Inst Basic
Specialities Basic instruction,
childrens' rides
1 full time instructor
Ave No 5 Horses, 9 Ponies
Courses WP, YT, Short, Ev, Hol
Facilities
Outdoor Manege 40 x 20 fl lt
SJ: Nov, 1 Paddock
CC: Basic, 10 Schooling
Lec Rm, Vis Aids, Chng Rm, Wait Rm
Hacking

Livery Full, P/T, DIY
Schooling General
Exclusions Wt Limit, 14 st, Age Limit, 5+,
No casual hire
Location Between Daventry and
Stockton

WEST MIDLANDS

BOURNE VALE STABLES
Little Hardwick Road, Aldridge,
Walsall, West Midlands, WS9 0SQ
Tel 0121 353 7174
Contact Mrs P Cooper
Riding School, Training Centre Inst
Riding & Jumping
Staff Chief Instructor Mr P Waterhouse
(BHSII)
Plus 2 full time instructors
Ave No 15 Horses, 15 Ponies
Courses WP, Short, P/T
Facilities
Covered School 20 x 40 gly
Outdoor Manege 25 x 40 fl lt
SJ: Nov, 1 Paddock
Lec Rm, Vis Aids, Chng Rm, Wait Rm
Hacking
Livery Full, School
Schooling General, to Med Dress, to
SJ GR C
Exclusions Wt Limit, 14st, Age Limit, 5
Location 8 miles north of Birmingham,
4 miles from Sutton Coldfield and 4
miles from Walsall

BROOKFIELDS RIDING
& LIVERY CENTRE
Cannock Road, Shareshill,
Wolverhampton,
West Midlands, WV10 7LZ
Tel 01922 414090
Contact The Proprietor
Riding School Inst Riding & Jumping
Staff Chief Instructor Miss C Commins
(BHSAI)
Plus 3 full time instructors
Ave No 10 Horses, 10 Ponies
inc 1 El Dress, 1 SJ GR C, 1 SJ Jun C,
1 SJ Jun A, RDA 10
Courses WP, YT, Short, Ev, P/T
Facilities
Covered School 61 x 26 gly
Covered School 43 x 24 gly
Outdoor Manege 122 x 61 fl lt
Outdoor Manege 24 x 24 fl lt
SJ: Grade C, 1 Paddock
CC: Gallops
Lec Rm, Vis Aids, Chng Rm, Showers,
Wait Rm, Tack Shop
Hacking

Livery Full, P/T, Break, School, Grass
Schooling General, Break, to SJ GR C,
to HT Nov
Accom S, Tw, Caravan, SC
Exclusions Wt Limit, 18st, Age Limit, 3

FARMHOUSE STABLES
The Farmhouse, Marston,
Sutton Coldfield,
West Midlands, B76 0DW
Tel 01675 475959
Contact Mr & Mrs P J Gee
Training Centre Inst Riding & Jumping
Staff Chief Instructor Mr M P J Gee
(BHSII)
Plus 1 full time instructor
Ave No 9 Horses
inc 1 El Dress, 1 SJ GR C, 1 HT Int
Courses WP, Short, Ev, P/T
Facilities
Outdoor Manege 43 x 25 fl lt
SJ: Nov
CC: Basic, Nov, Banks, Water, Gallops
Chng Rm, Showers, Wait Rm
Hacking
Livery Full, Break, School, Hunt
Schooling Break, to Med Dress, to SJ
GR C
Location Off A4097 2 miles exit 9, M42

KINGSWOOD EQUESTRIAN TRUST
Kingswood Equestrian Centre,
County Lane, Albrighton,
Nr Wolverhampton,
West Midlands, WV7 3AH
Tel 01902 374480
Contact Mr R Lickley
Riding School, Training Centre,
Facility Centre Inst Riding & Jumping
Specialities Showjumping
Horse walker
Staff Chief Instructor Mrs Helena
Fellows (BHSAI, BHS Int.SM)
Plus 3 full time instructors
Ave No 7 Horses, 15 Ponies
inc 1 El Dress, 1 Med Dress, 1 SJ GR C,
1 SJ GR B, 1 SJ GR A, 1 HT Adv
Courses WP, YT, Short, Ev, P/T, Hol
Facilities
Covered School 24 x 54 gly
Outdoor Manege 70 x 40 fl lt
SJ: Grade A, 2 Paddock
CC: Basic, Nov, Banks, Natural, Gallops
Lec Rm, Vis Aids, Chng Rm, Wait Rm,
Tack Shop
Livery Full, P/T, Break, School
Schooling General, to Med Dress, to SJ
GR B, to SJ GR A, to HT Adv
Accom Caravan, Cottage, SC
Exclusions Wt Limit, 12st7, Age Limit, 4,
No hacking

Location Off A41 5 miles from Wolverhampton, 2 miles from Jn 3 off M54

NORTH WORCESTERSHIRE EQUESTRIAN CENTRE

Inc Silvretta Haflinger Stud, Shangri-la, Woodfield Lane, Romsley, Halesowen, West Midlands, B62 OLR
Tel 01562 710245
Contact Miss H Blair
Riding School, Training Centre Inst Riding & Jumping
Staff Chief Instructor Mrs J A Houghton (BHSI)
Ave No 4 Horses, 11 Ponies
inc 1 El Dress, Endurance Horses
Courses WP, YT, Short, Ev, P/T, Hol
Facilities
Covered School 22 x 12
Outdoor Manege 60 x 40
SJ: Nov, 1 Paddock
Lec Rm, Vis Aids
Hacking
Livery Full, Break, School, Hunt, Grass
Schooling General, Break, to El Dress
Exclusions Wt Limit, 17st, Age Limit, 3
Location Off the A491 between Kidderminster, Bromsgrove, Halesowen & Stourbridge. 5 miles from Jn 4 on the M5

STOURTON HILL STABLES

Bridgnorth Road, Stourton, Stourbridge, West Midlands, DY7 5BQ
Tel 01384 872865
Contact Mrs Helen Lord
Riding School, Training Centre Inst Riding & Jumping
2 full time instructors
Ave No 12 Ponies
Courses WP, Hol
Facilities
Outdoor Manege 20 x 50 fl lt
SJ: Nov, 1 Paddock
CC: Banks, 14 Schooling
Lec Rm, Vis Aids, Chng Rm, Wait Rm, Tack Shop
Hacking
Exclusions Wt Limit, 10st, Age Limit, 7
Location A458 4 miles from Stourbridge, 11 miles from Bridgnorth

WISHAW RIDING CENTRE

Bulls Lane, Wishaw, Sutton Coldfield, West Midlands, B76 9QW
Tel 0121 313 1663
Contact Mrs M Bevan
Riding School, RDA Inst Riding & Jumping

Staff Chief Instructor Mrs M Bevan (BHSAI, BHS Int.SM)
Plus 1 full time instructor
Ave No 10 Horses, 8 Ponies
inc 1 El Dress, 1 Adv Dress, 1 SJ GR C, 1 HT Adv
Courses WP, Short, Ev, P/T, Hol
Facilities
Covered School 43 x 18 gly
Outdoor Manege 20 x 40
Outdoor Manege 23 x 45
SJ: Grade C, 1 Paddock
CC: Water, 6 Schooling
Lec Rm, Vis Aids, Wait Rm
Hacking
Livery Full, P/T
Schooling General, to Nov Dress
Accom S, Db
Exclusions Wt Limit, 15st, Age Limit, 3
Location 8 miles from Birmingham, 2 1/2 miles from Sutton Coldfield

SHROPSHIRE

BERRIEWOOD FARM

Condover, Shrewsbury, Shropshire, SY5 7NN
Tel 01743 718252
Contact Mrs S M L Lock & Mrs P A Cowdy
Riding School, Training Centre, Facility Centre, RDA - NVQ centre
Level 3 Inst to BHSII
Specialities Career training
Staff Chief Instructor Mrs Felicity Fletcher (BHSI)
Plus 6 full time instructors
Ave No 28 Horses, 27 Ponies
inc 4 El Dress, 1 Med Dress, 2 SJ GR C
Courses WP, YT, Short, Ev, P/T, Hol
Facilities
Covered School 46 x 21 gly
Outdoor Manege 60 x 20 fl lt
Outdoor Manege 40 x 40
SJ: Nov, 1 Paddock
CC: Course, Basic, Nov, Int, Banks, Water, Natural
Lec Rm, Vis Aids, Chng Rm, Showers, Wait Rm, Tack Shop
Hacking
Livery Full, P/T, School, Grass
Schooling General
Accom Dor, FB
Exclusions Wt Limit, 15st, Age Limit, 3, No hunting or unescorted hacking

BOW HOUSE FARM
RIDING SCHOOL

Bow House Farm, Bishops Castle, Shropshire, SY9 5HY
Tel 01588 638427

Contact Miss C Meddins
Riding School Inst Riding & Jumping
Staff Chief Instructor Miss C A Meddins
(BHSAI)
Plus 1 full time instructor
Ave No 10 Horses, 5 Ponies
Courses WP, YT, Short, Ev, P/T, Hol
Facilities
Outdoor Manege 55 x 32
Outdoor Manege 41 x 23
SJ: Nov, Grade C, 1 Paddock
CC: Course, Nov, Banks, Water,
Natural, Gallops, 60 Schooling
Lec Rm, Vis Aids, Chng Rm, Wait Rm
Hacking
Livery Full, School, Hunt, Grass
Schooling General, to Nov Dress, to
SJ GR C, to HT Nov
Location A489 3 miles south Bishops
Castle

LILLESHALL
EQUESTRIAN CENTRE
Child Pit Lane, Newport,
Shropshire, TF10 9AR
Tel 01952 677166
Contact Miss S Francis
Riding School Inst Riding & Jumping
Specialities Breeding & Showing
natives, especially Exmoors &
Shetlands etc
Staff Chief Instructor Miss S Francis
(BHSAI)
Plus 1 full time instructor
Ave No 2 Horses, 9 Ponies
Courses YT, Short, Ev, Hol
Facilities
Outdoor Manege 35 x 25
SJ: Nov
Hacking
Livery Full, P/T, DIY, Break
Schooling General, Break, to Nov Dress
Exclusions Wt Limit, 11st, Age Limit, 5,
No unescorted hacking
Location In the grounds of the National
Sports Centre, Lilleshall. Off Pave lane,
Newport, Salop

MILL FARM RIDING CENTRE
Hughley, Shrewsbury,
Shropshire, SY5 6NT
Tel 01746 785645
Contact Mrs E Bosworth
**Riding School, Training Centre,
Long Distance Riding** Inst Riding &
Jumping
Specialities Superb hacking, including
Wenlock Edge. Riding holidays for all.
Close to Jack Munton long distance
ride (72 miles). 2 day rides
1 full time instructor

Ave No 12 Horses, 12 Ponies
Courses YT, Short, Ev, P/T, Hol
Facilities
SJ: Nov, 1 Paddock
CC: Course, Basic, Nov, Banks, Water,
Natural
Lec Rm, Vis Aids, Chng Rm, Showers,
Tack Shop
Hacking
Livery Full, P/T, DIY, Break, School,
Hunt, Grass
Schooling General, Break, to Nov Dress
Accom Db, F, Dor, Caravan, Cottage,
FB, SC
Exclusions Wt Limit, 15st,
No unescorted riders
Location 3 miles from Much Wenlock

NORTH FARM
RIDING ESTABLISHMENT
Ludlow, Salop, SY8 2HD
Tel 01584 872026
Contact Mr P Dickin
Riding School, RDA. Forest Hacking.
Inst Basic
Staff Chief Instructor Mr P J Dickin
Plus 1 full time instructor
Ave No 8 Horses, 7 Ponies
inc RDA, Novice beginners
Courses YT
Facilities
SJ: Nov, 1 Paddock
Chng Rm, Showers
Hacking
Livery P/T
Schooling Break
Accom Dor, Caravan, FB
Exclusions Wt Limit, 15st7, Age Limit, 5,
No dogs on hacks. Mminimum age 5
Location 1 mile west of Ludlow

OSWESTRY EQUESTRIAN CENTRE
Carreg-y-Big, Selattyn,
Oswestry,
Shropshire, SY10 7HX
Tel 01691 654754
Contact Mrs Kay Brown
Riding School Inst Riding & Jumping
Staff Chief Instructor Miss Kate Butler
(BHSAI, BHS Int Teach)
Ave No 17 Horses, 10 Ponies
Courses YT, Short, Ev, P/T, Hol
Facilities
Covered School 45 x 26 gly
Outdoor Manege 40 x 20
SJ: Nov
CC: Basic, Nov
Lec Rm, Vis Aids, Wait Rm
Hacking
Livery Full, School, Hunt
Accom Tw, FB

P G L ADVENTURE
c/o PGL Travel Ltd,
Boreatton Park, Baschurch,
Shrewsbury, Salop, SY4 2EZ
Tel 01989 764211 HQ
Contact Mr A Prince
Childrens Holiday Centre. Inst Basic
2 full time instructors
Ave No 8 Horses, 56 Ponies
Courses Hol
Facilities
SJ: 1 Paddock
Lec Rm, Vis Aids, Chng Rm, Showers,
Wait Rm
Accom Dor, Caravan, FB
Exclusions Age Limit, 8 to 13

PRESCOTT EQUESTRIAN CENTRE
Baschurch, Shrewsbury,
Shropshire, SY4 2DR
Tel 01939 260712
Contact Mrs J C Haydon
Riding School, Training Centre Inst
to BHSAI
Specialities Career training
4 full time instructors
Ave No 15 Horses, 19 Ponies
Courses WP, YT, Short, Ev, P/T, Hol
Facilities
Covered School 47 x 27 gly
Covered School 12 x 27 gly
Outdoor Manege 60 x 40 fl lt
Outdoor Manege 60 x 20 fl lt
SJ: Nov, Grade C, Grade B, Grade A,
1 Paddock
CC: Course, Int, Banks, Water, Natural
Lec Rm, Vis Aids, Chng Rm, Wait Rm,
Tack Shop
Hacking
Livery Full, P/T, DIY, School, Hunt,
Grass
Schooling General, to Nov Dress, to
SJ GR C, to HT Nov
Accom S, SC
Exclusions Wt Limit, 16st
Location Between A5 and A528,
7 miles from centre of Shrewsbury

RED CASTLE RIDING CENTRE
Selattyn, Nr Oswestry,
Shropshire, SY10 7LL
Tel 01691 659704
Contact Mr & Mrs M J Wilding
Riding School Inst Basic
Specialities Childrens riding
Staff Chief Instructor Mrs V G Wilding
Ave No 2 Horses, 12 Ponies
Courses Short
Facilities
Outdoor Manege 40 x 40
SJ: Nov

CC: Basic, Water, Natural, 6 Schooling
Lec Rm, Vis Aids, Chng Rm, Showers,
Wait Rm
Hacking
Exclusions Wt Limit, 12st,
Age Limit, 4 to 18, No casual hire
Location 5 miles out of Oswestry

TELFORD EQUESTRIAN CENTRE
Lodge Bank Farm, Granville Road,
Muxton, Telford,
Shropshire, TF10 8PB
Tel 01952 619825
Contact Mr M Khan
Riding School, Equestrian Centre
Inst Basic
Specialities Instruction in riding and
jumping
Staff Chief Instructor Mr M Z Khan
(BHSAI)
Ave No 11 Horses, 10 Ponies
Courses WP, YT, Short, Ev, Hol
Facilities
Covered School 55 x 18
Outdoor Manege 61 x 18 fl lt
SJ: Grade B, 1 Paddock
CC: Course
Lec Rm, Vis Aids, Wait Rm, Tack Shop
Hacking
Livery Full, P/T, Break, School, Hunt,
Grass
Schooling General, Break, to Med
Dress, to SJ GR C
Exclusions Only escorted riding
Location 2 miles from Jn 4 off M54 &
5 minutes from Telford Town Centre

TONG RIDING CENTRE
Church Farm, Tong, Shifnal,
Shropshire, TF11 8PW
Tel 01902 372352
Contact Mrs Garside Bates &
Mrs Russell
Riding School, Training Centre, RDA
Inst to BHSII
Specialities Career training
Staff Chief Instructor Mrs Garside-
Bates (BHSI)
Plus 3 full time instructors
Ave No 22 Horses, 9 Ponies
inc 3 El Dress, 3 Med Dress, 1 Adv
Dress, 4 SJ GR C, 1 SJ GR B, 2 HT Int
Courses WP, YT, Short, Ev, P/T, Hol
Facilities
Covered School 40 x 20 gly
SJ: Nov, 1 Paddock
CC: Course, Nov, Banks, Water,
Natural, 30 Schooling
Lec Rm, Vis Aids, Chng Rm, Wait Rm
Hacking
Livery Full, P/T, School, Grass

Schooling General, to Med Dress, to SJ GR C, to HT Nov
Accom S, Tw, Cottage, SC
Exclusions Wt Limit, 15st, Age Limit, 4, No unaccompanied riding
Location On A41, 1/4 mile north Jn 3 M54

TRENCH VILLA STABLES
The Trench, Ellesmere,
Shropshire, SY12 0LR
Tel 01691 623950
Contact Mrs H M Rathmill
Riding School, Training Centre Inst Riding & Jumping
Specialities Providing safe, enjoyable riding and jumping, with experienced and qualified staff. RDA
Staff Chief Instructor Mr K Richards (BHSII, BHS SM)
Plus 1 full time instructor
Ave No 8 Horses, 9 Ponies
inc 2 SJ GR C, 2 SJ Jun C, 3 Novice horse trials
Courses WP, YT, Short, Ev, P/T, Hol
Facilities
Covered School 27 x 15 gly
SJ: Grade C
Lec Rm, Vis Aids, Wait Rm, Tack Shop
Livery Full, P/T, DIY, Break, School
Schooling General, Break, to El Dress, to SJ GR C
Exclusions Wt Limit, 14st,
No unescorted hacking
Location Off A528 between Ellesmere and Overton. 1 mile from Ellesmere turn right towards Penley, stables 400yds on right

WALFORD COLLEGE
Baschurch, Nr Shrewsbury,
Shropshire, SY4 2HL
Tel 01939 262100
Contact Mrs J Hemmings
Riding School, Training Centre, Facility Centre Inst to BHSII
Specialities Career training
Staff Chief Instructor Mr A Tyler (BHSI)
Plus 5 full time instructors

Ave No 35 Horses, 5 Ponies
Courses WP, Short, Ev, P/T
Facilities
Covered School 60 x 30
Outdoor Manege 60 x 30
SJ: Nov, 1 Paddock
CC: Course, Nov, Banks, Water, Natural, 25 Schooling
Lec Rm, Vis Aids, Wait Rm
Livery Full, P/T, School
Schooling General, to El Dress, to SJ GR C, to HT Nov
Accom S, FB
Location On B5067 between Shrewsbury - Oswestry

THE WYKE OF SHIFNAL
Shifnal,
Shropshire, TF11 9PP
Tel 01952 460560
Contact Mr R J C & Linda Phillips & S D Phillips
Riding School, Training Centre, Facility Centre, RDA and Sidesaddle Inst Riding & Jumping
Staff Chief Instructor Mr R J C Phillips (BHSII, BHS SM)
Plus 3 full time instructors
Ave No 16 Horses, 7 Ponies
inc 2 El Dress, 2 Med Dress, 1 HT Adv
Courses WP, YT, Short, Ev, P/T, Hol
Facilities
Covered School 42 x 21 gly
Outdoor Manege 25 x 62 fl lt
Outdoor Manege 20 x 40 fl lt
SJ: Nov, Grade C, 2 Paddock
CC: Course, Nov, Banks, Water, Natural, 30 Schooling
Lec Rm, Vis Aids, Chng Rm, Wait Rm, Tack Shop
Hacking
Livery Full, P/T, Break, School, Hunt
Schooling General, Break, to Med Dress, to HT Int
Accom S, Tw, Db, F, Cottage, FB, SC
Exclusions Wt Limit, 12st5,
Hacking as part of lessons only
Location Just off A4169 1 mile south-west of Shifnal and 3 miles from Jn 4 on M54

Riding in the East

BEDFORDSHIRE ◆ CAMBRIDGESHIRE ◆ ESSEX
HERTFORDSHIRE ◆ NORFOLK ◆ SUFFOLK

BEDFORDSHIRE

BACKNOE END EQUESTRIAN CENTRE
Keysoe Road, Thurleigh,
Bedfordshire, MK44 2DZ
Tel 01234 772263
Contact Miss S L Dodson
Riding School Inst Riding & Jumping
Staff Chief Instructor Miss S Dodson
(BHSII)
Plus 2 full time instructors
Ave No 3 Horses, 2 Ponies
Courses YT, Short, Ev, P/T
Facilities
Outdoor Manege 60 x 20
SJ: Nov, 2 Paddock
Chng Rm, Showers, Wait Rm
Hacking
Livery Full, Break, School
Schooling General
Exclusions Wt Limit, 13st, Age Limit, 6,
No casual hire
Location Jn 12 off M1, 7 miles north of
Bedford

ROCKLANE RIDING CENTRE
Orchard Farm, Ivinghoe Aston,
Leighton Buzzard,
Beds, LU7 9DL
Tel 01525 222402
Contact Mrs J Joyce
Riding School Inst Riding & Jumping
Specialities All round tuition
Staff Chief Instructor Mr J Tossell
(BHSAI)
Ave No 6 Horses, 8 Ponies
Courses WP, YT, Ev, P/T, Hol
Facilities
Outdoor Manege 20 x 40 fl lt
SJ: Nov, 1 Paddock
CC: 3 Schooling
Chng Rm
Exclusions Wt Limit, 15st
Location Off the B489 between
Dunstable & Leighton Buzzard

TINSLEY'S RIDING SCHOOL
Green Lane, Clapham,
Bedfordshire, MK41 6EX
Tel 01234 268556
Contact Mr & Mrs Black
Riding School Inst Basic
Staff Chief Instructor Mrs Black (BHSII)
Ave No 5 Horses, 8 Ponies
Courses Ev, Hol
Facilities
Outdoor Manege 20 x 40 fl lt
SJ: Nov, 1 Paddock
CC: Basic, Nov, Natural, 10 Schooling
Wait Rm
Hacking
Livery DIY
Schooling General, to Nov Dress
Exclusions Wt Limit, 13st, Age Limit, 6,
No unescorted hacks
Location 1 mile north of Bedford A6
from Bedford, turn off into Green Lane
in Clapham, Riding School in Green
Lane

CAMBRIDGESHIRE

THE COLLEGE OF WEST ANGLIA
Landbeach Road, Milton,
Cambs, CB4 6DB
Tel 01223 860701
Contact Miss C A Ratcliffe
**Riding School, Training Centre,
Facility Centre** Inst to BHSII
Specialities Career training
Staff Chief Instructor Miss C A Ratcliffe
(BHSII, BHS SM)
Plus 6 full time instructors
Ave No 23 Horses, 2 Ponies
inc 3 El Dress, 2 Med Dress, 3 SJ GR
C, 2 SJ GR B, Side Saddle
Courses WP, YT, Short, Ev, P/T
Facilities
Covered School 20 x 40 gly
Outdoor Manege 30 x 60
SJ: Nov, 1 Paddock

CC: Banks, Natural, Gallops, 14
Schooling
Lec Rm, Vis Aids, Chng Rm, Showers,
Wait Rm
Livery P/T, Break
Schooling General, Break, to Med
Dress, to SJ GR C, to HT Int
Exclusions Wt Limit, 14st, Age Limit, 7
Location Just off Jn A45/A10

CONQUEST LIVERY
AND RIDING CENTRE
Conquest Drove, Farcet Fen,
Cambs, PE7 3DH
Tel 01733 240967
Contact Mr E Butler
Livery
1 full time instructor
Facilities
Outdoor Manege 20 x 40 fl lt
Outdoor Manege 20 x 30
SJ: Nov, 1 Paddock
Chng Rm, Wait Rm
Livery Full, P/T, DIY, Grass
Exclusions Wt Limit, 12st, Age Limit, 7
Location 2 miles south of
Peterborough

CROSS LEYS FARM
ST JOHN'S WOOD LIVERY YARD
Leicester Road, Thornhaugh,
Peterborough,
Cambridgeshire, PE8 6NS
Tel 01780 782609
Contact W A Fuller & Son
Livery
Specialities DIY livery
Facilities
Outdoor Manege 25 x 40 fl lt
Chng Rm, Wait Rm
Livery Full, P/T, DIY, Hunt
Exclusions No stallions taken for livery
Location Off A47, 3 miles from A1

GRANGE FARM
EQUESTRIAN CENTRE
Wittering Grange, Wansford,
Peterborough,
Cambridgeshire, PE8 6NR
Tel 01780 782459
Contact Mr & Mrs R Dunlop
Riding School Inst Riding & Jumping
Staff Chief Instructor Mrs A Shelton
(BHSAI, BHS Int Teach, BHS Int.SM)
Plus 4 full time instructors
Ave No 30 Horses, 40 Ponies
inc 4 El Dress
Courses YT
Facilities
Covered School 40 x 20 gly

Covered School 40 x 20
Outdoor Manege 70 x 30 fl lt
Outdoor Manege 65 x 30 fl lt
Outdoor Manege 110 x 42 fl lt
SJ: Nov
CC: Course, Basic, Nov, Banks, Water,
Natural, Gallops
Lec Rm, Vis Aids, Chng Rm, Showers,
Wait Rm, Tack Shop
Hacking
Livery Full, P/T, Break, School, Grass
Schooling General, Break, to Nov
Dress, to SJ GR C, to HT Nov
Exclusions Wt Limit, 16st, Age Limit, 3,
No unescorted hacks
Location Between A1 & A47, 10 miles
from Peterborough & 5 miles from
Stamford

HAGGIS FARM STABLES
Cambridge Road, Barton,
Cambridge, CB3 7AT
Tel 01223 460353
Contact Mrs B J Morris-Lowe
Riding School Inst Riding & Jumping
Specialities Pony Club activites
2 full time instructors
Ave No 8 Horses, 12 Ponies
inc 1 El Dress, 2 HT Int
Courses WP, YT, Short
Facilities
Covered School 36 x 18
Outdoor Manege 20 x 40
SJ: Nov, 1 Paddock
CC: Course, Basic, Banks, Water,
Natural
Lec Rm, Vis Aids, Chng Rm, Wait Rm
Hacking
Livery Full
Exclusions Wt Limit, 14st, Age Limit, 3,
No casual hire
Location 1/4 mile from Jn 12 of M11

LYNCH FARM EQUESTRIAN CLUB
Wistow Way, Orton Wistow,
Peterborough,
Cambridgeshire, PE2 6XA
Tel 01733 234445
Contact Mr D M Brown
Riding School, Training Centre Inst
Riding & Jumping
3 full time instructors
Ave No 11 Horses, 11 Ponies
inc 3 Med Dress
Courses WP, YT, Short, Ev, P/T, Hol
Facilities
Covered School 37 x 20 gly
SJ: Nov, 1 Paddock
CC: Natural, 5 Schooling
Lec Rm, Vis Aids, Chng Rm, Wait Rm
Hacking

Livery Full, P/T, Break, School, Hunt
Schooling General, to Med Dress, to HT Nov
Exclusions Wt Limit, 13st, Age Limit, 5, No unescorted hacking
Location 1 1/2 miles from A1 by Alwalton

PARK HOUSE LIVERY
91 High Street, Harston,
Cambridgeshire, CB2 5PZ
Tel 01223 870075
Contact Mrs Carol King
Riding School, Facility Centre Inst Basic
Specialities Instruction for beginners to the more experienced, with emphasis on Dressage training
Staff Chief Instructor Mrs Carol King Plus 1 full time instructor
Ave No 3 Horses, 11 Ponies inc 1 El Dress
Courses WP, YT, Short, Ev, Hol
Facilities
Outdoor Manege 20 x 40 fl lt
SJ: Nov, 1 Paddock
CC: Course, Basic, Banks, Natural, Gallops
Lec Rm, Vis Aids, Chng Rm, Wait Rm
Livery Full, P/T, Break, School, Hunt, Grass
Schooling General, Break, to Med Dress, to SJ GR C, to HT Nov
Accom S, Db, Cottage, SC
Exclusions Wt Limit, 15st, Age Limit, 5, No hacking
Location J11 off M11 centre of Harston village

RECTORY FARM STABLES
Rectory Farm, Graveley, Huntingdon,
Cambridge, PE18 9PP
Tel 01480 830336
Contact Mrs S N Pembroke
Livery
Hacking
Livery P/T, DIY
Exclusions No casual clients
Location Between A1 & A14, 6 miles south of Huntingdon

SWISS COTTAGE RIDING STABLES
Longacre Farm, School Road,
Marshland St James, Wisbech,
Cambridgeshire, PE14 8EZ
Tel 01945 430315
Contact Ms K J Whitby
Riding School, Facility Centre Inst Basic
Specialities Novice and nervous riders

Staff Chief Instructor Mrs K J Whitby
Ave No 3 Horses, 13 Ponies
Courses WP
Facilities
Outdoor Manege 25 x 45 fl lt
SJ: Nov, 1 Paddock
Lec Rm, Vis Aids, Chng Rm, Wait Rm
Hacking
Exclusions Wt Limit, 14.7 st, Age Limit, 3, No casual hire. Compulsory assesment lesson
Location 3 miles from Wisbech town centre, 2 miles off A47

ESSEX

ALDBOROUGH HALL EQUESTRIAN CENTRE LTD
Aldborough Hatch, Ilford,
Essex, IG2 7TE
Tel 0181 590 1433
Contact Mr A R S Garrett
Riding School, Training Centre, Facility Centre Inst Riding & Jumping
Staff Chief Instructor Mr A R S Garrett (BHSII, BHS SM) Plus 5 full time instructors
Ave No 20 Horses, 16 Ponies inc 4 El Dress, 3 Med Dress, 4 Adv Dress, 2 SJ GR C, 2 SJ GR B, 3 SJ GR A, 1 HT Int, Breed competition horses BWB & HIS
Courses WP, Short, Ev, P/T
Facilities
Covered School 24 x 60 gly
Outdoor Manege 50 x 90 fl lt
Outdoor Manege 20 x 40
SJ: Grade A, 1 Paddock
CC: Course, Basic, Adv, Banks, Water, Natural, Gallops, 100 Schooling
Lec Rm, Vis Aids, Chng Rm, Showers, Wait Rm
Livery Full, Break, School
Schooling General, Break, to Med Dress, to Adv Dress, to SJ GR A, to HT Int
Accom S, Tw, SC
Exclusions Wt Limit, 14st7, Age Limit, 4
Location 3/4 mile off A12. 3 miles M11. A406 Red Bridge roundabout east of M11

ASHTREE EQUESTRIAN CENTRE
Little Waltham, Chelmsford,
Essex, CM3 3PA
Tel 01245 362424
Contact Mr G Weal & Miss J Weal
Riding School, Training Centre,

Facility Centre Inst Basic
Staff Chief Instructor Miss J Weal
Ave No 8 Horses, 14 Ponies
inc 1 El Dress, 2 SJ Jun C
Courses WP, YT, Short, Ev, P/T, Hol
Facilities
Covered School 20 x 40
SJ: Nov, Grade C
Lec Rm, Vis Aids, Chng Rm, Wait Rm
Hacking
Livery Full, Break, School, Hunt
Schooling General, Break, to El Dress,
to SJ GR C, to HT Nov
Exclusions Wt Limit, 14st,
Age Limit, 2 1/2, No Casual Hire
Location 4 miles from Chelmsford City
Centre off the A130

BARROW FARM GROUP
RIDING FOR THE DISABLED
Barrow Farm, Highwood,
Chelmsford, Essex, CM1 3QR
Tel 01277 821538
Contact Miss A E Mitchell
Riding School, RDA Inst Riding &
Jumping
Staff Chief Instructor Miss A E Mitchell
(BHSAI, BHS Int Teach)
Plus 1 full time instructor
Ave No 14 Ponies
inc RDA
Facilities
Covered School 20 x 40
Outdoor Manege 25 x 50
Lec Rm, Vis Aids, Wait Rm
Hacking
Exclusions Wt Limit, 12st, Only able to
teach RDA riders
Location Between Writtle and
Blackmore, 2 miles off A414

BROOK FARM
EQUESTRIAN CENTRE
Radwinter, Saffron Walden,
Essex, CB10 2TH
Tel 01799 599262
Contact Ms N Gooding
Riding School, Training Centre Inst
Basic
3 full time instructors
Ave No 10 Horses, 15 Ponies
inc 2 El Dress, 1 Med Dress
Courses WP, YT, Short, Ev, P/T
Facilities
Covered School 42 x 22 gly
Outdoor Manege 40 x 20 fl lt
SJ: Nov, 1 Paddock
Chng Rm, Wait Rm, Tack Shop
Hacking
Livery Full, P/T, Break, School
Schooling General, Break, to Nov

Dress, to El Dress
Exclusions Age Limit, 3,
No riders over 14st
Location B1054, 5 miles from Saffron
Walden, 8 miles from Haverhill

BURCHES RIDING SCHOOL
Gt Burches Road, Thundersley,
Essex, SS7 3NF
Tel 01268 776654
Contact Mr & Mrs G J Bush
Riding School Inst Riding & Jumping
Specialities Dressage
Staff Chief Instructor Mrs L D Bush
(BHSAI)
Plus 1 full time instructor
Ave No 5 Horses, 13 Ponies
inc 1 El Dress
Courses WP, YT, Short, Ev, P/T, Hol
Facilities
Outdoor Manege 20 x 40 fl lt
Outdoor Manege 15 x 30 fl lt
SJ: Nov, 1 Paddock
Lec Rm, Vis Aids, Wait Rm, Tack Shop
Hacking
Livery Full, P/T, DIY, School
Schooling General, to El Dress, to SJ
GR C, to HT Nov
Exclusions Wt Limit, 14st, Age Limit, 5,
No casual hire
Location Off A127 between Rayleigh
and Hadleigh

DANBURY CARRIAGE
DRIVING CENTRE
Chamberlains Farm, Sporehams Lane,
Danbury, Essex, CM3 4AJ
Tel 01245 226745
Contact Mr T & Mrs D Selway
Training Centre, Facility Centre,
Livery, Carriage Driving Centre
Specialities Competition driving and
livery
Staff Chief Instructor Mr T Selway
Ave No 3 Horses
inc 3 driving horses
Courses WP, Short, Ev, P/T, Hol
Facilities
Outdoor Manege 24 x 40 fl lt
Lec Rm, Vis Aids, Chng Rm, Wait Rm
Livery Full, Break, School
Schooling Break
Location 3 miles off A12 east of
Chelmsford

DE'BEAUVOIR FARM LIVERY YARD
Church Road, Ramsden Heath,
Nr Billericay, Essex, CM11 1PW
Tel 01268 711302
Contact Mr & Mrs Hinde

Livery
Facilities
CC: Natural, 6 Schooling
Livery Full, P/T, DIY
Location Off the A129 between Wickford and Billericay

**EASTMINSTER
SCHOOL OF RIDING**
Hooks Hall Farm, The Chase,
Rushgreen, Romford, Essex, RM7 0SS
Tel 01708 447423
Contact Mr & Mrs Ackland
Riding School Inst Riding & Jumping
Staff Chief Instructor Mrs A Ackland
(BHSAI, BHS Int Teach)
Plus 3 full time instructors
Ave No 16 Horses, 19 Ponies
inc 3 El Dress, 4 SJ GR C, 2 SJ GR B,
2 SJ GR A
Courses WP, YT, Short, Ev, P/T
Facilities
Covered School 15 x 30
Outdoor Manege 30 x 60 fl lt
SJ: Grade B, 1 Paddock
CC: Course, Basic, Banks, Water,
Natural
Lec Rm, Vis Aids, Wait Rm
Hacking
Livery Full, P/T, DIY, School, Grass
Schooling General, to El Dress, to SJ
GR B
Exclusions Wt Limit, 14st, Age Limit, 5,
Escorted only following assessment
lesson
Location On A125, 15 miles from
London, 2 miles from Romford

ELMWOOD EQUESTRIAN CENTRE
Elm Farm, Maldon Road,
Burnham-on-Crouch,
Essex, CM0 8NT
Tel 01621 783216/784330
Contact Mr & Mrs J & A Hull
Livery
Specialities Livery of all types,
specialising in DIY
1 full time instructor
Facilities
Outdoor Manege 20 x 40 fl lt
Outdoor Manege 40 x 60 fl lt
SJ: Nov, 1 Paddock
CC: Basic, 5 Schooling
Lec Rm, Vis Aids, Chng Rm, Showers,
Wait Rm
Hacking
Livery Full, P/T, DIY, Break, School,
Grass
Schooling General, Break
Location
On B1010 between Althorne - Burnham

FOREST LODGE RIDING SCHOOL
Epping Road, (Nr City Limits),
Epping, Essex, CM16 5HW
Tel 01992 812137
Contact Mr B Patrick
Riding School Inst Basic
Specialities Basic instruction in riding
and jumping, specialising in children
1 full time instructor
Ave No 1 Horses, 15 Ponies
Courses Ev, P/T, Hol
Facilities
Covered School 15 x 45 gly
Lec Rm, Vis Aids, Chng Rm, Wait Rm
Hacking
Livery Full, P/T
Exclusions Wt Limit, 12st, Age Limit, 2,
Subject to competency
Location On B1393 between Epping &
Loughton, 3 miles from Jn 26 of M25

FOXHOUND RIDING SCHOOL
Baker Street, Orsett,
Essex, RM16 3LJ
Tel 01375 891367
Contact Mr D Creamer
Riding School, Training Centre Inst
Riding & Jumping
Staff Chief Instructor Mrs M Cox
(BHSAI)
Plus 2 full time instructors
Ave No 6 Horses, 10 Ponies
inc 3 El Dress
Courses YT, Ev, P/T, Hol
Facilities
Covered School 20 x 40 gly
Outdoor Manege 20 x 35 fl lt
SJ: Nov, Grade C, 1 Paddock
CC: Course, Basic, Nov, Water, Natural
Chng Rm, Wait Rm, Tack Shop
Hacking
Livery Full, P/T, DIY, Break, School,
Hunt, Grass
Schooling General, Break, to El Dress,
to SJ GR C, to HT Nov
Exclusions Wt Limit, 15st, Age Limit, 5,
No unaccompanied hiring
Location 10 minutes from M25.
15 minutes from Dartford Tunnel

HAYCOCKS LIVERY STABLES
Blue Row, East Mersea Road,
West Mersea, Colchester, Essex
Tel 01206 383974
Contact Mrs C Conway &
Mrs C Hewes
Livery
Facilities
Outdoor Manege 20 x 40 fl lt
Wait Rm
Livery DIY

Location 8 miles north of Colchester on B1026

HIGH BEECH RIDING SCHOOL
Packsaddle Farm, Pynest Green Lane, Waltham Abbey,
Essex, EN9 3QL
Tel 0181 508 8866
Contact Mr A J Taylor
Riding School Inst Riding & Jumping
Staff Chief Instructor Mr A J Taylor
Plus 5 full time instructors
Ave No 14 Horses, 11 Ponies
Courses WP, YT, Ev, Hol
Facilities
Covered School 18 x 37
SJ: Nov, 1 Paddock
Lec Rm, Vis Aids, Wait Rm
Hacking
Schooling General, to Nov Dress
Exclusions Wt Limit, 13st5, Age Limit, 7, No casual hire
Location 1 mile from Jn 26 on M25 between Waltham Abbey and Loughton

HILL FARM EQUESTRIAN TRAINING CENTRE
Hill Farm, Pan Lane, East Hanningfield, Chelmsford, Essex, CM3 8BJ
Tel 01245 400115
Contact Mr R Lawrence
Riding School, Training Centre Inst to BHSAI
Specialities Career training
3 full time instructors
Ave No 16 Horses, 10 Ponies inc 1 El Dress
Courses WP, YT, Short, Ev, P/T
Facilities
Covered School 40 x 20 gly
Outdoor Manege 50 x 20 fl lt
SJ: Nov, 8acre Paddock
Lec Rm, Vis Aids, Chng Rm
Hacking
Livery Full, P/T, DIY, Break, School, Hunt, Grass
Schooling General, Break, to El Dress, to SJ GR C
Accom S, Tw, SC
Exclusions Wt Limit, 15st, Age Limit, 4, No casual hiring
Location 5 miles south of Chelmsford off A130

JUBILEE FARM HOUSE
Newney Green, Writtle, Chelmsford, Essex, CM1 3SF
Tel 01245 422442
Contact Mr & Mrs Turner
Livery

Specialities Most types of livery with excellent bridleway hacking.Horse transportation service available
Ave No 6 Horses
Facilities
SJ: Nov, 3 Paddock
Chng Rm, Wait Rm
Livery Full, P/T, DIY, Hunt, Grass
Exclusions No stallions
Location 1 mile off A414, 2 miles from Writtle

LONGWOOD EQUESTRIAN CENTRE
Lelant, Dry Street, Laindon, Basildon, Essex, SS16 5NG
Tel 01268 541177
Contact Mr I Lewington & Partners
Riding School Inst Basic
2 full time instructors
Ave No 5 Horses, 8 Ponies
Courses WP, YT
Facilities
SJ: Nov, Grade A
Lec Rm, Vis Aids, Chng Rm, Showers, Wait Rm, Tack Shop
Hacking
Livery DIY
Schooling General, Break, to SJ GR A
Exclusions Wt Limit, 14st, Age Limit, 8, No casual hire
Location 1 mile from Basildon town centre. 2 miles from A13

LYNFORD NEW FARM
Runwell Road, Wickford, Essex, SS11 7PS
Tel 01268 562818
Contact Mr D Knox
Livery, Shows
Ave No 14 Horses, 14 Ponies
Facilities
Covered School 23 x 18
SJ: Nov, 2 Paddock
Tack Shop
Livery DIY
Location On the A132 between Wickford and Rettendon Turnpike

MOOR END STABLES
Great Sampford, Saffron Walden, Essex, CB10 2RQ
Tel 01799 586338
Contact Miss S J Green
Livery
Staff Chief Instructor Miss S Ahlquist (BHSAI, BHS Int Teach)
Plus 3 full time instructors
Facilities
Covered School 20 x 60
Outdoor Manege 20 x 40 fl lt

Outdoor Manege 20 x 40 fl lt
SJ: Nov, Grade C, 1 Paddock
CC: Course, Basic, Nov, Int, Banks, Natural
Lec Rm, Vis Aids, Chng Rm, Showers, Wait Rm
Hacking
Livery Full, P/T, DIY, Break, School, Hunt, Grass
Schooling General, Break, to El Dress, to SJ GR C
Accom S, Tw, FB
Location B1053 between Saffron Walden and Thaxted

RAWRETH EQUESTRIAN CENTRE
Church Road, Rawreth,
Wickford, Essex, SS11 8SH
Tel 01268 733008
Contact Mrs L D Jack
Riding School, Training Centre Inst
Basic
Staff Chief Instructor Mrs L D Jack (BHSAI)
Plus 2 full time instructors
Ave No 8 Horses, 11 Ponies
Courses WP, YT, Short, Ev, P/T, Hol
Facilities
Covered School 32 x 17
Outdoor Manege 20 x 60 fl lt
SJ: Nov, 1 Paddock
CC: 8 Schooling
Lec Rm, Vis Aids, Chng Rm, Wait Rm
Hacking
Livery Full, P/T, Break, School, Hunt
Schooling General, to Nov Dress, to SJ GR C
Exclusions Wt Limit, 15st, Age Limit, 5, No casual hire
Location 1/2 mile west of A13

RAYNE RIDING CENTRE
Fairy Hall Lane, Rayne,
Braintree, Essex, CM8 8SZ
Tel 01376 322231
Contact Mr & Mrs B R Pewter
Riding School, Training Centre, Facility Centre, RDA Inst to BHSAI
Staff Chief Instructor Mrs C Armstrong (BHSAI, BHS Int Teach, BHS Int.SM)
Plus 2 full time instructors
Ave No 17 Horses, 17 Ponies
inc 1 El Dress, 1 SJ GR B
Courses WP, Short, Ev, P/T, Hol
Facilities
Covered School 20 x 40 gly
Outdoor Manege 23 x 60 fl lt
SJ: Nov, Grade C, 1 Paddock
CC: Banks, Natural, 5 Schooling
Lec Rm, Vis Aids, Chng Rm, Showers, Wait Rm

Hacking
Livery Full, P/T, Break, School, Hunt
Schooling General, Break, to Nov Dress, to El Dress, to Med Dress, to SJ GR C, to SJ GR B, to HT Nov, to HT Int
Accom Caravan, Cottage, SC
Exclusions Wt Limit, 18st, Age Limit, 4, No casual hire
Location Off A120 1 mile from Rayne village centre

RUNNINGWELL EQUESTRIAN CLUB
Warren Road, Rettendon,
Chelmsford, Essex, CM6 5DG
Tel 01268 711221
Contact Mr & Mrs A I Bowman
Riding School, Training Centre Inst
Riding & Jumping
Specialities Western Hacking
Staff Chief Instructor Miss K Marshall (BHSII)
Plus 3 full time instructors
Ave No 20 Horses, 6 Ponies
inc 3 El Dress, 3 Med Dress, 2 Adv Dress, 6 SJ GR C, 1 SJ GR B, 1 SJ GR A, 1 SJ Jun C, 1 SJ Jun A
Courses WP, Ev
Facilities
Covered School 41 x 20 gly
Covered School 38 x 20
Outdoor Manege 40 x 20 fl lt
Outdoor Manege 15 x 15
SJ: Grade A, 1 Paddock
CC: Banks, Water, Natural, Gallops, 15 Schooling
Lec Rm, Vis Aids, Chng Rm, Showers, Wait Rm
Hacking
Livery Full, P/T, DIY, Break, School
Schooling General, Break, to Med Dress, to SJ GR A
Accom S, Db, Dor, SC
Exclusions Age Limit, 3, No horse hire
Location Off A130 between Wickford and Chelmsford

SHOPLAND HALL EQUESTRIAN CENTRE
Shopland Road, Rochford,
Essex, SS4 1LT
Tel 01702 543377
Contact Mrs J S & Miss A L Murrell
Riding School, Training Centre Inst
Riding & Jumping
Specialities Instruction in riding and jumping
Staff Chief Instructor Miss A Murrell (BHSII)
Plus 5 full time instructors
Ave No 8 Horses, 19 Ponies
inc 3 SJ GR C

Courses WP, YT, Short, Ev, P/T, Hol
Facilities
Covered School 24 x 30 gly
Outdoor Manege 22 x 66 fl lt
SJ: Nov, 2 Paddock
CC: Course, Basic, Banks, Natural, Gallops
Lec Rm, Vis Aids, Chng Rm, Wait Rm, Tack Shop
Hacking
Livery Full, Break, School
Schooling General, Break, to El Dress, to SJ GR C, to HT Nov
Accom S, Tw, SC
Exclusions Wt Limit, 16st, Age Limit, 2, No casual hire
Location Off the B1013 three miles north of Rochford

TIPTREE EQUESTRIAN CENTRE
Simpsons Lane, Tiptree,
Essex, CO5 0PP
Tel 01621 815552
Contact Miss M Dicks
Riding School, Facility Centre Inst Basic
Staff Chief Instructor Miss Michaela Dicks
Plus 1 full time instructor
Ave No 5 Horses, 6 Ponies
Courses Short, Ev, P/T, Hol
Facilities
Covered School 30 x 50 gly
Outdoor Manege 30 x 40 fl lt
SJ: Nov
Lec Rm, Vis Aids, Chng Rm, Showers, Wait Rm
Hacking
Livery Full, P/T, DIY, Break, School, Hunt
Schooling General, Break, to Med Dress, to SJ GR C
Exclusions Wt Limit, 15st, Age Limit, 5, No casual hire
Location Off the B1023 between Tiptree and Maldon

WEST BOWERS
West Bowers Farm, Woodham Walter, Maldon, Essex, CM9 6RZ
Tel 01245 222819
Contact Mr C Warner
Livery
Ave No 7 Horses, 3 Ponies
Facilities
Covered School 30 x 18
SJ: 1 Paddock
CC: Natural, 12 Schooling
Livery Full, P/T, DIY, Grass
Location 3 miles north of A414 between Chelmsford and Maldon

WOODREDON RIDING SCHOOL
Woodredon Farm Lane, Upshire,
Waltham Abbey, Essex, EN9 3SX
Tel 01992 714312/711144
Contact Mr D L Gill
Riding School Inst Riding & Jumping
Staff Chief Instructor Mrs K Gill
Plus 3 full time instructors
Ave No 14 Horses, 14 Ponies inc 1 Med Dress
Courses Short, Ev, P/T, Hol
Facilities
Covered School 37 x 23 gly
Outdoor Manege 20 x 60
SJ: Nov, 1 Paddock
CC: Basic, Banks, Natural, Gallops, 12 Schooling
Lec Rm, Vis Aids, Wait Rm
Hacking
Livery Full, P/T, Break, School
Schooling General, to Adv Dress
Exclusions Wt Limit, 14st, Age Limit, 5, No novices hacking
Location Off A121, 1/2 mile from Jn 26 on the M25

WRITTLE COLLEGE
Cow Watering Lane, Writtle,
Chelmsford, Essex, CM1 3SD
Tel 01245 420705
Contact Mr G J Andrews
Training Centre Inst to BHSII
8 full time instructors
Ave No 30 Horses
Courses Short, Ev, P/T
Facilities
Covered School 26 x 51 gly
Outdoor Manege 20 x 40 fl lt
Outdoor Manege 25 x 65
SJ: Nov, 1 Paddock
CC: Course, Basic, Nov, Banks, Water, Natural
Lec Rm, Vis Aids
Livery Full, P/T, Break, School, Grass
Schooling General, Break, to El Dress, to Med Dress, to HT Nov
Accom FB
Exclusions Wt Limit, 13st, No casual clients
Location West of Chelmsford, 3/4 mile off A414

HERTFORDSHIRE

BAMBERS GREEN RIDING CENTRE
Takeley, Bishops Stortford,
Herts, CM22 6PE
Tel 01279 870320
Contact Mr I Dobson
Riding School, Training Centre,

Facility Centre Inst Riding & Jumping
2 full time instructors
Ave No 8 Horses, 7 Ponies
Courses Short, Ev, P/T, Hol
Facilities
Outdoor Manege 20 x 40 fl lt
SJ: Nov, 1 Paddock
CC: Course, Basic, 17 Schooling
Lec Rm, Vis Aids, Chng Rm
Hacking
Livery Full, P/T, Break, School
Schooling General, Break, to Med
Dress
Exclusions Wt Limit, 14st,
Age Limit, 3 1/2, No casual hire
Location 1/2 mile north off A120 at
Little Lanfield, midway between
Dunmow and Bishops Stortford

CONTESSA RIDING CENTRE
Willow Tree Farm, Colliers End,
Nr Ware, Hertfordshire, SG11 1EN
Tel 01920 821792/821496
Contact Miss T Layton
**Riding School, Training Centre,
Competition Yard** Inst to BHSII
Specialities Holiday courses. Inst in
Riding & Jumping BHSI Dressage.
Dressage courses with schoolmasters
up to Grand Prix. Examination training
courses, holiday courses
Staff Chief Instructor Miss T Layton
(BHSI)
Plus 5 full time instructors
Ave No 25 Horses, 8 Ponies
inc 6 El Dress, 4 Med Dress,
4 Adv Dress, 2 SJ GR C
Courses WP, YT, Short, Ev, P/T, Hol
Facilities
Covered School 20 x 45
Outdoor Manege 60 x 25 fl lt
SJ: Nov, 1 Paddock
CC: Basic, Natural, 10 Schooling
Lec Rm, Vis Aids, Chng Rm, Showers,
Wait Rm
Hacking
Livery Break, School
Schooling General, Break, to Med
Dress, to Adv Dress, to SJ GR C, to HT
Nov
Accom S, Tw, Caravan, SC
Exclusions Wt Limit, 15st,
No casual hire
Location 3 miles north of Ware on the
A10

COUNTY LIVERY
Dene House, Longmeadow Stables,
Ashendene Road, Bayford,
Hertfordshire, SG13 8PX
Tel 01992 511423

Contact Mr K Patient
Livery
Specialities Livery & Hacking
2 full time instructors
Ave No 3 Horses, 2 Ponies
Facilities
Outdoor Manege 20 x 40 fl lt
SJ: Nov
Chng Rm
Hacking
Livery Full, P/T, Break, School
Schooling General, Break
Exclusions No Hacking without
assesment ride
Location Between Broxbourne and
Newgate Street

FOREST STABLES RIDING CENTRE
Leapers Lane, Great Hallingbury,
Bishops Stortford,
Hertfordshire, CM22 7TR
Tel 01279 758051
Contact Mr & Mrs Glen
Riding School, Facility Centre Inst
Basic
Specialities Beginners and hacking
Staff Chief Instructor Mrs P A Glen
Plus 2 full time instructors
Ave No 8 Horses, 13 Ponies
inc 3 SJ GR C
Courses WP, Short, Ev, P/T, Hol
Facilities
Outdoor Manege 20 x 40 fl lt
Outdoor Manege 20 x 40 fl lt
SJ: Nov
Lec Rm, Vis Aids, Wait Rm
Hacking
Livery P/T
Exclusions Wt Limit, 13st , Age Limit, 4,
No casual hire, all hacks subject to
assessment
Location Off A120 2 miles from Jn 8,
M11

GREENACRES EQUESTRIAN
Lower Luton Road, Harpenden,
Hertfordshire, AL5 5EG
Tel 01582 760612
Contact Mr & Mrs P H Woor
Riding School Inst Riding & Jumping
Staff Chief Instructor Mrs K Tynan
Plus 5 full time instructors
Ave No 14 Horses, 14 Ponies
inc 4 SJ GR C, 1 SJ GR B, 2 SJ GR A,
1 SJ Jun C
Courses Short, Ev, P/T, Hol
Facilities
Covered School 128 x 82 gly
Outdoor Manege 39 x 25
SJ: Nov, Grade C, Grade B, Grade A,
1 Paddock

CC: Water, Natural, 3 Schooling
Hacking
Livery Full, P/T, DIY, Break, School, Grass
Schooling General, Break, to El Dress, to SJ GR A, to HT Nov
Accom Tw
Exclusions Age Limit, 3, No casual hiring
Location On the B652 between Harpenden and Luton

HALLINGBURY HALL EQUESTRIAN CENTRE
Little Hallingbury, Bishop's Stortford, Hertfordshire, CM22 2RP
Tel 01279 730348
Contact Mrs S Hardwick
Riding School, Training Centre Inst Riding & Jumping
Specialities Dressage shows held, unaffiliated and affiliated, up to Grand Prix
Staff Chief Instructor Miss E Firth (BHSII)
Plus 2 full time instructors
Ave No 15 Horses, 12 Ponies inc 5 El Dress, 2 Med Dress, 4 SJ GR C, 2 HT Int
Courses WP, YT, Short, Ev, P/T, Hol
Facilities
Covered School 20 x 40 gly
Outdoor Manege 25 x 45 fl lt
Outdoor Manege 30 x 20 fl lt
Outdoor Manege 20 x 60
SJ: Nov, Grade A, 1 Paddock
CC: Course, Nov, Int, Banks, Water, Natural, Gallops, 36+ Schooling
Lec Rm, Vis Aids, Chng Rm, Showers, Wait Rm, Tack Shop
Livery Full, DIY, Break, School
Schooling General, Break, to Med Dress, to SJ GR B, to HT Int
Accom S, Tw, Db, Cottage, SC
Exclusions Wt Limit, 12st7, Age Limit, 4, No casual hacking without assessment lesson
Location On A1060 3 miles south of Bishop's Stortford

HASTOE HILL RIDING SCHOOL
Tring, Herts, HP23 6LU
Tel 01442 828909
Contact Mr & Mrs R Jarman
Riding School, Facility Centre Inst Basic
Specialities Teaching children and nervous riders
Staff Chief Instructor Miss Jackie Richardson (BHSII)
Plus 2 full time instructors

Ave No 8 Horses, 9 Ponies
Courses WP, Short, Ev, P/T, Hol
Facilities
Covered School 32 x 17 gly
Outdoor Manege 25 x 45 fl lt
SJ: Grade A, 1 Paddock
Lec Rm, Vis Aids, Wait Rm
Hacking
Livery Full, P/T, School, Hunt
Schooling General, to El Dress, to SJ GR B
Accom S, SC
Exclusions Wt Limit, 15st, Age Limit, 3, No casual hire
Location 8 miles from Aylesbury, Jn 20 M25 off A41. On the borders of Buckinghamshire, Hertfordshire and Bedfordshire

HIGH HERTS RIDING SCHOOL
High Herts Farm, Pimlico, Hemel Hempstead, Herts, HP3 8ST
Tel 01923 269265
Contact Mr P Waterhouse & Mrs P Couldridge
Riding School, Training Centre Inst Riding & Jumping
Specialities General Instruction, Livery, Hacking, Courses & Shows, Horse walker installed
Staff Chief Instructor Miss S Legg (BHSAI)
Plus 1 full time instructor
Ave No 8 Horses, 15 Ponies inc 1 SJ GR C
Courses WP, YT, P/T, Hol
Facilities
Covered School 40 x 20
Outdoor Manege 40 x 20 fl lt
SJ: Nov, 1 Paddock
CC: Course, Nov, Int, Banks, Natural, Vis Aids, Wait Rm, Tack Shop
Hacking
Livery Full, P/T, DIY, Break, School
Schooling General, Break, to Nov Dress, to SJ GR C, to HT Nov
Exclusions Wt Limit, 13st, Age Limit, 4, No unescorted hacking
Location Close to Jn 8 on the M1 and M25, between Watford and Hemel Hemstead

HOSKINS FARM LIVERY STABLES
High Wych, Sawbridgeworth, Hertfordshire, CM21 0LD
Tel 01279 722165
Contact P & K Backshall & Wood
Facility Centre, Livery
2 full time instructors
Facilities
Outdoor Manege 45 x 50

SJ: Nov, 1 Paddock
Wait Rm
Hacking
Livery Full, P/T, School, Hunt
Exclusions No horses for hire
Location Off A414 between High
Wycombe/Gilstone

OAKLANDS COLLEGE
EQUESTRIAN CENTRE
Oaklands Campus, Hatfield Road,
St Albans, Hertfordshire, AL4 0JA
Tel 01727 850651
Contact Mr R Thomas
Training Centre, Facility Centre,
Livery Inst Riding & Jumping
5 full time instructors
Ave No 28 Horses, 4 Ponies
inc 2 El Dress, 1 SJ GR C
Courses WP, YT, Short, Ev, P/T, Hol
Facilities
Covered School 20 x 40
Outdoor Manege 20 x 60 fl lt
SJ: Nov
CC: Basic, 12 Schooling
Lec Rm, Vis Aids, Wait Rm
Livery Full
Schooling General, Break, to Nov
Dress, to El Dress, to SJ GR C
Accom S, FB
Location M25 Jn 21 2 miles from
St Albans City Centre

PATCHETTS EQUESTRIAN CENTRE
Hilfield Lane , Aldenham,
Wattford, Herts, WD2 8DP
Tel 01923 855776/852255
Contact Thc Proprietor
Riding School, Training Centre,
Facility Centre Inst to BHSII
Specialities General tuition -
specialised instruction - livery & shows
Staff Chief Instructor Mrs W Hawkes
(BHSII, BHS SM)
Plus 10 full time instructors
Ave No 25 Horses, 15 Ponies
inc 4 El Dress, 2 Med Dress,
3 SJ GR C, 1 SJ GR B
Courses WP, Short, Ev, P/T, Hol
Facilities
Covered School 60 x 20 gly
Covered School 20 x 50
Outdoor Manege 20 x 60 fl lt
Outdoor Manege 20 x 40
Outdoor Manege 20 x 80
SJ: Nov, Grade C, Grade A
CC: Course, Basic, Nov, Int, Banks,
Water
Lec Rm, Vis Aids, Chng Rm, Showers,
Wait Rm, Tack Shop
Hacking

Livery Full, P/T, School
Schooling General, Break, to Nov
Dress, to El Dress, to Med Dress, to SJ
GR B, to HT Nov
Accom S, Tw, Db, FB
Exclusions Wt Limit, 13st, Age Limit, 6,
No unescorted hacks
Location Adjacent to Jn 5 Ml. M25
Jn 19 clockwise, 21A anti-clockwise

ROSE HALL FARM
Sarratt, Rickmansworth,
Herts, WD3 4PA
Tel 01442 833269
Contact Mrs S V Higgs
Riding School Inst Riding & Jumping
Specialities General Instruction,
Livery, Hacking, Events & Hunter Trials
Staff Chief Instructor Mrs D Ripper
Ave No 12 Horses, 14 Ponies
inc Hunters
Courses YT, Short, Ev, Hol
Facilities
Outdoor Manege 25 x 45
Outdoor Manege 20 x 40 fl lt
SJ: Nov, Grade B, 1 Paddock
CC: Course, Basic, Nov, Banks, Water,
Natural
Wait Rm
Hacking
Livery Full, DIY, Break, School, Hunt
Schooling General, Break, to Nov
Dress, to SJ GR C, to HT Int
Exclusions Wt Limit, 13st7, Age Limit, 5,
No casual hiring, No unesorted rides
Location 1/2 mile north west of Sarratt
Village, 5 minutes from M25 Jn 18 & 20

SOUTH MEDBURN FARM
South Medburn Farm, Watling Street,
Elstree, Herts, WD6 3AA
Tel 0181 953 1420
Contact Mrs M L Rose
Riding School, Training Centre Inst
to BHSAI
Specialities Schooling / Dressage
8 full time instructors
Ave No 10 Horses, 6 Ponies
inc 1 Med Dress, 1 SJ GR C
Courses WP, YT, Short
Facilities
Covered School 60 x 22
Covered School 40 x 20
Outdoor Manege 60 x 20 fl lt
Outdoor Manege 40 x 20
SJ: Nov, Grade C, 1 Paddock
CC: Course, Basic, Nov, Banks, Water,
15 Schooling
Lec Rm, Vis Aids, Chng Rm, Wait Rm
Hacking
Livery Full, Break, School, Hunt

Schooling General, Break, to Nov
Dress, to Med Dress
Accom Tw, Cottage, SC
Exclusions Wt Limit, 13st, Age Limit, 6
Location Off A41, 14 miles from the
centre of London

TEWIN HILL EQUESTRIAN CENTRE
Tewin Hill Farm, Tewin Hill, Tewin,
Hertfordshire, AL6 0LL
Tel 01438 718501
Contact Ms Linda Redman
Facility Centre, Livery
Specialities Catering for all types of
livery
2 full time instructors
Ave No 55 Horses
Courses WP
Facilities
Outdoor Manege 30 x 60 fl lt
SJ: Nov
CC: Course, Basic, Water, Natural
Chng Rm, Wait Rm
Livery Full, P/T, DIY, Break, School,
Hunt, Grass
Location Jn 6 off A1(M) 3 miles west of
Welwyn Garden City

NORFOLK

BLACKBOROUGH END
EQUESTRIAN CENTRE
The Stables, East Winch Road,
Blackborough End, Kings Lynn,
Norfolk, PE32 1SF
Tel 01553-841212
Contact Mr C G Nash
Riding School, Training Centre,
Facility Centre Inst Riding & Jumping
2 full time instructors
Ave No 10 Horses, 12 Ponies
inc 2 SJ GR C
Courses WP, YT, Short, Ev, P/T, Hol
Facilities
Covered School 20 x 40 gly
Outdoor Manege 20 x 40
SJ: Nov, Grade C, 1 Paddock
Lec Rm, Vis Aids, Chng Rm, Tack
Shop
Hacking
Livery Full, P/T, DIY, Break, School,
Hunt, Grass
Schooling General, Break, to Nov
Dress, to SJ GR C
Accom Dor, FB
Exclusions Wt Limit, 14st, Age Limit, 3,
No casual hire
Location Off A47 Swaffham Road,
3 miles from Kings Lynn

EASTON COLLEGE
EQUESTRIAN CENTRE
Easton College, Easton,
Norwich, Norfolk
Tel 01603 741779
Contact Mrs C Good
Training Centre Inst Riding & Jumping
3 full time instructors
Ave No 18 Horses
inc 9 El Dress, 8 SJ GR C
Courses YT, Short, Ev, P/T, Hol
Facilities
Covered School 25 x 40
SJ: Nov, 1 Paddock
Lec Rm, Vis Aids, Chng Rm, Showers,
Wait Rm
Accom S, FB
Exclusions Wt Limit, 13st, Age Limit, 12,
No casual hire
Location Off A47 situated on Norfolk
County Showground

FOREST LODGE RIDING CENTRE
Sandy Hill Lane, Weybourne, Holt,
Norfolk, NR25 7HW
Tel 01263 588578
Contact Mr & Mrs T Davies
Riding School, Training Centre Inst
Basic
Specialities Instruction for novices and
beginners
Staff Chief Instructor Mrs L J Davies
(BHSAI), Plus 2 full time instructors
Ave No 11 Horses, 14 Ponies
Courses WP, YT, Short, P/T, Hol
Facilities
Outdoor Manege 25 x 50
SJ: Nov
CC: Banks, Natural, Gallops, 10 Schooling
Lec Rm, Vis Aids, Chng Rm, Showers,
Wait Rm
Hacking
Livery Full, P/T, DIY, Break, School, Grass
Schooling General, Break, to Nov Dress
Exclusions Wt Limit, 14 stone,
No casual hire
Location 3/4 mile from A148 between
Holt and Cromer

GRANGE FARM LIVERY
Spixworth, Norwich,
Norfolk, NR10 3PR
Tel 01603 898272
Contact Messrs D M Cook
Livery
Ave No 14 Horses, 12 Ponies
Facilities
Covered School 17 x 42
SJ: 2-3ac Paddock
Location 4 miles north of Norwich
between the A140 and B1150

IVY FARM EQUESTRIAN CENTRE
c/o 31 Brackenwood, Necton,
Swaffham, Norfolk, PE37 8EU
Tel 01760 722125
Contact Mrs B Bates &
Mrs B T Lawrence
Riding School Inst Riding & Jumping
Staff Chief Instructor Miss B T Bates
(BHSAI)
Plus 1 full time instructor
Ave No 3 Horses, 9 Ponies
Courses WP, YT
Facilities
SJ: Nov, 1 Paddock
Lec Rm, Vis Aids, Chng Rm, Wait Rm
Hacking
Livery Full, P/T, DIY, Break, School
Schooling General, Break, to El Dress,
to Med Dress
Exclusions Wt Limit, 10st7, Age Limit, 5,
No unaccompanied hacking
Location 1 mile off A47, 5 miles from
Swaffham. Ivy Farm, Holme Hale,
Thetford, Norfolk

RECTORY ROAD RIDING SCHOOL
Old Rectory, Suffield,
Norwich, NR11 7ER
Tel 01263 761367
Contact Mrs W Garrett
Riding School Inst Riding & Jumping
Staff Chief Instructor Mrs L Coller
(BHSAI, BHS Int.SM)
Ave No 4 Horses, 18 Ponies
inc 1 SJ GR C, 2 SJ Jun C
Courses Ev, Hol
Facilities
Covered School 24 x 18
SJ: Nov, 1 Paddock
Hacking
Livery Full, P/T, Break, School
Schooling General, Break, to Nov
Dress, to SJ GR C
Exclusions Wt Limit, 12st, Age Limit, 4
Location Off B145 between North
Walsham and Aylesham

ROSE ACRE RIDING STABLES
Back Mundesley Road, Gimingham,
Mundesley, Norfolk, NR11 8HN
Tel 01263 720671
Contact Mrs J Self
Riding School, Training Centre Inst
Riding & Jumping
Staff Chief Instructor Mrs J Self
(BHSAI, BHS Int Teach)
Ave No 3 Horses, 2 Ponies
inc 2 El Dress, 1 SJ GR B, 1 SJ Jun C
Courses WP, YT, Short, Ev, P/T
Facilities
Outdoor Manege 18 x 35 fl lt

SJ: Grade A, 1 Paddock
CC: Course, Basic, Banks, Water
Lec Rm, Vis Aids, Chng Rm, Wait Rm
Hacking
Livery Full, P/T, DIY, School, Hunt,
Grass
Schooling General, to Nov Dress, to El
Dress, to SJ GR C, to SJ GR B, to SJ
GR A, to HT Nov
Exclusions Wt Limit, 13st, Age Limit, 4,
No unescorted rides
Location 6 miles from Cromer, just off
B1159 coast road

RUNCTON HALL STUD
North Runcton, Kings Lynn,
Norfolk
Tel 01553 840676
Contact Mr & Mrs J R Stilgoe
Riding School Inst Riding & Jumping
1 full time instructor
Ave No 2 Horses, 5 Ponies
inc 1 SJ GR C
Courses WP, Short, P/T
Facilities
Covered School 15 x 32
Outdoor Manege 30 x 44
SJ: Grade B, Grade A, 1 Paddock
CC: Course, Basic, Banks, Water
Lec Rm, Vis Aids
Hacking
Livery Full, P/T, DIY, Break, School,
Hunt, Grass
Schooling General, Break, to Nov
Dress, to El Dress, to SJ GR C, to SJ
GR B, to HT Nov, to HT Int
Exclusions Wt Limit, 16st, Age Limit, 5,
No casual hire
Location Centre of village 1 mile from
A10

SALHOUSE EQUESTRIAN CENTRE
The Street, Salhouse, Norwich,
Norfolk, NR13 6RW
Tel 01603 720921/782749
Contact Mr R C Fielder
Riding School Inst Riding & Jumping
2 full time instructors
Ave No 19 Horses, 4 Ponies
inc 1 Med Dress
Courses Short, Ev, P/T
Facilities
Covered School 61 x 24 gly
Covered School 30 x 12
Outdoor Manege 80 x 30
SJ: Nov, 1 Paddock
CC: Course, Basic, Nov
Lec Rm, Vis Aids, Chng Rm, Showers,
Wait Rm
Hacking
Schooling General

Exclusions Age Limit, 9.
No casual hire
Location 5 miles south of Norwich off
the B1151

STRUMPSHAW RIDING CENTRE
Buckenham Road, Strumpshaw,
Norwich, Norfolk, NR13 4NP
Tel 01603 712815
Contact Miss W Murray
Riding School, Training Centre Inst
Riding & Jumping
Staff Chief Instructor Miss W Murray
(BHSII)
Plus 3 full time instructors
Ave No 7 Horses, 8 Ponies
inc 1 El Dress, 1 Med Dress,
1 SJ GR C
Courses YT, Short, Ev, P/T, Hol
Facilities
Covered School 43 x 23 gly
Covered School 24 x 12 gly
Outdoor Manege 40 x 30 fl lt
Outdoor Manege 17 x 30
SJ: Nov, 2 Paddock
CC: Banks, 10 Schooling
Lec Rm, Vis Aids, Wait Rm
Hacking
Livery Full, P/T, DIY, Break, School
Schooling General, Break, to El Dress,
to SJ GR C, to HT Nov
Accom S, Tw, FB
Exclusions Wt Limit, 13st, Age Limit, 5
Location 7 miles east of Norwich, just
off A47 Gt Yarmouth road

TOP FARM EQUESTRIAN CENTRE
Field Road, Weston Longville,
Norwich, Norfolk, NR9 5JN
Tel 01603 872247/872662
Contact Ms Le'Fevre
**Riding School, Training Centre,
Facility Centre, Holiday Centre** Inst
Riding & Jumping
Staff Chief Instructor Mr D Hutchinson
Ave No 16 Horses, 12 Ponies
Courses WP, YT, Short, Ev, P/T, Hol
Facilities
Covered School 60 x 20 gly
Outdoor Manege 60 x 20
SJ: Nov, 1 Paddock
Lec Rm, Vis Aids, Chng Rm, Showers,
Wait Rm
Hacking
Livery Full, P/T, DIY, Break, School,
Hunt, Grass
Schooling General, Break, to Med
Dress, to SJ GR A, to HT Nov
Accom S, Tw, Db, Dor, FB
Exclusions Wt Limit, 18st, Age Limit, 5,
No casual hire

Location 1 mile off A1067, 10 miles
west of Norwich

WEST RUNTON RIDING STABLE
West Runton, Cromer,
Norfolk, NR27 9QH
Tel 01263 837339
Contact Mrs J M V Bakewell
**Riding School, Norfolk Shire Horse
Centre** Inst Riding & Jumping
2 full time instructors
Ave No 12 Horses, 12 Ponies
Courses YT
Facilities
Covered School 30 x 20
SJ: Nov
Lec Rm, Vis Aids, Wait Rm
Hacking
Livery P/T
Exclusions No casual hire
Location Between Cromer and
Sheringham on north Norfolk coast

WEYBOURNE EQUESTRIAN CENTRE
The Barn, Cherry Trees,
Sandy Hill Lane, Weybourne,
Norfolk, NR25 7HW
Tel 01263 588260
Contact Mrs T Swift
Riding School, Training Centre Inst
Basic
Staff Chief Instructor Mr Mark Westley
(BHSAI)
Ave No 5 Horses, 7 Ponies
inc 3 El Dress, 2 SJ GR C
Courses WP, YT, Short, Ev, P/T, Hol
Facilities
Outdoor Manege 44 x 20 fl lt
SJ: Grade C, 1 Paddock
Lec Rm, Vis Aids, Wait Rm
Hacking
Livery Full, P/T, DIY, Break, School,
Hunt, Grass
Schooling General, Break, to Nov
Dress, to SJ GR C, to HT Nov
Accom Caravan, Cottage, FB, SC
Exclusions Wt Limit, 15st, Age Limit, 5,
No casual hire
Location 1 1/2 miles off A148. Between
Holt & Sheringham

WILLOW FARM RIDING SCHOOL
Ormesby St Margaret,
Great Yarmouth, Norfolk, NR29 3QE
Tel 01493 730297
Contact Mrs J Russell
Riding School Inst Riding & Jumping
Staff Chief Instructor Mrs J Russell
Plus 1 full time instructor
Ave No 4 Horses, 10 Ponies

Courses YT, Short, Ev
Facilities
Covered School 12x 25
Outdoor Manege 23 x 37 fl lt
SJ: Nov, 1 Paddock
CC: Basic, Nov, Water, Natural,
10 Schooling
Lec Rm, Vis Aids, Chng Rm, Wait Rm
Hacking
Livery Full, P/T, DIY, Grass
Exclusions Wt Limit, 14st, Age Limit, 6,
No casual hire
Location On A149 5 miles from Great
Yarmouth and 20 miles from Norwich

WILLOW END
EQUESTRIAN CENTRE
Kemps Corner, Pulham St Mary,
Diss, Norfolk, IP21 4YH
Tel 01379 608296
Contact Mrs S I Vincent
Riding School Inst Riding & Jumping
Staff Chief Instructor Miss S Martin
(BHSAI)
Ave No 10 Horses, 10 Ponies
Facilities
CC: Banks, 14 Schooling
Chng Rm, Showers, Wait Rm
Hacking
Livery P/T
Schooling General, Break, to El Dress
Accom F, Dor, FB
Exclusions Wt Limit, 14st, Age Limit, 4,
No casual hire
Location Off B1134, 1 1/2 miles from
Pulham St Mary

SUFFOLK

BRITISH RACING SCHOOL
Snailwell Road, Newmarket,
Suffolk, CB8 7NU
Tel 01638 665103
Contact The Director
Training Centre
Specialities Careers within the racing
industry
Staff Chief Instructor Mr R Sidebottom
Plus 5 full time instructors
Ave No 51 Horses, 2 Ponies
inc General riding & Race exercise riding
Courses WP, YT, Short, P/T
Facilities
Covered School 25 x 40 gly
Lec Rm, Vis Aids, Chng Rm, Showers,
Wait Rm
Accom Tw, Db, Cottage, FB
Exclusions Wt Limit, 11st7,
Age Limit, 16

Location one mile from Newmarket
town centre off A142

GROVE HOUSE
EQUESTRIAN CENTRE
Grove House Farm, Hall Road,
Spexhall, Halesworth,
Suffolk, IP19 0RR
Tel 01986 781502
Contact Mr D J Keegan
Livery
Specialities Riding for beginners and
novices particularly dressage and
eventing
1 full time instructor
Facilities
Outdoor Manege 21 x 61 fl lt
SJ: Grade C, 1 Paddock
Wait Rm
Livery Full, Break, School, Hunt
Schooling General, Break, to El Dress,
to SJ GR B
Location 2 miles north of Halesworth
off the A144

HAWKINS FARM RIDING STABLES
Mendlesham Green,
Stowmarket, Suffolk, IP14 5RB
Tel 01449 766264
Contact Mrs F M Harrison
Riding School, Training Centre Inst
Basic
Specialities Career training
Staff Chief Instructor Mrs Fiona Mary
Harrison (BHSAI)
Plus 1 full time instructor
Ave No 6 Horses, 19 Ponies
Courses WP, Short, Ev, P/T, Hol
Facilities
Outdoor Manege 30 x 60 fl lt
Outdoor Manege 15 x 30 fl lt
SJ: Nov
CC: Basic, Banks, Water, Natural, 9
Schooling
Lec Rm, Vis Aids, Chng Rm, Wait Rm
Hacking
Livery P/T, School
Schooling General, to El Dress
Exclusions Wt Limit, 14st, Age Limit, 3,
No Casual hire
Location 1.5 miles off the A140
between Bury St Edmunds and Ipswich

NEWTON HALL
EQUITATION CENTRE
Swilland, Ipswich, Suffolk, IP6 9LT
Tel 01473 785616
Contact Mrs R E Theobald
Riding School, Training Centre Inst
to BHSAI

Specialities Tailor made long or short career training courses
Staff Chief Instructor Mrs R E Theobald (BHSI)
Plus 9 full time instructors
Ave No 24 Horses, 30 Ponies
inc 3 El Dress, 4 SJ GR C, 3 SJ Jun C
Courses WP, YT, Short, Ev, P/T, Hol
Facilities
Covered School 12 x 27
Outdoor Manege 30 x 60 fl lt
SJ: Nov, Grade C, 1 Paddock
CC: Course, Basic, Banks, Water, Natural, 20 Schooling
Lec Rm, Vis Aids, Wait Rm
Hacking
Livery Full, P/T, Break, School, Hunt
Schooling General, Break, to Nov Dress, to El Dress, to SJ GR C, to HT Nov
Accom S, Tw, Db, F, Dor
Exclusions Wt Limit, 18st,
No unescorted hacking or casual hire
Location Off the B1077, 5 miles north east of Ipswich and 1 mile from Swillan village

PAKEFIELD RIDING SCHOOL
Carlton Road, Lowestoft,
Suffolk, NR33 0NA
Tel 01502 572257
Contact Mrs T Hardy
Riding School, Training Centre, Vaulting Inst Riding & Jumping
Staff Chief Instructor Miss A Hardy (BHSAI)
Plus 1 full time instructor
Ave No 10 Horses, 14 Ponies
inc 1 El Dress, Vaulting/Showing/RDA
Courses WP, YT, Hol
Facilities
Covered School 23 x 15 gly
Outdoor Manege 23 x 30 fl lt
SJ: 1 Paddock
Lec Rm, Vis Aids, Chng Rm, Wait Rm, Tack Shop
Hacking
Livery Full, Break, School
Schooling General, Break, to Nov Dress
Exclusions Wt Limit, 16st, Age Limit, 3, No hunting hiring
Location Carlton road, 1 mile Lowestoft

POPLAR PARK EQUESTRIAN TRAINING CENTRE
Heath Road, Hollesley,
Woodbridge, Suffolk, IP12 3NA
Tel 01394 411023
Contact Mr Mike Daniell
Riding School, Training Centre Inst

Riding & Jumping
Specialities Career training
1 full time instructor
Ave No 11 Horses, 4 Ponies
Courses WP, YT, Short, Ev, P/T, Hol
Facilities
Covered School 18 x 37
Outdoor Manege 40 x 50 fl lt
Outdoor Manege 20 x 40
SJ: Grade A, 1 Paddock
CC: Course, Nov, Int, Banks, Water, Natural, Gallops, 40 Schooling
Lec Rm, Vis Aids, Chng Rm, Showers, Wait Rm
Hacking
Livery Full, P/T, Break, School, Hunt, Grass
Schooling General, Break, to El Dress, to SJ GR C, to HT Int, to HT Adv
Accom S, SC
Exclusions Wt Limit, 15st, Age Limit, 6, No casual hire. No hunting hire
Location Off B1083, 6 miles off A12, east of Woodbridge

POPLAR FARM RIDING STABLES
Brockley Green, Hundon,
Sudbury, Suffolk, CO10 8DS
Tel 01440 786595
Contact Ms Kay V Bryant
Riding School, Facility Centre Inst Basic
Specialities Nervous riders children and adults, help given for regaining confidence
Staff Chief Instructor Ms K Bryant
Ave No 2 Horses, 7 Ponies
Courses Short, Ev, P/T, Hol
Facilities
Covered School 15 x 30
Outdoor Manege 25 x 45
SJ: Grade C
Lec Rm, Vis Aids, Chng Rm, Wait Rm
Hacking
Livery DIY
Schooling General, Break, to Nov Dress, to SJ GR C
Accom Tw, Cottage, SC
Exclusions Wt Limit, 13st7, Age Limit, 4, No casual hire
Location 4 miles from Haverhill off the A143 between Kedington and Hundon

VALLEY FARM RIDING & DRIVING CENTRE
Wickham Market,
Woodbridge, Suffolk, IP13 0ND
Tel 01728 746916
Contact Mrs S Ling
Riding School, Vaulting Inst Riding & Jumping

Specialities Riding for beginners,
driving and vaulting
Staff Chief Instructor Mrs Sarah Ling
(BHSAI)
Plus 3 full time instructors
Ave No 11 Horses, 19 Ponies
inc 1 El Dress, Voltige, Carriage
Driving, Polocrosse, Western
Courses WP, YT, Ev, P/T, Hol
Facilities
Covered School 8 x 18 gly
Covered School 15 x 35 gly
SJ: Nov, 1 Paddock

CC: Course, Banks, Water, Natural,
Gallops
Lec Rm, Vis Aids
Hacking
Livery Full, P/T, DIY, Break, School,
Grass
Schooling General, Break, to El Dress
Accom Db, FB
Exclusions Wt Limit, 19st,
No casual hire
Location 1/2 mile from Wickham
Market off the B1078

Riding in London

ALDERSBROOK RIDING SCHOOL & LIVERY STABLE
Empress Avenue, London, E12 5HW
Tel 0181 530 4648
Contact Mrs I Thorne
Riding School Inst Riding & Jumping
Staff Chief Instructor Mr N Dollimore (BHSAI)
Ave No 4 Horses, 8 Ponies
Courses Ev
Facilities
Outdoor Manege 20 x 40 fl lt
Outdoor Manege 25 x 55 fl lt
Outdoor Manege 20 x 18
SJ: Nov
Lec Rm, Vis Aids, Chng Rm, Wait Rm
Hacking
Livery Full, P/T, DIY, Break, School
Schooling General, Break
Exclusions Wt Limit, 15st, Riders to be assessed before hacking
Location Off A117 between Manor Park and Wanstead

BELMONT RIDING CENTRE
Belmont Farm, The Ridgeway,
Mill Hill, London, NW7 1QT
Tel 0181 906 1255
Contact Mr A Reid
Riding School, Training Centre, Facility Centre Inst to BHSII
Specialities Career training and Polo tuition
Staff Chief Instructor Miss C G Robinson (BHSI)
Plus 3 full time instructors
Ave No 14 Horses, 14 Ponies
inc 1 El Dress, 1 Med Dress, 1 Adv Dress, 1 SJ GR C, Novice Eventers
Courses WP, Short, Ev, P/T, Hol
Facilities
Covered School 40 x 20 gly
Outdoor Manege 23 x 50 fl lt
Outdoor Manege 85 x 50 fl lt
Outdoor Manege 23 x 50
SJ: Grade C, Grade B, Grade A, 1 Paddock

CC: Course, Basic, Nov, Int, Water, Natural, Gallops, 20 Schooling
Lec Rm, Vis Aids, Chng Rm, Showers, Wait Rm
Hacking
Livery Full, Break, School, Hunt, Grass
Schooling General, Break, to Adv Dress, to SJ GR C
Accom S, SC
Exclusions Wt Limit, 13st, Age Limit, 4, No hiring
Location 7 miles from centre of London

CIVIL SERVICE RIDING CLUB
Royal Mews, Buckingham Palace Road, London, SW1W 0QH
Tel 0171 930 7232
Contact Hon Treasurer
Riding School Inst Riding & Jumping
Ave No 6 Horses, 2 Ponies
Wait Rm
Exclusions Wt Limit, 13st, Age Limit, 16, Members only

DULWICH RIDING SCHOOL
Dulwich Common,
London, SE21 OSU
Tel 0181 693 2944
Contact Mr J T Bellman
Riding School Inst Riding & Jumping
1 full time instructor
Ave No 7 Horses, 7 Ponies
Courses WP, YT
Schooling General, Break
Exclusions Wt Limit, 11st, Age Limit, 10, No casual hire
Location Off A205 on Dulwich Common

EALING RIDING SCHOOL
Gunnersbury Avenue, Ealing,
London, W5 3XD
Tel 0181 992 3808
Contact Miss I Lockyer

Riding School Inst Basic
Specialities Basic instruction, School contract, Livery
2 full time instructors
Ave No 8 Horses, 19 Ponies inc 1 SJ GR C
Courses WP, YT, Short, Ev, Hol
Facilities
Outdoor Manege 40 x 25 fl lt
Outdoor Manege 25 x 25 fl lt
Outdoor Manege 40 x 25 fl lt
SJ: Nov, 1 Paddock
Lec Rm, Vis Aids, Chng Rm, Wait Rm, Tack Shop
Schooling General, to El Dress, to SJ GR C
Exclusions Wt Limit, 14st, Age Limit, 5, No unescorted riding

GOULDS GREEN RIDING SCHOOL
Goulds Green, Hillingdon, Middlesex, UB8 3DG
Tel 01895 446256
Contact Mrs G Jupp
Riding School, Tack shop Inst Riding & Jumping
Specialities General instruction, livery, hacking, childrens courses
4 full time instructors
Ave No 4 Horses, 8 Ponies
Courses WP, Ev, P/T, Hol
Facilities
Outdoor Manege 25 x 75 fl lt
Outdoor Manege 68 x 22
SJ: Nov
Lec Rm, Vis Aids, Wait Rm, Tack Shop
Hacking
Livery Full, P/T, DIY, Grass
Exclusions Wt Limit, 14st, Age Limit, 3, No unescorted/unsupervised riding
Location 2 miles from Jn 4 on M4

HYDE PARK RIDING STABLES
63 Bathurst Mews,
London, W2 2SB
Tel 0171 723 2813
Contact Richard Briggs OBE
Riding School Inst Riding & Jumping
Staff Chief Instructor Miss Fiona Granger
Ave No 6 Horses, 6 Ponies
Courses WP
Facilities
Outdoor Manege 80 x 30
Outdoor Manege 20 x 40
SJ: Nov
Tack Shop
Hacking
Schooling General, to Nov Dress

Exclusions Wt Limit, 13st/14st, Age Limit, 5, All riding escorted
Location Hyde Park

KENTISH TOWN CITY FARM
1 Cressfield Close, London, NW5 4BN
Tel 0171 916 5421/0
Contact Mr M Magennis
Riding School Inst Basic
1 full time instructor
Ave No 3 Horses, 3 Ponies inc RDA
Courses YT
Facilities
Outdoor Manege 25 x 45 fl lt
SJ: Nov
Lec Rm, Vis Aids, Chng Rm
Exclusions Wt Limit, 11st, Age Limit, 8
Location Off Grafton Road, Kentish Town

KINGS OAK EQUESTRIAN CENTRE
Theobald Park Road, Enfield, Middlesex, EN2 9BL
Tel 0181 363 7868
Contact Mrs J P Gill
Riding School Inst Riding & Jumping
Staff Chief Instructor Mrs J P Gill (BHSAI)
Ave No 8 Horses, 14 Ponies
Courses Short, Hol
Facilities
Covered School 24 x 42 gly
Outdoor Manege 20 x 30 fl lt
SJ: Nov, Grade C, Grade A
CC: Basic, Banks, Water, Natural, 10 Schooling
Chng Rm, Wait Rm
Hacking
Livery Full, P/T, DIY, Break, School
Schooling General, Break, to Nov Dress, to SJ GR A, to HT Nov
Exclusions Wt Limit, 16st, Age Limit, 4, No inexperienced riders taken on hacks
Location 3 miles from M25 Jn 25 on the A10

LEE VALLEY REGIONAL PARK AUTHORITY
Lee Valley Riding Centre, Leabridge Road, Leyton, London, E10 7QL
Tel 0181 556 2629
Contact Mrs C Kirkby-Ivory
Riding School, Training Centre Inst to BHSAI
Specialities Career training, side saddle and driving instruction

4 full time instructors
Ave No 13 Horses, 9 Ponies
inc 3 El Dress
Courses WP, YT, Short, Ev, P/T, Hol
Facilities
Covered School 20 x 40 gly
Outdoor Manege 52 x 20 fl lt
SJ: Nov, 1 Paddock
CC: Course, Nov, Banks, Natural,
Gallops
Lec Rm, Vis Aids, Chng Rm, Showers,
Wait Rm, Tack Shop
Livery P/T
Schooling General, to Med Dress, to
SJ GR C, to HT Nov
Accom S, Db, Caravan, SC
Exclusions Wt Limit, 14st, Age Limit, 5
Location On A104, 3 miles from M11

LOWDHAM LODGE
EQUESTRIAN CENTRE
Pole Hill Road, Hillingdon,
Middlesex, UB10 0QE
Tel 0181 813 5800
Contact Ms S Parker
Riding School, Training Centre,
Facility Centre Inst Basic
Specialities Instruction for novice and
nervous riders, stable management
courses also offered
Staff Chief Instructor Miss Sue Parker
Plus 2 full time instructors
Ave No 5 Horses, 8 Ponies
inc 1 El Dress, 1 SJ GR C
Courses WP, Short, Ev, P/T, Hol
Facilities
Outdoor Manege 20 x 40 fl lt
Outdoor Manege 40 x 35 fl lt
SJ: Nov
Chng Rm, Wait Rm
Hacking
Livery Full, P/T, DIY, Break, School
Schooling General, Break
Exclusions Wt Limit, 13st, Age Limit, 3,
No casual hire, assesment lesson
before hacking
Location M4 Jn 4 off the A4020
between Uxbridge and Hayes

MUDCHUTE EQUESTRIAN CENTRE
Pier Street, London, E14 9HP
Tel 0171 515 0749
Contact Mr James Harling
Riding School, City farm Inst Basic
Staff Chief Instructor Mr James Harling
(BHSAI, BHS Int.SM)
Plus 1 full time instructor
Ave No 6 Horses, 8 Ponies
Courses WP, Short, Hol

Facilities
Outdoor Manege 30 x 50
SJ: Nov, 1 Paddock
CC: Basic, Nov, Banks, Natural, Gallops,
10 Schooling
Lec Rm, Vis Aids, Chng Rm, Showers,
Wait Rm
Schooling General, to Nov Dress, to
Med Dress, to SJ GR C
Exclusions Wt Limit, 13st, Age Limit, 7
Location 2 miles off A13 between
Canning Town and Poplar

NEWHAM RIDING SCHOOL
& ASSOCIATION
The Docklands Equestrian Centre,
2 Claps Gate Lane, Beckton,
London, E6 4JF
Tel 0171 511 3917
Contact Miss L Greaves
Riding School Inst Basic
4 full time instructors
Ave No 10 Horses, 10 Ponies
Courses YT
Facilities
Covered School 20 x 60 gly
Outdoor Manege 20 x 40 fl lt
SJ: Nov
Livery DIY
Exclusions Wt Limit, 12st, Age Limit, 5
Location Adjacent London City Airport

PARK LANE STABLES
Park Lane, Teddington,
Middlesex, TW11 0HY
Tel 0181 977 4951
Contact Mr M P Dailly
Riding School Inst Basic
Staff Chief Instructor Mr M Dailly
(BHSAI, BHS Int Teach)
Ave No 5 Horses, 6 Ponies
Courses Short, P/T, Hol
Chng Rm
Hacking
Exclusions Wt Limit, 11, Age Limit, 3,
No casual hire
Location 3 miles from A3, adjacent to
Teddington High St

ROSS NYE'S
8 Bathurst Mews, London, W2 2SB
Tel 0171 262 3791
Contact Mr R Nye
Riding School, General Hacking Inst
Riding & Jumping
Specialities Career training, Pony Club
& RDA

Staff Chief Instructor Miss K Nye
(BHSAI, BHS Int Teach)
Plus 1 full time instructor
Ave No 7 Horses, 9 Ponies
Courses WP, Short, P/T, Hol
Facilities
Outdoor Manege 67 x 25
Outdoor Manege 37 x 25
SJ: Nov
Chng Rm
Hacking
Exclusions Wt Limit, 14st, Age Limit, 7
Location North side of Hyde Park.
Nearest tube is Lancaster Gate

STAG LODGE STABLES
Robin Hood Gate, Richmond Park,
London, SW15 3RS
Tel 0181 974 6066
Contact Mr B Johnson
Riding School, Training Centre Inst
Basic
Specialities Hacking & Instruction for
young children
Ave No 7 Horses, 11 Ponies
Courses WP, Short, Hol
Facilities
Outdoor Manege 30 x 12 fl lt
Lec Rm, Vis Aids, Chng Rm, Showers,
Wait Rm, Tack Shop
Hacking
Livery Full, School
Schooling General
Accom S, Db, SC
Exclusions Wt Limit, 14st,
Age Limit, 2 1/2, No casual hire
Location On A3 between Robin Hood
roundabout and Richmond Park

SUNBURY RIDING SCHOOL
Fordbridge Road, Sunbury-on-Thames,
Middlesex, TW16 6AS
Tel 01932 789792
Contact Miss A Hodgson
Riding School Inst Basic
2 full time instructors
Ave No 5 Horses, 8 Ponies
Courses WP, YT, Short, Ev, P/T, Hol
Facilities
Outdoor Manege 20 x 60
SJ: Nov, Grade A, 1acre Paddock
CC: Water, Natural
Lec Rm, Vis Aids, Chng Rm, Wait Rm
Livery Full, P/T, DIY, Break, Grass
Schooling General, Break, to Nov
Dress, to El Dress, to SJ GR B
Exclusions Wt Limit, 18st, Age Limit, 3,
No casual hire
Location B375 2 miles from Jn 1 M3

SUZANNE'S RIDING SCHOOL
Brookshill Drive, Harrow Weald,
Middlesex, HA3 6SB
Tel 0181 954 3618
Contact Mrs S Marczak
Riding School, Training Centre,
Facility Centre Inst to BHSII
Specialities The school places great
emphasis on classical equitation and
trains in high school dressage
Staff Chief Instructor Mr Julian
Marczak
Plus 2 full time instructors
Ave No 31 Horses, 43 Ponies
inc All Riding Club & Pony Club events
Courses WP, YT, Short, Ev, P/T, Hol
Facilities
Covered School 30 x 15 gly
Outdoor Manege 20 x 40 fl lt
Outdoor Manege 50 x 30
Outdoor Manege 57 x 18 fl lt
SJ: Nov, 1 Paddock
CC: Course, Basic, Nov, Int, Banks,
Water, Natural, Gallops
Lec Rm, Vis Aids, Chng Rm
Hacking
Livery Full, P/T, School, Hunt, Grass
Schooling General, Break, to Med
Dress, to SJ GR B, to HT Int
Accom S, Tw, Cottage, FB, SC
Exclusions Wt Limit, 14st, Age Limit, 5

TRENT PARK EQUESTRIAN CENTRE
Bramley Road, Southgate,
London, N14 4XG
Tel 0181 363 9005
Contact Mr K Beaven
Riding School, Training Centre Inst
to BHSII
Staff Chief Instructor Mr K Beaven
(BHSI)
Plus 7 full time instructors
Ave No 30 Horses, 16 Ponies
inc 2 El Dress, 2 SJ GR C, 3 SJ GR A,
2 HT Int
Courses WP, YT, Hol
Facilities
Covered School 24 x 67 gly
Outdoor Manege 18 x 67 fl lt
Outdoor Manege 46 x 18 fl lt
SJ: Grade C, Grade B, Grade A,
1 Paddock
CC: Course, Basic, Nov, Natural
Lec Rm, Vis Aids, Chng Rm, Wait Rm
Hacking
Livery Full, P/T, Break, School
Schooling General, Break, to El Dress,
to SJ GR C, to HT Nov
Accom S, SC
Exclusions Wt Limit, 14st7,
Age Limit, 5, No casual hire

Location Jn 24 off M25. Off A111 200yds from Oakwood Underground Station

**WILLOWTREE
RIDING ESTABLISHMENT**
The Stables, Ronver Road,
London, SE12
Tel 0181 857 6438
Contact Mr & Mrs E A Massey
Riding School Inst Riding & Jumping
Staff Chief Instructor Miss J Johansson Massey
Ave No 17 Horses, 14 Ponies
Courses WP, YT
Facilities
Covered School 37 x 18 gly
Outdoor Manege 51 x 31 fl lt
SJ: Nov
Lec Rm, Vis Aids, Chng Rm, Wait Rm
Schooling General, to Nov Dress
Exclusions Wt Limit, 12st, Age Limit, 4
Location Off South Circular between Catford, Lewisham and Bromley

WIMBLEDON VILLAGE STABLES
24a/b, High Street,
Wimbledon,
London, SW19 5DX
Tel 0181 946 8579
Contact Mrs C Andrews
Riding School, Training Centre Inst to BHSAI
Specialities Small groups, career training

Staff Chief Instructor Mrs C Stevenson (BHSI)
Plus 7 full time instructors
Ave No 11 Horses, 6 Ponies
Courses WP, YT, Short, P/T, Hol
Facilities
Outdoor Manege 80 x 20
Outdoor Manege 40 x 100
SJ: 1 Paddock
Lec Rm, Vis Aids, Chng Rm, Wait Rm
Hacking
Livery Full, P/T, School
Schooling General, to Nov Dress, to SJ GR C
Exclusions Wt Limit, 14st, Age Limit, 2, No unaccompanied hacking
Location Rear of Dog and Fox pub, at Jn of High Street with Church Road. 5 minutes walk from train and tube

**THE WORMWOOD SCRUBS
PONY CENTRE**
Woodmans Mews, Scrubs Lane,
c/o 30 Sunningdale Avenue, East Acton,
London, W3 7NS
Tel 0181 740 0573
Contact Sr Mary Joy Langdon
Riding School, Training Centre, RDA Centre Inst Riding & Jumping
Ave No 8 Horses, 16 Ponies
Courses WP, YT, Short, Ev
Facilities
Covered School 30 x 40 gly
SJ: Nov
Lec Rm, Vis Aids, Chng Rm, Showers, Wait Rm
Exclusions Wt Limit, 10st, Age Limit, 5

Riding in the South East

KENT ◆ SURREY
EAST SUSSEX ◆ WEST SUSSEX

KENT

APPLETREE STABLES
Starvenden Lane, The Common,
Cranbrook, Kent, TN17 2AN
Tel 01580 713833
Contact Mrs Nuthall
Riding School, Training Centre Inst
Riding & Jumping
Staff Chief Instructor Mrs V Nuthall (BHSI)
Ave No 6 Horses, 10 Ponies
inc 1 El Dress, 2 SJ GR C
Courses WP, Short, P/T
Facilities
Outdoor Manege 20 x 40 fl lt
Outdoor Manege 20 x 40 fl lt
SJ: Nov, Grade C, 1 Paddock
CC: Basic, Nov, Banks, Water,
9 Schooling
Lec Rm, Vis Aids, Chng Rm
Hacking
Livery Full, P/T, DIY, Break, School,
Hunt, Grass
Schooling General, Break,
to SJ GR C, to HT Nov
Exclusions Wt Limit, 14st
Location 1 1/2 miles north of
Cranbrook A229

BEDGEBURY LEISURE
Bedgebury School Riding Centre,
Goudhurst, Kent, TN17 2SH
Tel 01580 211602
Contact Mr S Gregory
Riding School, Training Centre Inst
to BHSAI
Specialities Career training
Staff Chief Instructor Mr S Gregory
(BHSAI, BHS Int Teach, BHS Int.SM)
Plus 5 full time instructors
Ave No 18 Horses, 18 Ponies
inc 2 Med Dress, 1 SJ GR C,

2 SJ Jun C, 2 HT Int
Courses WP, Short, P/T, Hol
Facilities
Covered School 44 x 22
Covered School 60 x 20
Outdoor Manege 20 x 40 fl lt
Outdoor Mancgc 25 x 30 fl lt
SJ: Nov, 1 Paddock
CC: Course, Basic, Nov, Banks, Water,
Natural, 30 Schooling
Lec Rm, Vis Aids, Wait Rm
Hacking
Livery Full, P/T, Break, School, Hunt
Schooling General, Break, to Med
Dress, to SJ GR B, to HT Int
Accom S, Tw, FB
Exclusions Wt Limit, 12st, Age Limit, 4,
No casual hiring
Location On B2079 between
Goudhurst and Flimwell

BLUE BARN EQUESTRIAN CENTRE
Blue Barn Farm, Great Chart,
Ashford, Kent, TN26 1JS
Tel 01233 621183/622933
Contact Mrs S M Draper
Riding School, Training Centre Inst
Riding & Jumping
3 full time instructors
Ave No 10 Horses, 14 Ponies
inc 1 Med Dress, 1 SJ GR A, 1 HT Int
Courses WP, YT, Short, Ev, P/T, Hol
Facilities
Covered School 67 x 21 gly
Covered School 37 x 21
Outdoor Manege 40 x 20 fl lt
SJ: Grade A, 3 Paddock
CC: Banks, Water, Natural, Gallops,
10 Schooling
Lec Rm, Vis Aids, Chng Rm, Wait Rm
Hacking
Livery Full, P/T, DIY, Break, School,
Hunt, Grass

Schooling General, Break, to El Dress,
to SJ GR A, to HT Adv
Accom S, Db, Cottage, SC
Exclusions Wt Limit, 16st,
No unescorted rides
Location On the A28, between Ashford
and Bethersden

BRADBOURNE RIDING
& TRAINING CENTRE
Bradbourne Vale Road,
Sevenoaks, Kent, TN13 3DH
Tel 01732 453592
Contact Mr P G Felgate
**Riding School, Training Centre, RDA
Centre** Inst Riding & Jumping
Staff Chief Instructor Mrs E F Felgate
(BHSAI)
Plus 3 full time instructors
Ave No 13 Horses, 28 Ponies
inc RDA Ponies
Courses WP, Hol
Facilities
Covered School 18 x 30
Outdoor Manege 20 x 60 fl lt
SJ: Nov, 1 Paddock
CC: Course, Basic, Nov, Banks, Water,
Natural
Lec Rm, Vis Aids, Chng Rm, Showers,
Wait Rm
Livery Full, P/T, Break, School
Schooling General, Break, to El Dress,
to SJ GR C, to HT Nov
Accom Caravan, FB, SC
Exclusions Wt Limit, 18st, Age Limit, 6
Location On A25 at the Jn with the
A21, North of Sevenoaks

CALLUM PARK RIDING CENTRE
Lower Halstow, Nr Sittingbourne,
Kent, ME9 7ED
Tel 01795 844978/844258
Contact Mr J & Mrs L McGee
Riding School Inst Riding & Jumping
Specialities Able to tailor courses for
the individual requirements of the client
Staff Chief Instructor Mrs L McGee
(BHSAI)
Plus 3 full time instructors
Ave No 10 Horses, 10 Ponies
Courses WP, Short, Ev, P/T, Hol
Facilities
Covered School 26 x 42 gly
SJ: Nov
Lec Rm, Vis Aids, Wait Rm
Hacking
Livery Full, Break, School, Hunt
Schooling General, Break, to Nov
Dress, to SJ GR C, to HT Nov
Exclusions Age Limit, 3.
Escorted instructional riding only

Location Between the Medway Towns
and Sittingbourne via M2, A2, A249

CHAUCER RIDING
AND LIVERY STABLES
Kake Street, Waltham,
Nr Canterbury, Kent, CT4 5SB
Tel 01227 700396
Contact Miss C Johnston
**Riding School, Training Centre,
Facility Centre** Inst Riding & Jumping
Staff Chief Instructor Miss C Johnston
(BHSAI, BHS Int.SM, BHS Int Teach)
Ave No 1 Horses, 7 Ponies
Courses WP, Ev, P/T, Hol
Facilities
Covered School 20 x 40 gly
SJ: Nov
Chng Rm
Hacking
Livery Full, P/T, Break, School
Schooling General, to Nov Dress
Exclusions Wt Limit, 13st, Age Limit, 4,
No unaccompanied riders
Location In the centre of the village

CHAVIC PARK STABLES
Jail Lane, Biggin Hill,
Kent, TN16 3AU
Tel 01959 572090
Contact Mrs G Palmer
Riding School, Training Centre Inst
Riding & Jumping
Staff Chief Instructor Mrs G Palmer
(BHSII)
Plus 2 full time instructors
Ave No 2 Horses, 6 Ponies
inc 1 El Dress, 1 SJ GR C, 4 Driving
ponies
Courses WP, YT, Short, Ev, P/T, Hol
Facilities
Covered School 20 x 40 gly
Outdoor Manege 30 x 60
SJ: Nov, Grade C, 1 Paddock
CC: Course, Basic, Nov, Banks, Water,
Natural
Lec Rm, Vis Aids, Wait Rm
Livery Full, P/T, DIY, Break, School,
Hunt, Grass
Schooling General, Break, to Nov
Dress, to SJ GR C
Exclusions Wt Limit, 13st,
No casual hiring
Location Centre of Biggin Hill, off A233

CHELSFIELD RIDING SCHOOL
Church Road, Chelsfield,
Orpington, Kent, BR6 7SN
Tel 01689 855603
Contact Miss J M Golding

Riding School, Facility Centre Inst
Riding & Jumping
Staff Chief Instructor Miss J M Golding
Plus 5 full time instructors
Ave No 10 Horses, 10 Ponies
Facilities
Covered School 20 x 40 gly
Outdoor Manege 20 x 30 fl lt
SJ: Nov, 1 Paddock
CC: Course, Basic
Chng Rm, Wait Rm
Livery Full, Grass
Exclusions Wt Limit, 14st, Age Limit, 6,
No unescorted hacking
Location 1/2 mile off A224, 1 1/2 miles
from M25, 1/2 mile off A21

COBHAM MANOR RIDING CENTRE
Water Lane, Thurnham,
Maidstone, Kent, ME14 3LU
Tel 01622 738497/738871
Contact Mr & Mrs J Brumer
**Riding School, Training Centre,
Facility Centre** Inst Riding & Jumping
Specialities Children and Adults riding
holidays & recreational riding
Staff Chief Instructor Mrs C Hall (BHSII)
Plus 3 full time instructors
Ave No 18 Horses, 23 Ponies
Courses WP, YT, Short, Ev, P/T, Hol
Facilities
Covered School 37 x 18 gly
Outdoor Manege 50 x 27 fl lt
Outdoor Manege 40 x 20 fl lt
Outdoor Manege 60 x 30 fl lt
SJ: Nov
CC: Course, Nov, Banks, 20 Schooling
Lec Rm, Vis Aids, Wait Rm, Tack Shop
Hacking
Livery Full, P/T, DIY, Break, School,
Hunt, Grass
Schooling General, Break, to Nov
Dress, to HT Nov
Accom S, Tw, Db, SC
Exclusions Wt Limit, 14st, Age Limit, 4
Location M20 follow signs to Bearsted

COOMBE WOOD STABLES
Coombe Wood Lane, Hawkinge,
Kent, CT18 7BZ
Tel 01303 893332
Contact Mr & Mrs M Fuller
Facility Centre, Livery
Facilities
Covered School 24 x 42
CC: Basic
Hacking
Livery DIY
Exclusions No casual hire
Location Off A260 between Hawkinge
& Folkestone

CORNILO RIDING
Sutton Court Farm, Sutton-by-Dover,
Kent, CT15 5DF
Tel 01304 375033
Contact Mrs B D Fuller
Riding School Inst Basic
Staff Chief Instructor Mrs Marina
Aunger (BHSII)
Ave No 10 Horses, 17 Ponies
Courses YT, Short, Hol
Facilities
Covered School 12 x 14
Outdoor Manege 20 x 40 fl lt
SJ: Nov, 1 Paddock
CC: Course, Basic, Banks, Water,
Natural
Hacking
Exclusions Escorted hacking only
Location Signposted from Jn of A2 &
A256 north of Dover

GOODNESTONE COURT EQUESTRIAN
Goodnestone Court, Graveney,
Faversham, Kent, ME13 9BZ
Tel 01795 535806
Contact Miss A L Bones
Riding School, Training Centre Inst
to BHSAI
Specialities Career training. Evening
courses run for BHS stages
Staff Chief Instructor Miss A L Bones
(BHSII, BHS SM)
Plus 1 full time instructor
Ave No 8 Horses, 4 Ponies
inc 1 SJ GR C, 1 SJ GR B, 1 SJ Jun C,
1 HT Nov
Courses WP, Short, Ev, P/T, Hol
Facilities
Covered School 18 x 14
Outdoor Manege 22 x 40 fl lt
SJ: Nov, Grade C, 1 Paddock
CC: Banks, 9 Schooling
Lec Rm, Vis Aids, Chng Rm
Hacking
Livery Full, School, Hunt, Grass
Schooling General, to Nov Dress, to
SJ GR C, to HT Nov
Exclusions Wt Limit, 14st, Age Limit, 6,
No casual hire
Location Between Faversham and
Graveney

HADLOW COLLEGE EQUESTRIAN CENTRE
Hadlow, Tonbridge,
Kent, TN11 0AL
Tel 01732 852204
Contact Mr D L Payne

Riding School, Training Centre, Facility Centre Inst to BHSAI
Specialities Training of students to BHSAI
Staff Chief Instructor Mr D L Payne (BHSII, BHS SM)
Plus 3 full time instructors
Ave No 21 Horses, 1 Ponies
inc 2 El Dress, 2 SJ GR C, 1 HT Int
Courses YT, Short, Ev, P/T
Facilities
Outdoor Manege 30 x 60
Outdoor Manege 40 x 50
SJ: Nov, Grade C, 2 Paddock
CC: Basic, Banks, Water, Natural, 8 Schooling
Lec Rm, Vis Aids, Chng Rm, Showers, Wait Rm
Hacking
Livery Full, P/T, Break, School
Schooling General, Break, to Nov Dress, to El Dress, to Med Dress, to SJ GR C, to SJ GR B, to SJ GR A, to HT Nov, to HT Int
Accom S, FB, SC
Exclusions Wt Limit, 12st 7, Age Limit, 12
Location Off the A26, in the village of Hadlow, 4 miles from Tonbridge

HEIGHTS RIDING STABLES
Westerham Heights Farm,
Westerham Hill, Westerham,
Kent, TN16 2ED
Tel 01959 571953
Contact Mrs M Burton
Riding School, Training Centre Inst to BHSAI
Specialities Career training
Staff Chief Instructor Mrs M Burton (BHSAI, BHS Int.SM)
Plus 2 full time instructors
Ave No 12 Horses, 12 Ponies
inc 1 El Dress, 2 SJ GR C, 2 SJ Jun C, 1 HT Int
Courses WP, YT, Short, Ev, P/T, Hol
Facilities
Outdoor Manege 46 x 30 fl lt
SJ: Nov, Grade B, 1 Paddock
CC: Natural, 10 Schooling
Lec Rm, Vis Aids, Wait Rm
Hacking
Livery Full, P/T, DIY, School, Hunt, Grass
Schooling General, to El Dress, to SJ GR C, to HT Nov
Exclusions Wt Limit, 14st, No unescorted hacking
Location Situated on the A233, 15 miles from London, 5 miles from the M25

HONNINGTON EQUESTRIAN CENTRE
Vauxhall Lane, Southborough,
Kent, TN4 OXD
Tel 01892 546230
Contact The Manager
Riding School, Training Centre Inst Riding & Jumping
Specialities Nervous and novice riders. Vaulting
2 full time instructors
Ave No 20 Horses, 30 Ponies
Courses Short, Ev, P/T, Hol
Facilities
Covered School 23 x 47 gly
Outdoor Manege 20 x 40 fl lt
Outdoor Manege 20 x 60
SJ: Nov, 1 Paddock
CC: Basic, Banks, Gallops, 8 Schooling
Lec Rm, Vis Aids, Chng Rm, Wait Rm
Hacking
Livery Full, P/T, DIY, Break, School
Schooling General, Break, to Nov Dress
Exclusions Wt Limit, 16st

HORSESHOES RIDING SCHOOL
Dean Street, East Farleigh,
Maidstone, Kent, ME15 OPR
Tel 01622 746161
Contact Mr & Mrs R Hargreaves
Riding School, Training Centre, Facility Centre Inst Riding & Jumping
Specialities Riding for all the family
Staff Chief Instructor Mr S Hargreaves (BHSAI)
Ave No 10 Horses, 16 Ponies
inc 2 SJ GR C, 2 HT Int
Courses WP, Short, Ev, Hol
Facilities
SJ: Nov
Lec Rm, Vis Aids, Chng Rm, Wait Rm
Hacking
Schooling General, Break, to Nov Dress, to SJ GR C, to HT Nov
Exclusions Wt Limit, 15st, Age Limit, 5
Location Maidstone A229 to Hastings turn right at Linton crossroads, turn right at 2nd crossroads 'Dean Street', we are 1/4 mile on left next to Horseshoes pub

LIMES FARM EQUESTRIAN CENTRE
Pay Street, Hawkinge,
Folkestone, Kent, CT18 7DZ
Tel 01303 892335
Contact Miss A Berry BHSI
Riding School, Training Centre, Facility Centre, Holiday Clinics Inst to BHSII
Specialities Career training, NVQ & BHS stage exams
Staff Chief Instructor Miss A Berry (BHSI)
Plus 8 full time instructors

Ave No 16 Horses, 11 Ponies
inc 3 El Dress, 2 Med Dress, 5 SJ GR
C, 1 SJ GR B, 5 SJ Jun C, 2 HT Int
Courses WP, YT, Short, Ev, P/T, Hol
Facilities
Covered School 70 x 25
Outdoor Manege 60 x 25 fl lt
SJ: Nov, Grade C, Grade B, Grade A,
2 Paddock
CC: Course, Basic, Nov, Banks, Water,
Natural, 30 Schooling
Lec Rm, Vis Aids, Chng Rm, Wait Rm
Hacking
Livery Full, P/T, DIY, Break, School,
Grass
Schooling General, Break, to Nov
Dress, to El Dress, to Med Dress, to
Adv Dress, to SJ GR C, to SJ GR B, to
SJ GR A, to HT Nov, to HT Int, to HT
Adv
Accom S, Tw, Dor, FB, SC
Exclusions Wt Limit, 14st7, Age Limit, 4
Location Turn off A260 Canterbury -
Folkstone road opposite Black Horse
public house, Densole. Turn into Pay
Street. Limes Farm approx 1/4 mile on
right

LODGE HILL SADDLE CLUB
Lodge Hill Training Area, Shed 25,
Nr Chattenden Barracks, Hoo,
St Werburgh, Rochester, Kent
Tel 01634 822618
Contact Lt Colonel J B Olley
Riding School Inst Riding & Jumping
Specialities Recreational riding for
beginners, novices and children
Staff Chief Instructor Mrs Clare
Stockley
Plus 2 full time instructors
Ave No 17 Horses, 7 Ponies
Courses WP, YT, Short, Ev, P/T
Facilities
Covered School 80 x 20
Outdoor Manege 25 x 40
SJ: Nov
Lec Rm, Vis Aids, Chng Rm, Showers,
Wait Rm
Hacking
Livery Full, P/T, School, Hunt, Grass
Exclusions Wt Limit, 14st, Age Limit, 3,
Escorted hacking only
Location Off A228 between
Chattenden & St Werburgh

MANNIX STUD
Nightingale Farm, Whiteacre Lane,
Waltham, Canterbury,
Kent, CT4 5SR
Tel 01227 700349
Contact Mrs J Goddard

**Riding School, Training Centre,
Childrens holiday centre** Inst Riding &
Jumping
Ave No 12 Horses, 31 Ponies
Courses WP, YT, Short, Ev, P/T, Hol
Facilities
Covered School 60 x 80 gly
Outdoor Manege 60 x 100
SJ: Nov, 1 Paddock
CC: Course, Basic, Banks, Water,
Natural
Lec Rm, Vis Aids, Chng Rm, Showers
Hacking
Livery Full, P/T
Accom S, Tw, F, Dor, FB
Exclusions Wt Limit, 16st, Age Limit, 3,
No adults on riding holidays
Location Between Ashford and
Canterbury

MOUNT MASCAL STABLES
Vicarage Road, Bexley,
Kent, DA5 2AW
Tel 0181 300 3947
Contact Mr J C Window
Riding School Inst Basic
Specialities Beginners, children and
weekend riders
6 full time instructors
Ave No 20 Horses, 20 Ponies
inc 1 El Dress, 1 SJ GR C
Courses WP, Ev, Hol
Facilities
Covered School 60 x 20 gly
Outdoor Manege 40 x 20 fl lt
SJ: Grade C, 2 Paddock
CC: Course, Basic, Nov, Banks, Water,
Natural
Lec Rm, Vis Aids, Chng Rm, Wait Rm
Hacking
Livery Full, DIY, Break, School, Hunt,
Grass
Schooling General, Break, to Nov
Dress, to El Dress, to SJ GR C, to HT
Nov
Accom S, Db, SC
Exclusions Wt Limit, 18st, Age Limit, 5,
Outside instructors except on a club
basis
Location Outskirts of Bexley Village,
1 mile from A2 & M20

NELSON PARK RIDING CENTRE
St Margarets Road, Woodchurch,
Birchington, Kent, CT7 0HJ
Tel 01843 822251
Contact Mrs S Matthews
**Riding School, Training Centre,
Facility Centre** Inst to BHSAI
Specialities Career training, NVQ
Levels 1-3

Staff Chief Instructor Mrs S Matthews
(BHSAI, BHS Int.SM)
Plus 2 full time instructors
Ave No 9 Horses, 11 Ponies
inc 1 El Dress
Courses WP, YT, Short, Ev, P/T, Hol
Facilities
Covered School 21 x 42
Outdoor Manege 20 x 40 fl lt
Outdoor Manege 20 x 35 fl lt
SJ: Nov, 1 Paddock
CC: Course, Basic, Nov, Banks
Lec Rm, Vis Aids, Chng Rm, Showers,
Wait Rm, Tack Shop
Hacking
Livery Full, P/T, School, Grass
Schooling General, to Nov Dress, to
SJ GR C, to HT Nov
Accom Caravan
Exclusions Wt Limit, 17st, Age Limit, 2,
No casual hiring
Location 1 mile off A253, between
Birchington and Ramsgate

OATHILL RIDING CENTRE
Pound Lane, Molash,
Nr Canterbury, Kent, CT4 8HQ
Tel 01233 740573
Contact Mrs L Topp
Riding School Inst Riding & Jumping
Specialities Childrens' and Adults'
riding holidays
3 full time instructors
Ave No 12 Horses, 10 Ponies
Courses Hol
Facilities
Outdoor Manege 20 x 40 fl lt
SJ: Nov, 1 Paddock
CC: Natural, Gallops, 11 Schooling
Lec Rm, Vis Aids, Chng Rm, Wait Rm
Hacking
Livery Full, P/T, Break, School, Hunt,
Grass
Schooling General, Break, to Nov
Dress
Accom Tw, F, FB
Exclusions Wt Limit, 16st, Age Limit, 4,
No unaccompanied riding
Location A252 between Charing and
Canterbury

RIDING FARM STABLES
Riding Lane, Hildenborough,
Tonbridge, Kent, TN11 9LN
Tel 01732 838717
Contact Mr J & Mrs S Gosling
Riding School Inst Riding & Jumping
Specialities Riding & Jumping for
Adults and children. Beginners,
Novices or Individuals wishing to
improve their riding

Staff Chief Instructor Mrs S Gosling
Plus 2 full time instructors
Ave No 14 Horses, 9 Ponies
inc 3 SJ GR C
Courses WP, Short, P/T
Facilities
Covered School 38 x 22 gly
Outdoor Manege 35 x 30 fl lt
SJ: Nov, Grade C, 1 Paddock
CC: Course, Basic, Banks, Water,
Natural
Chng Rm, Wait Rm
Livery Full, P/T, Hunt, Grass
Schooling General, to Nov Dress, to SJ
GR C, to HT Nov
Exclusions Wt Limit, 14st, Age Limit, 4,
No hacking
Location Off A21 between Sevenoaks
and Tonbridge, 6 miles from Jn 6 off M25

**ROOTING STREET FARM
RIDING CENTRE**
Rooting Street Farm, Little Chart,
Ashford, Kent. TN27 0PX
Tel 01233 840434
Contact Mrs J Rogers BHSI
**Training Centre, Facility Centre,
Livery**
Specialities Career training
1 full time instructor
Ave No 3 Horses, 1 Ponies
inc 1 El Dress, 2 SJ GR C
Facilities
Outdoor Manege 20 x 60 fl lt
Outdoor Manege 40 x 20
SJ: Nov, 1 Paddock
CC: 10 Schooling
Lec Rm, Vis Aids, Chng Rm, Showers,
Wait Rm
Livery Full, P/T, DIY, Break, School,
Grass
Schooling General, Break, to Nov
Dress, to Med Dress, to HT Nov
Exclusions Wt Limit, 13st7,
No casual hiring
Location Main road between Hothfield
and Little Chart. 2 1/2 miles from A20

TAYLOR'S RIDING ESTABLISHMENT
Casita, Waverley Avenue,
Minster-on-Sea,
Sheerness, Kent, ME12 2JL
Tel 01795 872203
Contact Mr & Mrs R W Hayler
**Riding School, Training Centre,
Facility Centre, Residential Courses.**
Inst Riding & Jumping
Specialities Facilities for disabled riders
and the deaf, including cart for wheelchair
Staff Chief Instructor Mrs Y Hayler
(BHSAI)

Plus 2 full time instructors
Ave No 11 Horses, 10 Ponies
inc 1 El Dress, 1 SJ GR C
Courses WP, YT, Short, Ev, P/T, Hol
Facilities
Covered School 18 x 24 gly
Outdoor Manege 24 x 49 fl lt
SJ: Nov, Grade C, 1 Paddock
Lec Rm, Vis Aids, Chng Rm, Showers,
Wait Rm
Livery Full, DIY, Break, School, Grass
Schooling General, Break, to Nov
Dress, to SJ GR C, to HT Nov
Accom Db, FB
Exclusions Wt Limit, 13st, Age Limit, 4,
No hacking
Location 1 mile from seafront,
10 minutes from Bridge/Sheerness.
Phone for directions

**TOLLGATE
RIDING STABLES**

Contact Mr W Prielipp & Miss C Curtis

This
establishment
is currently
re-locating.

Please
contact
the British Horse Society
RS&RR Office
on 01926 707 700
for further details.

TREWINT FARM STABLES
Gills Green, Hawkhurst,
Kent, TN18 5AD
Tel 01580 752272
Contact Mrs S J Barbour
**Riding School, Training Centre,
Breaking & schooling** Inst Riding &
Jumping
Specialities Career training
Staff Chief Instructor Mrs S J Barbour
(BHSAI, BHS Int Teach, BHS Int.SM)
Ave No 4 Horses, 13 Ponies
inc 1 SJ GR C

Courses WP, Short, Ev, P/T, Hol
Facilities
Outdoor Manege 24 x 40 fl lt
SJ: Nov
CC: Nov, Banks, Water, Natural,
Gallops, 4 Schooling
Lec Rm, Vis Aids, Chng Rm, Showers,
Wait Rm
Hacking
Livery Full, P/T, Break, School, Hunt,
Grass
Schooling General, Break, to Nov
Dress, to SJ GR C, to HT Nov
Accom Tw, FB
Exclusions Wt Limit, 14st
Location On outskirts of Hawkhurst
village, adjoining Bedgebury Forest

WHITELEAF RIDING CENTRE
Lower Road, Teynham,
Nr Sittingbourne, Kent, ME9 9BY
Tel 01795 522512
Contact Mrs M Olley
Riding School Inst Riding & Jumping
Specialities Instruction for all levels
from beginners to advanced riding &
jumping, courses in stable management,
Dressage instruction to Prix St George
Staff Chief Instructor Miss N Radlett
Plus 1 full time instructor
Ave No 6 Horses, 7 Ponies
Courses WP, Short, Ev, P/T, Hol
Facilities
Covered School 23 x 23 gly
Outdoor Manege 20 x 60 fl lt
SJ: Nov, 1 Paddock
CC: Natural, 15 Schooling
Chng Rm, Wait Rm
Hacking
Livery Full, P/T, Break, School, Hunt
Schooling General, Break, to Adv
Dress, to SJ GR C, to HT Int
Exclusions No unescorted hacking

SURREY

BARNFIELD RIDING SCHOOL
Parkfields Road, Off Park Road,
Kingston, Surrey, KT2 5LL
Tel 0181 546 3616
Contact Ms J Grayson
Riding School, Training Centre Inst
Riding & Jumping
Staff Chief Instructor Mrs J Grayson
(BHS SM)
Plus 2 full time instructors
Ave No 6 Horses, 5 Ponies
Courses WP, YT, Short, Ev, P/T, Hol
Facilities
Outdoor Manege 20 x 40 fl lt

SJ: Nov
Wait Rm
Hacking
Livery Full
Schooling General, to El Dress
Exclusions Wt Limit, 12st, Age Limit, 2,
Must be assessed before joining a
group hack
Location Between the Kingston and
Ham gates of Richmond Park

BEECHWOOD RIDING SCHOOL
Hillboxes Farm, Marden Park,
Woldingham, Surrey, CR3 7JD
Tel 01883 342266
Contact Miss J Garnham
Riding School, Training Centre Inst
Riding & Jumping
Staff Chief Instructor Miss J Garnham
(BHSAI)
Plus 2 full time instructors
Ave No 12 Horses, 12 Ponies
inc 2 El Dress, 1 SJ GR C
Courses Short, Hol
Facilities
Covered School 20 x 20
Outdoor Manege 20 x 60
Outdoor Manege 50 x 30
Outdoor Manege 20 x 40
Outdoor Manege 20 x 60
SJ: 1 Paddock
CC: Basic, Banks, Water, Natural,
6 Schooling
Lec Rm, Vis Aids, Chng Rm, Showers,
Wait Rm
Hacking
Livery Full
Schooling General, Break, to El Dress
Exclusions Wt Limit, 13st, Age Limit, 7,
No casual hire or YTS
Location Marden Park (North Downs).
Jn 6 M25

BURSTOW PARK RIDING CENTRE
Antlands Lane, Horley,
Surrey, RH6 9TF
Tel 01293 820766
Contact Mrs S Hart
Riding School Inst Riding & Jumping
Specialities Childrens instruction
Staff Chief Instructor Mrs S Hart
Plus 3 full time instructors
Ave No 3 Horses, 15 Ponies
inc 5 El Dress
Courses WP, YT
Facilities
Covered School 20 x 40 gly
Outdoor Manege 91 x 183 fl lt
Outdoor Manege 30 x 49 fl lt
SJ: Nov, 1 Paddock
CC: 10 Schooling

Lec Rm, Vis Aids, Chng Rm, Wait Rm
Livery Full, P/T, School
Schooling General, to El Dress
Exclusions Wt Limit, 12st, Age Limit, 2,
No casual hire
Location Off exit 10 of M23. Follow
Copthorne sign. Left to end of road, then
right. Stables next place on the right

CLOCK TOWER RIDING CENTRE
Brighton Road, Tadworth,
Surrey, KT20 6QZ
Tel 01737 832874
Contact Mr G B Ayling-Rouse
Riding School, Training Centre Inst
Riding & Jumping
Specialities Hacking and Novice
Instruction
Staff Chief Instructor Miss F Skyrme
(BHSII)
Plus 1 full time instructor
Ave No 9 Horses, 8 Ponies
inc 1 El Dress
Courses WP, Short, Ev, P/T
Facilities
Outdoor Manege 34 x 21 fl lt
Outdoor Manege 18 x 18 fl lt
SJ: Nov
Lec Rm, Vis Aids, Chng Rm, Showers,
Wait Rm
Hacking
Livery Full, P/T, Grass
Schooling General, Break
Exclusions Wt Limit, 13st, Age Limit, 5,
No unescorted riding
Location On A217 between Kingswood
and Banstead Cross

CRANLEIGH SCHOOL
Horseshoe Lane, Cranleigh,
Surrey, GU6 8QQ
Tel 01483 276426/273666
Contact Mrs J J Hennessy
Riding School, Public School Inst
Basic
Staff Chief Instructor Mrs J J Hennessy
(BHSAI)
Ave No 7 Horses, 8 Ponies
inc 1 El Dress, 1 SJ GR A
Courses WP, YT, Short, Ev, P/T, Hol
Facilities
Outdoor Manege 50 x 20
SJ: Nov, 1 Paddock
CC: Banks, Water, Natural, 12 Schooling
Lec Rm, Vis Aids, Chng Rm, Showers,
Wait Rm
Hacking
Livery Full, P/T, Break
Schooling General, Break, to Med
Dress, to SJ GR C, to HT Nov
Accom S, Dor, FB

Exclusions Wt Limit, 13st, Age Limit, 6
Location Off A281 from Guildford to
Horsham

DIAMOND CENTRE
FOR HANDICAPPED RIDERS
Woodmansterne Road,
Carshalton, Surrey
Tel 0181 643 7764
Contact Mr H Henn
Riding School, Disabled riders only
Inst Riding & Jumping
Staff Chief Instructor Miss L Lord
Plus 6 full time instructors
Ave No 15 Horses, 17 Ponies
Courses WP
Lec Rm, Vis Aids, Chng Rm
Exclusions Wt Limit, 12st, Age Limit, 5

DORKING RIDING CENTRE
c/o 6 Ranmore Road, Croydon,
Surrey, CR0 5QA
Tel 01306 881718
Contact Mr & Mrs R B Colbran
Riding School, Training Centre Inst
Riding & Jumping
Specialities Instruction for the novice
rider and hacking
Staff Chief Instructor Miss W Brooke
Plus 1 full time instructor
Ave No 5 Horses, 10 Ponies
Courses WP, YT, Short, Ev, P/T, Hol
Facilities
Covered School 17 x 34 gly
Outdoor Manege 20 x 40
SJ: Nov
CC: Basic, Natural, 3 Schooling
Lec Rm, Vis Aids, Chng Rm, Wait Rm
Hacking
Accom S, Cottage, SC
Exclusions Wt Limit, 15st, Age Limit, 4,
No casual hire,
1/2 hr assessment lesson
Location Downs Meadow, Ranmore
Road, Dorking, Surrey. Jn 9 M25,
3/4 mile from Dorking town centre

EBBISHAM FARM
LIVERY STABLES
Ebbisham Lane, Walton-on-the-Hill,
Tadworth, Surrey, KT20 7SA
Tel 01737 812568
Contact Mrs L Bubb
Livery
Specialities Working pupil courses
Staff Chief Instructor Mr R J Beisiegel
(BHSII)
Courses WP
Facilities
Outdoor Manege 40 x 45 fl lt

Outdoor Manege 20 x 40 fl lt
SJ: Nov, 1 Paddock
CC: Course, Nov, Banks, Natural
Chng Rm, Showers, Wait Rm
Livery Full, Break, School, Hunt
Schooling to El Dress, to HT Nov
Accom S, Db, Cottage, SC
Location Between Tadworth and
Epsom

FARLEIGH COURT RIDING CENTRE
Farleigh Court Road, Warlingham,
Surrey, CR6 9PX
Tel 01883 627364
Contact Mr & Mrs J Baird
Riding School Inst Basic
Specialities Children
Staff Chief Instructor Mrs D Baird
(BHSAI, BHS Int.SM)
Plus 2 full time instructors
Ave No 9 Horses, 9 Ponies
Courses WP, Short, Hol
Facilities
Covered School 18 x 37 gly
Outdoor Manege 18 x 55 fl lt
SJ: Nov, 2 Paddock
CC: Course, Basic, Banks, Natural,
20 Schooling
Lec Rm, Vis Aids, Wait Rm
Hacking
Livery Full, P/T
Schooling General, to Nov Dress
Exclusions Wt Limit, 17st, Age Limit, 4,
No casual hire
Location North Downs, 5 miles from
centre of Croydon

FENNS FARM RIDING CENTRE
Fenns Lane, West End,
Nr Chobham, Surrey, GU24 9QF
Tel 01483 797349/359
Contact Mrs S Hulbert
Riding School, Facility Centre Inst
Basic
Specialities Sound instruction for
novice adults and children, and
excellent hacking.Also Polo instruction
2 full time instructors
Ave No 3 Horses, 9 Ponies
Courses WP, Short, Ev, P/T, Hol
Facilities
Outdoor Manege 40 x 45 fl lt
SJ: Nov, 1 Paddock
CC: Basic, Banks, Natural, 6 Schooling
Lec Rm, Vis Aids, Chng Rm, Wait Rm
Hacking
Livery Full, P/T, DIY, Break, School,
Hunt
Schooling General, Break, to Nov
Dress, to SJ GR A, to HT Nov
Exclusions Wt Limit, 13st, Age Limit, 3,

No casual Hire
Location Junction 3 M3 off A322
between Guildford and Bagshot

GARSON FARM STABLES
Winterdown Road, West End,
Esher, Surrey, KT10 8LS
Tel 01372 462026
Contact Ms S Timpson
Riding School, Training Centre Inst
Riding & Jumping
Specialities Teaching students and
livery. Emphasis on dressage
Staff Chief Instructor Ms S Timpson
(BHSII, BHS SM)
Plus 4 full time instructors
Ave No 4 Horses, 2 Ponies
inc 2 Med Dress
Courses WP, YT, Short, Ev, P/T, Hol
Facilities
Outdoor Manege 60 x 20
SJ: Grade C, 1 Paddock
CC: Basic, 12 Schooling
Chng Rm, Wait Rm
Hacking
Livery Full, P/T, Break, School, Grass
Schooling General, Break, to Med
Dress, to SJ GR C, to HT Nov
Exclusions Wt Limit, 12st,
No casual hire
Location M25 jnc 10 off A307 Cobham
to Esher Road

GREEN LANE STABLES
Green Lane (Off Garth Road),
Morden, Surrey, SM4 6SE
Tel 0181 337 3853
Contact Ms Lynda Goodson
Riding School Inst Basic
Staff Chief Instructor Mrs Leslie Bielcki
Plus 1 full time instructor
Ave No 6 Horses, 8 Ponies
Facilities
Outdoor Manege 75 x 35 fl lt
SJ: Nov
Chng Rm, Wait Rm
Hacking
Exclusions Wt Limit, 16st, Age Limit, 6
Location 2 miles from A3, 2 miles from
Marden Central Station

GREENWAYS FARM & STABLES
Lower Eashing, Godalming,
Surrey, GU7 2QF
Tel 01483 414741
Contact Mrs M Sprake (snr)
Riding School Inst Basic
Staff Chief Instructor Mr Mark Sprake
(BHSAI)
Plus 1 full time instructor

Ave No 8 Horses, 8 Ponies
Courses Hol
Facilities
Outdoor Manege 40 x 20 fl lt
SJ: Nov, 1 Paddock
CC: 7 Schooling
Lec Rm, Vis Aids, Chng Rm
Hacking
Livery Hunt, Grass
Exclusions Wt Limit, 13st, Age Limit, 8,
No casual hire
Location Off the A3, 5 miles south of
Guildford

HUNTERSFIELD FARM
RIDING CENTRE
Fairlawn Road, off Croydon Lane,
Banstead, Surrey, SM7 3AU
Tel 0181 643 1333
Contact Mr & Mrs D Horley
Riding School, Training Centre Inst
Riding & Jumping
Staff Chief Instructor Mrs M Pattison
(BHSII)
Plus 1 full time instructor
Ave No 7 Horses, 12 Ponies
inc 1 Med Dress
Courses WP, Short, Ev, Hol
Facilities
Covered School 20 x 40
SJ: Nov
Lec Rm, Vis Aids, Chng Rm, Wait Rm
Hacking
Livery Full, P/T, School
Schooling General, Break, to SJ GR C
Exclusions Wt Limit, 13st, Age Limit, 5,
No unescorted hacks, no hiring

HURSTFIELDS EQUESTRIAN CENTRE
Hurst Road, Walton-on-the-Hill,
Tadworth, Surrey, KT20 5BD
Tel 01737 814305/813750
Contact Mrs K Gostling
Facility Centre, Livery, Grass livery
1 full time instructor
Facilities
Outdoor Manege 20 x 60 fl lt
SJ: Nov, Grade C, 1 Paddock
CC: Course, Basic, Banks, Water,
Natural
Livery Full, P/T, Break, School, Grass
Exclusions Clients on own horses only
Location Walton-on-the-Hill, between
Tadworth and Epsom Downs

KILN COTTAGE STABLES
Kiln Cottage, Badshot Farm Lane,
Badshot Lea, Farnham,
Surrey, GU9 9HY
Tel 01252 333200

Contact Mrs Angela Andrew
Riding School, Training Centre Inst
Basic
Staff Chief Instructor Mrs A Andrew
(BHSAI)
Plus 2 full time instructors
Ave No 15 Horses, 10 Ponies
inc Dressage & Event horses suitable
for AI students
Courses WP, YT, Short, Ev, P/T, Hol
Facilities
Outdoor Manege 20 x 35
SJ: Grade C, 1 Paddock
CC: Water, Natural, 6 Schooling
Lec Rm, Vis Aids, Chng Rm
Hacking
Livery Full, P/T, Break, School, Hunt,
Grass
Schooling General, Break, to Nov
Dress, to SJ GR C, to HT Nov
Exclusions Wt Limit, 15st, Age Limit, 5,
Assesment required for hacking.
No casual hire
Location 1 mile from Farnham town
centre, on Aldershot Road

THE KINGSTON RIDING CENTRE
38 Crescent Road,
Kingston-upon-Thames,
Surrey, KT2 7RG
Tel 0181 546 6361
Contact Messrs J & L Mastroianni
Riding School Inst to BHSAI
Specialities Career training, courses
tailor made to suit individuals
6 full time instructors
Ave No 20 Horses, 6 Ponies
Courses WP, Short, Ev, P/T, Hol
Facilities
Covered School 20 x 40
Outdoor Manege 20 x 60
SJ: Nov
CC: Course, Nov, Banks, Natural
Lec Rm, Vis Aids, Chng Rm, Wait Rm
Hacking
Livery Full, Break, School, Hunt
Schooling General, Break, to El Dress,
to Med Dress, to SJ GR C, to HT Nov
Accom Db, Dor, SC
Exclusions Wt Limit, 13st7, Age Limit, 3,
No casual hire
Location 400 yds from Kingston Gate
of Richmond Park

LANGSHOT EQUESTRIAN CENTRE
Gracious Pond Road, Chobham,
Surrey, GU24 8HJ
Tel 01276 856949
Contact Mesdames HJ Stevenson &
LE Kingsnorth
Riding School, Training Centre,

Facility Centre Inst Riding & Jumping
Staff Chief Instructor Mrs P Heimann-
Tootell
Plus 3 full time instructors
Ave No 12 Horses, 17 Ponies
Courses WP, YT, Short, Ev, P/T, Hol
Facilities
Covered School 20 x 60
Outdoor Manege 60 x 20 fl lt
Outdoor Manege 20 x 40 fl lt
SJ: Nov, Grade C, Grade B, Grade A,
1 Paddock
CC: Course, Nov, Banks, Water,
Natural
Lec Rm, Vis Aids, Chng Rm
Hacking
Livery Full, P/T
Schooling General, Break
Exclusions Wt Limit, 13st, Age Limit, 6,
No private hire
Location Between Chertsey and
Woking

LOWER FARM RIDING & LIVERY STABLES
Stoke Road, Stoke D'Abernon,
Cobham, Surrey
Tel 01932 867545/86699
Contact Mrs H Lambourn &
Mrs J Brown
Riding School Inst Riding & Jumping
Staff Chief Instructor Miss Emma
Brady
Plus 2 full time instructors
Ave No 15 Horses, 10 Ponies
Courses Short, Ev, Hol
Facilities
SJ: Nov, 0.5 Paddock
CC: Water, 11 Schooling
Lec Rm, Vis Aids, Chng Rm, Wait Rm,
Tack Shop
Livery Full, P/T, School
Schooling General, to El Dress, to HT
Nov
Exclusions Wt Limit, 13st,
No casual hire
Location Off A3 at Cobham

OLDENCRAIG EQUESTRIAN CENTRE & STUD
Tandridge Lane, Lingfield,
Surrey, RH7 6LL
Tel 01342 833317
Contact Mr I Winfield
Riding School, Training Centre, Stud
Inst Riding & Jumping
Specialities Accredited centre for NVQ
levels 1-3
2 full time instructors
Ave No 12 Horses, 6 Ponies
inc 3 El Dress, 1 Med Dress, 4 SJ GR C

Courses WP, YT, Ev, P/T, Hol
Facilities
Covered School 40 x 20 gly
Outdoor Manege 20 x 60
Outdoor Manege 40 x 30 fl lt
SJ: Nov, Grade C, 1 Paddock
Lec Rm, Vis Aids, Chng Rm, Showers,
Wait Rm
Hacking
Livery Full, P/T, Break, School, Hunt
Schooling General, Break, to Adv
Dress, to SJ GR B
Exclusions Wt Limit, 15st, Age Limit, 5,
No casual hire
Location Tandridge Lane on the corner
of B2029, between Blindley Heath and
Lingfield, just off A22 in Blindley Heath

ORCHARD COTTAGE
RIDING STABLES
Babylon Lane, Lower Kingswood,
Tadworth, Surrey, KT20 6XA
Tel 01737 241311
Contact Mr P R Howell
Riding School Inst Riding & Jumping
Specialities Childrens courses
Staff Chief Instructor Miss A Vickery
(BHSAI, BHS Int Teach)
Plus 3 full time instructors
Ave No 10 Horses, 11 Ponies
Courses Short, Ev, P/T, Hol
Facilities
Covered School 40 x 20
SJ: Nov, 1 Paddock
CC: Course, Basic, Nov, Banks,
Natural
Lec Rm, Vis Aids, Chng Rm, Wait Rm
Hacking
Exclusions Wt Limit, 15st, Age Limit, 5,
No casual hiring
Location Jn 8 off M25, off the A217

PARWOOD EQUESTRIAN CENTRE
Westwood Lane, Normandy,
Guildford, Surrey, GU3 2JE
Tel 01483 810087
Contact Mr H S Goold
**Riding School, Training Centre,
Facility Centre** Inst Riding & Jumping
Specialities Instruction in riding and
jumping
3 full time instructors
Ave No 11 Horses, 9 Ponies
Courses WP, Short, Ev, P/T, Hol
Facilities
Covered School 20 x 55 gly
Outdoor Manege 20 x 60 fl lt
SJ: Nov, 1acre Paddock
CC: Banks, Natural, 5 Schooling
Lec Rm, Vis Aids, Showers, Wait Rm
Hacking

Livery Full, P/T, DIY, Break, School,
Grass
Schooling General, Break, to Nov
Dress, to El Dress, to SJ GR C
Exclusions Wt Limit, 16st, Age Limit, 6,
No casual hire
Location Between Guildford and
Aldershot off A323

THE ROYAL ALEXANDRA
& ALBERT SCHOOL
Gatton Park, Reigate,
Surrey, RH2 0TW
Tel 01737 642818
Contact Mr E P Earle
Riding School, Boarding School Inst
Riding & Jumping
Specialities Childrens riding instruction
Staff Chief Instructor Mrs L Stone (BHSAI)
Plus 1 full time instructor
Ave No 4 Horses, 3 Ponies
Courses WP, Short, Ev, P/T, Hol
Facilities
Outdoor Manege 25 x 40 fl lt
SJ: Nov, Grade C, 1 Paddock
Lec Rm, Vis Aids, Chng Rm, Showers,
Wait Rm
Hacking
Schooling General, Break, to El Dress,
to SJ GR C
Accom S, Tw, Dor, FB
Exclusions Wt Limit, 14st, Age Limit, 5,
No casual hire
Location 12 miles from Gatwick Airport,
1 mile from Jn 8 of M25

SOUTH WEYLANDS
EQUESTRIAN CENTRE
Esher Road, Hersham,
Walton-on-Thames, Surrey, KT12 4LJ
Tel 01372 463010
Contact Mrs P Bushnell
Riding School, Training Centre Inst
Riding & Jumping
Staff Chief Instructor Mrs P Bushnell
(BHSI)
Plus 1 full time instructor
Ave No 9 Horses, 14 Ponies
Courses WP, Ev, P/T, Hol
Facilities
Covered School 41 x 15 gly
Covered School 26 x 18 gly
Outdoor Manege 60 x 20
Outdoor Manege 80 x 25
SJ: Nov, 1 Paddock
CC: Course, Basic
Lec Rm, Vis Aids, Chng Rm, Wait Rm,
Tack Shop
Livery School
Schooling General, Break, to Med
Dress

Accom S, Tw, SC
Exclusions Wt Limit, 11st, Age Limit, 5
Location On A244 between Esher and Weybridge

TRUXFORD RIDING CENTRE
Thursley Road, Elstead,
Surrey, GU8 6LW
Tel 01252 702086
Contact Mr C Peter Edmondson
Riding School, Training Centre Inst
Riding & Jumping
Staff Chief Instructor Miss B Hill
Plus 1 full time instructor
Ave No 10 Horses, 6 Ponies
inc 2 El Dress
Courses WP, YT, Short, Ev, P/T, Hol
Facilities
Covered School 35 x 20
Outdoor Manege 20 x 40 fl lt
SJ: Nov, 1 Paddock
CC: Gallops
Lec Rm, Vis Aids, Chng Rm, Showers,
Wait Rm
Hacking
Livery Full, P/T, Break, School, Hunt
Schooling General, Break, to El Dress,
to SJ GR C
Accom Tw, SC
Exclusions Wt Limit, 16st, Age Limit, 5,
No casual hire
Location Between A31 & A3 1 mile
from Elstead village

WEYBRIDGE EQUESTRIAN CENTRE
Grenside Road (off Grotto Road),
Weybridge, Surrey, KT13 8QB
Tel 01932 248544
Contact Miss B Wilson &
Miss J Morgan
Riding School, Training Centre Inst
Basic
Specialities Teaching children and
childrens courses
Ave No 5 Horses, 12 Ponies
Courses WP, YT, Short, Ev, P/T, Hol
Facilities
Outdoor Manege 20 x 40 fl lt
Outdoor Manege 20 x 60
SJ: Nov, 1 Paddock
Lec Rm, Vis Aids, Chng Rm, Showers,
Wait Rm
Hacking
Livery Full, P/T, DIY, Break, School
Schooling General, Break, to Nov
Dress
Exclusions Wt Limit, 14stone,
No casual hire.
Body protectors compulsory
Location J11 off M25. 1 mile from
Weybridge town centre

WILDWOODS RIDING CENTRE
Ebbisham Lane, Walton-on-the-Hill,
Tadworth, Surrey, KT20 5BH
Tel 01737 812146
Contact Mrs A C Chambers
Riding School, Training Centre Inst
to BHSAI
Specialities Nervous beginners,
UK Chasers, Mockhunting and Beach
rides. Day rides, Childrens' day & week
courses - non residential
Staff Chief Instructor Mrs A Chambers
(BHSII)
Plus 1 full time instructor
Ave No 12 Horses, 7 Ponies
inc 1 El Dress, 4 SJ GR C, 3 17hh+
Hunters
Courses WP, Short, Ev, P/T, Hol
Facilities
Outdoor Manege 15 x 45 fl lt
Outdoor Manege 20 x 40
SJ: Nov, Grade C, 2 Paddock
CC: Course, Basic, Nov, Banks, Water,
Natural, Gallops, 20 Schooling
Lec Rm, Vis Aids, Chng Rm, Showers,
Wait Rm
Hacking
Schooling General, Break, to El Dress,
to SJ GR C, to HT Nov
Exclusions Wt Limit, 16st7,
Age Limit, 3 1/2, No casual hire
Location Foot of Epsom Downs

WISHANGER EQUESTRIAN CENTRE
Frensham Lane, Churt,
Surrey, GU10 2QG
Tel 01252 792604
Contact Ms J R Norkett
Riding School, Training Centre Inst
to BHSAI
Staff Chief Instructor Mr N Rapley (BHSII)
Plus 3 full time instructors
Ave No 15 Horses, 25 Ponies
inc 1 El Dress, 1 Med Dress, 1 SJ GR
C, 1 SJ Jun C, Driving Ponies
Courses WP, YT, Short, Ev, P/T, Hol
Facilities
Covered School 15 x 30
Outdoor Manege 60 x 30
Outdoor Manege 22 x 50 fl lt
Outdoor Manege 15 x 30
SJ: Nov
Lec Rm, Vis Aids, Chng Rm, Showers,
Wait Rm
Hacking
Livery Full, P/T, Break, School, Hunt,
Grass
Schooling General, Break, to Med
Dress, to SJ GR C, to HT Nov
Accom S, Caravan, FB
Exclusions Wt Limit, 14st, Age Limit, 4,
No casual hire

Location Off A287 between Farnham
& Hindhead

EAST SUSSEX

CANTERS END RIDING SCHOOL
Hadlow Down, Uckfield,
East Sussex, TN22 4HP
Tel 01825 830213
Contact Miss V Grove
Riding School Inst Basic
Specialities Children
Staff Chief Instructor Miss V Grove
Ave No 5 Horses, 4 Ponies
Facilities
Covered School 14 x 27
CC: Natural, 5 Schooling
Hacking
Exclusions Wt Limit, 13st, Age Limit, 4,
No casual hire
Location On 272 between Buxted and
Heathfield

ENGLISH LANGUAGE
AND EQUESTRIAN CENTRE
Friars Gate Farm, Marden Hill,
Crowborough,
East Sussex, TN6 1XH
Tel 01892 661195
Contact Mr D R C Forsyth
Riding School, Facility Centre,
English language school Inst Riding
& Jumping
Staff Chief Instructor Mrs H Garner
(BHSII)
Ave No 7 Horses, 1 Ponies
Facilities
Covered School 34 x 14
Outdoor Manege 52 x 26
SJ: Nov, 1 Paddock
CC: Basic
Lec Rm, Vis Aids, Wait Rm
Hacking
Livery P/T
Accom Tw, FB
Exclusions Wt Limit, 12st, Age Limit, 9,
No unescorted riding
Location 1 1/2 miles from
Crowborough, off the B2188

FOLKINGTON MANOR STABLES
Folkington, Nr Polegate,
East Sussex, BN26 5SD
Tel 01323 482437
Contact Mr A Stacy-Marks
Livery
1 full time instructor
Ave No 17 Horses
Facilities

Outdoor Manege 25 x 60 fl lt
SJ: Nov, 8 acs Paddock
CC: Basic, Water, Natural, Gallops,
9 Schooling
Lec Rm, Vis Aids, Wait Rm, Tack Shop
Hacking
Livery Full, P/T, DIY, Break, School,
Hunt, Grass
Schooling General, Break, to Nov
Dress, to SJ GR C, to HT Nov
Accom S, Db, SC
Exclusions none for livery yard
Location is situated 1/2 mile west of
Polgate, signposted off A27

GATEWOOD FARM RIDING SCHOOL
Robin Post Lane, Wilmington,
East Sussex, BN26 6RP
Tel 01323 483709
Contact Mr & Mrs K Quicke
Riding School Inst Riding & Jumping
Specialities summer picnic rides on the
South Downs
Staff Chief Instructor Mr G Booth
(BHSAI)
Plus 1 full time instructor
Ave No 10 Horses
Courses YT, Hol
Facilities
Covered School 18 x 24
Outdoor Manege 60 x 100
SJ: Nov, 1 Paddock
CC: Basic, Nov, Natural, Gallops,
11 Schooling
Vis Aids, Chng Rm, Wait Rm
Hacking
Schooling General
Exclusions Wt Limit, 12st - 13st,
Age Limit, 12
Location Take the A27 to Wilmington
Crossroads. Turn northwards into
Thornwell Road, go over the railway line,
carry on until you see Robin Post Lane.
Turn up here and Gatewood Farm is the
last property on the left

GOLDEN CROSS
EQUESTRIAN CENTRE
Chalvington Road, Golden Cross,
Hailsham, East Sussex, BN27 3SS
Tel 01825 872311
Contact Miss B A Huckle
Riding School, Training Centre,
Facility Centre Inst Riding & Jumping
Specialities Competition Centre
Staff Chief Instructor Mrs J Hartwell
(BHSII)
Plus 1 full time instructor
Ave No 8 Horses, 12 Ponies
inc 1 El Dress, 3 SJ GR C
Courses WP, YT, P/T

Facilities
Covered School 26 x 52 gly
Outdoor Manege 20 x 40 fl lt
SJ: Nov, Grade A, 1 Paddock
Chng Rm, Wait Rm
Hacking
Livery Full, P/T, DIY, Break, School,
Hunt, Grass
Schooling General, Break, to Nov
Dress, to SJ GR C, to HT Nov
Exclusions Wt Limit, 16st, Age Limit, 3,
No casual hire or unassessed casual
hacking
Location Off A22 between Uckfield
and Hailsham

HIGHAM FARM
Chapel Lane, Guestling,
Hastings,
East Sussex, TN35 4HP
Tel 01424 812636
Contact Miss C Green
Training Centre, Livery, Side Saddle
Inst to BHSI
Specialities Teaching of side saddle
and dressage to music
Staff Chief Instructor Miss CA Green
(BHSI)
Ave No 7 Horses
inc 3 El Dress, 2 Med Dress, 1 Adv
Dress, 2 SJ GR C, 1 SJ GR B,
2 Side Saddle
Courses Short, Ev, P/T, Hol
Facilities
Outdoor Manege 20 x 60 fl lt
Outdoor Manege 20 x 20
SJ: Nov, Grade A, 1 Paddock
CC: Banks, Water, Natural
Lec Rm, Vis Aids, Wait Rm
Livery Full, P/T, Break, School
Schooling General, Break, to Adv
Dress, to SJ GR C, to HT Nov
Exclusions Wt Limit, 12st7,
Age Limit, 12,
No hiring for hacking or hunting
Location Off A259 between Hastings
and Guestling Green

HYLANDS STABLES
2 Highlands Farm Cottages,
Arlington Road West, Nr Hailsham,
East Sussex, BN27 3RD
Tel 01323 846797
Contact Mrs M J Tattersall
Riding School Inst Basic
Staff Chief Instructor Mrs M J Tattersall
(BHSII)
Plus 1 full time instructor
Ave No 1 Horses, 4 Ponies
inc 1 Med Dress, 1 SJ Jun A
Courses WP, YT, Short, P/T

Facilities
Outdoor Manege 40 x 20 fl lt
Hacking
Livery Full, P/T, Break, School, Hunt
Schooling General, Break, to Nov
Dress, to El Dress, to SJ GR C, to HT
Nov
Exclusions Wt Limit, 14st,
No casual hire
Location Off A22 between Eastbourne
and Oakfield or Uckfield and Polegate

MEADOWBANK
EQUESTRIAN CENTRE
Downash, Hailsham,
East Sussex, BN27 2RP
Tel 01323 848777
Contact Mrs Stella Vincent
Riding School, Training Centre Inst
Riding & Jumping
Specialities Novice riders preparing for
stages I & II
Staff Chief Instructor Mrs S L Vincent
(BHSAI, BHS Int.SM)
Ave No 6 Horses, 11 Ponies
inc 2 El Dress, 1 HT Int
Courses Short, Ev, Hol
Facilities
Outdoor Manege 20 x 40 fl lt
SJ: Nov, 1 Paddock
CC: Banks, Natural, 15 Schooling
Lec Rm, Vis Aids, Chng Rm, Showers,
Wait Rm
Hacking
Livery Full, P/T, DIY, Break, School,
Grass
Schooling General, Break, to El Dress
Exclusions Wt Limit, 15st, Age Limit, 3,
No casual hire
Location East of A22, 1 1/2 miles from
Hailsham town centre

PLUMPTON COLLEGE
Equine & Animal Studies Unit,
Plumpton, Lewes,
East Sussex, BN7 3AE
Tel 01273 890454
Contact Mr J Campbell
Training Centre, Competitions Inst to
BHSII
Specialities Career training
7 full time instructors
Ave No 57 Horses
inc 1 Med Dress
Courses YT, Short, Ev, P/T, Hol
Facilities
Covered School 23 x 44 gly
Outdoor Manege 20 x 60 fl lt
SJ: Nov, Grade C, 1 Paddock

CC: Course, Basic
Lec Rm, Vis Aids, Chng Rm, Showers,
Wait Rm
Hacking
Livery Full, P/T, DIY, School
Schooling to Adv Dress
Accom S, FB
Exclusions Wt Limit, 14st,
No casual hire
Location Off B2116 approx 5 miles
from Lewes

WEST SUSSEX

ARUNDEL FARM RIDING
AND DRIVING CENTRE
Park Place, Arundel,
West Sussex
Tel 01903 882061
Contact Mrs J Leggett
Riding School Inst Riding & Jumping
Specialities Driving instruction from
novice to advanced
Staff Chief Instructor Mr N O'Nions
(BHSII)
Plus 2 full time instructors
Ave No 9 Horses, 10 Ponies
inc 2 Med Dress
Courses WP, YT, Hol
Facilities
Covered School 37 x 18
Outdoor Manege 27 x 15 fl lt
SJ: Nov, 1 Paddock
CC: Basic, Banks, 7 Schooling
Lec Rm, Vis Aids, Chng Rm, Wait Rm
Hacking
Livery Full, P/T, School
Exclusions Wt Limit, 13st7, Age Limit,
4, No hacking for the inexperienced
Location Just off A27 on the outskirts
of Arundel, on the A284

BELMOREDEAN STUD
& LIVERY STABLES
Little Champions Farm,
Maplehurst Road, West Grinstead,
West Sussex, RH13 6RN
Tel 01403 864635/864587
Contact Miss L M Hartnett
Facility Centre, Livery
Courses WP, YT
Facilities
Covered School 60 x 20
Outdoor Manege 60 x 20
Chng Rm, Wait Rm
Livery Full, P/T, School, Hunt, Grass
Schooling General
Location 5 miles south of Horsham off
the A272

BRINSBURY COLLEGE
North Heath,
Pulborough,
West Sussex, RH20 1DL
Tel 01798 877400
Contact Miss C Green
Training Centre Inst to BHSII
Specialities Career training
5 full time instructors
Ave No 36 Horses
inc 5 Side Saddle Horses
Courses WP, YT, Short, Ev, P/T
Facilities
Covered School 21 x 40 gly
Outdoor Manege 30 x 60 fl lt
Outdoor Manege 25 x 45
SJ: Nov, 1 Paddock
CC: Natural, 16 Schooling
Lec Rm, Vis Aids
Accom Tw, FB
Exclusions Wt Limit, 13st, Age Limit, 16

DITCHLING COMMON STUD
Burgess Hill,
West Sussex, RH15 0SE
Tel 01444 236678/871900
Contact Mr P G M Dudeney
Riding School Inst to BHSII
Specialities Career training and
Mounted Skill at Arms training
Staff Chief Instructor Mr P J M Dudeney
(BHSII, BHS SM, BHS T)
Plus 1 full time instructor
Ave No 24 Horses, 18 Ponies
Courses Short, Ev, P/T, Hol
Facilities
Covered School 40 x 22 gly
Covered School 42 x 19
Outdoor Manege 20 x 40 fl lt
SJ: Grade B, 1 Paddock
CC: Course, Nov, Banks, Water,
10 Schooling
Lec Rm, Vis Aids, Showers, Wait Rm
Livery Full, P/T, DIY, Break, School
Schooling General, Break, to HT Nov
Accom S, SC
Exclusions Wt Limit, 12st7,
No casual hire
Location Off B2112 between Haywards
Heath and Ditchling

EASTWOOD STUD FARM
Graffham, Nr Petworth,
West Sussex, GU28 0QF
Tel 01798 867570
Contact Miss E K Wilder
Riding School Inst Riding & Jumping
Specialities Driving to competition level.
Help for schooling is taken from Mr Bill
Noble who is resident not far away
1 full time instructor

Ave No 5 Horses, 8 Ponies
inc 1 Med Dress, 1 SJ GR C, Driving
horses
Courses WP, Short, P/T, Hol
Facilities
Outdoor Manege 21 x 44 fl lt
SJ: Nov, 1 Paddock
Chng Rm, Showers, Wait Rm
Hacking
Livery Full, P/T, Break, School, Hunt,
Grass
Schooling General, Break, to Med
Dress, to SJ GR C, to HT Int
Accom Tw, FB, SC
Exclusions Wt Limit, 18st, Age Limit, 3,
No casual hire
Location 5 miles south of Petworth, off
A285

**GRANGEFIELD
CHILDRENS RIDING SCHOOL**
Grangefield, Bepton,
Nr Midhurst,
West Sussex, GU29 0JB
Tel 01730 813538
Contact Miss W Sugden
Riding School Inst Riding & Jumping
Staff Chief Instructor Miss W Sugden
(BHSAI)
Ave No 2 Horses, 8 Ponies
Facilities
Outdoor Manege 40 x 20
SJ: Nov, 1 Paddock
CC: Basic, 7 Schooling
Hacking
Livery P/T
Exclusions Age Limit, 4, No hunting

**HANGLETON FARM
EQUESTRIAN CENTRE**
Hangleton Farm, Hangleton Lane,
Ferring, Nr Worthing,
Sussex, BN12 6PP
Tel 01903 240352/240696
Contact Mr C Ellis
**Riding School, Training Centre,
Facility Centre** Inst Riding & Jumping
Specialities Career and Competition
training
Staff Chief Instructor Miss A Todd
(BHSII, BHS SM)
Plus 2 full time instructors

Ave No 13 Horses, 11 Ponies
inc 2 Med Dress, 1 SJ GR C,
1 SJ GR B
Courses WP, Ev, P/T, Hol
Facilities
Outdoor Manege 100 x 40 fl lt
Outdoor Manege 100 x 40 fl lt
SJ: Nov, Grade A, 1 Paddock
CC: 10 Schooling
Lec Rm, Vis Aids, Chng Rm, Showers,
Wait Rm
Hacking
Livery Full, DIY, Break, School
Schooling General, Break, to Med
Dress, to SJ GR A, to HT Int
Accom S, Tw, F
Exclusions Age Limit, 5,
No casual hire
Location North of A259, between
Worthing and Littlehampton

**LAVANT HOUSE
EQUESTRIAN CENTRE**
Lavant House, Lavant,
Chichester,
West Sussex, PO18 9AB
Tel 01243 530460
Contact Mrs L A Thomson
**Riding School, Training Centre,
Facility Centre, Boarding School** Inst
Riding & Jumping
Specialities Career Students working
towards BHS exams
Staff Chief Instructor Miss M J Claxton
(BHSAI, BHS SM)
Plus 2 full time instructors
Ave No 3 Horses, 10 Ponies
Courses WP, YT, Short, Ev, P/T, Hol
Facilities
Outdoor Manege 30 x 40
SJ: Grade C, 1 Paddock
Lec Rm, Vis Aids, Wait Rm
Hacking
Livery Full, P/T, DIY, Break, School,
Hunt
Schooling General, Break, to Med
Dress, to SJ GR C, to HT Int
Exclusions Wt Limit, 13st,
No Casual Hire, Assessment lesson
prior to hack
Location Off A286 between Chichester
and Midhurst in grounds of Lavant
School

Riding in the South

BERKSHIRE ◆ BUCKINGHAMSHIRE
HAMPSHIRE ◆ ISLE OF WIGHT
OXFORDSHIRE

BERKSHIRE

BEARWOOD RIDING CENTRE
Mole Road, Sindlesham,
Wokingham, Berks, RG11 5GB
Tel 01189 760010
Contact Mrs K Coles
Riding School, Training Centre,
Facility Centre Inst Riding & Jumping
2 full time instructors
Ave No 6 Horses, 5 Ponies
Courses WP, YT, Short, P/T, Hol
Facilities
Covered School 20 x 40 gly
Outdoor Manege 20 x 60 fl lt
SJ: Nov
CC: Banks, 2 Schooling
Lec Rm, Vis Aids, Wait Rm
Hacking
Livery Full, P/T, School, Hunt
Schooling General, to El Dress
Exclusions Wt Limit, 13st
Location B3030 between Arborfield
(A327) and Winnersh (A329)

BERKSHIRE COLLEGE
OF AGRICULTURE
Hall Place, Burchetts Green,
Maidenhead, Berkshire, SL6 6QR
Tel 01628 824444
Contact Mr P Thorn Bsc(Hons) MCIM
Riding School, Training Centre,
Facility Centre Inst to BHSII
Specialities Career training
Staff Chief Instructor Miss C Lopresti
(BHSI)
Plus 8 full time instructors
Ave No 40 Horses, 4 Ponies
inc 6 El Dress, 1 Adv Dress, 4 SJ GR
C, 4 HT Int
Courses YT, Short, Ev, P/T, Hol
Facilities
Covered School 60 x 40
Outdoor Manege 40 x 40

SJ: Nov, Grade C
CC: Course, Basic, Banks, Gallops,
20 Schooling
Lec Rm, Vis Aids
Hacking
Livery P/T, School, Grass
Schooling General, to El Dress, to SJ
GR C
Accom S, Tw, Caravan, FB
Exclusions Wt Limit, 13st, Age Limit, 16,
College students only

BERKSHIRE RIDING CENTRE
Crouch Lane, Winkfield,
Berkshire, SL4 4TN
Tel 01344 883331
Contact Mr & Mrs T G F Lord
Livery
Specialities Training with own horse for
competition
Courses WP
Facilities
Covered School 22 x 50 gly
Outdoor Manege 25 x 70
SJ: Nov, 1 Paddock
Lec Rm, Vis Aids, Wait Rm
Livery Full, P/T, Break, School, Hunt
Schooling General, to Adv Dress, to SJ
GR A, to HT Nov
Exclusions Training with own horse
Location Off A332 between Ascot &
Windsor

BLACKNEST GATE
RIDING CENTRE
Blacknest Gate, Mill Lane,
Sunninghill, Berkshire, SL5 0PS
Tel 01344 876871
Contact Miss K Cox & Miss S Quest
Riding School Inst Riding & Jumping
Specialities Hacking in Windsor Great
Park
Staff Chief Instructor Miss Kate Cox
Plus 3 full time instructors

Ave No 8 Horses, 4 Ponies
inc 2 SJ GR C
Courses Short, Ev, P/T, Hol
Facilities
Covered School 24 x 11
Outdoor Manege 83 x 37 fl lt
SJ: Nov, Grade C
Chng Rm, Showers, Wait Rm
Hacking
Livery Full, P/T, Break, School, Hunt
Schooling General, Break, to Nov
Dress, to SJ GR C, to HT Nov
Exclusions Age Limit, 4,
No casual hire
Location West of Great Park

BRADFIELD RIDING CENTRE
The Maltings, Bradfield,
Berks, RG7 6AJ
Tel 0118 974 4048
Contact Mrs J A White
Riding School Inst Riding & Jumping
Specialities General instruction,
Livery, Childrens Holiday Courses -
Shows
Staff Chief Instructor Mrs J A White
(BHSAI)
Plus 1 full time instructor
Ave No 13 Horses, 12 Ponies
Courses WP, Short, Ev, P/T
Facilities
Covered School 26 x 46
SJ: Nov
CC: Course, Basic, Banks, Natural
Hacking
Livery Full, P/T, DIY, Break, School,
Hunt, Grass
Schooling General, Break, to Nov
Dress, to SJ GR C, to HT Nov
Exclusions Wt Limit, 13st,
No casual hiring

CLOUD STABLES
SCHOOL OF EQUITATION
Church Lane, Arborfield,
Reading, Berks, RG2 9JA
Tel 01734 761522
Contact Mr W A Patrick
Riding School, Training Centre Inst
Riding & Jumping
1 full time instructor
Ave No 16 Horses, 5 Ponies
inc 1 El Dress, RDA
Courses WP, YT, Short, Ev, P/T, Hol
Facilities
Covered School 30 x 26 gly
Covered School 25 x 12
Outdoor Manege 20 x 40
SJ: Nov, Grade C, 1 Paddock
CC: Course, Basic, Nov, Banks, Water,
Natural, 25 Schooling

Lec Rm, Vis Aids, Chng Rm, Showers,
Wait Rm
Livery Full, Break, School, Hunt
Schooling General, Break, to Nov
Dress, to El Dress, to Med Dress, to SJ
GR C, to HT Nov
Accom Caravan
Exclusions Wt Limit, 12st
Location Take the turning off A327
between Shinfield and Arborfield Cross

HALL PLACE
EQUESTRIAN CENTRE
Little Heath, Tilehurst,
Reading, Berks, RG31 5TX
Tel 01734 426938
Contact Mrs J Vincent
Riding School, Training Centre,
Facility Centre Inst Riding & Jumping
Specialities General instruction,
Hacking & Shows, RDA
Staff Chief Instructor Miss S Scanlan
(BHSAI)
Plus 3 full time instructors
Ave No 10 Horses, 10 Ponies
inc 1 El Dress, 1 SJ GR C, 1 SJ Jun C
Courses WP, YT, Short, Ev, P/T
Facilities
Covered School 27 x 46 gly
Outdoor Manege 78 x 76
SJ: Nov, Grade C, Grade B, 1 Paddock
CC: Course, Basic, Nov, Banks, Water,
Natural
Lec Rm, Vis Aids, Chng Rm, Wait Rm,
Tack Shop
Hacking
Livery Full, P/T, DIY, School, Hunt,
Grass
Schooling General, to Nov Dress, to El
Dress, to SJ GR C, to SJ GR B, to HT
Nov, to HT Int
Exclusions No unescorted rides
Location Jn 12 M4 between Reading
and Pangbourne

THE SPANISH BIT
RIDING SCHOOL & LIVERY
Elm Farm, Boveney Road,
Dorney Common, Nr Windsor,
Berkshire, SL4 6QD
Tel 01628 661275
Contact Mr & Mrs K M Harris
Riding School Inst Riding & Jumping
Specialities General instruction,
Courses at most levels, Livery, hacking
5 full time instructors
Ave No 8 Horses, 14 Ponies
Courses WP
Facilities
Covered School 40 x 20 gly
Outdoor Manege 40 x 25 fl lt

SJ: Nov, 1 Paddock
CC: Banks, Natural, 5 Schooling
Chng Rm, Wait Rm
Hacking
Livery Full, P/T, School
Schooling General
Accom S, Tw, Cottage
Exclusions Wt Limit, 14st, Age Limit, 6,
No hacking without escort
Location Between Maidenhead, Slough
and Windsor, 5 minutes off M4 Jn 7

TIDMARSH STUD
Maidenhatch, Tidmarsh,
Reading, Berkshire, RG8 8HP
Tel 01734 744840
Contact Mrs F Harter
Riding School Inst Basic
Specialities Instruction in riding &
jumping, horses produced for
competitions, breaking and schooling
Staff Chief Instructor Mr John Harter
Plus 2 full time instructors
Ave No 3 Horses, 4 Ponies
inc 2 HT Int
Courses WP
Facilities
Outdoor Manege 20 x 40 fl lt
SJ: Nov, 1 Paddock
CC: Basic, Natural, 7 Schooling
Showers
Hacking
Livery Full, P/T, DIY, Break, School,
Hunt, Grass
Schooling General, Break, to Med
Dress, to SJ GR B, to HT Adv
Exclusions No casual hire
Location Turn off A340 opposite the
Greyhound public house, first left into
Dark Lane, first left again

WHITELOCKS FARM
RIDING SCHOOL
Garsons Lane, Maidens Green,
Bracknell, Berkshire, RG12 6JA
Tel 01344 890522
Contact Miss Gillian Jordan
Riding School, RDA Inst Riding &
Jumping
Specialities General instruction,
Novice children
Staff Chief Instructor Mrs Belinda
Crocker
Plus 3 full time instructors
Ave No 9 Horses, 9 Ponies
Courses WP, YT, Short, Ev, P/T, Hol
Facilities
Outdoor Manege 40 x 20 fl lt
Outdoor Manege 20 x 20 fl lt
Outdoor Manege 40 x 20 fl lt
SJ: Nov, 1 Paddock

Wait Rm
Hacking
Livery Full, P/T, Break, School
Schooling General, Break, to Nov Dress
Exclusions Wt Limit, 15st,
No casual hire
Location Between Bracknell and
Winkfield on A330

BUCKINGHAMSHIRE

AESCWOOD FARM
Rawlings Lane, Seer Green,
Buckinghamshire, HP9 2RQ
Tel 01494 875048
Contact Mr & Mrs Holbrook
Riding School Inst Basic
Specialities Children
Staff Chief Instructor Mrs M Campbell
Ave No 15 Ponies
Courses YT, Short, Ev, P/T, Hol
Facilities
Covered School 75 x 40
Outdoor Manege 24 x 14
Lec Rm, Vis Aids, Chng Rm, Wait Rm
Hacking
Exclusions Wt Limit, 12st, Age Limit, 3,
No casual hire
Location Jn 2 M40, 3 miles from
Beaconsfield town centre

BOUNDARY ROAD FARM
& RIDING SCHOOL
Boundary Road, Taplow,
Buckinghamshire, SL6 0EZ
Tel 01628 602869
Contact Mr Frederick James Morris
MBE
Riding School Inst Basic
Specialities Riding instruction for
children and nervous adults
Staff Chief Instructor Miss A Manning
Plus 1 full time instructor
Ave No 7 Horses, 13 Ponies
Courses YT, Short, Ev, P/T, Hol
Facilities
Outdoor Manege 20 x 40
SJ: Nov
Chng Rm, Wait Rm
Hacking
Exclusions No unescorted hacking

BRAWLINGS FARM
RIDING CENTRE
Brawlings Lane, Chalfonts, St Peter,
Bucks, SL9 0RE
Tel 01494 872132
Contact Mr & Mrs D G Edwards

Riding School, Training Centre Inst
Riding & Jumping
Specialities General instruction, RDA,
Riding Club
Staff Chief Instructor Mrs J A Edwards
(BHSII)
Plus 8 full time instructors
Ave No 15 Horses, 14 Ponies
Courses WP, P/T
Facilities
Covered School 20 x 40 gly
Outdoor Manege 20 x 60 fl lt
SJ: Nov, Grade C, 1 Paddock
CC: Course, Basic, Nov, Banks,
Natural
Lec Rm, Vis Aids, Chng Rm
Hacking
Livery Full, P/T, School
Schooling General, to El Dress, to SJ
GR C, to HT Nov
Exclusions Wt Limit, 12st7, Age Limit, 5,
No casual hiring
Location Chorleywood, Chalfonts

CORHAM STABLES
Sandpit Lane, Bledlow,
Aylesbury, Bucks, HP17 9QQ
Tel 01844 342119
Contact Mrs V J List
Riding School Inst Riding & Jumping
Specialities General instruction, Show
jumping, Livery, Hacking
2 full time instructors
Ave No 6 Horses, 10 Ponies
inc 2 SJ GR C
Courses WP, YT, Short, Ev, P/T, Hol
Facilities
Outdoor Manege 37 x 18 fl lt
SJ: Nov, Grade C, 1 Paddock
Lec Rm, Vis Aids, Chng Rm, Wait Rm
Hacking
Livery Full, P/T, Break, School, Hunt,
Grass
Schooling General, Break, to Nov
Dress, to SJ GR C, to SJ GR B
Exclusions Wt Limit, 16st, Age Limit, 3,
No unescorted hacking
Location Off B4009

HARTWELL RIDING STABLES
Oxford Road, Aylesbury,
Bucks, HP17 8NP
Tel 01296 748641
Contact Mr H Herring
Riding School Inst Riding & Jumping
Specialities General Instruction -
Children, Riding Club, Hacking
Staff Chief Instructor Miss D Smith
(BHSII)
Ave No 8 Horses, 8 Ponies
Courses YT, Ev, P/T

Facilities
Outdoor Manege 40 x 20 fl lt
Outdoor Manege 40 x 20 fl lt
SJ: Nov, 1 Paddock
CC: Course, Basic, Banks, Natural
Vis Aids, Chng Rm, Wait Rm
Livery Full, P/T, Break, School, Grass
Schooling General, Break, to Nov
Dress
Accom S, SC
Exclusions Wt Limit, 13st, Age Limit, 6
Location Just outside Aylesbury on
A418

**LOUGHTON MANOR
EQUESTRIAN CENTRE**
Redland Drive, Childs Way,
Loughton, Milton Keynes, MK5 8AZ
Tel 01908 666434
Contact Mr J P Mitchell
Riding School, Training Centre Inst
Riding & Jumping
Specialities General instruction,
Career students, Livery, Holiday
courses & Shows
Staff Chief Instructor Miss D Dye
(BHS Int.SM, BHS Int Teach)
Plus 1 full time instructor
Ave No 16 Horses, 16 Ponies
inc 3 Med Dress, 2 SJ GR C, 1 HT Int
Courses WP, YT, Short, Ev, P/T, Hol
Facilities
Covered School 30 x 15 gly
Outdoor Manege 20 x 55 fl lt
SJ: Nov, Grade A, 2 Paddock
CC: Course, Basic, Int, Banks, Water,
Natural
Lec Rm, Vis Aids, Wait Rm, Tack Shop
Hacking
Livery Full, P/T, Break, School
Schooling General, Break, to Med
Dress, to SJ GR C
Accom S, Tw, F, SC
Exclusions Wt Limit, 15st, Age Limit, 3,
No casual riding
Location Jn 14 off M1, 10 minutes
along Childs Way

LOWER FARM STABLES
Castle Road, Lavendon, Olney,
Buckinghamshire, MK46 4JG
Tel 01234 712692
Contact R A Gregory
Riding School, Training Centre Inst
Riding & Jumping
Staff Chief Instructor Miss K Gregory
(BHSII, BHS SM)
Ave No 7 Horses, 7 Ponies
inc 1 El Dress, 2 SJ GR C
Courses WP, Short, Ev, P/T, Hol
Facilities

Outdoor Manege 25 x 40 fl lt
SJ: Nov, Grade C, 2acre Paddock
CC: Banks, Natural, 6 Schooling
Lec Rm, Vis Aids, Chng Rm, Wait Rm
Hacking
Livery Full, P/T, Break, School, Hunt,
Grass
Schooling General, Break, to El Dress,
to SJ GR C
Accom S, FB
Exclusions Wt Limit, 13st, Age Limit, 5,
No casual hire
Location Jn 14 M1, off A428 between
Milton Keynes and Bedford

MECA RIDING CENTRE
Wooburn Common Road,
Wooburn Common,
High Wycombe, Bucks, HP10 0JS
Tel 01628 529666
Contact Mr & Mrs R Tickell
Riding School Inst to BHSAI
Specialities General instruction,chil-
dren,nervous adults,holiday courses
Staff Chief Instructor Mrs P Tickell
Plus 3 full time instructors
Ave No 13 Horses, 15 Ponies
inc 1 El Dress, 1 SJ GR C, 1 HT Int
Facilities
SJ: Grade C, 1 Paddock
CC: Natural, Gallops, 15 Schooling
Lec Rm, Vis Aids, Chng Rm, Wait Rm
Hacking
Livery Full, Grass
Exclusions Wt Limit, 15st, Age Limit, 6,
No casual hire - assessment lesson

RADNAGE HOUSE
RIDING SCHOOL
Green End Road, Radnage,
High Wycombe, Bucks, HP14 4BZ
Tel 01494 483268
Contact Mr & Mrs R H Pitt
Riding School, Training Centre,
Facility Centre Inst Riding & Jumping
Specialities Adult instruction & hacking
Staff Chief Instructor Miss A Strathdee
(BHSII)
Plus 2 full time instructors
Ave No 15 Horses
inc 1 Med Dress
Courses WP, Short, Ev, P/T, Hol
Facilities
Covered School 37 x 18 gly
Outdoor Manege 37 x 18 fl lt
SJ: Nov, 1 Paddock
CC: Course, Basic, Nov, Banks, Water,
Natural
Lec Rm, Vis Aids, Chng Rm
Hacking
Livery Full, Break, School, Hunt

Schooling General, Break, to El Dress,
to SJ GR C, to HT Nov
Accom SC
Exclusions Wt Limit, 12st7,
Age Limit, 12, No unescorted hacking
Location Chiltern Hills between High
Wycombe and Stonechurch

SHANA RIDING SCHOOL
New Road, Walters Ash,
High Wycombe, Bucks, HP14 4UZ
Tel 01494 562200/563449
Contact Mr R Huggard
Riding School, Training Centre,
Facility Centre Inst Basic
Specialities General instruction, shows
& holiday courses
Staff Chief Instructor Mrs J M Huggard
(BHSAI)
Plus 7 full time instructors
Ave No 18 Horses, 12 Ponies
inc 4 El Dress, 4 SJ GR C, Specialist
Instructional Courses
Courses WP, Ev, P/T, Hol
Facilities
Covered School 46 x 29 gly
Covered School 29 x 22
Outdoor Manege 20 x 40 fl lt
SJ: Nov, Grade C, 5 Paddock
CC: Course, Basic, Nov, Banks, Water,
Natural, 20 Schooling
Lec Rm, Vis Aids, Chng Rm, Showers,
Wait Rm, Tack Shop
Hacking
Livery Full, P/T, DIY, Break, School
Schooling General, Break, to Nov
Dress, to SJ GR C, to HT Nov
Accom S, Db, SC
Exclusions Wt Limit, 16st, Age Limit, 3,
No horse hire for hunting, all hacks
escorted
Location Between Naphill village and
RAF Strike Command, adjacent to
Bradenham and Lacey Green off A4010

SHARDELOES FARM
EQUESTRIAN CENTRE
Cherry Lane, Amersham,
Buckinghamshire, HP7 0QF
Tel 01494 432577
Contact Mr T Williams & Ms S King
Riding School, Facility Centre Inst
Basic
3 full time instructors
Ave No 6 Horses, 9 Ponies
Courses WP, Short, Ev, P/T, Hol
Facilities
Covered School 21 x 30
Outdoor Manege 25 x 65
SJ: Grade C, 1 Paddock
CC: Course, Basic, Natural, Gallops

Lec Rm, Vis Aids, Chng Rm, Showers, Wait Rm
Hacking
Livery Full, P/T, Break, School, Hunt, Grass
Schooling General, Break, to El Dress, to SJ GR C, to HT Adv
Exclusions Wt Limit, 14st, Age Limit, 5, No casual Hire. Compulsory back protectors
Location J18 M25 off A404 between Amersham and High Wycombe

**SNOWBALL FARM
EQUESTRIAN CENTRE**
Snowball Farm, Dorneywood Road, Burnham, Buckinghamshire, SL1 8EH
Tel 01628 666222
Contact Mrs S Western-Kaye
Riding School, Training Centre Inst Riding & Jumping
Specialities General instruction, Livery, Hacking and Shows
4 full time instructors
Ave No 15 Horses, 15 Ponles
Courses WP, Short, Ev, P/T, Hol
Facilities
Covered School 55 x 25 gly
Covered School 49 x 25
Outdoor Manege 20 x 40 fl lt
SJ: Nov, 1 Paddock
CC: Course, Basic, Nov, Banks, Water, Natural, 40 Schooling
Vis Aids, Chng Rm, Wait Rm, Tack Shop
Hacking
Livery Full, P/T, Break, School, Grass
Schooling General, to HT Nov
Accom S, Tw, Caravan, Cottage, SC
Exclusions Wt Limit, 14st,
No casual hire
Location Between M4 Jn 7 and M40 Jn 2 north of Burnham

STOWE RIDINGS
Blackpit Farm, Silverstone Road, Stowe, Bucks, MK18 5LJ
Tel 01280 812363
Contact Mr & Mrs P W Wheeler
Riding School, Training Centre, Facility Centre Inst Riding & Jumping
6 full time instructors
Ave No 16 Horses, 16 Ponies
inc 3 Med Dress, 4 SJ GR C
Courses WP, YT, Short, Ev, P/T, Hol
Facilities
Covered School 30 x 67 gly
Outdoor Manege 60 x 40 fl lt
Outdoor Manege 40 x 20 fl lt
SJ: Nov, 1 Paddock
CC: Course, Nov, Banks, Water,

Gallops, 35 Schooling
Lec Rm, Vis Aids, Chng Rm, Wait Rm
Hacking
Livery Full, P/T, Break, School, Hunt
Schooling General, Break, to Med Dress, to SJ GR C
Accom Tw, Dor, Cottage, FB
Exclusions Wt Limit, 15st, Age Limit, 5, No casual hire
Location Off the A43 at Silverstone, between Dadford and Silverstone Circuit

TUDOR STUD
Chinnor Road, Bledlow Ridge, Nr High Wycombe,
Buckinghamshire, HP14 4AE
Tel 01494 481324
Contact Ms Sandra Barr
Riding School Inst Basic
Specialities General instruction, livery, hacking & Dressage
Staff Chief Instructor Ms Sandra Barr Plus 1 full time instructor
Ave No 7 Horses, 12 Ponies
inc General Purpose
Courses WP, Short, Ev, P/T
Facilities
Covered School 35 x 20
SJ: Nov
Lec Rm, Vis Aids, Wait Rm
Hacking
Livery Full, P/T, Break, School, Hunt
Schooling General, Break, to Nov Dress, to Med Dress, to SJ GR C
Exclusions Wt Limit, 13st, Age Limit, 5, All rides escorted
Location On A40, 1 mile from Jn 5 of M40

HAMPSHIRE

ARNISS RIDING & LIVERY STABLES
Godshill, Fordingbridge, Hampshire
Tel 01425 654114
Contact Miss A Finn
Riding School, RDA Inst Basic
Staff Chief Instructor Miss A Finn (BHSAI)
Ave No 10 Horses, 10 Ponies
Facilities
Outdoor Manege 20 x 40 fl lt
Outdoor Manege 60 x 60
SJ: Nov
Chng Rm, Wait Rm
Hacking
Livery Full, P/T, Break, School, Grass
Schooling General, Break
Exclusions Wt Limit, 16st, Age Limit, 5
Location On B3078

BROADLANDS RIDING CENTRE
Lower Paice Lane, Medstead,
Alton, Hampshire, GU34 5PX
Tel 01420 563382
Contact Mrs S M Stratford
Riding School, Training Centre, RDA
Inst Riding & Jumping
Specialities Career training and
Childrens Holiday courses
Staff Chief Instructor Mrs S M Stratford
(BHSAI)
Plus 1 full time instructor
Ave No 4 Horses, 8 Ponies
Courses WP, YT, Short, P/T, Hol
Facilities
Covered School 32 x 18
SJ: Nov, 1 Paddock
CC: Basic, Natural
Lec Rm, Vis Aids, Chng Rm
Livery Full, Break, School
Schooling General, to Nov Dress, to
HT Nov
Accom Tw, FB
Exclusions Wt Limit, 11st, Age Limit, 9,
No casual hire
Location Between Alton and Alresford,
off A31

BROCKS FARM
LIVERY & RIDING CENTRE
Brocks Farm, Longstock,
Stockbridge, Hampshire, SO20 6DF
Tel 01264 810090
Contact Mrs & Miss J & L Burtenshaw
Riding School, Training Centre Inst
Riding & Jumping
Staff Chief Instructor Mrs P Teggin
(BHSII)
Ave No 9 Horses, 12 Ponies
inc 1 El Dress, 4 Med Dress, 2 Adv
Dress, 3 SJ GR C, Ponies working at
medium - advanced
Facilities
Outdoor Manege 60 x 20 fl lt
SJ: Nov, Grade C, 1 Paddock
CC: 8 Schooling
Vis Aids
Hacking
Livery Full, Break, School
Schooling General, Break, to Adv
Dress, to SJ GR C, to HT Nov
Exclusions Wt Limit, 14st, Age Limit, 4,
No casual hire
Location Test Valley

BURLEY-VILLA
EQUESTRIAN CENTRE
Bashley Common Road,
New Milton, Hampshire, BH25 5SM
Tel 01425 610278
Contact Miss P M E Carter-Pennington

Riding School, Western Riding Inst
Riding & Jumping
Specialities Western style trail riding in
the New Forest
1 full time instructor
Ave No 10 Horses, 10 Ponies
inc 1 El Dress, 1 SJ GR C, 1 SJ Jun C,
1 SJ Jun A
Courses WP, YT, Short, Ev, P/T, Hol
Facilities
Covered School 55 x 21 gly
Outdoor Manege 40 x 20 fl lt
SJ: Nov, Grade A, 1 Paddock
CC: Banks
Lec Rm, Vis Aids, Chng Rm, Showers,
Wait Rm
Hacking
Livery Full, P/T, DIY, Break, School,
Hunt
Schooling General, Break, to El Dress,
to SJ GR A
Accom S, Tw, Db, F, FB
Exclusions Wt Limit, 16st, Age Limit, 3,
No unescorted riders
Location On B3058 north of New Milton

CATHERSTON STUD
Manor Farm, Hurstbourne Priors,
Whitchurch, Hampshire, RG28 7SE
Tel 01256 892045
Contact Mrs A G Loriston-Clarke
**Training Centre, Facility Centre,
Livery, Stud & show centre** Inst all
BHS
Staff Chief Instructor Mrs Jennie
Loriston-Clarke FBHS (FBHS)
Plus 5 full time instructors
Ave No 15 Horses, 2 Ponies
inc 2 El Dress, 2 Med Dress, 2 Adv
Dress, 2 SJ GR C, 2 SJ GR B,
2 SJ Jun C, 4 HT Int, 1 Side Saddle &
2 Racehorses
Courses WP, YT, Short, Ev, Hol
Facilities
Covered School 60 x 26 gly
Covered School 34 x 17
Outdoor Manege 60 x 28
SJ: Nov, Grade C, Grade B, Grade A
CC: Banks, Water, Natural, Gallops,
10 Schooling
Lec Rm, Vis Aids, Chng Rm, Showers,
Wait Rm
Livery Full, P/T, Break, School, Hunt,
Grass
Schooling General, Break, to Adv
Dress, to SJ GR A, to HT Adv
Accom S, Tw, Cottage, FB, SC
Exclusions Wt Limit, 11st, Age Limit, 16,
Private lessons on clients' horses only
Location On B3400 between
Whitchurch & Andover. Easy access
from A34 & A303

117

**FIR TREE FARM
EQUESTRIAN CENTRE**
Ogdens, Fordingbridge,
Hants, SP6 2PY
Tel 01425 654744
Contact Mr & Mrs K Simmonds
Riding School Inst Riding & Jumping
1 full time instructor
Ave No 9 Horses, 8 Ponies
Courses WP, YT, Short, Ev, P/T
Facilities
Outdoor Manege 20 x 60 fl lt
SJ: Nov
Hacking
Livery Full, P/T, Break, School
Schooling General, Break, to El
Dress, to Med Dress
Exclusions Wt Limit, 15st, Age Limit, 4,
No unaccompanied hacks
Location 2 miles from Fordingbridge.
Off the A388 to Hyde, Ogdens is on the
edge of the New Forest

**FLANDERS FARM
RIDING CENTRE**
Silver Street, Hordle,
Lymington, Hants, SO4 6DF
Tel 01590 682207
Contact Mr & Mrs Driver
**Riding School, Training Centre,
Driving - wedding, funerals, forest
drives** Inst Riding & Jumping
Staff Chief Instructor Mrs T S J
McIntyre (BHSAI)
Plus 1 full time instructor
Ave No 10 Horses, 10 Ponies
Courses WP, YT, Short, P/T, Hol
Facilities
Covered School 18 x 43
Outdoor Manege 20 x 40
SJ: Nov, 1 Paddock
CC: Course, Basic
Lec Rm, Vis Aids, Chng Rm, Wait Rm
Hacking
Livery Full, P/T, Break, School, Hunt,
Grass
Schooling General, Break, to Nov
Dress, to SJ GR C
Exclusions Wt Limit, 16st,
No casual, appointments only
Location Between Lymington and New
Milton

**FORT WIDLEY
EQUESTRIAN CENTRE**
Portsdown Hill Road, Cosham,
Portsmouth, PO6 3LS
Tel 01705 324553
Contact Ms Joanne Barringer
Riding School Inst Riding & Jumping
Specialities Instruction in riding and

jumping, childrens' activities
Ave No 15 Horses, 15 Ponies
Courses Short, Ev, P/T, Hol
Facilities
Covered School 40 x 20
Outdoor Manege 20 x 40
Lec Rm, Vis Aids, Chng Rm, Showers,
Wait Rm
Hacking
Livery Full, P/T, DIY, Grass
Schooling General
Accom Dor, FB
Exclusions Wt Limit, 17st,
No unescorted rides
Location 4 miles from Portsmouth city
centre

**GLENEAGLE
EQUESTRIAN CENTRE**
Allington Lane, West End,
Southampton,
Hampshire, SO3 3HQ
Tel 01703 473164/473370
Contact Mrs D K Day
**Riding School, Training Centre,
Facility Centre, Hunting Hire-Rescue
& Rehabilitation Centre** Inst Riding &
Jumping
Staff Chief Instructor Mrs D K Day
Plus 5 full time instructors
Ave No 10 Horses, 10 Ponies
inc 1 SJ GR C, 4 Cross Country
Courses WP, YT, Short, Ev, P/T, Hol
Facilities
Outdoor Manege 160 x 80 fl lt
Outdoor Manege 40 x 24
SJ: Nov, 1 Paddock
CC: Course, Basic, Nov, Int, Banks,
Natural, Gallops, 26 Schooling
Lec Rm, Vis Aids, Chng Rm, Wait Rm,
Tack Shop
Hacking
Livery Full, P/T, DIY, Break, School,
Hunt, Grass
Schooling General, Break, to Nov
Dress, to HT Nov
Accom S, Tw, Db, FB
Exclusions Wt Limit, 16st, Age Limit, 4
Location Off old A27, between West
End and Durley

**HORSESHOE CENTRE
FOR HANDICAPPED RIDERS**
Picketts Hill, Headley,
Nr Borden, Hampshire, GU35 8TB
Tel 01428 713858
Contact Mr & Mrs C W Turner
**Riding School, Disabled and
handicapped riders** Inst Basic
Location Off A325 between Borden
and Farnham

INADOWN FARM LIVERY STABLES
Newton Valence, Alton,
Hampshire, GU34 3RB
Tel 01420 588439
Contact Mrs F Janson
Riding School Inst Riding & Jumping
Specialities In house Riding Club
Staff Chief Instructor Miss F McDonand
(BHSII, BHS SM)
Ave No 6 Horses, 16 Ponies
inc 1 SJ GR C
Facilities
Outdoor Manege 20 x 60
SJ: Nov
Chng Rm
Hacking
Livery Full, P/T, DIY, School, Grass
Schooling General, to Nov Dress, to
SJ GR C, to HT Nov
Exclusions Wt Limit, 14st, Age Limit, 3,
No casual hire, no hunting hire
Location Off A32, 2 miles south of
Alton

MERRIE STUD RIDING SCHOOL
Corhampton Farm, Corhampton,
Southampton, SO3 3NB
Tel 01489 877564
Contact Mrs J D N Shaw
Riding School, Training Centre, stud
Inst Riding & Jumping
Staff Chief Instructor Mrs J D N Shaw
(BHSAI)
Plus 1 full time instructor
Ave No 14 Ponies
inc 1 El Dress
Courses WP, YT, Short, Ev, P/T, Hol
Facilities
Covered School 9 x 12
Outdoor Manege 40 x 20 fl lt
SJ: Nov
CC: Course, Basic, Nov, Banks, Water,
Natural
Chng Rm, Wait Rm
Hacking
Livery Full, P/T, DIY, Break, School,
Hunt, Grass
Schooling General, Break, to El Dress,
to HT Nov
Accom Tw
Exclusions Wt Limit, 11st7, Age Limit, 6,
No casual hire
Location On B3035 just off A32 by
Corhampton roundabout

THE NAVAL RIDING CENTRE
HMS Dryad, Southwick,
Nr Fareham, Hampshire, PO17 6EJ
Tel 01705 379974
Contact Cdr B W Holden-Crawford,
Mr G Passmore

Riding School, Training Centre Inst to
BHSI
Specialities Career training
Staff Chief Instructor Mr A Noordijk (BHSI)
Plus 11 full time instructors
Ave No 25 Horses, 15 Ponies
inc 5 El Dress, 1 Med Dress, 1 Adv
Dress, 8 SJ GR C, 2 SJ Jun C
Courses WP, YT, Short, Ev, P/T, Hol
Facilities
Covered School 65 x 25
Covered School 45 x 20
Outdoor Manege 50 x 65
SJ: Nov, Grade C, Grade B, 1 Paddock
CC: Course, Basic, Nov, Water, Natural
Lec Rm, Vis Aids, Chng Rm, Wait Rm
Hacking
Livery Full, Break
Schooling General, Break, to Med
Dress, to SJ GR C, to HT Nov
Exclusions Age Limit, 5, No casual hire.
No hunting
Location 10 minutes from exit 11 on
M27

NEW PARK MANOR & STABLES
Lyndhurst Road, Brockenhurst,
Hampshire, SO42 7QH
Tel 01590 623919
Contact Miss A Lawson
Riding School Inst Riding & Jumping
Specialities Flexible service to cus-
tomers. Pub or picnic rides plus special
offers on lessons for regular clients
Staff Chief Instructor Miss A Lawson
(BHSAI)
Plus 1 full time instructor
Ave No 7 Horses, 3 Ponies
inc 4 El Dress
Courses WP, Short, Ev, P/T, Hol
Facilities
Outdoor Manege 20 x 40
CC: Basic
Chng Rm, Wait Rm
Hacking
Livery Full, P/T, DIY, Break, School,
Hunt, Grass
Schooling General, Break, to Nov Dress
Accom S, Tw, Db, F, FB
Exclusions Wt Limit, 14st, Age Limit, 3,
Road work
Location On A337 between
Brockenhurst and Lyndhurst. Direct
access onto New Forest

QUEEN ELIZABETH COUNTRY PARK RIDING
Gravel Hill, Horndean,
Waterlooville, Hampshire, PO8 0QE
Tel 01705 599669
Contact Mrs S Binder & Mrs J Whatley

Riding School Inst Basic
Specialities Endurance riders and their horses are welcome for fittening. Extensive hacking as small groups or individuals through spectacular countryside with access to the South Downs bridleways, including trail riding holidays
Staff Chief Instructor Mrs S Binder (BHSAI)
Plus 1 full time instructor
Ave No 11 Horses
Courses Short, Ev, P/T
Lec Rm, Vis Aids
Hacking
Exclusions Wt Limit, 13,
No unescorted hacking
Location Off A3, 4 miles south of Petersfield

QUOB STABLES
Church Croft Farm, Durley Brook Road, Durley, Southampton, SO32 2AR
Tel 01703 694657
Contact Mrs E Davies
Riding School Inst Riding & Jumping
Specialities Instruction in riding & jumping
Ave No 7 Horses, 9 Ponies
Courses WP, Short, Ev, P/T, Hol
Facilities
Outdoor Manege 30 x 50 fl lt
SJ: Nov, 2 Paddock
Chng Rm, Showers, Wait Rm
Hacking
Livery Full, P/T, School, Hunt
Schooling General
Exclusions No unescorted hacking
Location Between West End and Durley near Jn / off M27

RUSSELL EQUESTRIAN CENTRE
Black Farm Gaters Hill, Westend, Southampton, Hampshire, SO3 3HT
Tel 01703 473693
Contact Mrs C A Boulton
Riding School, Training Centre, RDA
Inst Riding & Jumping
Staff Chief Instructor Mrs W Dalton (BHSAI)
Ave No 10 Horses, 10 Ponies
Courses WP, YT, Ev, P/T, Hol
Facilities
Outdoor Manege 25 x 25 fl lt
Outdoor Manege 23 x 43 fl lt
SJ: Grade C, Grade B, Grade A, 1 Paddock
CC: Course, Basic, Banks, Water, Natural, Gallops
Lec Rm, Vis Aids, Wait Rm
Hacking
Livery P/T, DIY, Break, School, Grass

Schooling General, Break, to Nov Dress, to SJ GR C, to HT Nov
Accom Caravan, SC
Exclusions Wt Limit, 13st, Age Limit, 2 1/2, No casual hacking - assessment first

✳ RYCROFT SCHOOL OF EQUITATION
New Mill Lane, Eversley, Hampshire, RG27 0RA
Tel 01189 732761
Contact Mr & Mrs W Hundley
Riding School, Training Centre, Facility Centre Inst to BHSAI
Specialities Career training
Staff Chief Instructor Mrs Fiona Hunter-Inglis (BHSI)
Plus 5 full time instructors
Ave No 35 Horses, 10 Ponies
inc 2 Med Dress, 2 SJ GR C, 1 SJ GR B, 1 SJ GR A, 2 HT Int, 10 Scurry Ponies (5 pairs)
Courses WP, YT, Short, Ev, P/T, Hol
Facilities
Covered School 50 x 25 gly
Outdoor Manege 70 x 30
Outdoor Manege 40 x 20
SJ: Nov, Grade C, Grade B, Grade A, 1 Paddock
CC: Course, Nov, Banks, Water, Natural
Lec Rm, Vis Aids, Chng Rm, Wait Rm, Tack Shop
Hacking
Livery Full, P/T, Break, School, Hunt
Schooling General, Break, to El Dress, to SJ GR C, to SJ GR B, to SJ GR A, to HT Nov, to HT Int
Accom S, Tw, Db
Exclusions Wt Limit, 12st, No casual hire
Location Off the A327 between Reading & Farnborough

SCHOOL FARM EQUESTRIAN
School Farm Equestrian Centre, Romsey Road, Lockerley, Hants, SO51 0JA
Tel 01794 341196
Contact Miss Kay Waterman
Training Centre, Facility Centre, Livery
Specialities Dressage training
2 full time instructors
Courses WP, YT, Short, Ev, P/T, Hol
Facilities
Covered School 20 x 60
Outdoor Manege 20 x 60 fl lt
SJ: Nov, Grade C, Grade B, 1 Paddock
CC: Course, Basic, Nov, Banks, Natural

Lec Rm, Vis Aids
Hacking
Livery Full, P/T, DIY, Break, School, Hunt, Grass
Schooling General, Break, to Adv Dress, to SJ GR C, to HT Int
Accom S, Cottage, SC
Exclusions No casual hire, not a Riding School

SHERECROFT FARM EQUESTRIAN CENTRE & PINKMEAD FARM EQUESTRIAN
Mill Hill, Botley,
Southampton, Hampshire, SO30 2GY
Tel 01489 783087
Contact Ms Stephene King
Riding School Inst Riding & Jumping
Specialities Courses tailored to individual needs, with exam training to BHSAI
Staff Chief Instructor Mrs S King (BHSII) Plus 3 full time instructors
Ave No 2 Horses, 13 Ponies
Courses WP, YT, Short, Ev, P/T, Hol
Facilities
Outdoor Manege 20 x 40 fl lt
SJ: Grade C, 1 Paddock
CC: Course, Nov, Banks, Water, Natural
Chng Rm
Hacking
Livery Full, P/T, DIY, Break, School, Hunt
Schooling General, Break, to Nov Dress, to SJ GR C, to HT Nov
Exclusions Wt Limit, 13st, Age Limit, 4, No unescorted hacking
Location Near to Botley Station on A344

SPARSHOLT COLLEGE
Winchester,
Hampshire, SO21 2NF
Tel 01962 776441/776895
Contact Mr T D Jackson
Training Centre Inst to BHSAI
Specialities Career Student training
Staff Chief Instructor Miss K Hampshire (BHSII) Plus 3 full time instructors
Ave No 17 Horses, 3 Ponies
Facilities
Outdoor Manege 30 x 60 fl lt
SJ: Nov
Lec Rm, Vis Aids
Hacking
Livery Break
Exclusions All riding under instruction
Location On A272 between Stockbridge and Winchester

STOCKBRIDGE RIDING SCHOOL
Winton Hill, Stockbridge,
Hants, SO20 6HN
Tel 01264 810727
Contact Mr & Mrs J H Wrayton
Riding School Inst Basic
Staff Chief Instructor Mr J H Wrayton
Ave No 9 Horses, 3 Ponies
Courses Hol
Facilities
Outdoor Manege 40 x 20 fl lt
Outdoor Manege 40 x 60 fl lt
SJ: Nov, 1 Paddock
CC: Natural, Gallops, 5 Schooling
Lec Rm, Vis Aids, Chng Rm, Showers, Wait Rm
Hacking
Livery Full, Break, School, Hunt
Schooling General, Break, to Nov Dress
Accom Tw, FB
Exclusions Wt Limit, 13st, Age Limit, 6
Location On the A272 between Stockbridge & Winchester

WELLINGTON EQUESTRIAN EDUCATION WELLINGTON RIDING
Basingstoke Road,
Heckfield, Hook,
Hampshire, RG27 0LJ
Tel 0118 932 6308
Contact Mr J Goodman
Riding School, Training Centre, Competition yard/Riding vacations.
Inst to BHSI
Specialities Career training
5 full time instructors
Ave No 48 Horses, 40 Ponies inc 2 Adv Dress, 1 SJ GR C, 1 HT Adv
Courses WP, YT, Short, Ev, P/T, Hol
Facilities
Covered School 41 x 20 gly
Outdoor Manege 20 x 60 fl lt
Outdoor Manege 60 x 30 fl lt
Outdoor Manege 25 x 15
Outdoor Manege 60 x 40
Outdoor Manege 25 x 20
SJ: Nov, Grade C, Grade B, 1 Paddock
CC: Course, Basic, Nov, Int, Banks, Water, Gallops, 40 Schooling
Lec Rm, Vis Aids, Chng Rm, Wait Rm, Tack Shop
Hacking
Livery Full, Break, School, Grass
Schooling General, Break, to Adv Dress, to SJ GR A, to HT Adv
Accom Tw, Dor, FB
Exclusions Wt Limit, 14st
Location On A33 between Reading and Basingstoke

ISLE OF WIGHT

BRICKFIELDS
EQUESTRIAN CENTRE
Newham Road, Binstead,
Nr Ryde, Isle of Wight, PO33 3TH
Tel 01983 566801/615116
Contact Mrs P Legge
Riding School, Training Centre,
Facility Centre, Trekking Centre,
Shire Horse/Miniature Pony Tourist
Centre Inst Basic
3 full time instructors
Ave No 20 Horses, 22 Ponies
iinc 1 El Dress, 1 Med Dress, 1 SJ GR C,
1 SJ GR B, 1 SJ Jun C, 1 HT Int
Courses WP, YT, Short
Facilities
Covered School 49 x 28 gly
Outdoor Manege 55 x 30 fl lt
Outdoor Manege 60 x 30
Outdoor Manege 80 x 100
SJ: Nov, 1 Paddock
Lec Rm, Vis Aids, Chng Rm, Wait Rm,
Tack Shop
Hacking
Livery Full, P/T, DIY, Break, School,
Hunt
Schooling General, Break
Exclusions Wt Limit, 16st
Location Off A3054 signed to Shire
Centre

OXFORDSHIRE

THE ASTI STUD & SADDLERY
Millaway Farm, Goosey,
Nr Faringdon, Oxon, SN7 8PA
Tel 01367 710288
Contact Mrs R Rowland
Riding School, Training Centre,
Facility Centre Inst Basic
Specialities One to one lessons for
children and nervous adults
Staff Chief Instructor Mrs P Hintz
(BHSAI)
Ave No 3 Horses, 4 Ponies
inc 1 SJ GR C, 1 SJ Jun C
Courses WP, Hol
Facilities
Outdoor Manege 20 x 40 fl lt
SJ: Grade C, 1 Paddock
CC: Course, Basic, Water, Natural
Lec Rm, Vis Aids, Chng Rm, Showers,
Wait Rm, Tack Shop
Hacking
Livery Full, P/T, DIY, Break, School,
Hunt, Grass
Schooling General, Break, to Nov
Dress, to SJ GR C, to HT Int

Exclusions Wt Limit, 14st, Age Limit, 3,
No casual hire
Location Between Wantage and
Farringdon off the A417

COTSWOLD TRAINING CENTRE
93 Shilton Road, Carterton,
Oxon, OX18 1EN
Tel 01993 842262
Contact Mrs C A Hogg
Training Centre, Facility Centre,
Livery
Specialities Career Students,
Courses, Competition Livery
Staff Chief Instructor Mrs C A Hogg
(BHSAI, BHS Int Teach)
Plus 1 full time instructor
Courses WP, YT, Short, Ev, P/T
Facilities
Outdoor Manege 60 x 30 fl lt
SJ: Nov, Grade C, Grade B, 1 Paddock
CC: Course, Basic, Nov, Banks,
Water, Natural, 17 Schooling
Lec Rm, Vis Aids, Chng Rm, Showers
Livery Full, P/T, DIY, School, Hunt
Schooling General, to Med Dress, to
SJ GR C, to HT Nov
Accom S, Tw, FB
Exclusions No casual hiring
Location On B4020 off A40, Burford,
midway between Oxford and
Cheltenham

EWELME PARK STABLE YARD
Ewelme Park, Park Corner, Nettlebed,
Henley, Oxon, RG9 6DZ
Tel 01491 642273
Contact Mrs B Chen
Livery
Specialities First class off road
hacking and a personal service
Ave No 18 Horses
Facilities
Outdoor Manege 22 x 41
Chng Rm, Wait Rm
Livery Full, P/T
Location J5 M40, 5 miles from
Henley-on-Thames

MANNANAN STABLES
The Coach House, Rosehill,
Henley-on-Thames, Oxon, RG9 3EB
Tel 01628 824078
Contact Mrs P R Stacey
Facility Centre, Livery
Specialities High quality livery service
and schooling facilities for hire
Staff Chief Instructor Mrs P R Stacey
(BHSAI)
Plus 1 full time instructor

Facilities
Outdoor Manege 60 x 20 fl lt
Outdoor Manege 60 x 20
Outdoor Manege 40 x 20
SJ: Grade C, 1 Paddock
CC: Course, Int, Banks, Water, Natural, Gallops
Hacking
Livery Full, P/T, DIY, School, Grass
Exclusions No horses for hire
Location On A4130 between Henley & Maidenhead

NEW HOUSE LIVERY
New House Farm, Hanney Road,
Southmoor, Abingdon,
Oxon, OX13 5HR
Tel 01865 821180
Contact Mrs P S Blanchard
Livery
Specialities All types of livery service. Facilities for hire. Creche. Pony Club Camps
Ave No 10 Horses, 10 Ponies
Facilities
Outdoor Manege 60 x 20
SJ: Nov, 5acr Paddock
CC: Banks, Water, Natural, 10 Schooling
Lec Rm, Vis Aids, Chng Rm, Showers
Hacking
Livery Full, P/T, DIY, School, Hunt, Grass
Schooling General, to SJ GR C
Accom FB
Exclusions No casual hiring
Location Off A420 near Kingston Bagpuize near Abingdon, Didcot, Wantage & Faringdon

OAKFIELD RIDING SCHOOL
Great Coxwell, Faringdon,
Oxon, SN7 7LU
Tel 01367 240126
Contact Mr D C Farrow
Riding School Inst Riding & Jumping
Specialities Specialising in teaching nervous novice adults
Staff Chief Instructor Miss M A Goodwin
Plus 3 full time instructors
Ave No 14 Horses, 13 Ponies
Courses WP, Short, Ev, P/T
Facilities
Outdoor Manege 20 x 40
SJ: Nov, 1 Paddock
CC: Banks, Water, Natural, 6 Schooling
Lec Rm, Vis Aids
Hacking
Schooling General
Exclusions Wt Limit, 15st, Age Limit, 4

STANDLAKE EQUESTRIAN CENTRE
Downs Road, Standlake,
Witney,
Oxfordshire, OX8 9UH
Tel 01865 300099
Contact Mr & Mrs Pillans
Riding School, Training Centre, Facility Centre Inst Basic
Specialities Absolute novices and nature trail rides. Saddle seat equitation up to advanced level. Also writer of The Biblical approach to Horsemanship
Staff Chief Instructor Mrs Suzanne Pillans (BHSAI)
Ave No 4 Horses, 6 Ponies
inc 3 El Dress
Courses WP, YT, Short, Ev, P/T, Hol
Facilities
Covered School 37 x 18 gly
SJ: Nov, 1 Paddock
CC: Course, Basic, Banks, Water, Natural, Gallops
Lec Rm, Vis Aids, Chng Rm, Showers, Wait Rm
Hacking
Livery Full, P/T, DIY, Break, School
Schooling General, Break, to El Dress
Exclusions Age Limit, 4, No casual hire
Location Off A415 1 mile from Standlake village

TURVILLE VALLEY STUD
Turville,
Henley-on-Thames,
Oxon, RG9 6QU
Tel 01491 638338
Contact Mrs A Fois
Riding School, Training Centre, Classical Riding. Lusitano Stud Inst Riding & Jumping
Specialities Classical Riding, Career Students, Stud. General Instruction, Camps & Holiday Courses
Staff Chief Instructor Mrs A Fois
Plus 1 full time instructor
Ave No 7 Horses, 15 Ponies
inc 3 El Dress, 2 Med Dress, 4 Adv Dress, Classical Dressage
Courses WP, Short, P/T, Hol
Facilities
Outdoor Manege 20 x 40 fl lt
Outdoor Manege 25 x 50
Lec Rm, Vis Aids, Chng Rm, Wait Rm
Hacking
Schooling General, to Adv Dress
Accom Cottage, SC
Exclusions Wt Limit, 11st7, Age Limit, 2, No hunting or unescorted hacks, No Adult beginners
Location 4 miles from Jn 5 of M40

**VALLEY FARM
EQUESTRIAN CENTRE**
Shotteswell, Nr Banbury,
Oxon, OX17 1HZ
Tel 01295 730576
Contact Mrs D A Faulkner
Riding School Inst Riding & Jumping
Specialities General instruction -
hacking - livery - summer camps
Staff Chief Instructor Mrs S Ellard (BHSII)
Plus 2 full time instructors
Ave No 12 Horses, 12 Ponies
Courses WP, Short, Ev, P/T, Hol
Facilities
Covered School 24 x 46 gly
Outdoor Manege 20 x 40 fl lt
SJ: Nov
CC: 5 Schooling
Lec Rm, Vis Aids, Wait Rm
Hacking
Livery Full, P/T, Break, School
Schooling General, Break, to Nov
Dress
Exclusions Wt Limit, 15st,
No casual hire
Location 3 miles north of Banbury,
close to M40

**WATERSTOCK HOUSE
TRAINING CENTRE**
Waterstock, Nr Oxford,
Oxfordshire, OX33 1JS
Tel 01844 339616
Contact Mr & Mrs J Walker
Riding School, Training Centre Inst
Riding & Jumping
Specialities Instruction at all levels.
Training for competition. Schooling &
breaking
Staff Chief Instructor Mr Mark Smith
Ave No 6 Horses
inc 1 SJ GR C, 1 SJ GR B
Courses WP, Short, P/T, Hol
Facilities
Covered School 20 x 40
Outdoor Manege 80 x 35
SJ: Nov, Grade A, 1 Paddock
CC: Basic, Nov, Int, Adv, Banks, Water,
Natural, 20 Schooling
Lec Rm, Vis Aids, Chng Rm, Wait Rm,
Tack Shop
Livery Full, Break, School, Grass
Schooling General, Break, to El Dress,
to SJ GR A, to I IT Adv
Accom S, Tw, F, Dor, FB
Exclusions Wt Limit, 11st, Age Limit, 13
Location 2 miles from Jn 7 of M40;
7 miles east of Oxford, 50 miles west of
London

Riding in the South West

AVON ◆ CORNWALL ◆ DEVON ◆ DORSET
GLOUCESTERSHIRE ◆ SOMERSET
WILTSHIRE

AVON

AVON RIDING CENTRE FOR THE DISABLED
Kings Weston Road, Henbury,
Nr Bristol, BS10 7QT
Tel 0117 959 0266
Contact Mrs B Grant
Riding School, Training Centre, Riding for the Disabled Inst Riding & Jumping
3 full time instructors
Ave No 12 Horses, 16 Ponies
Courses YT, Short, Ev, P/T, Hol
Facilities
Covered School 56 x 26 gly
Outdoor Manege 40 x 20 fl lt
SJ: Nov, Grade C, 1 Paddock
CC: Course, Basic, Natural, Gallops, 20 Schooling
Lec Rm, Vis Aids, Chng Rm
Hacking
Livery Break, School
Schooling General, Break, to Nov Dress
Exclusions Wt Limit, 12st, Age Limit, 7, Hacking only for competent or accompanied riders

CLEVEDON RIDING CENTRE
Clevedon Lane, Clevedon,
Avon, BS21 7AG
Tel 01275 858699
Contact R A & J A Sims
Riding School Inst Riding & Jumping
Staff Chief Instructor Miss S Sims (BHSAI)
Ave No 9 Horses, 5 Ponies

Courses WP, YT
Facilities
Outdoor Manege 40 x 80 fl lt
SJ: Nov, Grade C, 1 Paddock
CC: Course, Basic, Nov
Wait Rm
Hacking
Livery Full, Grass
Schooling General, Break
Exclusions Wt Limit, 16st,
No casual hire
Location Off B3124, between Clevedon and Portishead

HARTLEY WOOD RIDING CENTRE
King Lane, Clutton Hill,
Clutton, Bristol, Avon, BS18 4QQ
Tel 01761 452063
Contact Mrs R Withey
Riding School, Training Centre Inst Riding & Jumping
Staff Chief Instructor Mrs R Withey (BHSII)
Plus 3 full time instructors
Ave No 17 Horses, 8 Ponies
Courses WP, Short, Ev, P/T, Hol
Facilities
Outdoor Manege 24 x 48 fl lt
Outdoor Manege 25 x 50
SJ: Nov, 1 Paddock
CC: Course, Nov, Banks, Water, Natural
Lec Rm, Vis Aids, Wait Rm
Hacking
Livery Full, P/T, Break, School, Hunt, Grass
Schooling General, Break, to Nov Dress, to SJ GR C, to HT Nov
Exclusions Wt Limit, 15st, Age Limit, 4
Location 10 miles from Bath, Bristol and Wells off A37 or A39

KINGSWESTON STABLES
Kingsweston Road, Bristol,
BS11 0UX
Tel 01179 828929
Contact Mr R Slaughter
Riding School Inst Riding & Jumping
Staff Chief Instructor Mrs H McEwan-Smith (BHSAI)
Ave No 6 Horses, 10 Ponies
Facilities
Outdoor Manege 25 x 37
SJ: Nov
CC: Basic, Natural, 9 Schooling
Chng Rm
Hacking
Livery Full, P/T, DIY, Grass
Schooling General
Exclusions Wt Limit, 12st,
No casual hire, all rides escorted
Location 4 miles north west from
centre of Bristol

LEYLAND COURT
RIDING SCHOOL
Trench Lane, Northwoods,
Winterbourne, Bristol, BS36 1RY
Tel 01454 773163
Contact Mr M D Irish
Livery
Staff Chief Instructor Mrs A J Irish
(BHSAI)
Plus 1 full time instructor
Ave No 7 Horses, 10 Ponies
Courses WP
Facilities
Outdoor Manege 90 x 50 fl lt
SJ: Nov
CC: Course, Basic, Natural,
22 Schooling
Lec Rm, Vis Aids, Chng Rm, Wait Rm,
Tack Shop
Hacking
Livery Full, P/T, DIY, Break, School,
Hunt, Grass
Schooling General, Break
Exclusions Wt Limit, 18st, Age Limit, 4,
No beginners or novice riders for
hacking
Location North east off M5/M4
interchange, Almondsbury, north Bristol

MENDIP RIDING CENTRE
Lyncombe Lodge, Churchill
Avon, BS19 5PQ
Tel 01934 852335
Contact Mrs Lee
Riding School, Trekking Centre Inst
Riding & Jumping
3 full time instructors
Ave No 10 Horses, 15 Ponies
Courses Hol

Facilities
Outdoor Manege 20 x 60
SJ: Nov, 1 Paddock
CC: Course, Basic, Nov, Int
Lec Rm, Vis Aids, Chng Rm
Hacking
Schooling General, Break, to Nov
Dress, to El Dress
Accom S, Tw, Db, F, Dor, FB
Exclusions Wt Limit, 17st, Age Limit, 3
Location 3 miles from Jn 21 on M3

URCHINWOOD MANOR
EQUITATION CENTRE
Congresbury, Avon, BS19 5AP
Tel 01934 833248
Contact Capt P J Hall
**Riding School, Training Centre,
Stud/schooling & breaking.** Inst to
BHSII
Specialities Career training
Staff Chief Instructor Miss B E Pool
(BHSI)
Plus 3 full time instructors
Ave No 17 Horses, 15 Ponies
inc 4 Med Dress, 1 Adv Dress,
1 SJ GR C, 1 HT Int, 4 Side Saddle,
4 Hunters
Courses WP, YT, Short, Ev, P/T, Hol
Facilities
Covered School 24 x 54 gly
Outdoor Manege 20 x 50 fl lt
SJ: Nov, Grade C, 1 Paddock
CC: Basic, Nov, Banks, Water, Natural,
Gallops
Lec Rm, Vis Aids, Showers, Wait Rm,
Tack Shop
Hacking
Livery Full, Break, School, Grass
Schooling Break, to Adv Dress,
to HT Int
Accom S, Tw, F, Dor, FB
Exclusions No unaccompanied hacks
Location Off A370 between
Congresbury and Bristol

WELLOW
TREKKING CENTRE
Little Horse Croft Farm,
Wellow, Bath, BA2 8QE
Tel 01225 834376
Contact Mr & Mrs F R Shellard
Trekking Centre, Livery, RDA Inst
Basic
3 full time instructors
Ave No 21 Horses, 11 Ponies
inc Tekking
Facilities
Outdoor Manege 37 x 24 fl lt
Wait Rm
Hacking

Livery Full, P/T, DIY, Hunt, Grass
Location Wellow village, 6 miles south of Bath

WHITE CAT STABLES
Howsmoor Lane, Lyde Green,
Emersons Green,
South Gloucestershire, BS16 7AH
Tel 0117 956 4370/0226
Contact Miss P E Gough
Riding School Inst Riding & Jumping
Staff Chief Instructor Miss P Gough (BHSAI)
Ave No 7 Horses, 10 Ponies
Courses WP, YT, Hol
Facilities
SJ: Nov
CC: Course, Basic
Lec Rm, Vis Aids
Livery Full
Schooling General, Break
Exclusions Age Limit, 5

CORNWALL

CHIVERTON RIDING CENTRE
Silverwell, Blackwater,
Truro, Cornwall, TR4 8JQ
Tel 01872 560471
Contact Mrs S A Fawdry & Miss V Jane
Riding School, Training Centre Inst Riding & Jumping
Specialities Career training
Staff Chief Instructor Miss V Jane (BHSII)
Plus 2 full time instructors
Ave No 10 Horses, 9 Ponies
inc 8 El Dress, 4 Med Dress,
1 Adv Dress
Courses WP, YT, Short, Ev, P/T
Facilities
Covered School 22 x 44 gly
Outdoor Manege 20 x 60
SJ: Nov, Grade B
CC: Basic, Nov, Int
Lec Rm, Vis Aids, Chng Rm, Wait Rm
Hacking
Livery Full, P/T, DIY, Break, School
Schooling General, Break, to Med Dress, to SJ GR B, to HT Int
Accom S, Tw, Db, FB
Exclusions Wt Limit, 13st, Age Limit, 5
Location 3 1/2 miles from Truro, off B3277, 1/4 mile from A30

DUCHY COLLEGE
Home Farm, Stoke Climsland,
Callington, Cornwall, PL17 8PB
Tel 01579 370769

Contact Mr A S Counsell
Riding School, Training Centre, Facility Centre Inst to BHSI
Specialities Career training
Staff Chief Instructor Miss J Batty-Smith (BHSI)
Plus 9 full time instructors
Ave No 70 Horses, 10 Ponies
inc 4 El Dress, 2 Med Dress, 8 SJ GR C, 2 SJ GR B, 1 SJ Jun C, 3 HT Int,
Competition Driving Horses, Single Pair & Tandem
Courses YT, Short, Ev, P/T, Hol
Facilities
Covered School 60 x 25 gly
Covered School 20 x 40
Outdoor Manege 70 x 27 fl lt
SJ: Nov, Grade A, 2 Paddock
CC: Course, Basic, Nov, Int, Banks, Water, Natural, Gallops, 60 Schooling
Lec Rm, Vis Aids, Chng Rm, Showers, Wait Rm
Livery Full, P/T, School
Schooling General, Break, to Adv Dress, to SJ GR B, to HT Int
Accom S, Tw, Db, Dor, Cottage, FB
Exclusions Wt Limit, 14st, Age Limit, 10
Location Off A388 between Callington and Launceston

ELM PARK EQUESTRIAN CENTRE
Meadow Springs, North Beer, Boyton,
Nr Launceston, Cornwall, PL15 8NP
Tel 01566 785353
Contact Mr & Mrs D L Shaw
Riding School, Training Centre Inst Basic
Specialities Beginners and nervous riders, and specialist jumping tuition
Staff Chief Instructor Mr Barry Shaw (BHSAI)
Ave No 4 Horses, 7 Ponies
inc 1 Med Dress
Courses WP, YT, Short, Ev, P/T, Hol
Facilities
Covered School 37 x 20
SJ: Nov
CC: 4 Schooling
Lec Rm, Vis Aids
Livery Full, P/T, DIY, Grass
Schooling General, to Nov Dress, to SJ GR C
Exclusions No unaccompanied riding or hacking
Location 6 miles north of Launceston, off B3254

GOOSEFORD RIDING SCHOOL
Gooseford Farm, St Mellion,
Nr Saltash, Cornwall, PL12 6RT
Tel 01579 350715

Contact W A & K P Bock
Riding School Inst Basic
Specialities Fun teaching for both children and adults
Staff Chief Instructor Mrs Alison Smith (BHSAI)
Ave No 5 Horses, 4 Ponies
Courses WP
Facilities
Outdoor Manege 50 x 30
SJ: Nov
Lec Rm, Vis Aids, Chng Rm
Hacking
Livery Full, Break, School
Schooling General, Break, to Nov Dress
Exclusions Wt Limit, 15st, Age Limit, 4, No unaccompanied hacking
Location Between Ashton & St Dominic

GOOSEHAM BARTON STABLES
Morwenstow, Bude,
Cornwall, EX23 9PG
Tel 01288 331204
Contact Mr R Hamilton
Trekking Centre Inst Basic
Ave No 10 Horses, 17 Ponies
Courses YT
Hacking
Accom Cottage, SC
Exclusions Wt Limit, 16st, Age Limit, 3
Location 3 miles off A39 north Devon/Cornwall border, between Bideford and Bude

LAKEFIELD EQUESTRIAN CENTRE
Pendavey Farm, Camelford,
Cornwall, PL32 9TX
Tel 01840 213279
Contact Miss Monk & Mr & Mrs Perring
Riding School Inst Riding & Jumping
Specialities Instruction in riding and stable management
Staff Chief Instructor Miss R L Monk (BHSAI)
Ave No 3 Horses, 5 Ponies
Courses WP, Short, Ev, P/T, Hol
Facilities
Outdoor Manege 20 x 40
SJ: Nov, 1 Paddock
Chng Rm
Hacking
Livery Full
Exclusions No unescorted hacking
Location On B3266 north of Camelford

THE MANOR RIDING CENTRE
Veryan, Nr Truro,
Cornwall, TR2 5PW
Tel 01872 501574

Contact Mrs J Trethowan
Riding School, Training Centre, Facility Centre Inst Riding & Jumping
Specialities Produce classical thinking riders
1 full time instructor
Ave No 5 Horses, 10 Ponies
inc 3 El Dress, 1 SJ GR C
Courses WP, YT, Short, Ev, P/T, Hol
Facilities
Covered School 24 x 15
Outdoor Manege 57 x 25
SJ: Nov
CC: Banks, 10 Schooling
Lec Rm, Vis Aids, Wait Rm
Hacking
Livery Full, P/T, DIY, Break, School, Hunt, Grass
Schooling General, Break, to El Dress, to SJ GR C
Exclusions Wt Limit, 13st, Age Limit, 5, Only experienced riders for beach hacks

OLD MILL STABLES
Rejarne Farm, Lelant Downs,
Hayle, Cornwall, TR27 6LN
Tel 01736 753045
Contact Miss SV Renowden & Miss MM Scotting
Riding School Inst Basic
Staff Chief Instructor Miss S V Renowden
Plus 1 full time instructor
Ave No 13 Horses, 10 Ponies
inc 3 El Dress, 3 Med Dress
Facilities
Covered School 20 x 35 gly
Outdoor Manege 20 x 40
Lec Rm, Vis Aids, Chng Rm
Hacking
Livery Full, School, Grass
Schooling General, to Med Dress, to HT Nov, to HT Int
Exclusions Wt Limit, 12st7, Age Limit, 7, No unaccompanied hacking, no hunters for hire
Location A30 by-passing Hayle, end of by-pass take St Ives Road, at 2nd roundabout turn left. Sign says 'holiday route for day visitors to St Ives'. Stables are 1 mile on left - well signposted

ROMANY WALKS RIDING STABLES
Ludgvan, Penzance,
Cornwall, TR20 8EJ
Tel 01736 740838
Contact Mrs A McCallum
Riding School, Training Centre Inst Basic
Specialities Beginners and nervous riders

Ave No 6 Horses, 9 Ponies
inc 2 El Dress
Courses WP, YT, Short, Ev, P/T, Hol
Facilities
SJ: Nov
CC: Basic, Banks, Water, Natural,
Gallops, 10 Schooling
Lec Rm, Vis Aids, Wait Rm
Hacking
Livery Full, P/T, Break, School
Schooling General, Break, to El Dress,
to HT Nov
Exclusions Wt Limit, 14st, Age Limit, 5,
No casual hire, assesment before
hacking
Location 3 miles east of Penzance off
the A30

**ST LEONARDS
EQUITATION CENTRE**
St Leonards, Polson, Launceston,
Cornwall, PL15 9QR
Tel 01566 775543
Contact Mr A B T Reeve
**Riding School, Training Centre,
Facility Centre, Competition Training
Yard.** Inst to BHSAI
Specialities Career training
Staff Chief Instructor Mr A B T Reeve
(BHSAI)
Plus 6 full time instructors
Ave No 5 Horses, 6 Ponies
inc 3 El Dress, 2 SJ GR C
Courses WP, YT, Short, Ev, P/T, Hol
Facilities
Outdoor Manege 20 x 40 fl lt
SJ: Nov, Grade A, 1 Paddock
CC: Course, Basic, Nov, Int, Adv,
Banks, Water, Natural, Gallops,
50 Schooling
Lec Rm, Vis Aids, Chng Rm, Showers,
Wait Rm, Tack Shop
Hacking
Livery Full, P/T, DIY, Break, School,
Hunt
Schooling General, Break, to El Dress,
to SJ GR B, to HT Int
Accom Tw, Db, F, Cottage, FB, SC
Exclusions Wt Limit, 20st, Age Limit, 4,
No unaccompanied rides
Location 1 mile from Launceston town
centre on the A388 to Polson

ST VEEP RIDING STABLES
St Veep, Lerryn,
Lostwithiel, Cornwall, PL22 0PA
Tel 01208 873521
Contact Mrs E M Barron
Riding School Inst Basic
Specialities Getting children started at
an early age not only in riding but also

in horse care and management
Staff Chief Instructor Miss Josephine
Barron (BHSAI)
Ave No 3 Horses, 11 Ponies
Courses YT, Hol
Facilities
Outdoor Manege 20 x 40
SJ: Nov
Chng Rm, Showers, Wait Rm
Hacking
Schooling General, Break, to Nov
Dress, to SJ GR C, to HT Nov
Accom Tw, FB
Exclusions Wt Limit, 15st, Age Limit, 4,
No unaccompanied hacking
Location St Veep is 1 1/2 miles south of
Lerryn

**TM INTERNATIONAL
SCHOOL OF HORSEMANSHIP**
Sunrising Riding Centre,
Henwood, Liskeard,
Cornwall, PL14 5BP
Tel 01579 362895
Contact Captain T Moore
Riding School, Training Centre Inst to
BHSAI
Specialities Career training
Staff Chief Instructor Miss K M Tyrrell
Plus 3 full time instructors
Ave No 12 Horses, 13 Ponies
inc 4 El Dress, 5 SJ GR C, 7 SJ Jun C,
Arab Stallion at Stud
Courses WP, YT, Short, Ev, P/T, Hol
Facilities
Outdoor Manege 22 x 41
Outdoor Manege 20 x 20
SJ: Nov, Grade C, 1 Paddock
CC: Course, Basic, Nov, Banks, Natural
Lec Rm, Vis Aids, Chng Rm, Showers,
Wait Rm
Hacking
Livery P/T, Break, School
Schooling General, Break, to El Dress,
to SJ GR C, to HT Nov
Accom Tw, F, Dor, Caravan, FB, SC
Exclusions Wt Limit, 14st, Age Limit, 4
Location On the edge of Bodmin Moor,
6 1/2 miles north of Liskeard

TIMBERDOWN RIDING SCHOOL
Lidwell, Callington, Cornwall, PL17 8LJ
Tel 01579 370577
Contact Mr & Mrs A J Dourof
Riding School Inst Basic
Specialities Nervous riders, children &
adults. Pony care stable management
classes
Ave No 4 Horses, 10 Ponies

Courses YT
Facilities
Outdoor Manege 20 x 40
SJ: Nov
CC: Basic
Hacking
Livery Break
Schooling General
Accom Tw, FB
Exclusions Wt Limit, 14st, Age Limit, 2
Location Off Horsebridge road from
Stoke Climsland

TREGURTHA DOWNS RIDING SCHOOL

Marazion, Penzance,
Cornwall, TR20 9LD
Tel 01736 711422
Contact Mr & Mrs P Richards
Riding School Inst Riding & Jumping
2 full time instructors
Ave No 10 Horses, 6 Ponies
Facilities
Outdoor Manege 30 x 30
SJ: Grade C, 1 Paddock
CC: Course, Int, Banks, Water, Natural,
Gallops, 54 Schooling
Chng Rm, Wait Rm
Hacking
Livery Full, P/T, DIY, Break, School,
Hunt, Grass
Schooling General, Break, to Nov
Dress, to SJ GR A, to HT Nov
Exclusions Wt Limit, 15st, Age Limit, 6
Location Off Marazion by-pass

TRENANCE RIDING SCHOOL

Trenance Leisure Area,
Trenance Lane, Newquay,
Cornwall, TR7 1AU
Tel 01637 872699
Contact Mrs J Burt
**Riding School, Trekking Centre,
Superb coastal/beach riding** Inst
Basic
1 full time instructor
Ave No 12 Horses, 12 Ponies
Facilities
Outdoor Manege 37 x 18
SJ: Nov
CC: Basic, Nov, Water, Natural
Lec Rm, Vis Aids, Wait Rm
Hacking
Livery Full, P/T, Break, School, Grass
Schooling General, Break, to Nov
Dress
Exclusions Wt Limit, 16st,
Age Limit, 5,
Hunting/unaccompanied riders
Location Edge of town, adjacent to
river estuary

WHEAL BULLER RIDING SCHOOL

Buller Hill, Redruth,
Cornwall, TR16 6ST
Tel 01209 211852
Contact Mrs J A Dallimore
**Riding School, Training Centre,
Facility Centre, Trekking Centre** Inst
Riding & Jumping
1 full time instructor
Ave No 15 Horses, 30 Ponies
inc 3 El Dress, 1 Med Dress, 3 SJ GR
C, 5 Gold series endurance horses,
3 Novice HT
Courses WP, YT, Short, Ev, P/T, Hol
Facilities
Covered School 20 x 40
Outdoor Manege 20 x 40
SJ: Nov
CC: Basic, Banks, Water, Natural,
16 Schooling
Lec Rm, Vis Aids, Chng Rm, Wait Rm
Hacking
Livery Full, Break, School, Hunt
Schooling General, Break, to Nov
Dress, to El Dress, to SJ GR C, to HT
Nov
Accom Tw, Db, Dor, FB
Exclusions No unaccompanied
hacking
Location 1 mile from Redruth on the
B3297 to Helston

DEVON

ABIGAIL EQUESTRIAN CENTRE

Woodway Street, Chudleigh,
Newton Abbot,
Devon, TQ13 OJU
Tel 01626 852167
Contact Mrs L M Saunders
Riding School, RDA Inst Riding &
Jumping
Staff Chief Instructor
Miss G C Saunders
Ave No 5 Horses, 5 Ponies
inc Dressage-Elem/Nov, SJ-Novice
Courses YT
Facilities
Covered School 27 x 14
SJ: Nov, 1 Paddock
Hacking
Livery Full, P/T, DIY, Hunt, Grass
Schooling General, Break, to Nov
Dress
Exclusions Wt Limit, 16st,
Unaccompanied hacking
Location 1/4 mile east of Chudleigh
town centre

BABLEIGH RIDING SCHOOL
Bableigh House, Landkey,
Barnstaple, Devon, EX32 0NT
Tel 01271 830242
Contact Mrs V A Coles
Riding School Inst Basic
Specialities Courses offered in
conjunction with North Devon College
Staff Chief Instructor Mrs V A Coles
Plus 2 full time instructors
Ave No 8 Horses, 12 Ponies
inc 2 El Dress
Courses WP, YT, Short, Ev, P/T
Facilities
Outdoor Manege 44 x 22 fl lt
SJ: Nov, 1 Paddock
CC: Course, Nov, Banks
Lec Rm, Vis Aids, Chng Rm
Hacking
Livery Full, P/T
Schooling General, Break, to Nov
Dress, to El Dress
Exclusions Wt Limit, 14st, Age Limit, 6,
No casual hire
Location Off A361, 1 1/2 miles from
the centre of Landkey

BICTON
COLLEGE OF AGRICULTURE
East Budleigh, Budleigh Salterton,
Devon, EX9 7BY
Tel 01395 562300
Contact Mr P J Cook
Training Centre Inst to BHSI
Specialities Career training
4 full time instructors
Ave No 36 Horses, 1 Ponies
inc 1 El Dress, 1 Med Dress, 1 Adv
Dress, 1 SJ GR C
Courses YT, Short, Ev, P/T
Facilities
Covered School 20 x 40
Outdoor Manege 20 x 40
Outdoor Manege 30 x 60
SJ: Grade B, 1 Paddock
CC: Basic, Nov, Banks, Natural
Lec Rm, Vis Aids, Chng Rm, Showers,
Wait Rm
Livery Break, School
Schooling General, Break, to Adv
Dress, to SJ GR A, to HT Int
Accom S, Tw, F, Dor, FB, SC
Exclusions Age Limit, 16
Location On A367 between Budleigh
Salterton and Colaton Raleigh

BUDLEIGH SALTERTON
RIDING SCHOOL
Dalditch Lane, Budleigh Salterton,
Devon, EX9 7AS
Tel 01395 442035/443920

Contact Mrs B J Howick
Riding School, Training Centre Inst
Riding & Jumping
Staff Chief Instructor Mrs M Howick
(BHSAI)
Plus 4 full time instructors
Ave No 13 Horses, 13 Ponies
inc Breeding of German Warmbloods
Courses WP, YT, Short, Ev, P/T, Hol
Facilities
Outdoor Manege 25 x 50 fl lt
SJ: Nov, 1 Paddock
Lec Rm, Vis Aids, Chng Rm, Wait Rm
Hacking
Livery Full, P/T, DIY, Break, School,
Hunt, Grass
Schooling General, Break, to Nov
Dress, to SJ GR C, to HT Nov
Exclusions Wt Limit, 16st,
No unaccompanied hacks

CLOVELLY DONKEYS
76 High Street, Clovelly,
Bideford, Devon, EX39 5TJ
Tel 01237 431659
Contact Ms Susan Green
Specialities Led Donkey Rides and
Woodland Hacks
1 full time instructor
Ave No 2 Horses, 11 Ponies
Hacking
Exclusions Wt Limit, 6st for Donkeys,
9 1/2st for Mules
Location Clovelly Donkey Stables

COLLACOTT EQUESTRIAN CENTRE
Kings Nympton, Umberleigh,
North Devon, EX37 9TP
Tel 01769 572725
Contact Mrs J Sherar & Ms V Vant
Riding School, Training Centre,
Facility Centre Inst Basic
Specialities Very good facilities,
excellent accommodation, idyllic setting,
small and friendly riding school
Staff Chief Instructor Mrs Claire Withers
(BHSII)
Ave No 4 Horses, 7 Ponies
inc 1 SJ Jun C
Courses WP, YT, Short, Ev, P/T
Facilities
Outdoor Manege 20 x 40 fl lt
SJ: Nov, 1 Paddock
CC: Basic, Natural, 12 Schooling
Lec Rm, Vis Aids, Chng Rm, Showers,
Wait Rm
Hacking
Livery Full, P/T, DIY, Break, School,
Hunt, Grass
Schooling General, Break, to Nov
Dress, to HT Nov

Accom Tw, F, Caravan, Cottage, FB, SC
Exclusions Wt Limit, 15st
Location 3 miles south of S Molton, I mile north of Kings Nympton

CROSS COUNTRY EXMOOR
Great Rapscott, South Molton,
Devon, EX36 3EL
Tel 01598 760247
Contact Mr A G Hill
Riding School Inst Riding & Jumping
Specialities The stimulation and motivation of riders up to an advanced horse trials level
1 full time instructor
Ave No 10 Horses
inc 2 HT Int
Courses Short, Hol
Facilities
Covered School 41 x 20
SJ: Grade B, 3 Paddock
CC: Course, Adv, Banks, Water, Natural, Gallops, 100 Schooling
Lec Rm, Vis Aids, Chng Rm, Showers, Wait Rm
Hacking
Livery Full, Break, School, Hunt
Schooling General, Break, to El Dress, to SJ GR C, to HT Int
Accom Tw, Db, FB
Exclusions Wt Limit, 13st, Age Limit, 7
Location 2 miles north of Aller Cross roundabout

DEVENISH PITT RIDING SCHOOL
Farway, Nr Colyton,
Devon, EX13 6EG
Tel 01404 871355
Contact Mrs M A Banks
Riding School, Beginners hacks Inst Riding & Jumping
Specialities Family run business. Childrens Days - fully supervised, Family rides, Birthday rides/gymkhanas, Mini Cross Country Course
Staff Chief Instructor Mrs A Smith (BHSAI)
Plus 3 full time instructors
Ave No 8 Horses, 12 Ponies
Courses WP, Short, P/T, Hol
Facilities
Covered School 24 x 30
SJ: Nov, 1 Paddock
CC: Banks, Water, Natural, 8 Schooling
Lec Rm, Vis Aids, Chng Rm, Wait Rm, Tack Shop
Hacking
Livery Full, P/T, DIY, Break, School, Hunt, Grass

Schooling General, Break, to Nov
Dress, to HT Nov
Accom Tw, Db, F, Cottage, SC
Exclusions Wt Limit, 16st, Age Limit, 3, No unacompanied hacking
Location Farway Valley

DITTISCOMBE
EQUESTRIAN CENTRE
Slapton, Kingsbridge,
Devon, TQ7 2QF
Tel 01548 581049
Contact Mrs A Farleigh & Mr M Rogers
Riding School, Facility Centre, Trekking Centre, Backing/Breaking & Schooling Inst Basic
Staff Chief Instructor Mrs Alex Farleigh
Ave No 5 Horses, 8 Ponies
inc 2 El Dress, 1 Med Dress, Driving
Courses Short, Ev, P/T, Hol
Facilities
Covered School 15 x 40
Outdoor Manege 20 x 40 fl lt
SJ: Nov, Grade C, 1 Paddock
CC: Course, Basic, Nov, Banks, Water, Natural, Gallops
Showers
Hacking
Livery Full, P/T, DIY, Break, School, Hunt, Grass
Schooling General, Break, to Nov
Dress, to El Dress, to SJ GR C, to HT Nov
Accom Db, FB
Exclusions Wt Limit, 14st, Age Limit, 2 1/2
Location 2 miles north west of Slapton, mid district Kingsbridge, Totnes and Dartmouth, 15 miles south of Λ38

EASTLAKE FARM RIDING STABLES
Eastlake Farm, Belstone,
Okehampton, Devon, EX20 1QT
Tel 01837 52513
Contact Mr D Saunders
Trekking Centre
Staff Chief Instructor Miss C D White
Ave No 5 Horses, 17 Ponies
Courses YT
Hacking
Schooling General
Exclusions Wt Limit, 20st
Location 1 1/2 miles south east of Okehampton, off old A30 on the edge of Dartmoor

FITZWORTHY RIDING
Fitzworthy, Corntown , Cornwood,
Nr Ivybridge, Devon, PL21 9PH
Tel 01752 837836

Contact Mrs B J Wilson
Riding School Inst Basic
Specialities Friendly atmosphere.
Holidays for children also
2 full time instructors
Ave No 10 Horses, 10 Ponies
inc 1 El Dress, 1 SJ GR C, 1 HT Int
Courses WP, Ev, Hol
Facilities
SJ: Nov
CC: Course, Basic, Banks, Natural
Lec Rm, Vis Aids, Chng Rm
Hacking
Accom F, FB
Exclusions Wt Limit, 13 1/2st
Location Lee Mill exit A38 signed to
Cornwood

GRANGE EQUESTRIAN CENTRE
Inwardleigh, Okehampton,
Devon, EX20 3DA
Tel 01837 52303
Contact Ms S Courtney
Riding School, Facility Centre Inst
Riding & Jumping
Specialities Career training
1 full time instructor
Ave No 6 Horses, 8 Ponies
Courses WP, YT, P/T
Facilities
Covered School 60 x 20 gly
Covered School 24 x 17
Outdoor Manege 20 x 40 fl lt
SJ: Nov, Grade C, Grade B, Grade A
CC: Basic, Nov, Int, Banks, Water
Showers, Tack Shop
Livery Full, P/T, DIY, Break, School,
Hunt, Grass
Schooling General, Break, to El Dress,
to SJ GR C, to HT Nov
Location On Northlaw road from
Okehampton

HIGH BULLEN FARM
Ilkerton, Barbrook, Lynton,
North Devon, EX35 6PH
Tel 01598 753318
Contact Mrs S Pettinger
Trekking Centre
Specialities Adult residential riding
holidays
Staff Chief Instructor Miss Joanne
Medland
Ave No 14 Horses
Chng Rm, Showers
Hacking
Accom Cottage, FB
Exclusions Age Limit, 16,
Residents only
Location Set above the Lyn Valley,
within the Exmoor National Park

HILLTOP RIDING SCHOOL
Pennsylvania Road, Exeter,
Devon
Tel 01392 251370
Contact Miss J Portbury
Riding School Inst Basic
Ave No 4 Horses, 9 Ponies
inc 1 El Dress
Courses WP, Short, Ev, P/T, Hol
Facilities
SJ: Nov
Chng Rm
Livery Full, Break, School, Hunt
Schooling General, Break, to Nov
Dress, to El Dress

HONEYSUCKLE FARM
EQUESTRIAN CENTRE
Haccombe-with-Combe,
Newton Abbot, Devon, TQ12 4SA
Tel 01626 355944
Contact Mr & Mrs I G Mackay
Riding School, Training Centre Inst to
BHSAI
Specialities Teaching
1 full time instructor
Ave No 7 Horses, 15 Ponies
inc 2 El Dress
Courses WP, YT, Short, Ev, P/T, Hol
Facilities
Covered School 16 x 32
Outdoor Manege 50 x 40 fl lt
SJ: Nov, Grade C
CC: Course, Basic, Nov, Int, Banks,
Water, Natural, Gallops
Lec Rm, Vis Aids, Chng Rm, Showers,
Wait Rm
Hacking
Livery Full, P/T, DIY, Break, School,
Grass
Schooling General, Break, to Nov
Dress, to HT !nt
Accom SC
Exclusions Wt Limit, 14st, Age Limit, 2,
No casual hire
Location Off B3195 between Newton
Abbot and Shaldon

LYDFORD HOUSE RIDING STABLES
Lydford, Okehampton,
Devon, EX20 4AU
Tel 01822 820347
Contact Mr R E Boulter
Riding School, Training Centre,
Riding Holidays Inst Riding & Jumping
Staff Chief Instructor Mrs C Knight
(BHSII)
Ave No 8 Horses, 8 Ponies
Courses WP, YT, Short, P/T, Hol
Facilities
Outdoor Manege 20 x 40

SJ: Nov, 1 Paddock
Lec Rm, Vis Aids, Chng Rm, Showers,
Wait Rm
Hacking
Livery Full, Break, School
Schooling General, Break, to Nov
Dress
Accom S, Tw, Db, F, FB
Exclusions Wt Limit, 14st7, Age Limit, 3,
No unescorted rides
Location Dartmoor - off A386 between
Okehampton and Tavistock

NEWHALL EQUESTRIAN CENTRE
Nr Killerton, Broadclyst,
Exeter, Devon, EX5 3LW
Tel 01392 462453
Contact Mrs J A Llewellin
Livery, National Trust Visitor Centre
Specialities Livery
Courses WP
Facilities
Covered School 60 x 90 gly
SJ: Nov, 1 Paddock
Lec Rm, Vis Aids, Chng Rm, Wait Rm
Livery Full, P/T, DIY, Break, School,
Hunt, Grass
Accom S, Db, FB
Location Off B3181, 3 miles from
Broadclyst. Follow signs for Killerton
Gardens

**NORTH DEVON
EQUESTRIAN CENTRE**
Shirwell, Barnstaple,
Devon, EX31 4HR
Tel 01271 850864
Contact Mr Paul Jennings & Ms Sarah
Jeffrey
Riding School, Training Centre Inst
Riding & Jumping
Specialities Instruction in Riding &
Jumping
Staff Chief Instructor Miss S Jeffery
(BHSAI, BHS Int.SM)
Plus 3 full time instructors
Ave No 9 Horses, 10 Ponies
inc 1 El Dress, 2 Med Dress, 1 SJ Jun C,
Driving & Side Saddle
Courses WP, YT, Short, P/T
Facilities
Outdoor Manege 20 x 60
SJ: Nov, 1 Paddock
CC: Banks, Water, Natural, 9 Schooling
Lec Rm, Vis Aids, Chng Rm, Wait Rm
Hacking
Livery Full, P/T, Break, School, Hunt
Schooling General, Break, to Nov
Dress, to El Dress
Exclusions Wt Limit, 15st, Age Limit, 4,
No hacking without assessment lesson

Location Off A39 6 miles north of
Barnstaple

OAKLANDS RIDING SCHOOL
Balls Farm Lane, Alphington,
Exeter, EX2 9JA
Tel 01392 272105
Contact Ms Joyce Newbery
Riding School Inst Basic
Staff Chief Instructor Miss D Watson
Plus 1 full time instructor
Ave No 20 Horses, 10 Ponies
Facilities
Covered School 21 x 12
Outdoor Manege 30 x 23
Outdoor Manege 30 x 23
SJ: Nov, 2 Paddock
CC: Course, Basic, Banks, Water,
Natural
Chng Rm, Wait Rm
Hacking
Livery Full, P/T, DIY, Break, School,
Hunt, Grass
Schooling General, Break, to Nov Dress
Exclusions Age Limit, 3
Location Off slip road of main A30 to
Okehampton

ROYLANDS RIDING STABLES
Noor Lane, Croyde Bay,
Braunton, Devon, EX33 1NU
Tel 01271 890898
Contact Mrs S G Maddocks
Riding School, Riding Holidays Inst
Riding & Jumping
Staff Chief Instructor Mr S G Maddocks
(BHSAI)
Ave No 5 Horses, 5 Ponies
inc 1 El Dress
Courses YT, Hol
Facilities
Outdoor Manege 20 x 40
SJ: Nov, 1 Paddock
CC: Basic, 10 Schooling
Lec Rm, Vis Aids, Chng Rm, Showers,
Wait Rm
Hacking
Livery Full, P/T, DIY, Break, School,
Hunt, Grass
Schooling General, Break, to El Dress,
to SJ GR C, to HT Nov
Accom S, Tw, Db, FB
Exclusions Wt Limit, 14st,
No unaccompanied rides

**SHILSTONE ROCK STUD &
TREKKING CENTRE**
Widecombe-in-the-Moor,
Newton Abbot, Devon, TQ13 7TF
Tel 01364 621281

Contact Mr & Mrs Newbolt-Young
Trekking Centre Inst Basic
Staff Chief Instructor Mrs D Mackwood
(BHSII)
Ave No 14 Horses, 36 Ponies
Facilities
Outdoor Manege 25 x 40
SJ: 1 Paddock
Chng Rm, Wait Rm
Hacking
Livery Full, Break, School, Hunt, Grass
Schooling General
Exclusions Wt Limit, 15st, Age Limit, 6,
No unescorted rides
Location 1 mile out of
Widdecombe/Ashburton

DORSET

BRYANSTON RIDING CENTRE
Bryanston School, Blandford Forum,
Dorset, DT11 0PX
Tel 01258 452411
Contact Miss P Longden - Head of
Riding
Riding School, Training Centre Inst
to BHSII
Specialities Instruction in Riding &
Jumping
Staff Chief Instructor Miss P Longden
(BHSI)
Plus 1 full time instructor
Ave No 8 Horses, 6 Ponies
Courses WP, YT
Facilities
Outdoor Manege 30 x 70
Outdoor Manege 20 x 40
CC: Course, Basic, Banks, Water,
Natural, 16 Schooling
Lec Rm, Vis Aids, Chng Rm, Showers,
Wait Rm
Hacking
Livery Full, P/T, School
Schooling General
Exclusions No unescorted hacking
Location Blandford Forum

CHURCH ROAD RIDING SCHOOL
63 Springfield Road, Broadway,
Weymouth, Dorset
Tel 01305 833272
Contact Mrs A Varney
Riding School Inst Basic
Staff Chief Instructor Mrs A Varney
(BHSAI)
Ave No 7 Horses, 7 Ponies
Courses YT, Short
Facilities
Outdoor Manege 20 x 40

SJ: Nov
CC: Nov
Location Sutton Points, Weymouth,
Dorset

FOREST LODGE
EQUESTRIAN CENTRE
Motcombe, Nr Shaftesbury,
Dorset, SP7 9PL
Tel 01747 851685
Contact Mr & Mrs R I Roberts
Riding School, Training Centre,
Facility Centre, RDA riding Inst Riding
& Jumping
Specialities Career training, affiliated
and unaffiliated shows
3 full time instructors
Ave No 24 Horses, 14 Ponies
Courses WP, YT, Short, Ev, P/T, Hol
Facilities
Covered School 61 x 27 gly
Outdoor Manege 46 x 23 fl lt
SJ: Nov, Grade C, 1 Paddock
CC: Course, Basic, Nov, Banks, Water,
Natural, Gallops
Lec Rm, Vis Aids, Chng Rm, Showers,
Wait Rm
Hacking
Livery Full, P/T, Break, School, Hunt,
Grass
Schooling General, Break, to El Dress,
to SJ GR C, to HT Nov
Accom S, Tw, Db, F, Dor, Cottage, FB,
SC
Exclusions Wt Limit, 15st,
Age Limit, 2 1/2, No unescorted hacking,
Trekking, hire, DIY livery
Location 2 miles from Shaftesbury,
Gillingham

THE FORTUNE CENTRE
OF RIDING THERAPY
Avon Tyrrell, Bransgore,
Christchurch, Dorset, BH23 8EE
Tel 01425 673297
Contact Mrs J Dixon-Clegg
Training Centre Inst Riding & Jumping
Specialities Full time further education
through Horsemastership for young
people 16 - 25 with special needs
9 full time instructors
Ave No 12 Horses, 12 Ponies
inc 1 El Dress, 1 Adv Dress
Courses Short
Facilities
Covered School 20 x 40
Covered School 20 x 18
Outdoor Manege 20 x 60
Outdoor Manege 20 x 40
SJ: Nov, 1 Paddock
CC: Natural, 6 Schooling

Lec Rm, Vis Aids, Chng Rm, Showers,
Wait Rm
Hacking
Accom S, Tw, Dor, FB
Exclusions Wt Limit, 12st,
No commercial work.
Riding therapists only
Location New Forest between
Bransgore and Burley

HIGHER POUND RIDING CENTRE
Higher Pound Farm, Monkton Wyld,
Nr Bridport, Dorset, DT6 6DD
Tel 01297 678747
Contact Miss Clare Blatchford
Trekking Centre
Specialities Hacking through
Charmouth Forest & Wooton Woods
Staff Chief Instructor Miss Clare
Blatchford
Plus 1 full time instructor
Ave No 3 Horses, 17 Ponies
Facilities
Covered School 30 x 15
SJ: Nov
Chng Rm, Wait Rm
Hacking
Livery Full, P/T, DIY, School, Hunt,
Grass
Accom S, Tw, Db, F, Cottage, SC
Exclusions Wt Limit, 14st, Age Limit, 3,
No private hire
Location Off A35 take B3165
Crewkerne Road at Hunters Lodge

IVERS HOUSE
Ivers Hains Lane, Marnhull,
Sturminster Newton, Dorset, DT10 1JU
Tel 01258 820164
Contact Mr P F Cheesman
Riding School Inst Basic
Specialities Young adults & children
with special needs
Staff Chief Instructor Mrs S Shuttler
Ave No 3 Ponies
Lec Rm, Vis Aids, Chng Rm, Showers,
Wait Rm
Hacking
Exclusions Residents only
Location On B3092 between
Sturminster Newton & Gillingham

KINGSTON MAURWARD COLLEGE
Dorchester, Dorset, DT2 8PY
Tel 01305 215063
Contact Miss Anne Tezer
Training Centre Inst Riding & Jumping
Specialities Student training & Equine
courses
1 full time instructor

Ave No 23 Horses, 1 Ponies
inc 4 El Dress, 2 Med Dress, 2 HT Int
Courses Short, Ev, P/T
Facilities
Outdoor Manege 65 x 65
SJ: Nov
Lec Rm, Vis Aids, Chng Rm
Exclusions Riding under instruction
only
Location Signposted off A35 south
east of Dorchester

LANEHOUSE EQUITATION CENTRE
Overbury Close, Weymouth,
Dorset, DT4 9UE
Tel 01305 770177
Contact Mr R H Addison
Riding School, Training Centre Inst
Riding & Jumping
Staff Chief Instructor Mr R H Addison
Plus 1 full time instructor
Ave No 4 Horses, 12 Ponies
inc general instruction - own horses
Courses WP, YT, Short, Ev
Facilities
Outdoor Manege 40 x 60 fl lt
SJ: Nov, Grade C, Grade B, Grade A,
1 Paddock
Lec Rm, Vis Aids, Chng Rm, Wait Rm
Hacking
Livery Full, P/T, Break, School
Schooling General, Break, to Nov
Dress, to SJ GR C, to HT Nov
Exclusions Wt Limit, 14st, Age Limit, 5

LEIGH EQUESTRIAN CENTRE
Three Gates, Leigh,
Sherborne, Dorset, DT9 6JQ
Tel 01963 210469/210323
Contact Miss S E Richards & Miss A J
Day
Training Centre, Livery
Staff Chief Instructor Miss S Richards
(BHSI)
Courses WP, YT, Short, Ev, P/T
Facilities
Covered School 20 x 40 gly
Outdoor Manege 20 x 40
SJ: Nov, Grade C, 1 Paddock
CC: Course, Basic, Nov, Banks,
Natural, 30 Schooling
Lec Rm, Vis Aids, Chng Rm, Showers,
Wait Rm
Livery Full, P/T, Break, School, Hunt,
Grass
Schooling General, Break, to Med
Dress, to SJ GR C, to HT Nov
Exclusions No casual hire,
No unescorted hacking
Location 3 miles off the A352 south of
Sherbourne

LULWORTH EQUESTRIAN CENTRE

Kennel Farm, Coombe Keynes, Wareham,
Dorset, BH20 5QR
Tel 01929 400396
Contact Mrs J Jesty
Riding School, Trekking Centre, Event training centre. Inst Riding & Jumping
1 full time instructor
Ave No 4 Horses, 6 Ponies
Courses YT, Hol
Facilities
Outdoor Manege 20 x 60 fl lt
SJ: Nov, Grade C, 1 Paddock
CC: Course, Nov, Banks, Water, Natural
Wait Rm
Hacking
Livery Full, P/T, DIY, Hunt, Grass
Schooling General, to Nov Dress, to HT Nov
Accom S, Tw, F, Caravan, Cottage, SC
Exclusions Wt Limit, 14st, Age Limit, 13, No unescorted hacking
Location Between Coombe Keynes and East Lulworth

POUND COTTAGE RIDING CENTRE

Luccombe Farm, Milton Abbas, Blandford, Dorset, DT11 0BD
Tel 01258 880057/451240
Contact Mrs J Hardy
Riding School, Training Centre, RDA Group Inst Riding & Jumping
Specialities Career training
Staff Chief Instructor Mrs J Hardy (BHSAI)
Plus 1 full time instructor
Ave No 5 Horses, 10 Ponies inc Show Ponies (Native)
Courses WP, YT, Short, Ev, P/T, Hol
Facilities
Outdoor Manege 30 x 15 fl lt
Outdoor Manege 20 x 40
SJ: Nov, 1 Paddock
CC: Course, Basic, Banks
Lec Rm, Vis Aids, Wait Rm, Tack Shop
Hacking
Livery Full, P/T, Break, School, Hunt
Schooling General, Break, to Nov Dress
Accom Dor, SC
Exclusions Wt Limit, 14st, Age Limit, 2, No unescorted rides
Location Off A354 between Winterbourne, Whitchurch and Milton Abbass

THE RAC SADDLE CLUB

Bovington Camp, Bovington, Nr Wareham, Dorset
Tel 01929 403580
Contact Mr Nutt
Riding School, Training Centre Inst Riding & Jumping
Staff Chief Instructor Miss A S Buchanan (BHS Int Teach)
Plus 5 full time instructors
Ave No 23 Horses, 17 Ponies
Courses WP, YT, Short, Ev, P/T, Hol
Facilities
CC: Course, Basic, Banks, Water, Natural
Lec Rm, Vis Aids, Chng Rm, Wait Rm
Livery Full, P/T, DIY, Break, School, Grass
Schooling General, Break, to Nov Dress, to SJ GR C, to HT Nov
Exclusions No unescorted riding
Location 7 miles from Wareham off A352

STOCKS FARM EQUESTRIAN CENTRE

Christchurch Road, West Parley, Dorset, BH22 8SQ
Tel 01202 570288
Contact Mr P Oliver
Riding School, Facility Centre Inst Riding & Jumping
Staff Chief Instructor Miss Anne Bryant (BHSAI)
Plus 2 full time instructors
Ave No 8 Horses, 14 Ponies
Courses WP, Short, Ev, P/T, Hol
Facilities
Covered School 20 x 40 gly
Outdoor Manege 20 x 40 fl lt
Outdoor Manege 20 x 60
SJ: Nov, Grade C, 1 Paddock
CC: 10 Schooling
Lec Rm, Vis Aids, Wait Rm, Tack Shop
Hacking
Livery Full, P/T, DIY, Break, School
Schooling General, Break, to Nov Dress, to El Dress, to SJ GR C, to HT Nov
Exclusions Wt Limit, 13st, Age Limit, 4
Location On unnumbered road between Hurn Airport and West Parley

GLOUCESTERSHIRE

CHELTENHAM LADIES COLLEGE RIDING CENTRE

Great Witcombe, Gloucester, GL3 4TR
Tel 01452 864259
Contact Mrs S McDermott

Riding School Inst Riding & Jumping
Staff Chief Instructor Ms Judith Unwin
(BHSAI)
Plus 1 full time instructor
Ave No 4 Horses, 6 Ponies
Courses WP, YT
Facilities
Covered School 27 x 18
Outdoor Manege 37 x 18
SJ: 1 Paddock
CC: Course, Basic, Banks, Water,
Gallops
Hacking
Livery Full, DIY, Grass
Accom Tw
Exclusions Students of Cheltenham
Ladies College only

COLTSMOOR RIDING CENTRE
Coltsmoor Farm, Coln St Aldwyns,
Cirencester, Glos, GL7 5AX
Tel 01285 750049/750291
Contact Mr A R & Miss V C Gee
Riding School, Facility Centre Inst
Riding & Jumping
Staff Chief Instructor Miss V C Gee
(BHSII)
Plus 1 full time instructor
Ave No 11 Horses, 14 Ponies
Courses WP
Facilities
Outdoor Manege 25 x 50
SJ: Grade C, 1 Paddock
CC: 15 Schooling
Tack Shop
Hacking
Livery Full, P/T, DIY, Break, School,
Hunt
Schooling General, Break, to El Dress,
to SJ GR C, to HT Nov
Exclusions Wt Limit, 14st7,
Age Limit, 2 1/2 to 65,
No dogs, No unescorted hacking
Location 3 miles south of Burford (A40)

HARTPURY COLLEGE
c/o Equine Department,
Hartpury House,
Gloucester, GL19 3BE
Tel 01452 700283/700678
Contact Mr J D Michaels FBHS
Training Centre, Facility Centre,
Horse Walker Inst to BHSI
Specialities Career training
Staff Chief Instructor Mr J D Michaels
(FBHS)
Plus 10 full time instructors
Ave No 80 Horses, 2 Ponies
inc 5 El Dress, 5 Med Dress, 3 SJ GR C,
2 SJ GR B, 4 HT Int
Courses YT, Short, Ev, P/T

Facilities
Covered School 24 x 60 gly
Covered School 22 x 60
Outdoor Manege 22 x 60 fl lt
Outdoor Manege 60 x 20
SJ: Nov, Grade C, Grade B, Grade A,
1 Paddock
CC: Course, Basic, Nov, Int, Adv,
Banks, Water, Natural, 40 Schooling
Lec Rm, Vis Aids, Tack Shop
Hacking
Livery DIY
Schooling General, to Adv Dress, to
SJ GR B, to HT Adv
Accom S, Tw, Dor, Cottage, FB, SC
Exclusions No casual clients
Location On A417 between Gloucester
and Ledbury

HUNTLEY SCHOOL OF EQUITATION
Woodend Farm, Huntley,
Glos, GL19 3EY
Tel 01452 830440
Contact Mrs T Freeman
Riding School, Training Centre Inst
to BHSI
Specialities Career training
Staff Chief Instructor Mrs C A Broad
FBHS (FBHS)
Plus 1 full time instructor
Ave No 30 Horses, 3 Ponies
inc 1 Med Dress, 1 Adv Dress,
2 SJ GR C
Courses WP, Short, Ev, P/T, Hol
Facilities
Covered School 20 x 40 gly
Outdoor Manege 20 x 60 fl lt
SJ: Nov, Grade C, 1 Paddock
CC: Course, Nov, Banks, Water,
Natural, Gallops
Lec Rm, Vis Aids
Livery Break, School
Schooling General, Break, to Adv
Dress, to SJ GR C, to HT Nov
Accom S, Tw, Dor, SC
Exclusions Age Limit, 10
Location On A40 midway between
Gloucester and Ross-on-Wye, opposite
garden centre

LITTLEDEAN RIDING CENTRE
Wellington Farm, Littledean,
Gloucestershire, GL14 2TO
Tel 01594 823955
Contact Mrs G M Chamberlain
Riding School, Training Centre,
Trekking Centre, RDA Inst to BHSAI
Staff Chief Instructor Ms Debbie James
(BHSII, BHS SM)
Plus 1 full time instructor
Ave No 19 Horses, 15 Ponies

Courses WP, YT, Short, Ev, P/T, Hol
Facilities
Outdoor Manege 20 x 30 fl lt
CC: 10 Schooling
Chng Rm
Exclusions Wt Limit, 16st,
Age Limit, 3 1/2,
No unaccompanied hacks
Location Off A4151 Littledean village,
side road signed Soudley

LONG DISTANCE
RIDING CENTRE
Fosseway, Bourton-on-the-Water,
Glos, GL54 2HL
Tel 01451 821101/820358
Contact Miss J P Davies
Riding School Inst Riding & Jumping
1 full time instructor
Ave No 8 Horses, 4 Ponies
Courses WP
Facilities
Outdoor Manege 43 x 21 fl lt
SJ: Nov, 1 Paddock
Chng Rm, Wait Rm
Hacking
Exclusions Wt Limit, 14st, Age Limit, 7,
No hunting
Location On A429, between Two
Turnings to Bourton-on-the-Water

NEWNHAM EQUESTRIAN CENTRE
Big Hyde Farm, Newnham-on-Severn,
Gloucester, GL14 1HQ
Tel 01594 516513
Contact Ms S L Charles
Riding School Inst Riding & Jumping
Specialities Individual competition
training for show jumping
Staff Chief Instructor Miss S Charles
(BHSAI)
Plus 1 full time instructor
Ave No 7 Horses, 8 Ponies
Courses WP, Short, Ev, P/T, Hol
Facilities
Covered School 46 x 19
Outdoor Manege 20 x 40 fl lt
SJ: Nov, Grade C
CC: Basic, Natural
Lec Rm, Vis Aids
Hacking
Livery Full, P/T, DIY, Break, School,
Hunt
Exclusions Escorted hacks only
Location Turn off A48 at Clock Tower
up Station Road into Hyde Lane

PLAYMATE
CHILDRENS RIDING SCHOOL
Hardwicke Mews, Elmstone Hardwicke,

Cheltenham, Glos, GL51 9TD
Tel 01242 680888
Contact Mrs J A Swambo
Riding School Inst Basic
Staff Chief Instructor Mrs J A Swambo
Ave No 14 Ponies
Facilities
Outdoor Manege 23 x 50 fl lt
Exclusions Wt Limit, 7st,
Age Limit, 2 to 12
Location 4 miles from Cheltenham

SUMMERHOUSE EDUCATION
& EQUITATION CENTRE
Hardwicke, Gloucester, GL2 4RG
Tel 01452 720288
Contact Mrs S R Weston
Riding School, Training Centre,
Facility Centre, RDA & NVQ Centre
Inst to BHSII
Specialities Career training
Staff Chief Instructor Mrs Helen A Gallop
(BHSI, BHS SM)
Plus 7 full time instructors
Ave No 21 Horses, 20 Ponies
inc 3 El Dress, 3 Med Dress, 2 SJ GR C,
3 HT Int, 1 HT Adv, Novice, Side Saddle
& RDA
Courses WP, Short, Ev, P/T, Hol
Facilities
Covered School 25 x 70 gly
Outdoor Manege 20 x 60 fl lt
SJ: Grade C
CC: Course, Nov, Banks, Water
Lec Rm, Vis Aids, Chng Rm, Showers,
Wait Rm
Hacking
Livery Full, P/T, DIY, Break, School
Schooling General, Break, to Med
Dress, to SJ GR C, to HT Int
Accom S, Caravan, SC
Exclusions Wt Limit, 16st, Age Limit, 3,
No casual hire, no hunting hire
Location On the B4008, next to Jn 12
off M5

THE TALLAND
SCHOOL OF EQUITATION
Church Farm, Siddington,
Cirencester, Gloucestershire, GL7 6EZ
Tel 01285 652318
Contact Mr & Mrs B Hutton
Riding School, Training Centre,
Facility Centre, Riding for the dis-
abled Inst all BHS
Specialities Competition horses and
riders trained for all disciplines, up to and
including International standard
Staff Chief Instructor Mrs M Sivewright
(FBHS)
Plus 8 full time instructors

Ave No 100 Horses, 18 Ponies
inc 10 El Dress, 10 Med Dress,
10 Adv Dress, 5 SJ GR C, 5 HT Int,
3 HT Adv, Side Saddle
Courses WP, Short, P/T, Hol
Facilities
Covered School 20 x 40 gly
Outdoor Manege 55 x 63
SJ: Nov, Grade A, 1 Paddock
CC: Basic, Nov, Int, Adv, Banks, Water,
Natural, Gallops
Lec Rm, Vis Aids, Chng Rm, Showers
Livery Full, Break, School, Hunt, Grass
Schooling General, Break, to Adv
Dress, to SJ GR C, to HT Adv
Accom S, Tw, Dor, FB
Exclusions Wt Limit, 12st7

SOMERSET

BRIMSMORE EQUESTRIAN CENTRE
Tintinhull Road, Yeovil, Somerset,
c/o 8 The Spinney, Sampsons Wood,
Yeovil, Somerset
Tel 01935 410854
Contact Mrs V Nye
Riding School Inst Basic
Specialities Childrens' lessons, adult
beginners and nervous riders
Staff Chief Instructor Mrs Victoria Nye
(BHSII)
Ave No 4 Horses, 8 Ponies
inc 1 El Dress
Courses WP, Ev, P/T, Hol
Facilities
Outdoor Manege 20 x 40 fl lt
Outdoor Manege 50 x 30
SJ: Nov
Lec Rm, Vis Aids, Chng Rm, Wait Rm
Livery Full, P/T, DIY, School, Hunt,
Grass
Schooling General, to Nov Dress
Exclusions Wt Limit, 14st, Age Limit, 6,
No hacking
Location 1 mile south of Yeovil, on the
Tintinhull road

BURCOTT RIDING SCHOOL
Burcott Lane, Wells,
Somerset, BA5 1NQ
Tel 01749 673145
Contact Mr N Payne & Miss N
Stephens
Riding School, Training Centre, RDA
Inst Riding & Jumping
Staff Chief Instructor Miss N Stephens
(BHSII)
Ave No 12 Horses, 25 Ponies
inc 1 SJ GR A
Courses WP, YT, Ev, P/T, Hol

Facilities
Outdoor Manege 60 x 30 fl lt
SJ: Nov, Grade C, 1 Paddock
CC: Course, Basic, Nov, Banks,
Natural
Lec Rm, Vis Aids
Hacking
Livery Full, Break, School, Hunt, Grass
Schooling General, Break, to Nov
Dress, to SJ GR C, to HT Nov
Accom S
Exclusions Wt Limit, 15st,
No casual hiring
Location 1 1/2 miles south of Wells

CANNINGTON COLLEGE EQUESTRIAN CENTRE
Cannington, Bridgwater,
Somerset, TA5 2LS
Tel 01278 655000
Contact Miss S Figg
**Riding School, Training Centre,
Facility Centre** Inst Riding & Jumping
Specialities Practical skills
Staff Chief Instructor Miss S Figg (BHS
Int Teach, BHS Int.SM)
Plus 7 full time instructors
Ave No 27 Horses, 4 Ponies
inc 2 Med Dress, 1 HT Adv
Courses YT, Short, Ev, P/T
Facilities
Covered School 40 x 20 gly
Outdoor Manege 44 x 33 fl lt
SJ: Nov, Grade C
CC: Basic, Natural, 7 Schooling
Lec Rm, Vis Aids, Chng Rm, Wait Rm
Livery Full, P/T, Break, School
Schooling General, Break, to El Dress,
to SJ GR C, to HT Nov
Accom S, Tw, FB
Exclusions Age Limit, 14
Location Off A39 at Cannington

CURLAND EQUESTRIAN CENTRE
Crosses Farm, Curland,
Taunton, Somerset, TA3 5SD
Tel 01460 234234
Contact Miss J Van Meeuwen &
Miss C Carey
Riding School, Training Centre Inst
Riding & Jumping
Staff Chief Instructor Miss Jackie Van
Meeuwen (BHSAI)
Plus 1 full time instructor
Ave No 8 Horses, 15 Ponies
Courses WP, Ev, P/T, Hol
Facilities
Covered School 37 x 18 gly
Outdoor Manege 64 x 26
SJ: Nov
Wait Rm

Hacking
Livery Full, P/T, Break, School, Hunt
Schooling General, Break, to Nov
Dress, to El Dress, to SJ GR C, to HT
Nov
Accom Caravan, SC
Exclusions Age Limit, 3,
No unaccompanied hacking
Location 5 miles south east of
Taunton, 15 mins from Jn 25 of M5 and
from A303. Village of Curland between
Taunton and Chard

**EBBORLANDS FARM
& RIDING CENTRE**
Wookey Hole, Wells,
Somerset, BA5 1AY
Tel 01749 672550
Contact Mrs E A Gibbs
**Riding School, Training Centre,
Trekking Centre, R D A** Inst Basic
Specialities Career training
Staff Chief Instructor Mrs J Yates
(BHSAI, BHS Int Teach)
Plus 3 full time instructors
Ave No 10 Horses, 3 Ponies
inc general purpose
Courses WP, YT, Short, Ev, P/T, Hol
Facilities
Covered School 43 x 19
Outdoor Manege 49 x 24
SJ: Nov, Grade C
CC: Course, Basic, Banks, Natural
Lec Rm, Vis Aids
Hacking
Livery Full, P/T, DIY, Break, School,
Hunt, Grass
Schooling General, Break, to El Dress,
to SJ GR C, to HT Nov
Accom Caravan, SC
Exclusions Wt Limit, 13st7, Age Limit, 6,
Casual hiring and hunting
Location 2 1/2 miles north west of
Wells

GREENHAM EQUESTRIAN CENTRE
Ridge Farm, Greenham,
Wellington, Somerset, TA21 0JS
Tel 01823 673024
Contact Miss S Edwards
Riding School Inst Riding & Jumping
1 full time instructor
Ave No 6 Horses, 7 Ponies
Courses YT, Short, Ev, P/T, Hol
Facilities
Outdoor Manege 20 x 40 fl lt
SJ: Nov, 1 Paddock
Chng Rm
Hacking
Livery P/T, School
Schooling General, Break, to Nov

Dress, to HT Nov
Exclusions Wt Limit, 11st, Age Limit, 3,
No casual hire, hacking to known clients
only
Location 3 miles from Wellington

GREGGS RIDING SCHOOL
Placket Lane, off West Coker Road,
Yeovil, Somerset, BA20 2HH
Tel 01935 423894
Contact Mrs L A Bennett
Riding School, RDA Inst Basic
Specialities Stable management and
horse welfare tuition in all lessons
Staff Chief Instructor Mrs L A Bennett
Ave No 4 Horses, 7 Ponies
inc 1 El Dress
Courses Short, Ev, P/T
Facilities
Outdoor Manege 40 x 40
SJ: Nov
CC: Course, Basic, Banks, Natural
Chng Rm
Hacking
Schooling General, to Nov Dress, to HT
Nov
Exclusions Wt Limit, 13st,
No unaccompanied hiring for hacking
Location On the A30, Placket Lane,
west of Yeovil, towards West Coker

KNOWLE RIDING CENTRE
Timberscombe, Minehead,
Somerset, TA24 6TZ
Tel 01643 841342
Contact Mr & Mrs J R Lamacraft
Riding School, Facility Centre Inst
Riding & Jumping
Ave No 35 Horses, 15 Ponies
inc 1 HT Int, Polo Ponies
Courses Hol
Facilities
Covered School 20 x 41 gly
SJ: Nov, 1 Paddock
CC: Course, Int, Banks, Water, Natural
Lec Rm, Vis Aids, Chng Rm, Showers,
Wait Rm
Hacking
Livery Full, P/T, DIY, Hunt, Grass
Schooling General, to Nov Dress,
to SJ GR C, to HT Nov
Accom S, Tw, Db, F, Dor, Cottage, FB
Exclusions No unaccompanied children
under 11 years
Location Off the A396, between Dunster
& Timberscombe

MILLFIELD SCHOOL
Street, Somerset, BA16 0YD
Tel 01458 442291

141

Contact Mr C S Martin
Riding School, Training Centre Inst
to BHSII
5 full time instructors
Ave No 35 Horses, 10 Ponies
inc 1 El Dress, 1 Med Dress, 1 Adv
Dress, 1 SJ GR C, 1 SJ GR B,
1 SJ Jun C, 1 HT Int
Courses WP, Hol
Facilities
SJ: Grade B, 1 Paddock
CC: Course, Basic, Nov, Banks, Water,
Gallops
Lec Rm, Vis Aids, Chng Rm
Livery Full, School
Schooling General, Break, to Nov
Dress, to Adv Dress, to SJ GR B, to HT
Nov
Accom S, FB
Exclusions Wt Limit, 13st, Age Limit, 6

PERITON PARK RIDING STABLES
off Periton Road, Middlecombe,
Nr Minehead,
West Somerset, TA24 8SW
Tel 01643 705970
Contact Mr & Mrs Borland
**Facility Centre, Livery, Riding sta-
bles (hunting)** Inst Basic
Specialities Heated Swimming Pool
Ave No 10 Horses, 2 Ponies
Chng Rm, Wait Rm
Hacking
Livery Full, P/T, DIY, Hunt, Grass
Accom Caravan, Cottage, SC
Exclusions Wt Limit, 14st, Age Limit, 7
Location South of Minehead off A39

PINE LODGE
RIDING HOLIDAYS ON EXMOOR
Higher Chilcott Farm, Dulverton,
Somerset, TA22 9QQ
Tel 01398 323559
Contact Mr & Mrs Bullman
Trekking Centre
Specialities Riding holiday on Exmoo,
open all year. Small groups according
to ability
Staff Chief Instructor Mrs R I Bullman
Ave No 12 Horses, 10 Ponies
Facilities
SJ: Nov
Chng Rm, Showers
Hacking
Accom Tw, Db, Cottage, FB
Exclusions Wt Limit, 14st, Age Limit, 4,
All rides escorted
Location Off A396 north of village of
Dulverton

PORLOCK VALE HOUSE
Porlock Weir,
Somerset, TA24 8NY
Tel 01643 862338
Contact Mr & Mrs K Youd
Riding School, Hotel Inst Riding &
Jumping
Staff Chief Instructor Mr S Rigby (BHS
Int.SM)
Plus 3 full time instructors
Ave No 21 Horses, 2 Ponies
Courses Hol
Facilities
Covered School 25 x 45 gly
Covered School 30 x 15
Outdoor Manege 38 x 16
SJ: Nov, 1 Paddock
CC: Course, Basic, Nov, Int, Banks,
Water, Natural
Lec Rm, Vis Aids, Chng Rm, Wait Rm
Hacking
Livery Full, P/T, DIY, Break, School,
Hunt, Grass
Schooling General, Break, to El Dress,
to HT Nov
Accom Tw, Db, FB
Exclusions Wt Limit, 13st7, Age Limit, 15,
No unescorted hacking
Location Off A39, 1 mile from Porlock

RODGROVE STUD
EQUESTRIAN CENTRE
Moor Lane, Wincanton,
Somerset, BA9 9QU
Tel 01963 371323
Contact Mrs A J Barfoot
**Riding School, Training Centre,
Facility Centre, RDA** Inst Riding &
Jumping
Specialities Instruction in riding &
jumping for beginers. Student training
to BHS AI
Staff Chief Instructor Mrs A Barfoot
(BHSII, BHS SM)
Ave No 6 Horses, 4 Ponies
inc 2 El Dress
Courses WP, Short, Ev, P/T, Hol
Facilities
Outdoor Manege 25 x 50 fl lt
Outdoor Manege 19 x 15
Outdoor Manege 60 x 40
SJ: Nov
CC: Basic, Natural, 6 Schooling
Lec Rm, Vis Aids, Chng Rm, Showers
Livery Full, P/T, Break, School, Hunt
Schooling General, Break, to Med
Dress, to SJ GR C, to HT Nov
Accom FB
Exclusions Wt Limit, 13 1/2st,
No unsupervised riding
Location On the outskirts of Wincanton

WILTSHIRE

BRYMPTON RIDING SCHOOL
Common Road, Whiteparish,
Salisbury, Wiltshire, SP5 2RD
Tel 01794 884386
Contact Mrs S A Near
Riding School Inst Basic
Staff Chief Instructor Mrs S A Near
Plus 2 full time instructors
Ave No 5 Horses, 10 Ponies
Courses Hol
Facilities
Outdoor Manege 30 x 50
SJ: Nov
Hacking
Accom Db, F, Dor, Caravan, FB
Exclusions Wt Limit, 15st, Age Limit, 4,
No unescorted hacking

GROVELY RIDING CENTRE
Water Ditchampton, Wilton,
Salisbury, Wiltshire, SP2 0JB
Tel 01722 742288
Contact Miss S Curtis & Miss G Dunne
Riding School Inst Basic
Staff Chief Instructor Miss Gerry Dune
Plus 2 full time instructors
Ave No 7 Horses, 13 Ponies
inc 2 SJ GR C
Courses WP, Short, Ev, P/T, Hol
Facilities
Outdoor Manege 40 x 38
SJ: Nov, 1 Paddock
Lec Rm, Vis Aids, Wait Rm
Hacking
Livery Full, P/T, DIY, Break, School, Hunt
Schooling General, Break, to Nov
Dress, to SJ GR C
Exclusions No unescorted hacking
Location 1 mile from Wilton town
centre off A30

HARRIS CROFT RIDING CENTRE
Binknoll Lane, Wootton Bassett,
Swindon, Wiltshire, SN4 8QS
Tel 01793 853388
Contact Mr R Nutland
Riding School Inst Riding & Jumping
1 full time instructor
Ave No 15 Horses, 24 Ponies
Facilities
Covered School 16 x 22
Outdoor Manege 40 x 80 fl lt
Outdoor Manege 60 x 30
CC: Course, Basic, Nov, Int, Banks,
Water, Natural
Chng Rm, Wait Rm
Hacking
Livery Full, P/T, DIY

HEDDINGTON WICK CHILDRENS RIDING SCHOOL,
Hicksfield, The Common, Heddington,
Calne, Wiltshire, SN11 0NZ
Tel 01380 850182
Contact Mrs I Gage
Riding School, RDA Inst Riding &
Jumping
Staff Chief Instructor Mrs I Gage (BHSAI)
Ave No 3 Horses, 13 Ponies
Courses Short, Hol
Facilities
Outdoor Manege 20 x 40
Outdoor Manege 20 x 19
SJ: Nov
Chng Rm, Showers
Hacking
Exclusions Wt Limit, 10st
Location Off A3102 Calne on outskirts
of Heddington

HEYWOOD EQUESTRIAN CENTRE
Church Road, Heywood,
Westbury, Wiltshire, BA13 4LP
Tel 01373 823476
Contact Mr & Mrs T Tanner
Riding School Inst Riding & Jumping
Staff Chief Instructor Mrs T Tanner
(BHSAI, BHS Int Teach)
Plus 3 full time instructors
Ave No 8 Horses, 7 Ponies
Courses WP, YT, Short, Ev, P/T, Hol
Facilities
Covered School 40 x 25 gly
Outdoor Manege 23 x 42 fl lt
Lec Rm, Vis Aids, Chng Rm, Showers,
Wait Rm
Hacking
Livery Full, P/T, DIY, Break, School,
Hunt
Schooling General, Break, to Nov Dress
Exclusions Wt Limit, 14st,
No unescorted hacking

HURDCOTT LIVERY STABLES
Winterbourne Earls,
Salisbury, Wilts, SP4 6HR
Tel 01980 611276
Contact Miss C C Bright
Livery
Specialities Rug cleaning and repair
service
Facilities
Outdoor Manege 60 x 20
SJ: Nov, 1 Paddock
Chng Rm, Showers, Wait Rm, Tack
Shop
Livery Full, P/T, DIY, Grass
Exclusions No hiring
Location 3 miles from Salisbury, off
A338 Marlborough road

INFANTRY SADDLE CLUB
Oxendene, Warminster,
Wiltshire, BA12 OD2
Tel 01985 222395/213925
Contact Major (Rtd) R B Sullivan-Tailyour
Riding School Inst Riding & Jumping
2 full time instructors
Ave No 10 Horses, 7 Ponies
Courses WP, Short, Ev, P/T, Hol
Facilities
Covered School 37 x 18 gly
Outdoor Manege 55 x 27
SJ: Grade C, 1 Paddock
CC: Course, Basic, Nov, Banks, Water,
Natural, 12 Schooling
Lec Rm, Vis Aids, Chng Rm, Wait Rm
Hacking
Livery Full, P/T, DIY, Break, School,
Grass
Schooling General, Break, to El Dress,
to SJ GR C, to HT Nov
Exclusions Wt Limit, 13st, Age Limit, 6

**LACKHAM COLLEGE
EQUESTRIAN CENTRE**
Lackham College, Lacock,
Chippenham, Wilts, SN15 2NY
Tel 01249 443111
Contact Mr E Williams
Riding School, Training Centre, RDA
Inst to BHSAI
Specialities Career training
Staff Chief Instructor Miss J Anthony
(BHSI), Plus 2 full time instructors
Ave No 29 Horses
inc 2 El Dress, 1 SJ GR B, 1 HT Int
Courses WP, Short, P/T, Hol
Facilities
Covered School 42 x 20
Outdoor Manege 60 x 40
SJ: Nov, Grade C, 1 Paddock
CC: Course, Basic, Nov, Natural
Lec Rm, Vis Aids, Chng Rm, Wait Rm
Livery Full
Accom S, FB
Exclusions Wt Limit, 13st, Age Limit, 16
Location Off A350 between
Chippenham and Melksham

**THE MARLBOROUGH DOWNS
RIDING CENTRE**
Rockley, Marlborough, Wiltshire,
c/o Manton Grange, Marlborough,
Wiltshire, SN8 4HQ
Tel 01672 511411
Contact Ms A Byrne & Ms G Carter
Riding School Inst Riding & Jumping
Specialities Our riding centre offers
stunning, unrivalled hacking over open
downland and the historic Ridgeway

Staff Chief Instructor Miss A Byrne
(BHSII), Plus 1 full time instructor
Ave No 7 Horses, 10 Ponies
inc 1 Adv Dress, 1 SJ GR C, 1 HT Int
Courses WP, YT, Hol
Facilities
SJ: Nov, 1 Paddock
CC: Basic, Banks, Natural, 12 Schooling
Lec Rm, Vis Aids, Wait Rm
Hacking
Livery Full, P/T, DIY, Break, School,
Hunt, Grass
Schooling General, Break, to El Dress,
to SJ GR C, to HT Int
Exclusions Wt Limit, 15st7, Age Limit, 5
Location Marlborough Downs

**PEWSEY VALE
WHITE HORSE RIDING CENTRE**
Church Road, Stanton St Bernard,
Marlborough, Wiltshire, SN8 4LJ
Tel 01672 851777
Contact Mr H M E Sheldon and Mrs J
Munby
Riding School Inst Riding & Jumping
Specialities Tuition for competition
riders
Staff Chief Instructor Mr H M E
Sheldon (BHSAI, BHS Int.SM)
Plus 2 full time instructors
Ave No 10 Horses, 12 Ponies
Courses WP, Short, Ev, P/T, Hol
Facilities
Covered School 32 x 46
Outdoor Manege 20 x 40
SJ: Nov
CC: Course, Nov, Banks, Water,
Natural
Showers, Wait Rm
Hacking
Livery Full, P/T, Break, School, Hunt,
Grass
Schooling General, Break, to Med
Dress, to SJ GR C, to HT Nov
Exclusions No unaccompanied
hacking
Location Pewsey Vale between
Marlborough/Pewsey/Devizes

**STONAR SCHOOL
EQUESTRIAN CENTRE**
Cottles Park, Atworth,
Melksham, Wiltshire, SN12 8NT
Tel 01225 790422
Contact Mrs C Homan
Riding School, Training Centre Inst
to BHSAI
Specialities Career training at girls
boarding school
Staff Chief Instructor Mr J Collins
(BHSII, BHS SM)

Plus 3 full time instructors
Ave No 27 Horses, 25 Ponies
Courses WP, YT, P/T
Facilities
Covered School 20 x 40 gly
Outdoor Manege 41 x 41 fl lt
SJ: Grade C
CC: Course, Nov, Banks, Water, Natural
Lec Rm, Vis Aids, Chng Rm, Showers, Wait Rm
Livery P/T
Accom S, Tw, Dor, FB

TOLLARD PARK EQUESTRIAN CENTRE
Tollard Royal, Salisbury,
Wilts, SP5 5PU
Tel 01725 516249
Contact Miss K Allen
Riding School Inst Riding & Jumping
Specialities Adult Individual training - schooling tuition with or without own horse, for competitions, BHS exams
1 full time instructor
Ave No 8 Horses, 2 Ponies
inc 2 HT Adv
Courses WP, Short, Ev, P/T, Hol
Facilities
Covered School 60 x 23 gly
Outdoor Manege 55 x 25 fl lt
SJ: Nov, 1 Paddock
Chng Rm, Showers
Hacking
Livery Full, P/T
Schooling General, Break, to Nov Dress, to Adv Dress, to SJ GR B
Exclusions Wt Limit, 14st
Location 5 miles south east of Shaftesbury, signposted just off the B3081

WHITE HORSE TREKKING CENTRE
Cleeve House, Codford,
Warminster, Wiltshire, BA12 0JZ
Tel 01985 850395
Contact Mr W D Puddy MBE
Trekking Centre Inst Basic
Specialities Leap frog trekking, ie 2 groups, 1 riding and 1 in mini bus changing over
Staff Chief Instructor Mrs S Smith
Ave No 20 Horses, 10 Ponies
Courses YT, Short, P/T, Hol
Facilities
SJ: Nov, 1 Paddock

CC: Course, Basic, Banks, Water, 20 Schooling
Exclusions Wt Limit, 12st, No unescorted rides
Location On A36 between Wylef and Warminster

WICKSTEAD FARM EQUESTRIAN CENTRE
Highworth, Swindon,
Wiltshire, SN6 7PP
Tel 01793 762265
Contact Mrs V Mace
Training Centre, Facility Centre, Livery
1 full time instructor
Facilities
Covered School 50 x 20 gly
Outdoor Manege 50 x 25
SJ: Nov
CC: Course, Basic, Nov, Banks, Water, Natural, Gallops
Chng Rm, Wait Rm
Livery Full, P/T, DIY, Break, School, Hunt, Grass
Schooling General, Break, to Nov Dress
Location Off Jn 15 M4

WIDBROOK ARABIAN STUD & EQUESTRIAN CENTRE
Widbrook, Trowbridge,
Bradford-on-Avon, Wilts, BA15 1UD
Tel 01225 862608
Contact Mrs D Griggs
Riding School, Training Centre, Stud, RDA Inst Riding & Jumping
2 full time instructors
Ave No 10 Horses, 10 Ponies
inc 1 El Dress
Courses WP, Short, Ev, P/T, Hol
Facilities
Covered School 20 x 40
Outdoor Manege 40 x 35
SJ: Nov, 1 Paddock
CC: Course, Basic, Water, Natural
Lec Rm, Vis Aids, Wait Rm
Hacking
Livery Full, P/T, Break, School, Grass
Schooling General, Break, to El Dress, to HT Nov
Exclusions Wt Limit, 14st, Age Limit, 6, No casual hire, experienced hack riders only
Location A363 midway between Bradford-on-Avon and Trowbridge

Riding in Scotland

BORDERS ◆ CENTRAL
DUMFRIES & GALLOWAY ◆ FIFE
GRAMPIAN ◆ HIGHLANDS ◆ LOTHIAN
STRATHCLYDE ◆ TAYSIDE

Note

Local government reorganisation has resulted in changes to the Scottish Regions. In this edition of *Where to Ride* the former Regional name is followed by the new Unitary Authority names for that area.

BORDERS

(Scottish Borders)

**HAZELDEAN
RIDING CENTRE**
Hassendeanburn, Nr Hawick,
Roxburghshire, TD9 8RU
Tel 01450 870419
Contact Mr Turnbull
Riding School, Facility Centre Inst
Riding & Jumping
Staff Chief Instructor Mrs Alison Brown
Ave No 5 Horses, 8 Ponies
Courses Hol
Facilities
Covered School 37 x 21 gly
Outdoor Manege 37 x 21
SJ: Nov
Chng Rm, Wait Rm
Hacking
Livery Full, Break, School
Schooling General, Break
Exclusions Wt Limit, 13st
Location Off A7 40 miles from Carlisle
& 50 miles from Edinburgh

**NENTHORN RIDING
& LIVERY STABLES**
Nenthorn, Kelso,
Roxburghshire, TD5 7RY
Tel 01573 224073
Contact Mrs A Allan
Riding School Inst Riding & Jumping
Staff Chief Instructor Miss Jennifer
Christie
Ave No 12 Horses, 20 Ponies

Facilities
Covered School 20 x 40 gly
Outdoor Manege 25 x 30
SJ: Nov
Lec Rm, Vis Aids
Hacking
Livery Full, P/T, Break, School
Schooling General
Exclusions Wt Limit, 15st, Age Limit, 4
Location 3 miles north of Kelso

CENTRAL

(Clackmannanshire, Falkirk, Stirling)

**DEVON LEISURE PARK
EQUESTRIAN CENTRE**
Fishcross, by Alloa,
Clackmannanshire, FK10 3AN
Tel 01259 769888
Contact Mr D Campbell
Facility Centre
Specialities The facilities may be hired
for a wide range of equestrian events
including Showing, Jumping, Dressage
and Training
2 full time instructors
Facilities
Covered School 60 x 30 gly
Outdoor Manege 86 x 76 fl lt
Outdoor Manege 40 x 20
Outdoor Manege 40 x 20
SJ: Grade A, 92acr Paddock
Lec Rm, Vis Aids, Wait Rm
Hacking
Schooling to El Dress, to SJ GR A

Location Easily accessed from M9.
From Alloa take Tillicoultry (A908) road
to Fishcross cross roads, turn right,
Centre is signposted

DRUMBRAE RIDING CENTRE
Drumbrae Farm, Bridge of Allan,
Stirlingshire, FK9 4L8
Tel 01786 832247
Contact Mrs D & Miss L McNicol
Riding School, Trekking Centre Inst
Riding & Jumping
Staff Chief Instructor Miss L McNicol
(BHSII)
Ave No 7 Horses, 26 Ponies
inc 3 SJ GR C
Courses WP, Short, Ev, P/T, Hol
Facilities
Covered School 44 x 17
Outdoor Manege 50 x 32 fl lt
SJ: Nov
CC: Course, Nov, Water, Natural
Lec Rm, Vis Aids, Chng Rm
Hacking
Schooling General, Break, to SJ GR C,
to HT Nov
Accom Caravan, SC
Exclusions Wt Limit, 13st7, Age Limit, 5
Location One mile north from Bridge of
Allan on. the Sherrifmuir road, take left
fork signed Pendreich

**LOMONDSIDE STUD
& EQUESTRIAN CENTRE**
Buchanan Home Farm, Drymen,
Glasgow, G63 OHU
Tel 01360 660481
Contact Misses E & P Rennie
Riding School, Training Centre, Stud
Inst to BHSAI
Specialities Career training, working
stud with two stallions, show yard
producing Hunters and Mountain &
Moorland ponies
Staff Chief Instructor Miss E Rennie
(BHSI)
Plus 1 full time instructor
Ave No 4 Horses, 6 Ponies
inc 3 El Dress, 3 stallions (1TB, 2 New
Forest)
Courses WP, YT, Short, Ev, P/T, Hol
Facilities
Covered School 40 x 20
SJ: Nov
CC: Basic, Water, 6 Schooling
Lec Rm, Vis Aids, Chng Rm, Showers,
Wait Rm
Hacking
Livery Full, P/T, Break, School, Hunt
Schooling General, Break, to Nov
Dress, to El Dress, to SJ GR C

Exclusions Wt Limit, 13st, Age Limit, 4,
Only experienced riders for hacking,
No dogs
Location Off the A811, 15 miles north of
Glasgow & 25 miles west of Sterling in
Buchanan Castle Estate

DUMFRIES
& GALLOWAY

(Dumfries & Galloway)

BAREND RIDING CENTRE
Sandy Hills, Dalbeattie,
Kirkcudbrightshire, DG5 4NU
Tel 01387 780663
Contact Mr & Mrs F Gourlay
**Riding School, Training Centre,
Trekking Centre** Inst to BHSAI
Specialities Career training, students
may bring their own horses
Staff Chief Instructor Miss Clare Wight
(BHSII)
Plus 2 full time instructors
Ave No 5 Horses, 7 Ponies
Courses WP, YT, Short, P/T, Hol
Facilities
Outdoor Manege 55 x 25
SJ: Nov
CC: Course, Basic, Banks, Water,
Natural, Gallops
Lec Rm, Vis Aids, Chng Rm
Hacking
Livery Full, P/T, DIY, Break, School
Schooling General, Break, to HT Nov
Accom Tw, Db, FB, SC
Exclusions Wt Limit, 14st, Age Limit, 6,
No children under 10 for trekking

BRIGHOUSE BAY TREKKING PONIES
Brighouse Bay Holiday Park,
Borgue, Kirkcudbright,
Dumfries & Galloway, DG6 4TS
Tel 01557 870267
Contact Mr T C Gillespie
Trekking Centre Inst Basic
2 full time instructors
Ave No 1 Horses, 16 Ponies
Chng Rm, Showers, Wait Rm
Hacking
Schooling General
Accom Caravan, Cottage, FB, SC
Exclusions Wt Limit, 15st, Age Limit, 8

DALESIDE EQUESTRIAN CENTRE
4 The Crescent, Eastriggs, Annan,
Dumfriesshire, DG12 6NW
Tel 01461 40409

Contact Mr David Murray
Facility Centre, Livery
Specialities Livery centre offering B&B
for horse and rider. Friendly yard with
good supervision
1 full time instructor
Facilities
Outdoor Manege 45 x 29
SJ: Nov, Grade C, 1 Paddock
Lec Rm, Vis Aids, Chng Rm, Wait Rm
Livery Full, DIY, School, Grass
Exclusions No Stallions
Location 3 miles north M74. Take A75
towards Dumfries, turn off to Eastriggs

FIFE

(Fife)

GLENROTHES RIDING CENTRE
Balgeddie Farm, Glenrothes,
Fife, KY6 3ET
Tel 01592 742428
Contact Mr & Mrs P H Gilbert
Riding School, Facility Centre,
Hacking Inst Riding & Jumping
Staff Chief Instructor Mr P H Gilbert
(BHSAI, BHS Int Teach)
Plus 1 full time instructor
Ave No 16 Horses, 6 Ponies
Courses YT, Ev, P/T, Hol
Facilities
Covered School 43 x 20 gly
Covered School 15 x 20
Outdoor Manege 60 x 20 fl lt
SJ: Nov
CC: Banks, Water, Natural
Lec Rm, Vis Aids, Wait Rm
Hacking
Livery Full, Break, School, Grass
Schooling General, Break, to Nov
Dress, to SJ GR C, to HT Nov
Exclusions Wt Limit, 16st, Age Limit, 6
Location Off A911 and A92, 25 miles
from Edinburgh and 10 miles from
Kinross

KINSHALDY RIDING STABLES
Kinshaldy Farm, Leuchars,
Fife, KY16 0DR
Tel 01334 838527
Contact Mr B H Collier
Riding School, Training Centre Inst
Riding & Jumping
Specialities Hacking in woodland and
beach setting
Lessons for riders of all abilities
Staff Chief Instructor Miss J F Wann
(BHSII)
Ave No 7 Horses, 4 Ponies

Courses YT, Short, Ev, Hol
Facilities
Outdoor Manege 120 x 20 fl lt
Outdoor Manege 45 x 25 fl lt
SJ: Nov
Lec Rm, Vis Aids, Chng Rm, Wait Rm
Hacking
Livery Full, P/T, Grass
Schooling General, Break, to Nov Dress
Exclusions Wt Limit, 18stone,
Age Limit, 5
Location North east of Leuchars RAF
Base. Follow signs for Kinshaldy Beach
for 4 miles on unclassified road

GRAMPIAN

**(Moray, Aberdeenshire,
City of Aberdeen)**

ERROLLSTON
EQUESTRIAN & LEISURE
Whitehill Leisure (Scot) Ltd,
Cruden Bay, Peterhead,
Aberdeenshire, AB42 7PJ
Tel 01779 812303
Contact Miss M Elrick
Riding School, Trekking Centre Inst
Riding & Jumping
Specialities Training and instruction
tailored to suit individual needs
3 full time instructors
Ave No 14 Horses, 12 Ponies
inc 1 Med Dress, 1 SJ GR C,
1 SJ GR B
Courses Short, Ev, P/T, Hol
Facilities
Covered School 15 x 30
Outdoor Manege 40 x 50
SJ: Nov, Grade A, 2 Paddock
CC: Course, Int, Banks, Water, Natural
Lec Rm, Vis Aids, Chng Rm, Wait Rm,
Tack Shop
Hacking
Livery Full, P/T, DIY, Break, School,
Hunt, Grass
Schooling General, Break, to Nov
Dress, to Adv Dress, to SJ GR A,
to HT Adv
Accom S, Tw, Db, F, Caravan, FB
Exclusions Wt Limit, 18st, Age Limit, 3
Location Follow A92 from Aberdeen,
turn off on A952

GLEN TANAR
EQUESTRIAN CENTRE
Glen Tanar, Aboyne,
Aberdeenshire, AB34 5EU
Tel 013398 86448/87042
Contact Mrs Jaqueline M Rider

Riding School Inst Riding & Jumping
Specialities Family riding holidays in an area of great scenic beauty on Royal Deeside. Hacking for experienced riders
Staff Chief Instructor Mrs N Carrington (BHSAI)
Plus 2 full time instructors
Ave No 11 Horses, 16 Ponies inc 8 El Dress, 4 Pony Club Standard Jumping Ponies
Courses YT, Ev, Hol
Facilities
Covered School 37 x 17
Outdoor Manege 40 x 20
SJ: Nov
Wait Rm
Hacking
Livery Full, Break, School, Grass
Schooling General, Break, to Nov Dress, to El Dress
Accom S, Tw, F, Cottage, FB, SC
Exclusions Wt Limit, 16st, Age Limit, 3+
Location Located in a Glen close to Royal Deeside in an area of hills and woods of outstanding natural beauty

HAYFIELD EQUESTRIAN CENTRE
Hazelhead Park, Aberdeen, AB15 8BB
Tel 01224 315703
Contact Mr & Mrs J A Crawford
Riding School, Training Centre Inst to BHSAI
Specialities Offers a friendly atmosphere for riders of all ages, from novice to Career training. Language teaching available for foreign students
Staff Chief Instructor Mr J A Crawford (BHSII, BHS SM)
Plus 4 full time instructors
Ave No 20 Horses, 20 Ponies inc 2 El Dress, 2 SJ GR C, 10 Med Polo
Courses WP, Short, P/T, Hol
Facilities
Covered School 30 x 45 gly
Covered School 28 x 22 gly
Outdoor Manege 60 x 40 fl lt
Outdoor Manege 30 x 45 fl lt
SJ: Grade C, 1acre Paddock
CC: Course, Nov, Int, Banks, Water, Natural, 50 Schooling
Lec Rm, Vis Aids, Chng Rm, Showers, Wait Rm, Tack Shop
Hacking
Livery Full, P/T, Break, School, Grass
Schooling General, Break, to El Dress, to SJ GR C, to HT Int
Accom S, Tw, Db, FB
Exclusions Wt Limit, 14st, Age Limit, 3

Location In Hazelhead Park, 3 miles from centre of Aberdeen

LADYMIRE EQUESTRIAN CENTRE
Ladymire Farm, Ellon, Aberdeenshire, AB41 9LH
Tel 01358 721075
Contact Mr & Mrs Chisholm
Riding School Inst Basic
Specialities Friendly atmosphere for riders of all ages from novice to career training
2 full time instructors
Ave No 7 Horses, 7 Ponies
Courses YT, Short, Ev, P/T, Hol
Facilities
Covered School 45 x 20 gly
SJ: Nov, 1 Paddock
Lec Rm, Vis Aids, Chng Rm, Wait Rm
Hacking
Livery Full, P/T, DIY, Break, School, Grass
Schooling General, Break, to Nov Dress
Accom S, Cottage, SC
Exclusions Wt Limit, 15st, Age Limit, 5
Location 15 miles north of Aberdeen on A92, turn right for Kirkton of Logie Buchan

TOMINTOUL RIDING CENTRE
St Bridget Farm, Tomintoul, Ballindalloch, Banffshire, AB37 9HS
Tel 01807 580210
Contact Mrs R McNiven
Trekking Centre, Trail Riding Inst Basic
1 full time instructor
Ave No 5 Horses, 11 Ponies
Courses Hol
Facilities
Outdoor Manege 25 x 40
Chng Rm, Wait Rm
Hacking
Livery Full, P/T, Break, School, Grass
Schooling General
Exclusions Wt Limit, 15st
Location 25 miles from Aviemore on A939

HIGHLANDS

(Highland)

ACHALONE ACTIVITIES
North Achalone, Halkirk, Caithness, Highlands, KW12 6XA
Tel 01847 831326
Contact Mrs M B Bain

Riding School Inst Riding & Jumping
1 full time instructor
Ave No 2 Horses, 12 Ponies
Courses Hol
Facilities
Outdoor Manege 22 x 45
SJ: 1 Paddock
Lec Rm, Vis Aids
Hacking
Livery Full, P/T, Grass
Schooling General
Accom Tw, Db, FB

HIGHLAND RIDING CENTRE
Borlum Farm, Drumnadrochit,
Inverness, IV3 6XN
Tel 01456 450220
Contact Mr A D Macdonald-Haig
**Riding School, Training Centre,
Facility Centre, Trekking Centre** Inst
Riding & Jumping
Staff Chief Instructor Mrs P Corker
(BHSII)
Plus 2 full time instructors
Ave No 12 Horses, 20 Ponies
inc Most horses available for disabled
riding
Courses YT, Short, Hol
Facilities
Covered School 20 x 40 gly
Outdoor Manege 40 x 40
SJ: Nov, 1 Paddock
CC: Course, Nov, Natural, Gallops,
5 Schooling
Lec Rm, Vis Aids, Chng Rm, Showers
Hacking
Livery Full, P/T, DIY, Break, School,
Grass
Schooling General, Break, to El Dress,
to HT Nov
Accom Tw, Db, F, Cottage, FB, SC
Exclusions Wt Limit, 14st7, Age Limit, 4
Location On A82 Inverness - Fort
William Road, 1 mile south of
Drumnadrochit

LOGIE FARM RIDING CENTRE
Glenferness,
Nairn, IV12 5XA
Tel 01309 651226
Contact Mrs A S D Hilleary
**Riding School, Training Centre,
Trekking Centre** Inst to BHSAI
Specialities Career training
Staff Chief Instructor Mrs J Simpson
(BHSAI)
Plus 3 full time instructors
Ave No 8 Horses, 13 Ponies
inc 2 El Dress, 1 Med Dress
Courses YT, Short, Ev, P/T, Hol

Facilities
Outdoor Manege 65 x 37
SJ: Nov, Grade C, 1 Paddock
CC: Course, Basic, Nov, Int, Banks,
Water, Natural, Gallops, 40 Schooling
Lec Rm, Vis Aids, Chng Rm, Showers,
Wait Rm
Hacking
Livery Full, P/T, Break, School, Grass
Schooling General, Break, to El Dress,
to SJ GR C, to HT Nov
Accom S, F, Caravan, Cottage, FB, SC
Exclusions Wt Limit, 13st, Age Limit, 4,
No unaccompanied hacking
Location 10 miles from Nairn on A939,
10 miles from Forres, 12 miles from
Grantown-on-Spey

LOTHIAN

**(Midlothian, East Lothian, West
Lothian, City of Edinburgh)**

APPIN EQUESTRIAN CENTRE
Drem, Nr North Berwick,
East Lothian, EH39 5AS
Tel 01620 880366
Contact Mrs A Montgomery
Riding School, Facility Centre Inst
Riding & Jumping
Staff Chief Instructor Miss S Bowden
(BHSAI, BHS Int Teach)
Plus 2 full time instructors
Ave No 12 Horses, 10 Ponies
inc 2 El Dress, 1 Med Dress, 1 SJ GR C
Courses Short, Ev, P/T
Facilities
Covered School 43 x 21 gly
SJ: Grade C, 1 Paddock
Lec Rm, Vis Aids, Chng Rm, Wait Rm
Livery Full, P/T, School, Grass
Schooling General, to El Dress, to
Med Dress, to SJ GR C, to HT Nov
Accom Caravan, SC
Exclusions Wt Limit, 13st7, Age Limit, 5,
No YTS/Hacking
Location 6 miles from North Berwick,
5 miles from Gullone

THE GRANGE RIDING CENTRE
West Calder, West Lothian, EH55 8PS
Tel 01506 871219
Contact Mrs E J Knight
Riding School Inst Riding & Jumping
Specialities Dressage training
Staff Chief Instructor Mrs E J Knight
(BHSII)
Plus 2 full time instructors
Ave No 4 Horses, 8 Ponies
inc 2 Med Dress

Courses WP, YT, Ev
Facilities
Covered School 46 x 21
Outdoor Manege 40 x 20 fl lt
SJ: Nov
Lec Rm, Vis Aids, Chng Rm, Wait Rm,
Tack Shop
Hacking
Livery Full, Break, School
Schooling General, Break, to Med
Dress
Exclusions Wt Limit, 14st, Age Limit, 5
Location 1 1/2 miles north of West
Calder on the B7015

HOUSTON FARM RIDING SCHOOL
1 Houston Mains, Broxburn,
West Lothian, EH52 6JX
Tel 01506 811351
Contact Ian, Elizabeth & Anne Comrie
Riding School, Training Centre,
Trekking Centre Inst Riding & Jumping
Specialities Training and instruction
tailored to suit individual needs
Staff Chief Instructor Miss A Comrie
(BHSII)
Plus 3 full time instructors
Ave No 26 Horses, 26 Ponies
inc 6 El Dress, 2 Med Dress, 3 Adv
Dress, 3 SJ GR C
Courses WP, YT, Short, Ev, P/T, Hol
Facilities
Covered School 46 x 23
Covered School 30 x 12
SJ: Nov, Grade C, Grade B, 1 Paddock
CC: Nov, Banks, Water, Natural,
20 Schooling
Lec Rm, Vis Aids, Chng Rm, Showers,
Wait Rm, Tack Shop
Hacking
Livery Full, P/T, DIY, Break, School,
Hunt
Schooling General, Break, to Nov
Dress, to El Dress, to Med Dress, to
Adv Dress, to SJ GR C, to SJ GR B,
to SJ GR A, to HT Nov
Exclusions Wt Limit, 15st, Age Limit, 3,
All riders any experience
Location 1 mile from M8, Jn 3

OATRIDGE
AGRICULTURAL COLLEGE
Ecclesmachan, Broxburn,
West Lothian, EH52 6NH
Tel 01506 854387
Contact Mr P Print FBHS
Training Centre Inst to BHSII
Specialities Career training
Staff Chief Instructor Miss S Morrison
(BHS SM, BHSII)
Plus 4 full time instructors

Ave No 45 Horses, 2 Ponies
inc 10 El Dress, 2 Med Dress,
10 SJ GR C
Courses WP, YT, Short, Ev, P/T
Facilities
Covered School 42 x 26 gly
Outdoor Manege 40 x 40 fl lt
Outdoor Manege 60 x 20
SJ: Nov, Grade C, 1 Paddock
CC: Course, Basic, Nov, Water, Natural
Lec Rm, Vis Aids, Chng Rm, Showers,
Wait Rm
Schooling General, Break, to Med
Dress, to SJ GR C, to HT Nov
Accom S, Cottage, FB, SC
Exclusions Wt Limit, 14st, Age Limit, 16,
No casual hire.Students only
Location On Bathgate Hills between
Edinburgh and Glasgow

TOWER FARM RIDING STABLES
85 Liberton Drive,
Edinburgh, EH16 6NS
Tel 0131 664 3375
Contact Mrs J Forrest
Riding School, Training Centre,
Facility Centre Inst Riding & Jumping
Specialities Mounted games, Vaulting
Staff Chief Instructor Mrs J Forrest
(BHSAI, BHS Int Teach)
Plus 5 full time instructors
Ave No 25 Horses, 40 Ponies
inc 2 El Dress, Side saddle
Courses WP, YT, Short, Ev, P/T
Facilities
Covered School 25 x 45 gly
Outdoor Manege 36 x 18 fl lt
Outdoor Manege 40 x 50 fl lt
SJ: Nov
CC: Course, Basic, Banks, Water,
Natural, 16 Schooling
Lec Rm, Vis Aids, Chng Rm, Wait Rm,
Tack Shop
Hacking
Livery Full, Break, School, Hunt, Grass
Schooling General, Break, to Nov
Dress, to El Dress
Accom Tw, SC
Location 3 miles south of city centre, off
A701

VETERINARY FIELD STATION
Easter Bush, Roslin,
Midlothian, EH25 9RG
Tel 0131 650 6284
Contact Miss K Banks
Riding School, Training Centre Inst to
BHSAI
Specialities Career training
Staff Chief Instructor Miss K Banks (BHSII)
Plus 1 full time instructor

151

Ave No 10 Horses, 3 Ponies
inc 1 El Dress, 1 Med Dress, 1 SJ Jun C
Courses WP, Short, Ev, P/T
Facilities
Covered School 40 x 20
SJ: Nov
Lec Rm, Vis Aids, Chng Rm, Showers,
Wait Rm
Hacking
Schooling General, to Nov Dress
Exclusions Wt Limit, 14st, Age Limit, 10
Location Off A701, 1 mile of Roslin

WESTMUIR RIDING CENTRE
Totley Wells Grange, Winchburgh,
West Lothian, EH52 6QJ
Tel 0131 331 2990
Contact Miss D Murray
Riding School, Training Centre Inst
Riding & Jumping
Specialities Career training
Staff Chief Instructor Miss Deborah
Murray (BHSAI, BHS Int Teach)
Plus 2 full time instructors
Ave No 10 Horses, 10 Ponies
Courses WP, YT, Short
Facilities
Covered School 36 x 23 gly
Outdoor Manege 46 x 23 fl lt
SJ: Nov, 1 Paddock
CC: Basic, Banks, Water, 12 Schooling
Lec Rm, Vis Aids, Chng Rm, Wait Rm
Hacking
Livery Full
Schooling General
Accom S, Tw, Caravan, Cottage, SC
Exclusions Wt Limit, 16st, Age Limit, 3,
Hacking for existing clients only
Location Between Winchburgh and
South Queensferry

WHITELOCH FARM RIDING & TREKKING STABLES
Macmerry,
East Lothian, EH33 1PQ
Tel 01875 613662
Contact Mrs Listy Montgomery-Davies
**Riding School, Training Centre,
Facility Centre, Trekking Centre** Inst
Basic
Specialities Small friendly yard,
confidence boosting, and prides itself
on very high safety standards
Staff Chief Instructor Mrs Listy
Montgomery-Davies
Plus 1 full time instructor
Ave No 3 Horses, 11 Ponies
Courses YT, Short, Ev, Hol
Facilities
Outdoor Manege 20 x 40 fl lt
SJ: Nov, 1 Paddock

CC: Natural, 9 Schooling
Lec Rm, Vis Aids, Chng Rm, Wait Rm
Hacking
Schooling General, to Nov Dress
Accom Db, FB
Exclusions Wt Limit, 13st, Age Limit, 5
Location On the A1 Tranent to
Haddington, turn off to the village of
Macmerry

STRATHCLYDE

**(Argyll & Bute, N Ayrshire,
E Ayrshire, S Ayrshire,
N Lanarkshire, S Lanarkshire,
E Dunbartonshire,
City of Glasgow, E Renfrewshire,
Renfreshire, Inverclyde)**

ARDFERN RIDING CENTRE
Craobh Haven, By Loch Gilphead,
Argyll, PA31 8QR
Tel 01852 500632/500270
Contact Mr & Mrs N Boase
Riding School, Trekking Centre Inst
Basic
Specialities Western Riding
1 full time instructor
Ave No 14 Horses
inc Western, Endurance
Courses Short, P/T, Hol
Facilities
Outdoor Manege 44 x 30
CC: Course, Basic, Water, Natural
Chng Rm, Wait Rm
Hacking
Livery Full, P/T, Break, School
Schooling General, Break, to Nov
Dress
Accom Tw, Db, Cottage, SC
Exclusions Wt Limit, 16st
Location Off A816 between Oban and
Lochgilphead, taking the Craobh Haven
road, do not approach via Ardfern

AYRSHIRE EQUITATION CENTRE
South Mains, Corton Road,
Ayr, KA6 6BY
Tel 01292 266267
Contact Mr K Galbraith
**Riding School, Training Centre,
Trekking Centre, Carriage Driving.**
Inst to BHSAI
Specialities Career training
Staff Chief Instructor Mrs L Galbraith
(BHSAI)
Plus 1 full time instructor
Ave No 15 Horses, 10 Ponies
Courses WP, YT, Short, Ev, P/T, Hol

Facilities
Outdoor Manege 50 x 25 fl lt
SJ: Nov, 1 Paddock
CC: Course, Basic, Nov
Lec Rm, Vis Aids, Chng Rm, Wait Rm,
Tack Shop
Hacking
Livery Full, P/T, Break, School, Hunt,
Grass
Schooling General, Break
Accom Db, Caravan, FB
Exclusions Wt Limit, 16st, Age Limit, 5
Location 1 1/2 miles east of Ayr - A713

BANKFOOT FARM RIDING SCHOOL
Inverkip, Renfrewshire, PA16 0DT
Tel 01475 521390
Contact Mrs D H Mathie
**Riding School, Training Centre,
Facility Centre** Inst Riding & Jumping
Specialities Clients can enjoy
instruction in one of two outdoor
arenas, beach rides and hacking
through the private lands of Ardgowan
within a beautiful rural setting
Staff Chief Instructor Mrs Doreen
Mathie (BHS Int Teach, BHSAI)
Ave No 5 Horses, 8 Ponies
inc 1 El Dress
Courses WP, Short, Ev, P/T
Facilities
Outdoor Manege 20 x 40 fl lt
Outdoor Manege 15 x 30 fl lt
SJ: Nov, 2 Paddock
CC: Basic, Natural, 10 Schooling
Lec Rm, Vis Aids, Chng Rm, Wait Rm,
Tack Shop
Hacking
Livery P/T, DIY, Break, School, Grass
Schooling General, Break, to Nov
Dress, to SJ GR C, to HT Nov
Exclusions Wt Limit, 14st, Age Limit, 6
Location On A78 between Greenock &
Inverkip

BARGOWER RIDING SCHOOL
Bargower Farm, Fiveways,
Nr Kilmarnock, Ayrshire, KA15JX
Tel 01563 884223
Contact Mr & Mrs M Cano
Riding School Inst Basic
Staff Chief Instructor Miss L Munro
(BHSAI)
Plus 1 full time instructor
Ave No 7 Horses, 11 Ponies
Courses YT
Facilities
CC: Nov, 12 Schooling
Lec Rm, Vis Aids, Chng Rm, Showers
Hacking
Livery Full

Schooling to El Dress, to SJ GR C
Exclusions Wt Limit, 13st, Age Limit, 5
Location On the A76, between
Kilmarnock and Mauchline

CAIRNHOUSE RIDING CENTRE
The Stables, Blackwaterfoot,
Isle of Arran, KA27 8EU
Tel 01770 860466
Contact Mrs D Murchie
Riding School, Trekking Centre Inst
Basic
Staff Chief Instructor Mrs Dawn Murchie
(BHSAI)
Plus 1 full time instructor
Ave No 6 Horses, 6 Ponies
Courses Hol
Facilities
Outdoor Manege 20 x 40
SJ: Nov
Chng Rm, Wait Rm
Hacking
Livery Full
Schooling General
Exclusions Wt Limit, 12.7st,
No unaccompanied riding
Location On B880 11 miles south west
of Brodick

**CASTLE RIDING CENTRE
& ARGYLL TRAIL RIDING**
Brenfield House, Brenfield,
Argyll, PA30 8ER
Tel 01546 603274
Contact Mrs T B Gray-Stephens
**Riding School, Training Centre,
Facility Centre, Trekking Centre** Inst to
BHSAI
Specialities Vaulting, Trail riding, Event
training & Endurance riding. Swimming
with horses and beach gallops
5 full time instructors
Ave No 17 Horses, 18 Ponies
inc 2 El Dress, 1 Med Dress, 2 SJ GR C,
2 SJ Jun C, 1 SJ Jun A, 2 HT Int,
2 Vaulting Horses, 1 side saddle
Courses WP, Short, P/T, Hol
Facilities
Outdoor Manege 40 x 40
SJ: Nov, 1 Paddock
CC: Course, Basic, Nov, Banks, Water,
Natural, Gallops
Lec Rm, Vis Aids, Chng Rm, Showers,
Tack Shop
Hacking
Livery Full, P/T, DIY, Break, School,
Grass
Schooling General, Break, to Nov
Dress, to El Dress, to Med Dress, to SJ
GR C, to SJ GR B, to HT Nov, to HT Int
Accom S, Tw, Db, F, Dor, Caravan,

Cottage, FB, SC
Exclusions Wt Limit, 15st7, heavier by arrangement, Age Limit, 2,
No unaccompanied children under 9yrs on holiday
Location On A83, 4 miles south of Lochgilphead

EASTERTON STABLES
Mugdock, Milngavie,
Glasgow, G62 8LG
Tel 0141 956 1518/2425
Contact Miss R Brown & Mr D Ralston
Riding School Inst Riding & Jumping
5 full time instructors
Ave No 10 Horses, 9 Ponies
Courses WP, YT, Short, Ev
Facilities
Covered School 18 x 37
Outdoor Manege 40 x 60 fl lt
SJ: Nov, Grade C, 1 Paddock
CC: Course, Basic, Nov, Int, Adv,
Banks, Natural, Gallops, 30 Schooling
Lec Rm, Vis Aids, Chng Rm, Wait Rm
Hacking
Livery Full, P/T, DIY, School, Grass
Schooling General, Break, to Nov
Dress, to El Dress
Accom S
Exclusions Wt Limit, 18st, Age Limit, 3
Location Off A81, 6 miles north of Glasgow

GLEDDOCH RIDING SCHOOL
Gleddoch Hotel Ltd,
Langbank, Renfrewshire, PA14 6YE
Tel 01475 540350
Contact Mr L W Conn
Riding School Inst Basic
Staff Chief Instructor Mrs C Smith (BHSAI)
Plus 1 full time instructor
Ave No 3 Horses, 8 Ponies
Courses Short
Facilities
Outdoor Manege 50 x 18
CC: Basic
Lec Rm, Vis Aids, Chng Rm
Hacking
Livery Full, P/T, Break, School, Grass
Schooling General, Break
Exclusions Wt Limit, 12st, Age Limit, 7,
No unaccompanied hacking
Location 10 miles west of Glasgow airport off A8

HAZELDEN
SCHOOL OF EQUITATION
Mearnskirk, Newton Mearns,
Glasgow, G77 6RR

Tel 0141 639 3011/3101
Contact Mr W Young
Riding School Inst Riding & Jumping
1 full time instructor
Ave No 6 Horses, 12 Ponies
Courses YT
Facilities
Covered School 31 x 25
SJ: Nov
CC: Basic, Water, 10 Schooling
Lec Rm, Vis Aids, Tack Shop
Hacking
Livery Full, Grass
Exclusions Wt Limit, 12st, Age Limit, 4
Location Off A77, 7 miles south of Glasgow

JUMPS EQUESTRIAN CENTRE
Yieldshield Road, Carluke,
Lanarkshire, ML8 4QY
Tel 01555 773206
Contact Mr W Freeman
Riding School Inst Riding & Jumping
Ave No 3 Horses, 8 Ponies
inc 8 RDA Ponies
Courses WP, YT, Short
Facilities
Covered School 20 x 60
Covered School 44 x 18
Outdoor Manege 20 x 40 fl lt
Outdoor Manege 90 x 110 fl lt
Outdoor Manege 20 x 40
SJ: Nov, Grade C, Grade B, Grade A,
3 Paddock
CC: Basic, Banks, Natural, 8 Schooling
Lec Rm, Vis Aids, Chng Rm, Showers,
Wait Rm
Hacking
Livery Full, P/T, DIY, Break, Grass
Schooling General, to El Dress,
to SJ GR A, to HT Nov
Accom FB, SC
Exclusions Wt Limit, 15st, Age Limit, 4
Location 1 1/2 miles east of Carluke,
off the A721

KELBURN RIDING CENTRE
Kelburn Country Centre,
Kelburn Estate, Fairlie,
Ayrshire, KA29 0BE
Tel 01475 568544
Contact Ms Anne Williamson
Riding School Inst Riding & Jumping
Specialities Riding Instruction and
stable management courses tailored to
individual needs. Recreational riders &
career students
Staff Chief Instructor Ms Anne
Williamson (BHSAI, BHS Int.SM)
Plus 2 full time instructors
Ave No 10 Horses, 15 Ponies

Courses WP, YT, Short, Ev, P/T, Hol
Facilities
Outdoor Manege 20 x 40
SJ: Nov, 1 Paddock
CC: Course, Basic, Nov, Banks, Water, Natural
Lec Rm, Vis Aids, Wait Rm
Hacking
Livery Full, P/T, DIY, Break
Schooling General, Break
Exclusions Wt Limit, 14st,
All escorted riding
Location One mile south of Largs on A78 at the Jn of A760

LETTERSHUNA RIDING CENTRE
Appin, Argyll, PA38 4BN
Tel 01631 730227
Contact Mr & Mrs D R Craig
Facility Centre, Trekking Centre, Livery
Staff Chief Instructor Miss Jane Thompson (BHSAI)
Plus 1 full time instructor
Ave No 3 Horses, 9 Ponies
Courses Hol
Facilities
Outdoor Manege 24 x 48
SJ: Nov
CC: Course, Basic, Water, Natural
Chng Rm
Hacking
Livery Full, Break, School, Grass
Schooling General, Break
Exclusions Age Limit, 7
Location On A828 midway between Oban and Fort William overlooking Loch Linnhe

MULL OF KINTYRE EQUESTRIAN CENTRE
Homeston Farm, Campbeltown, Argyll, PA28 6RL
Tel 01586 552437
Contact Mr Malcolm McArthur
Trekking Centre
Specialities Trail riding, Cross country, Beach rides and Picnic rides. Kintyre is a peninsula of rolling hills, magnificent beaches and sea-scapes
Ave No 5 Horses, 5 Ponies
Facilities
Covered School 35 x 15
Outdoor Manege 40 x 25
CC: Course, Basic
Lec Rm, Vis Aids, Chng Rm, Wait Rm
Hacking
Accom S, Tw, Db, FB
Exclusions Wt Limit, 15st, Age Limit, 5
Location A83 to Campbeltown then A842 towards Southend approx 3 miles

ROCKSIDE FARM TREKKING CENTRE
Bruichladdich, Isle of Islay, Strathclyde, PA49 7UT
Tel 01496 850231
Contact Mrs R French
Riding School, RDA Inst Riding & Jumping
Specialities Interesting rides with 2 miles of beach on own property, without road work
Staff Chief Instructor Mrs R French (BHSAI)
Plus 2 full time instructors
Ave No 12 Horses, 18 Ponies
inc 1 SJ GR C
Courses P/T, Hol
Facilities
Outdoor Manege 18 x 40
Chng Rm
Hacking
Livery Full, P/T, Break, School, Grass
Schooling General, Break
Exclusions Wt Limit, 15st, Age Limit, 6
Location Take right turn off A847, 2 miles before Bruichladdicy, towards Sanaigmore; 5 miles to riding centre

ROTHESAY RIDING CENTRE
Ardbrannan Farm, Canada Hill, Rothesay, Isle of Bute, PA20 9EN
Tel 01700 504971/505849
Contact Mr & Mrs Rooney
Riding School, Training Centre, Trekking Centre Inst Riding & Jumping
Specialities Trekking and Leisure Riding
Staff Chief Instructor Mrs Jane Rooney (BHSAI)
Plus 3 full time instructors
Ave No 2 Horses, 20 Ponies
Courses P/T, Hol
Facilities
Outdoor Manege 20 x 40
SJ: 2 Paddock
Lec Rm, Vis Aids, Chng Rm, Wait Rm
Hacking
Schooling General, Break, to El Dress
Accom Dor, SC
Exclusions Wt Limit, 12st, Age Limit, 2
Location One mile south of Rothesay on A844

SCOTTISH EQUI COMPLEX
Race Course Stables, Lanark, Strathclyde, ML11 9TA
Tel 01555 661853
Contact Mrs M A Taylor
Riding School Inst Riding & Jumping
Specialities Riding Holidays, unaccompanied children welcome

Staff Chief Instructor Mrs S Boyle
(BHSAI)
Plus 3 full time instructors
Ave No 12 Horses, 12 Ponies
inc 1 Med Dress, Western
Courses Short, Hol
Facilities
Outdoor Manege 37 x 24 fl lt
Outdoor Manege 50 x 25
SJ: Nov, 1 Paddock
CC: Course, Basic, Banks, Water,
Natural, Gallops, 12 Schooling
Lec Rm, Vis Aids, Chng Rm, Showers,
Wait Rm
Hacking
Livery Full, Break, School
Schooling General, Break, to Nov Dress
Accom S, Tw, FB
Exclusions Wt Limit, 14st, Age Limit, 4+

WOODEND EQUESTRIAN

Woodend Farm, Kilsyth,
North Lanarkshire, G65 0PZ
Tel 01236 822201
Contact Mr R Chalmers
**Riding School, Training Centre,
Facility Centre** Inst Riding & Jumping
Specialities A friendly atmosphere for
riders of all ages from novice to career
training
Staff Chief Instructor Miss Liz Nairn
Ave No 9 Horses, 7 Ponies
inc 2 El Dress, 1 SJ GR C
Courses YT, Short, Ev, P/T
Facilities
Covered School 55 x 23
Outdoor Manege 55 x 37
SJ: Nov, Grade C, 1 Paddock
CC: Natural, 8 Schooling
Lec Rm, Vis Aids, Chng Rm, Wait Rm
Hacking
Livery Full, DIY, School, Grass
Schooling General, Break, to Med
Dress, to SJ GR C
Exclusions Wt Limit, 14st
Location From Edinburgh M9, M876
then take the A803 to Kilsyth

TAYSIDE

**(Perthshire & Kinross, Angus,
City of Dundee)**

CRIEFF HYDRO

Strathearn Stables, Crieff Hydro Hotel,
Crieff, Perthshire, Tayside, PH7 3LO
Tel 01764 655555
Contact Mrs L Simpson
Riding School, Training Centre Inst

Basic
4 full time instructors
Ave No 6 Horses, 9 Ponies
inc 2 El Dress
Courses YT, Short, Ev, P/T, Hol
Facilities
Outdoor Manege 40 x 20 fl lt
SJ: Nov, 1 Paddock
CC: Banks, Water, Natural
Lec Rm, Vis Aids, Chng Rm, Showers
Hacking
Livery Full, P/T, DIY, Break, School,
Grass
Schooling General, Break
Accom S, Tw, Db, F, FB, SC
Exclusions Wt Limit, 14st, Age Limit, 6
Location Off A85 at Crieff

DENMILL STABLES & GLENPROSEN RIDING CENTRE

Kirriemuir, Angus, DD8 5QQ
Tel 01575 572757/575961
Contact Miss Victoria J Orr
**Riding School, Training Centre,
Facility Centre, Trekking Centre** Inst
Riding & Jumping
Staff Chief Instructor Miss Victoria
Jane Orr (BHSAI)
Plus 1 full time instructor
Ave No 8 Horses, 10 Ponies
inc 1 El Dress, 1 Med Dress, 1 Adv
Dress, 1 SJ GR C
Courses WP, YT, Short, Ev, P/T
Facilities
Outdoor Manege 25 x 45 fl lt
SJ: Nov, Grade C, 1 Paddock
Lec Rm, Vis Aids, Chng Rm, Wait Rm
Hacking
Livery Full, P/T, DIY, Break, School,
Grass
Schooling General, Break, to Adv
Dress, to SJ GR C
Exclusions Wt Limit, 16st, Age Limit, 4
Location Take B951 from Forfar to
Kirriemuir - 6 miles. Follow one way
system through the town, past filling
station turn right, foot of hill turn right,
and then left past scout hut

THE GLENEAGLES EQUESTRIAN CENTRE

Auchterarder, Perthshire, PH3 1NZ
Tel 01764 663507
Contact Mrs D Zajda BHSI
**Riding School, Training Centre,
Facility Centre** Inst to BHSI
Specialities Career training, Carriage
Driving, Vaulting and Side Saddle
Staff Chief Instructor Mrs D Zajda
(BHSI)
Plus 7 full time instructors

Ave No 23 Horses, 10 Ponies
inc 6 El Dress, 2 Med Dress,
2 Adv Dress, 6 SJ GR C, 1 SJ GR B,
1 SJ Jun C, 1 HT Int, 4 Side Saddle,
single/pair/team carriages
Courses WP, Short, Ev, P/T, Hol
Facilities
Covered School 37 x 75 gly
Covered School 20 x 40
Outdoor Manege 60 x 40 fl lt
SJ: Nov, Grade C, Grade B, Grade A,
1 Paddock
CC: Course, Basic, Nov, Int, Banks,
Water, Natural, 40 Schooling
Lec Rm, Vis Aids, Chng Rm, Showers,
Wait Rm, Tack Shop
Hacking
Livery Full, P/T, Break, School, Hunt
Schooling General, Break, to Adv
Dress, to SJ GR A, to HT Int
Accom S, Tw, Db, FB
Exclusions Wt Limit, 16st, Age Limit, 4
Location Off A9 between Perth and
Stirling

GLENFARG
RIDING SCHOOL
Smiddyhill, Glenfarg,
Perth, PH2 9NL
Tel 01577 830262
Contact Miss A Stocks
Riding School, RDA Inst Basic
Staff Chief Instructor Miss A Stocks
Ave No 7 Ponies
Courses Hol

Facilities
Covered School 30 x 21 gly
Outdoor Manege 20 x 42
SJ: Nov, 1 Paddock
CC: Basic, Banks, Water, Natural,
12 Schooling
Wait Rm
Hacking
Livery DIY
Schooling General
Exclusions Wt Limit, 10st5,
Age Limit, 5
Location 5 miles north of Kinross,
11 miles from Perth on B896, Jn 8 and
Jn 9 M90

ROWANLEA
RIDING SCHOOL
Westcotside, Barry, Carnoustie,
Angus, DD7 7SA
Tel 01382 532536
Contact Mr D Conchie
Riding School Inst Basic
Staff Chief Instructor Mr D Conchie
Plus 2 full time instructors
Ave No 8 Horses, 20 Ponies
Facilities
Outdoor Manege 40 x 100 fl lt
SJ: Nov
Chng Rm, Tack Shop
Hacking
Livery P/T, DIY, Break, School
Schooling General, Break, to SJ GR C
Exclusions Age Limit, 3
Location 7 miles from Dundee off A930

Riding in Wales

CLWYD ◆ DYFED & WEST GLAMORGAN
GWENT, SOUTH & MID GLAMORGAN
GWYNEDD ◆ POWYS

Note

Local government reorganisation has resulted in name and border changes to the counties of Wales. In this edition of *Where to Ride* the former county name is followed by the new unitary authority names for that area.

CLWYD

(Flintshire, Denbighshire, Wrexham, Aberconwy & Colwyn)

**CHAPEL FARM
EQUESTRIAN CENTRE**
Newbridge, Wrexham,
Clwyd, LL14 3AJ
Tel 01978 823470
Contact Mr K Wycherley
Riding School Inst Riding & Jumping
3 full time instructors
Ave No 9 Horses, 5 Ponies
Courses WP, YT, Short, Ev, P/T, Hol
Facilities
Outdoor Manege 30 x 60
SJ: Nov
Lec Rm, Vis Aids
Hacking
Schooling General
Exclusions Wt Limit, 15st, Age Limit, 5,
Escorted hacking only
Location one mile off A5 going towards
Llangollen

CLAREMONT EQUESTRIAN CENTRE
Llanychan, Ruthin,
Denbighshire, LL15 1UD
Tel 01824 703324
Contact Ms K Carman
Riding School, Training Centre Inst
to BHSAI
Specialities Teaching beginners,
novice and nervous riders. Students
trained to BHS Stage II and NVQ 2,
stable management and
Horse Owners' courses
Staff Chief Instructor Miss K Carman
(BHSII, BHS SM)

Ave No 10 Horses, 5 Ponies
inc 1 El Dress, 1 Med Dress,
1 Adv Dress, 1 SJ GR C, 1 HT Int
Courses WP, YT, Short, Ev, P/T, Hol
Facilities
Outdoor Manege 60 x 20 fl lt
SJ: Nov, 4acre Paddock
CC: Course, Basic
Lec Rm, Vis Aids, Chng Rm, Wait Rm,
Tack Shop
Hacking
Livery Full, P/T, DIY, Break, School,
Hunt, Grass
Schooling General, Break, to Nov
Dress, to El Dress, to Med Dress,
to Adv Dress, to SJ GR C, to HT Nov,
to HT Int
Accom Tw, Db, Cottage, SC
Exclusions Wt Limit, 14st,
No unescorted riding
Location 5 miles north of Ruthin on the
B5429

THE EQUESTRIAN CENTRE
Gresford Road, Hope,
Wrexham, Clwyd, LL12 9SD
Tel 01978 760356/761349
Contact Mr & Mrs M W Tytherleigh
Riding School, Training Centre Inst
to BHSAI
5 full time instructors
Ave No 20 Horses, 15 Ponies
Courses WP, YT, Short, Ev, Hol
Facilities
Covered School 61 x 30 gly
Outdoor Manege 40 x 20 fl lt
Outdoor Manege 45 x 40
SJ: Grade C, 1 Paddock
CC: Course, Nov, Banks, Water,
Natural, Gallops
Lec Rm, Vis Aids, Chng Rm, Wait Rm

Hacking
Schooling General, Break, to El Dress,
to SJ GR C, to HT Nov
Accom Tw, F, FB
Exclusions Wt Limit, 14st7
Location 8 miles Chester, 7 miles
Wrexham

PEACEHAVEN
RIDING CENTRE
Terrace Lane, Penyffordd,
Chester, Clwyd, CH4 0HB
Tel 01244 546819
Contact Mr & Mrs G Williams
Riding School, Training Centre Inst
Riding & Jumping
Specialities NVQ location up to level 3
Staff Chief Instructor Mrs V Williams
(BHS Int.SM)
Plus 1 full time instructor
Ave No 8 Horses, 13 Ponies
inc 1 El Dress
Courses YT, Short, Ev, P/T, Hol
Facilities
Outdoor Manege 20 x 45 fl lt
SJ: Nov, 1 Paddock
Lec Rm, Vis Aids, Chng Rm, Showers,
Wait Rm, Tack Shop
Hacking
Livery Full, P/T, Break, School
Schooling General, to Nov Dress,
to El Dress
Exclusions Wt Limit, 13st, Age Limit, 4,
No unaccompanied riding
Location 7 miles from Chester
(A5104), 10 miles from Wrexham and 1
mile from A55

TYNLLWYN
RIDING SCHOOL
Tynllwyn Farm, Bryn-y-Maen,
Colwyn Bay, Clwyd, LL28 5ER
Tel 01492 580224
Contact Mr W Lewis
Riding School Inst Riding & Jumping
Specialities Instruction in Riding &
Jumping for beginners and novice riders
3 full time instructors
Ave No 12 Horses, 7 Ponies
Courses WP, YT, Short, Ev, P/T
Facilities
Covered School 20 x 30 gly
Outdoor Manege 50 x 27
CC: Course
Lec Rm, Vis Aids, Chng Rm, Wait Rm
Hacking
Schooling General
Exclusions No unescorted hacking
Location Near Colwyn Bay on B5113

DYFED &
WEST GLAMORGAN

**(Cardiganshire, Pembrokeshire,
Carmarthenshire, Swansea,
Port Talbot)**

BOWLING RIDING SCHOOL
Rudbaxton, Haverfordwest,
Pembrokeshire, SA62 4DB
Tel 01437 741407/599
Contact Mrs J Gibson
Riding School, Training Centre Inst to
BHSII
Staff Chief Instructor Mr M Butcher
(BHSAI, BHS Int Teach)
Plus 2 full time instructors
Ave No 20 Horses, 20 Ponies
inc 8 El Dress, 1 SJ GR C, 1 SJ GR B
Courses YT, Short, Ev, P/T, Hol
Facilities
Covered School 40 x 20 gly
Outdoor Manege 60 x 30 fl lt
SJ: Nov, 1 Paddock
CC: Natural, Gallops, 8 Schooling
Lec Rm, Vis Aids
Hacking
Exclusions Wt Limit, 15st, Age Limit, 3
Location 3 miles north of Haverfordwest
off A40

CAEIAGO
Ffarmers, Llanwrda,
Dyfed, SA19 8LZ
Tel 01558 650303
Contact Mr, Mrs & Ms C Pollak
Trekking Centre, Trail Riding
1 full time instructor
Ave No 15 Horses
Courses Hol
Chng Rm, Showers
Hacking
Accom S, Tw, Db, FB
Exclusions Wt Limit, 15st, Age Limit, 18
Location 2 miles off the A482 between
Llandovery and Lampeter

CIMLA TREKKING
& EQUESTRIAN CENTRE
Hawdref Ganor Farm, Cimla Neath,
West Glamorgan, SA12 9SL
Tel 01639 644944
Contact Mr S Brown
Riding School, Trekking Centre, RDA
Inst Riding & Jumping
Staff Chief Instructor Miss C Brown
Plus 2 full time instructors
Ave No 14 Horses, 25 Ponies
Courses WP, Short, Ev, P/T, Hol
Facilities
Covered School 21 x 45 gly

Outdoor Manege 40 x 20 fl lt
SJ: Nov
Hacking
Livery Full, Break, School, Hunt
Schooling General, Break
Accom S, Tw, Db, F, Dor
Exclusions Escorted Hacks only
Location On B4287, approx 3 miles
east of Neath

CLYN-DU RIDING CENTRE
Clyn-du Farm, Burry Port, Llanelli,
Dyfed, SA16 0BZ
Tel 01554 832546
Contact Mrs R Vaughan-Jones
**Riding School, Training Centre,
Facility Centre, RDA (Two Group
Days)** Inst to BHSAI
Specialities Breaking, schooling and
nervous riders. Base for local Pony
Club
Staff Chief Instructor Mrs R Vaughan-
Jones (BHSAI)
Plus 1 full time instructor
Ave No 11 Horses, 17 Ponies
inc 5 El Dress, 3 SJ GR C,
3 compete regularly at RC & Novice
Courses WP, YT, Short, Ev, P/T, Hol
Facilities
Outdoor Manege 30 x 50
SJ: Nov, 2 Paddock
CC: Basic, Banks, Water, Natural,
14 Schooling
Lec Rm, Vis Aids, Chng Rm, Showers,
Wait Rm
Hacking
Livery Full, P/T, DIY, Break, School,
Hunt, Grass
Schooling General, Break, to Nov
Dress, to El Dress, to SJ GR C, to HT
Nov
Accom Cottage, FB, SC
Exclusions Wt Limit, 15st,
No unescorted rides
Location Just off A484, 10 miles from
Jn 48 of M4

COPLEY STABLES
Bishopston, Swansea,
West Glamorgan, S43 3JA
Tel 01792 234428
Contact Mrs W Hemns-Tucker
Riding School Inst Riding & Jumping
Staff Chief Instructor Mrs W Hemns-
Tucker (BHSII)
Ave No 4 Horses, 6 Ponies
Courses YT, Short, Ev, P/T, Hol
Facilities
Outdoor Manege 58 x 29 fl lt
SJ: Nov, 1 Paddock
Hacking
Livery Full, Break, School, Hunt, Grass
Schooling General, Break, to SJ GR C,

to HT Nov
Accom S, Tw, Db, F, FB, SC
Exclusions Wt Limit, 15st, Age Limit, 6,
Unescorted hacking and hunting
Location On B4436 Swansea to
Bishopstone road

DERWEN INTERNATIONAL
WELSH COB CENTRE
Ynyshir, Pennant, Llan-non,
Dyfed, SY23 5JN
Tel 01545 570250
Contact Mr I J Roscoe-Lloyd
Welsh cob stud
Specialities In hand showing,
Breeding, Schooling. Museum
1 full time instructor
Ave No 60 Ponies
Courses WP, Short, Ev, P/T
Facilities
Covered School 20 x 55
Chng Rm, Wait Rm
Livery Break
Schooling General, Break
Location Off A487 1 mile north of
Aberaeron

DINEFWR RIDING CENTRE
Creigau Llandyfan, Ammanford,
Dyfed, SA18 2UD
Tel 01269 850042
Contact Mr & Mrs T Jenner
**Riding School, Facility Centre, RDA
centre** Inst Riding & Jumping
Staff Chief Instructor Mrs P Jenner
(BHSAI)
Ave No 9 Horses, 11 Ponies
Courses WP, YT, Ev, P/T, Hol
Facilities
Covered School 20 x 40
Covered School 25 x 25
SJ: Nov, Grade C, 1 Paddock
CC: Course, Banks, Water, Gallops
Lec Rm, Vis Aids, Chng Rm, Showers,
Wait Rm
Hacking
Livery Full, P/T, Break, School, Hunt,
Grass
Schooling General, Break, to Nov Dress
Accom Db, Dor, FB
Exclusions Wt Limit, 14st,
Age Limit, 3 1/2,
No unaccompanied rides
Location 6 miles from Jn 49 on the M4.
2 miles from Carreg Lennen Castle

THE DYFED RIDING CENTRE
Maes-Y-Felin, Bridell, Cardigan,
Dyfed, SA43 3DG
Tel 01239 612594
Contact Mrs T Humfrey
Riding School Inst Riding & Jumping
Staff Chief Instructor Mr T Humfrey

(BHSII)
Ave No 7 Horses, 13 Ponies
inc 2 El Dress, 3 SJ GR C
Courses WP, YT, Short, Hol
Facilities
Covered School 32 x 19 gly
Outdoor Manege 40 x 20
SJ: Nov, 1 Paddock
CC: Course, Basic, Banks, Water,
Natural, Gallops
Lec Rm, Vis Aids, Chng Rm, Showers,
Wait Rm
Hacking
Livery Full, P/T, Break, School, Grass
Schooling General, Break, to El Dress,
to SJ GR C, to HT Nov
Accom Tw, FB
Exclusions Wt Limit, 15st
Location Off A478, 4 miles from
Cardigan

L & A HOLIDAY & RIDING CENTRE
Goytre, Port Talbot,
West Glamorgan, SA13 2YP
Tel 01639 885509
Contact Mr & Mrs A G Holden
Riding School, Facility Centre,
Trekking Centre Inst Riding & Jumping
3 full time instructors
Ave No 45 Horses, 34 Ponies
Courses WP, YT, P/T, Hol
Facilities
Covered School 43 x 21
Outdoor Manege 20 x 30
SJ: Grade C, Grade B, Grade A,
1 Paddock
CC: Basic, Nov, 17 Schooling
Lec Rm, Vis Aids, Chng Rm, Showers,
Wait Rm
Hacking
Livery P/T, Grass
Schooling General, to Med Dress,
to SJ GR C, to HT Nov
Accom S, Tw, F, Cottage, FB, SC
Location Off A48 at Port Talbot Rugby
Club

PEMBROKESHIRE RIDING CENTRE
Pennybridge Farm, Hundleton,
Pembroke, Dyfed, SA71 5RD
Tel 01646 682513
Contact Mr & Mrs E W Scourfield
Riding School, Stud Inst Riding &
Jumping
Staff Chief Instructor Mrs S P
Scourfield (BHS SM)
Plus 4 full time instructors
Ave No 12 Horses, 10 Ponies
inc 1 El Dress, 1 SJ GR C
Courses WP, YT, Short, Ev, P/T, Hol
Facilities
Covered School 44 x 27 gly
Outdoor Manege 18 x 37 fl lt

SJ: Grade A, 1 Paddock
CC: Course, Basic, Banks, Natural
Lec Rm, Vis Aids, Chng Rm, Tack Shop
Hacking
Livery Full, P/T, Break, School, Hunt,
Grass
Schooling General, Break, to Nov
Dress, to SJ GR C, to HT Nov
Accom S, Db, F, Dor, FB
Exclusions Wt Limit, 14st, Age Limit, 4,
No unescorted riding
Location 2 1/2 miles south west of
Pembroke on the B4320

PLAS-Y-WERN RIDING STABLES
Newquay, Dyfed, SA45 9ST
Tel 01545 580156
Contact Mrs A Miles
Trekking Centre
Specialities Hacking & Trekking
Staff Chief Instructor Mrs A Miles
Plus 1 full time instructor
Ave No 1 Horses, 7 Ponies
Facilities
Covered School 20 x 30
CC: Course, Basic, Banks, Water,
Natural, 18 Schooling
Chng Rm, Wait Rm
Hacking
Schooling General
Accom Cottage, SC
Exclusions Wt Limit, 14st, Age Limit, 5,
No unescorted riding
Location B4342, 1 mile from New Quay

RHEIDOL RIDING & HOLIDAY CENTRE
Felin Rhiw Arthen, Capel Bangor,
Aberystwyth, Ceredigion, SY23 4EL
Tel 01970 880863
Contact Mr & Mrs G J Evans
Riding School, Training Centre,
Trekking Centre, Riding Holidays/RDA
Inst Riding & Jumping
Specialities Beginners and Improvers
Staff Chief Instructor Miss I N Evans
(BHSAI, BHS Int Teach, BHS Int.SM)
Plus 2 full time instructors
Ave No 8 Horses, 6 Ponies
inc 1 El Dress
Courses YT, Short, Ev, Hol
Facilities
Outdoor Manege 40 x 20 fl lt
SJ: 1 Paddock
CC: Banks, Water, Natural, 22 Schooling
Lec Rm, Vis Aids, Chng Rm, Showers
Hacking
Livery Full, P/T, DIY, Break, School,
Grass
Schooling General, Break, to Nov Dress
Accom Caravan
Exclusions Wt Limit, 15st
Location Off A44 (T), 4 miles east of
Aberystwyth

WAUN FAWR FARM
Primrose Lane, Rhos, Pontardawe,
West Glamorgan, SA8 3EU
Tel 01792 830273
Contact Mrs F E Davies
Livery
Specialities DIY Livery
Facilities
Outdoor Manege 120 x 60 fl lt
Chng Rm, Showers, Wait Rm
Hacking
Livery DIY
Location Off A474, 3 miles north of
Neath

WELSH EQUITATION CENTRE
Pantyrathro Manor, Llangain,
Carmarthen,
Carmarthenshire, SA33 5AJ
Tel 01267 241226
Contact Mr & Mrs E Morgan
Riding School Inst Riding & Jumping
Specialities Instruction in riding &
jumping for beginners, novices and
children. Holiday accommodation for
horse and rider
2 full time instructors
Ave No 6 Horses, 8 Ponies
Courses WP, YT, Short, Ev, P/T, Hol
Facilities
Covered School 60 x 20 gly
SJ: Nov, Grade C
CC: Banks, 6 Schooling
Lec Rm, Vis Aids, Chng Rm, Showers,
Wait Rm
Hacking
Livery Full, P/T, DIY, Break, School,
Hunt
Schooling General, Break,
to SJ GR C, to HT Nov
Accom S, Tw, Db, Caravan, Cottage,
SC
Exclusions Wt Limit, 15st,
Instructional riding only
Location Five miles from Carmarthen
town on headland overlooking the
beautiful Towy Valley Estuary,
Carmarthen Bay, and Llanstephan
Beach

WOODLANDS RIDING SCHOOL
Vennaway Lane, Parkmill, Gower,
Nr Swansea,
West Glamorgan, SA3 2EA
Tel 01792 232704
Contact Miss T D Watts
Riding School, Training Centre, RDA
Inst Riding & Jumping
Staff Chief Instructor Miss T Watts
(BHSI)
Ave No 6 Horses, 19 Ponies
Courses WP, YT
Facilities

CC: Basic
Lec Rm, Vis Aids, Chng Rm, Wait Rm
Hacking
Livery Full, P/T, DIY, Break, School,
Grass
Schooling General, Break
Exclusions Wt Limit, 14st
Location Off A4118 to Pennard

GWENT, SOUTH & MID GLAMORGAN

**(Bridgend, Vale of Glamorgan,
Cardiff, Rhondda Cynon Taff,
Merthyr Tydfil, Caerphilly, Bleanau
Gwent, Torfaen)**

ARGAE HOUSE STABLES
St Andrews Major,
Dinas Powys,
Vale of Glamorgan, CF64 4HD
Tel 01222 515546
Contact Miss A V Roberts
Riding School, Training Centre Inst
Riding & Jumping
1 full time instructor
Ave No 10 Horses, 5 Ponies
inc 1 Med Dress, 2 SJ GR C, 3 HT Int,
4 Open Team Chaser
Courses Short, Ev, P/T
Facilities
Covered School 25 x 45 gly
Outdoor Manege 20 x 60
SJ: Nov, Grade C, 1 Paddock
CC: Course, Basic, Nov, Banks,
Natural
Chng Rm
Livery Full, Break, School, Hunt
Schooling General, Break, to El Dress,
to SJ GR C, to HT Nov, to HT Adv
Exclusions Wt Limit, 14st, No YTS,
No casual hire
Location 8 miles south of Jn 33 on M4,
9 miles from airport on A4050

CARDIFF RIDING SCHOOL
Pontcanna Fields,
Llandaff,
Cardiff, CF1 9LB
Tel 01222 383908
Contact Mrs P Pembridge
Riding School, Training Centre, RDA
Inst Riding & Jumping
Staff Chief Instructor Mrs P Pembridge
(BHSAI, BHS Int Teach, BHS Int.SM)
Plus 3 full time instructors
Ave No 16 Horses, 17 Ponies
Courses WP, Short, Ev, P/T, Hol

Facilities
Covered School 55 x 30 gly
Outdoor Manege 30 x 30 fl lt
SJ: Nov, Grade C, 1 Paddock
CC: Course, Basic, Nov, Banks,
Natural
Lec Rm, Vis Aids, Chng Rm, Showers,
Wait Rm
Hacking
Livery Full, P/T, Break, School, Hunt
Schooling General, Break, to El Dress,
to SJ GR C, to HT Int
Exclusions Age Limit, 4
Accompanied hacking only
Location On A48, 1 mile from centre of
Cardiff

GROES FARM STABLES
Groes Farm, Southerndown,
Bridgend, Mid Glamorgan, CF32 0RL
Tel 01656 880365
Contact Mrs Mary Morgan
Livery
Ave No 24 Horses
Livery Full, P/T, DIY
Location 15 minutes from Jn 5 off M4

GROESWEN RIDING STABLES
Ty Canol Farm, Caerphilly,
South Wales, CF83 2RL
Tel 01222 882319
Contact Ms C E Jones
Riding School Inst Riding & Jumping
Specialities Beginners, novice and
nervous riders - lessons for children
and adults
Staff Chief Instructor Miss Catherine
Jones
Ave No 6 Horses, 6 Ponies
Courses WP, YT
Facilities
SJ: Nov
Lec Rm, Vis Aids
Hacking
Livery DIY
Exclusions Age Limit, 5
No unescorted hacking
Location off A468, 6 miles M4 Jn.32

GWENT TERTIARY COLLEGE
Usk Centre, Usk,
Monmouthshire, NP5 1XJ
Tel 01291 672311
Contact Mrs J Challoner
Riding School, Training Centre Inst
Riding & Jumping
Staff Chief Instructor Ms Sarah
Spencer-Williams (BHSI)
Plus 6 full time instructors
Ave No 10 Horses, 10 Ponies
Courses WP, YT, Short, Ev, P/T, Hol
Facilities
Outdoor Manege 20 x 40

Outdoor Manege 80 x 40
SJ: Nov, 1 Paddock
Chng Rm, Showers, Wait Rm
Hacking
Schooling General
Accom S, Tw, Db, FB
Exclusions Wt Limit, 11st7, Age Limit, 8
Location On A472, 1 mile from Usk

LIEGE MANOR FARM
EQUESTRIAN CENTRE
Liege Manor Farm, Llancarfan Lane,
Bonvilston,
Vale of Glamorgan, CF5 6TQ
Tel 01446 781648
Contact Miss Sarah M Bassett
Riding School Inst Riding & Jumping
Specialities Recreational Riders, Career
Students, specialised instruction for com-
petitions. Courses individually tailored
Staff Chief Instructor Miss Sarah Bassett
Ave No 29 Horses, 10 Ponies
inc 2 Med Dress, 2 SJ GR C, 1 SJ GR B,
1 SJ Jun C, Horse Trial Novice
Courses WP, YT, Short, Ev, P/T, Hol
Facilities
Covered School 20 x 40 gly
SJ: Nov, Grade C, 1 Paddock
Hacking
Livery Full, Break, School, Hunt
Schooling General, Break, to Med
Dress, to SJ GR B, to HT Nov
Exclusions Wt Limit, 15st,
No unescorted riding
Location Off A48, between Cowbridge &
Cardiff

PANT-Y-SAIS
RIDING & TREKKING STABLES
Jersey Marine, Neath,
West Glamorgan, SA10 6JS
Tel 01792 816439
Contact Mr & Mrs D S Gorvett
Riding School, Trekking Centre, RDA
Inst Basic
Staff Chief Instructor Mrs J Gorvett
Plus 2 full time instructors
Ave No 6 Horses, 19 Ponies
Courses Hol
Facilities
Covered School 47 x 19 gly
Outdoor Manege 37 x 19
SJ: Nov, 1 Paddock
CC: 6 Schooling
Lec Rm, Vis Aids, Chng Rm, Showers
Hacking
Livery Full, P/T
Schooling General
Accom Dor, SC
Exclusions Wt Limit, 16st, Age Limit, 6
Location Adjacent to golf course, in
Jersey Marine

**PARC-LE-BREOS
RIDING HOLIDAY CENTRE**
Parkmill, Gower, Swansea,
West Glamorgan, SA3 2HA
Tel 01792 371636
Contact Mr J T Edwards
Trekking Centre
Staff Chief Instructor Miss D Handley
Plus 1 full time instructor
Ave No 5 Horses, 25 Ponies
Chng Rm, Showers, Wait Rm
Accom Db, F, FB
Exclusions Wt Limit, 13st7, Age Limit, 10
Location Off A4118, 10 miles from
centre of Swansea

PENCOED COLLEGE
Bridgend, Mid Glamorgan, CF35 5LG
Tel 01656 860202/860635
Contact Mr J Thomas
**Riding School, Training Centre,
Facility Centre** Inst to BHSAI
7 full time instructors
Ave No 35 Horses, 5 Ponies
Courses Short, Ev, P/T, Hol
Facilities
Covered School 20 x 40 gly
Covered School 30 x 60 gly
SJ: Grade C, 1 Paddock
CC: Course, Basic, Nov, Banks, Water,
30 Schooling
Lec Rm, Vis Aids, Wait Rm
Livery Full, P/T, Break, School
Schooling General, Break, to El Dress,
to SJ GR C, to HT Nov
Exclusions Wt Limit, 13.5st,
No casual hire
Location 1 mile off Jn 35 on M4

**PONDEROSA
EQUESTRIAN CENTRE**
Newport Road, New Inn,
Pontypool, Gwent, NP4 0TP
Tel 01495 762660
Contact Mr & Mrs R Davies
Riding School, Training Centre Inst
Riding & Jumping
Staff Chief Instructor Mrs A Davies
(BHSAI, BHS Int.SM)
Plus 1 full time instructor
Ave No 8 Horses, 10 Ponies
inc 1 SJ GR C
Courses WP, Short, Ev, P/T, Hol
Facilities
Covered School 18 x 35
Outdoor Manege 35 x 70 fl lt
SJ: Nov, 1 Paddock
CC: Banks, 6 Schooling
Lec Rm, Vis Aids, Chng Rm, Wait Rm,
Tack Shop
Hacking
Livery Break, School
Schooling General, Break, to SJ GR C

Exclusions Wt Limit, 13st, Age Limit, 5,
Experienced hacking only
Location Just off A4042, 5 miles from
M4 Jn 6

**SEVERNVALE
EQUESTRIAN CENTRE**
Tidenham, Chepstow, Gwent, NP6 7LL
Tel 01291 623412
Contact Mr E Winter
**Riding School, Training Centre,
Facility Centre** Inst Riding & Jumping
Staff Chief Instructor Mrs E Winter
(BHSI)
Plus 3 full time instructors
Ave No 8 Horses, 6 Ponies
inc 1 El Dress, 1 SJ GR C, 1 HT Int
Courses WP, YT, Short, Ev, P/T, Hol
Facilities
Covered School 20 x 41 gly
Outdoor Manege 20 x 41
SJ: Nov, Grade C, Grade B, 1 Paddock
CC: Course, Basic, Nov, Banks,
Natural, 20 Schooling
Lec Rm, Vis Aids, Chng Rm, Wait Rm
Hacking
Livery Full, P/T, DIY, Break, School,
Hunt, Grass
Schooling General, Break, to El Dress,
to SJ GR B, to HT Int
Exclusions Wt Limit, 15st, Age Limit, 3

**SOUTH WALES
EQUESTRIAN CENTRE**
Heol-y-Cyw, Bridgend,
Mid Glamorgan, CF35 6NH
Tel 01656 862959/860854
Contact Mr J R Jones
Riding School, Training Centre Inst
to BHSAI
4 full time instructors
Ave No 12 Horses, 15 Ponies
Courses WP, YT, Short, Ev, P/T
Facilities
Covered School 18 x 55 gly
Outdoor Manege 20 x 40
SJ: Grade A, 1 Paddock
CC: Course, Int, Banks, Water,
Gallops, 35 Schooling
Lec Rm, Vis Aids, Chng Rm, Wait Rm,
Tack Shop
Hacking
Livery Full, P/T, DIY, School, Grass
Schooling General, to El Dress, to SJ
GR B
Exclusions Age Limit, 5
Location 4 miles from Jn 35 on M4

SPRINGFIELD RIDING STABLES
Springfield House, St Brides,
Wentloog, Newport,
Gwent, NP1 9SR
Tel 01633 680610

Contact Mrs A & Miss C & J Turner
Riding School, Training Centre Inst
Riding & Jumping
Specialities Childrens' riding
instruction, childrens' riding holidays,
mini camp. Beginners, novices and
nervous riders
Staff Chief Instructor Miss J Turner
(BHSAI)
Plus 2 full time instructors
Ave No 2 Horses, 19 Ponies
inc 4 SJ GR C
Courses WP, Short, Ev, Hol
Facilities
Covered School 18 x 40
Outdoor Manege 20 x 40
SJ: Nov, 1 Paddock
CC: Banks, Natural
Lec Rm, Vis Aids, Chng Rm, Showers,
Tack Shop
Schooling General, to HT Nov
Accom Dor, FB
Exclusions Wt Limit, 11st,
All riding under instruction
Location On the coast road between
B4239 Newport-Cardiff

SUNNY BANK LIVERY YARD
Sunny Bank Farm, Rudry Road, Rudry,
Mid Glamorgan, CF83 3DT
Tel 01222 864943
Contact Miss T J Pesci
Livery
Ave No 10 Horses, 12 Ponies
Courses Short, Ev, P/T
Facilities SJ: Nov, Grade C
Livery Full, P/T, Break, School, Hunt
Location On the outskirt of Rudry
village

TALYGARN RIDING STABLES
Talygarn, Pontyclun,
Mid Glamorgan, CF72 9JT
Tel 01443 225107
Contact Mr & Mrs S J & C N Rogers
Riding School Inst Basic
Specialities Adults, Children,
Beginners and Experienced. Courses
for riding and stable management
arranged to suit individual needs
Staff Chief Instructor Miss Lisa
Kempshead (BHSAI)
Plus 1 full time instructor
Ave No 6 Horses, 10 Ponies
Courses WP, Short, Ev, P/T, Hol
Facilities
Outdoor Manege 20 x 60 fl lt
SJ: Nov, 1 Paddock
CC: Basic, Natural, 6 Schooling
Lec Rm, Vis Aids, Wait Rm
Exclusions All riding under instruction
Location On A4222 between
Pontyclun & Cowbridge

GWYNEDD

**(Aberconwy & Colwyn,
Caernarfonshire & Merioneth,
Anglesey)**

ABERCONWY EQUESTRIAN CENTRE
Wern Bach Farm, Garth Road,
Llangystenin, Llandudno Junction,
Gwynedd, LL31 9JF
Tel 01492 544362
Contact Mr & Mrs H V Bowen
Riding School, NVQ Approved
Location Inst Riding & Jumping
Staff Chief Instructor Mrs D Bowen
(BHSAI, BHS Int Teach, BHS Int.SM)
Ave No 6 Horses, 6 Ponies
inc 3 El Dress, 2 SJ GR C,
Lunge lesson horse
Courses WP, YT, Short, Ev, P/T, Hol
Facilities
Covered School 40 x 20
SJ: Nov, 1acre Paddock
Lec Rm, Vis Aids, Wait Rm, Tack Shop
Hacking
Livery Full, P/T, DIY, Break, School
Schooling General, Break, to Nov
Dress, to El Dress, to Med Dress,
to SJ GR C
Exclusions Wt Limit, 13st, Age Limit, 4,
No unescorted riding
Location 2 miles east of Llandudno
Junction, off A55 midway between
Colwyn Bay and Llandudno

ANGLESEY
EQUESTRIAN CENTRE
Tanrallt Newydd, Bodedern,
Gwynedd, LL64 3UE
Tel 01407 741378/741106
Contact Mrs E M Manson
**Riding School, Training Centre,
Facility Centre, RDA, Side Saddle** Inst
Riding & Jumping
Staff Chief Instructor Mrs S Moreland
(BHSII)
Plus 1 full time instructor
Ave No 12 Horses, 12 Ponies
inc 1 Med Dress, 2 SJ GR C,
1 SJ Jun C, Side Saddle
Courses YT, Ev, P/T, Hol
Facilities
Covered School 37 x 24 gly
Outdoor Manege 30 x 30
SJ: Grade C, 1 Paddock
CC: Nov, 2 Schooling
Lec Rm, Vis Aids, Chng Rm, Wait Rm
Hacking
Livery Full, P/T, DIY, Break, School, Grass
Schooling General, Break, to El Dress,
to SJ GR C, to HT Nov
Accom Tw, FB

Exclusions Wt Limit, 16st
Location B5109 off A5, 5 miles from
Holyhead and 14 miles from Bangor

COLEG MEIRION-DWYFOR
Glynllifon, Caernarfon,
Gwynedd, LL54 5DU
Tel 01286 830261
Contact Dr Ian Rees
**Training Centre, Facility Centre,
Livery** Inst to BHSAI
3 full time instructors
Ave No 16 Horses, 4 Ponies
Courses WP, YT, Short, Ev, P/T, Hol
Facilities
Outdoor Manege 20 x 60
SJ: Nov, 1 Paddock
CC: Basic, Nov, Banks, Water, Natural,
12 Schooling
Lec Rm, Vis Aids, Chng Rm, Showers
Livery Full, P/T, Break, School, Grass
Schooling General, Break, to El Dress,
to SJ GR C, to HT Nov
Accom S, Db, F, FB
Exclusions Wt Limit, 14st, Age Limit, 16,
No casual clients
Location On A499 from Caernarfon to
Phwelli, 5 miles outside Caernarfon

PINEWOOD RIDING STABLES
Sychnant Pass Road, Conwy,
Gwynedd, LL32 8BZ
Tel 01492 592256
Contact Mr & Miss Oldfield
Trekking Centre
Staff Chief Instructor Miss P J Oldfield
Plus 3 full time instructors
Ave No 20 Horses, 20 Ponies
Facilities
Outdoor Manege 35 x 28
Chng Rm, Wait Rm
Hacking
Exclusions Wt Limit, 16st, Age Limit, 5
Location Off A55, 1 mile from Conwy
and 5 miles from Llandudno

RHIWIAU RIDING CENTRE
Llanfairfechan, Gwynedd, LL33 0EH
Tel 01248 680094
Contact Miss R Hill
Riding School Inst Riding & Jumping
Specialities Unaccompanied childrens'
holidays, RDA, Nervous riders. No road
work, beautiful countryside overlooking
Menai Straits. BET exam centre & BET
courses
Staff Chief Instructor Miss S F Hill
Ave No 6 Horses, 14 Ponies
Courses WP, YT, Short, Ev, P/T, Hol
Facilities
Outdoor Manege 20 x 40
SJ: Nov, 1 Paddock
CC: Course, Basic, Banks, Natural
Lec Rm, Vis Aids, Chng Rm, Showers,

Wait Rm
Hacking
Accom S, Tw, F, Dor, Caravan, FB
Exclusions Wt Limit, 17st, Age Limit, 3
Location A55 midway between Bangor
and Conway

SNOWDONIA RIDING STABLES
Waunfawr, Caernarfon,
Gwynedd, LL55 4PQ
Tel 01286 650342
Contact Mrs R Z Thomas
**Riding School, Training Centre,
Trekking Centre** Inst to BHSII
Specialities Career training, courses
conducted in Welsh if required
Staff Chief Instructor Miss S Thomas
(BHSI)
Plus 3 full time instructors
Ave No 12 Horses, 12 Ponies
inc 2 El Dress, 1 Med Dress,
1 Adv Dress, 1 SJ GR C, 1 SJ Jun C
Courses WP, YT, Short, Ev, P/T, Hol
Facilities
Outdoor Manege 20 x 40 fl lt
SJ: Nov, 1 Paddock
CC: Basic, Banks, 5 Schooling
Lec Rm, Vis Aids, Chng Rm, Showers,
Wait Rm
Hacking
Livery Full, P/T, DIY, Break, School,
Grass
Schooling General, Break, to Med
Dress, to SJ GR C
Location 3 miles from Caernarfon on
the A4085

**TAL Y FOEL STUD FARM
& RIDING CENTRE**
Tal y Foel, Dwyran,
Anglesey, LL61 6LQ
Tel 01248 430377
Contact Dr J Hutchings
**Riding School, B & B for horse and
rider** Inst Riding & Jumping
Specialities Individual or small group
tuition, instructional courses for the
individual needs
1 full time instructor
Ave No 12 Horses, 9 Ponies
Courses WP, YT, Short, Ev, P/T, Hol
Facilities
Outdoor Manege 20 x 40
SJ: Nov
CC: Basic, Nov, Banks, Water, Natural,
15 Schooling
Lec Rm, Vis Aids, Showers, Wait Rm
Hacking
Livery Full
Accom S, Tw, Dor
Exclusions Wt Limit, 15st,
Escorted hacks only
Location Off A4080 north of Newborough

'THE YARD'
Bwlchgwyn, Aberdovey,
Gwynedd, LL35 0SG
Tel 01654 767443
Contact Mr J F R Davies
Livery
Ave No 7 Horses, 4 Ponies
Facilities
Outdoor Manege 20 x 40
SJ: Nov
Livery Full, P/T, DIY, Break, School,
Grass
Schooling General, Break
Location 1 mile from village, take
Copper Hill Lane

POWYS

BRYNGWYN RIDING CENTRE
The Old Rectory, Bryngwyn,
Newchurch, Kington,
Herefordshire, HR5 3QN
Tel 01497 851661
Contact Miss R O Miles
**Riding School, Trekking Centre,
Moorland & Mountain Rides** Inst
Basic
1 full time instructor
Ave No 8 Horses, 7 Ponies
Courses Short, Hol
Facilities
SJ: Nov, 1 Paddock
CC: Banks, Water, Natural, Gallops,
6 Schooling
Chng Rm, Showers, Wait Rm
Hacking
Accom S, Tw, Db, F, Cottage, FB, SC
Exclusions Wt Limit, 14st,
No unaccompanied children under 10
Location Off B4594, 10 miles from
Kington, between Newchurch and
Painscastle

**DAN-YR-OGOF
TREKKING CENTRE**
Abercrave,
Swansea, SA9 1GJ
Tel 01639 730049/730284
Contact Mrs S J Reynolds
Trekking Centre
Specialities Trekking
Staff Chief Instructor Mrs S J Reynolds
(BHS Int.SM)
Plus 2 full time instructors
Ave No 3 Horses, 7 Ponies
Facilities
SJ: Nov, 1 Paddock
Lec Rm, Vis Aids, Chng Rm
Hacking
Livery Full, P/T, DIY, Break, School,
Grass

Schooling General, Break
Accom Db, F, Caravan, Cottage, SC
Exclusions Wt Limit, 14st, Age Limit, 5,
No unescorted rides
Location On A4067 between
Sennybridge and Abercraf. Turn into
Dan-Yr-Ogof show caves, in bottom field

**GOLDEN CASTLE
RIDING STABLES**
Llangattock, Crickhowell,
Powys, NP8 1PY
Tel 01873 810469
Contact Ms Fiona-Jane Griffiths
Riding School Inst Riding & Jumping
Specialities Mainly childrens riding
lessons, although adults can be catered
for, but limited to smaller groups or
individuals
Staff Chief Instructor Mrs Fiona-Jane
Griffiths
Plus 2 full time instructors
Ave No 3 Horses, 11 Ponies
inc 1 SJ GR C, 1 SJ Jun C
Courses Short, Ev, P/T, Hol
Facilities
Covered School 20 x 25
Outdoor Manege 20 x 40
SJ: Nov
CC: Basic, Banks, Natural
Hacking
Livery Full, P/T, DIY, School, Hunt
Schooling General, to Nov Dress,
to SJ GR C, to HT Nov, to HT Adv
Exclusions Age Limit, 3,
Hacking for experienced riders only
Location Llangattock, near Crickhowell

THE HEART OF WALES
Tyddu Farm, Dolau,
Llandrindod Wells,
Powys, LD1 5TB
Tel 01597 851884
Contact Mr D E Thomas
Riding School Inst Basic
Staff Chief Instructor Mrs L C Hay
Plus 2 full time instructors
Ave No 20 Horses, 25 Ponies
inc Race Horses
Courses WP, YT, Short, Ev, P/T, Hol
Facilities
Outdoor Manege 60 x 30 fl lt
SJ: Nov, 1 Paddock
CC: Course, Basic, Nov, Int
Lec Rm, Vis Aids, Chng Rm, Showers,
Wait Rm
Hacking
Schooling General, Break, to Nov
Dress, to SJ GR C
Accom Dor, FB, SC
Exclusions Wt Limit, 16st, Age Limit, 4
Location Off A488, 7 miles from
Llandrindod Wells

THE LION ROYAL HOTEL & TREKKING

The Lion Royal Hotel,
Rhayader, Powys, LD6 5AB
Tel 01597 810202
Contact Mrs Collard
Trekking Centre, Riding holidays
Staff Chief Instructor Mrs Collard
Plus 1 full time instructor
Ave No 12 Horses, 12 Ponies
Accom S, Tw, Db, F, FB
Exclusions Wt Limit, 16st,
No unescorted hacks. Open between
May & October

LLANGORSE RIDING CENTRE

Gilach Farm, Llangorse,
Brecon, Powys, LD3 7UH
Tel 01874 658272
Contact Mrs I Preece
Riding School, Trekking Centre, RDA & Adventure Activity Centre Inst
Basic
Specialities Trekking, climbing,
canoeing, orienteering, gorge walking
Staff Chief Instructor Miss T Millichip
(BHSAI)
Plus 2 full time instructors
Ave No 35 Horses, 35 Ponies
Facilities
Outdoor Manege 20 x 50 fl lt
CC: Course, Basic, Water, Natural,
Gallops
Chng Rm, Showers, Wait Rm
Hacking
Accom Tw, Db, F, Dor, FB
Exclusions Wt Limit, 18st, Age Limit, 5
Location South east of Llangorse on
the B4560, 1 mile from Llangorse and
3 miles from Bwlch

RIVERSIDE RIDING CENTRE

Llwyncytrych, Glangrwney,
Crickhowell, Powys, NP8 1EE
Tel 01873 811873
Contact Miss Laura Nicklin
Riding School Inst Riding & Jumping
Specialities Childrens' riding, stable
management and small adult groups
Staff Chief Instructor Miss Laura
Nicklin (BHSAI)
Ave No 3 Horses, 10 Ponies

Courses YT, Short, Ev, P/T, Hol
Facilities
Outdoor Manege 20 x 40
SJ: Nov, 1 Paddock
CC: Course, Basic, Natural
Lec Rm, Vis Aids, Wait Rm
Hacking
Livery Full, P/T, DIY, Break, School,
Hunt
Schooling General, to SJ GR C
Exclusions Wt Limit, 12st,
All hacking escorted
Location On main A40 between
Abergavenny & Crickhowell

TRANS-WALES-TRAILS

Cwmfforest, Pengenffordd,
Talgarth, Brecon,
Powys, LD3 0EU
Tel 01874 711398
Contact Mr & Mrs M Turner
Riding School, Trekking Centre, Riding Holiday Centre Inst Basic
Specialities Trail Ride Specialists
Staff Chief Instructor Mr P Turner
(BHSAI)
Ave No 13 Horses, 2 Ponies
Courses Hol
Facilities
Covered School 40 x 20 gly
SJ: Nov
Lec Rm, Vis Aids, Chng Rm, Showers
Hacking
Livery Full, P/T, Grass
Accom S, Tw, Db, FB
Exclusions Wt Limit, 13st,
Age Limit, 12, No beginners

WERN RIDING CENTRE

Llangattock Hillside, Crickhowell,
Powys, NP8 1LG
Tel 01873 810899
Contact Mrs G Holland
Trekking Centre
1 full time instructor
Ave No 15 Horses, 15 Ponies
Chng Rm, Wait Rm
Hacking
Accom Cottage
Exclusions Wt Limit, 14st, Age Limit,
6, Open March-October
Location Llangattock Mountain,
2 miles from Crickhowell

Riding in Ireland

NORTHERN IRELAND

BALLYKNOCK RIDING SCHOOL
38 Ballyknock Road, Hillsborough,
Co Down, BT26 6EF
Tel 01846 692144
Contact Miss J J Howes
Riding School Inst Riding & Jumping
Staff Chief Instructor Miss J J Howes
(BHSAI)
Ave No 5 Horses, 10 Ponies
inc 1 Med Dress
Courses Ev, P/T, Hol
Facilities
Covered School 18 x 37
Outdoor Manege 49 x 27
SJ: Nov, 1 Paddock
CC: Banks, Natural, Gallops,
10 Schooling
Hacking
Livery Full, Break, School, Hunt, Grass
Schooling General, Break, to Nov
Dress, to SJ GR C, to HT Nov
Accom Caravan, FB
Exclusions No unaccompanied riding
Location Between Hillsborough and
Moira

**THE BEECHES
EQUESTRIAN CENTRE**
171 Ballycorr Road, Ballyclare,
Co Antrim, BT39 9DF
Tel 01960 352441
Contact Mr M Wilson
Trekking Centre, Livery
Specialities Excellent cross country,
the fences are suitable for pony club
and riding club. Hacking and trekking
on land or quiet back roads, Forestry
hills and valleys close to Belfast and
the Antrim coast
Ave No 28 Horses, 32 Ponies
inc 4 El Dress, 5 SJ GR C, 5 SJ Jun C
Courses Ev, P/T, Hol
Facilities
Covered School 58 x 28 gly
Outdoor Manege 40 x 20 fl lt
SJ: Nov, Grade C, Grade B, 2 Paddock
CC: Course, Int, Banks, Water, Natural,
50 Schooling
Lec Rm, Vis Aids, Wait Rm
Hacking

Livery Full, DIY, Break, School, Hunt,
Grass
Schooling General, Break, to Nov
Dress, to SJ GR C, to HT Nov
Exclusions Age Limit, 6
Location 15 miles north east of Belfast
city centre

BIRR HOUSE RIDING CENTRE
81 Whinney Hill,
Dundonald, BT16 0UA
Tel 01232 425858
Contact Mrs C McVeigh
Riding School Inst Basic
Specialities Family run friendly service,
competent instructors, children especially
Staff Chief Instructor Mrs C McVeigh
Ave No 13 Horses, 22 Ponies
Courses Short, Ev, P/T, Hol
Facilities
Covered School 43 x 18
Outdoor Manege 61 x 29
SJ: Grade C, 1 Paddock
CC: Course, Banks, Water, Natural
Livery DIY
Schooling General
Exclusions Age Limit, 6
Location Between Holywood and
Newtonnards

THE BURN EQUESTRIAN CLUB
Knockbracken Healthcare Park,
Saintfield Road, Belfast, BT8 8BH
Tel 01232 402384
Contact Mrs Jeanetta Harper
**Riding School, Riding Club/Carriage
Driving/Special needs training** Inst
Riding & Jumping
Staff Chief Instructor Miss J Aitken
(BHSAI)
Plus 2 full time instructors
Ave No 9 Horses, 10 Ponies
Courses WP, P/T, Hol
Facilities
Covered School 20 x 40
Outdoor Manege 40 x 60 fl lt
SJ: Nov
Lec Rm, Vis Aids, Chng Rm, Showers,
Wait Rm
Hacking
Livery Full, P/T, Grass
Exclusions Wt Limit, 15st, Age Limit, 6

DRUMAHEGLIS RIDING SCHOOL
89 Glenstall Road, Ballmoney,
Co Antrim, BT53 7NB
Tel 01265 665500
Contact Miss C Morton
Riding School Inst Riding & Jumping
Staff Chief Instructor Miss C Morton
(BHSAI)
Plus 1 full time instructor
Ave No 6 Horses, 6 Ponies
Courses YT, Hol
Facilities
Outdoor Manege 40 x 20 fl lt
SJ: Nov, 1 Paddock
CC: Banks, 12 Schooling
Lec Rm, Vis Aids, Chng Rm, Wait Rm
Hacking
Livery Full, Grass
Schooling General, to Nov Dress,
to SJ GR C, to HT Nov
Exclusions Age Limit, 4

**DRUMGOOLAND HOUSE
TREKKING CENTRE**
29 Dunnanew Road, Seaforde,
Co Down, BT30 8PJ
Tel 01396 811956
Contact Mr F & Miss M McLeigh
Trekking Centre
Specialities Scenic area, Mountains of
Mourne, forestry, beach rides. Golf for
family members not riding. Fishing,
mountain climbing, hiking & walking
Staff Chief Instructor Miss M McLeigh
Plus 1 full time instructor
Ave No 12 Horses, 8 Ponies
Facilities
Outdoor Manege 60 x 20 fl lt
SJ: Nov, 1 Paddock
Chng Rm, Showers
Hacking
Livery Full, Break, Grass
Accom Db, F, FB
Location Seaforde, Downpatrick,
Co. Down

EAST HOPE EQUESTRIAN CENTRE
71 Killynure Road West, Carryduff,
County Down, BT8 8EA
Tel 01232 813186
Contact Ms L J Adams
Riding School Inst Riding & Jumping
Staff Chief Instructor Ms L J Adams
(BHSI)
Ave No 2 Horses, 5 Ponies
inc 1 Med Dress
Courses WP
Facilities
Outdoor Manege 65 x 30
SJ: Nov
Livery Full, P/T, DIY, Grass

Schooling General, to Med Dress,
to SJ GR C
Accom S
Exclusions No unaccompanied riding

**ENNISKILLEN COLLEGE
OF AGRICULTURE**
Levaghy, Enniskillen,
Co Fermanagh, BT74 4GF
Tel 01365 344800
Contact Dr E Long, Principal
Training Centre, Facility Centre Inst
to BHSII
11 full time instructors
Ave No 4 Horses, 1 Ponies
inc 1 Brood mare & 3 young stock
Courses YT, Short, Ev, P/T
Facilities
Covered School 40 x 25 gly
Outdoor Manege 45 x 30
SJ: Grade C, 1 Paddock
CC: Course, Nov
Lec Rm, Vis Aids, Chng Rm, Showers,
Wait Rm
Hacking
Accom S, Tw, Dor, FB
Exclusions No hire to the general
public
Location Between Enniskillen and
Irvinestown

**GALGORM PARKS
RIDING SCHOOL**
112 Sand Road, Ballymena,
Co Antrim, BT42 1DN
Tel 01266 880269
Contact Ms S R Kyle
Riding School Inst Riding & Jumping
Staff Chief Instructor Ms S R Kyle
(BHSAI)
Ave No 8 Horses, 10 Ponies
Courses WP, YT, Hol
Facilities
Covered School 24 x 37 gly
Outdoor Manege 30 x 37 fl lt
SJ: Nov, 1 Paddock
Lec Rm, Vis Aids, Tack Shop
Schooling General
Location Between Ballymena and
Cullybackey

**GALGORM MANOR
EQUESTRIAN CENTRE**
136 Fenaghy Road, Ballymena,
BT42 1EA
Tel 01266 881222
Contact Mr T P Caves
**Riding School, Facility Centre,
Trekking Centre** Inst Riding & Jumping
Specialities Beautiful surroundings,

quality horses, first class tack. 80 acres of woodland and open plain along 1 1/2 miles of River Maire. No road work. Good safe, constructive tuition
2 full time instructors
Ave No 5 Horses, 5 Ponies
inc 4 El Dress, 1 Med Dress,
2 SJ GR C, 2 SJ Jun C
Courses WP, YT, Short, Ev, P/T, Hol
Facilities
Outdoor Manege 60 x 40 fl lt
SJ: Nov, Grade C, Grade B, 2 Paddock
CC: Basic, Banks, Water, Natural, Gallops, 10 Schooling
Lec Rm, Vis Aids, Chng Rm, Showers, Wait Rm
Hacking
Livery Full, Break, School, Hunt
Schooling General, Break, to Nov Dress, to El Dress, to SJ GR C, to SJ GR B, to HT Nov, to HT Int
Accom S, Tw, Db, F, FB, SC
Exclusions Age Limit, 4
Location Galgorm, Ballymena - Cullybackey. Galgorm Manor Hotel

HILL FARM RIDING CENTRE
47 Altikeeragh Road, Castlerock,
Co Londonderry, BT51 4SR
Tel 01265 848629
Contact Mrs Gabrielle Doherty
Riding School, Trekking Centre Inst Basic
Specialities Scenic, quiet, close to beach, Golf, swimming, hotels, forest walks & National Trust
Staff Chief Instructor Mrs G Doherty
Plus 2 full time instructors
Ave No 3 Horses, 9 Ponies
inc 1 El Dress, 3 SJ GR C, 1 SJ Jun C, 2 HT Int
Courses Short, P/T, Hol
Facilities
Outdoor Manege 42 x 22 fl lt
SJ: Nov, 1 Paddock
CC: Natural, 12 Schooling
Lec Rm, Vis Aids, Showers, Wait Rm
Livery Full, School
Schooling General, to Nov Dress, to SJ GR C, to HT Nov
Accom Dor, FB
Exclusions Wt Limit, 15st, Age Limit, 4+
Location Between Colraine and Portadown

ISLAND EQUESTRIAN CENTRE
49 Ballyrashane Road, Coleraine,
Co Londonderry, BT52 2NL
Tel 01265 42599
Contact Mrs J McCollum
Riding School, Training Centre Inst

Riding & Jumping
Staff Chief Instructor Mrs J McCollum (BHSAI, BHS SM, BHS Int Teach)
Ave No 4 Horses, 4 Ponies
Courses Short, Ev, P/T, Hol
Facilities
Outdoor Manege 20 x 60
SJ: Nov, 1 Paddock
CC: Basic, Nov, Banks, Water, Natural, 8 Schooling
Lec Rm, Vis Aids, Chng Rm, Wait Rm
Hacking
Livery Full, P/T, School, Hunt, Grass
Schooling General, to Nov Dress, to SJ GR C, to HT Nov
Accom S, Db, FB, SC
Exclusions Wt Limit, 12st
Location Between Coleraine and Ballycastle. 1 1/2 miles from Coleraine on B67

LAGAN VALLEY
EQUESTRIAN CENTRE
170 Upper Malone Road, Dunmurry,
Belfast, BT17 9JZ
Tel 01232 614853
Contact Mr & Mrs W Cave
Riding School, Training Centre, Facility Centre, RDA, RC Inst Basic
Staff Chief Instructor Mrs L Faloona (BHSAI)
Plus 2 full time instructors
Ave No 7 Horses, 10 Ponies
inc 2 SJ Jun A
Courses WP, YT, P/T, Hol
Facilities
Covered School 46 x 18 gly
Outdoor Manege 40 x 30 fl lt
SJ: Nov, Grade C, 1 Paddock
CC: Course, Basic, Nov, Banks, Water, Natural
Lec Rm, Vis Aids, Wait Rm
Hacking
Livery Full, P/T, DIY, Break, School, Hunt, Grass
Schooling General, Break, to Nov Dress, to SJ GR C, to HT Nov
Accom Caravan, SC
Exclusions Wt Limit, 15st, Age Limit, 8, No unaccompanied riding
Location Off outer ring road between Mary Peters track and Lady Dixon Park

LESSANS RIDING STABLES
126 Monlough Road, Saintfield,
Co Down, Northern Ireland
Tel 01238 510141
Contact Miss P Auret
Riding School, Training Centre Inst Riding & Jumping
Specialities General instruction, childrens'

camps and club, adult courses
Staff Chief Instructor Miss P Auret
(BHSII, BHS SM)
Plus 1 full time instructor
Ave No 10 Horses, 13 Ponies
Courses WP, YT, Short, Ev, P/T, Hol
Facilities
SJ: Nov
CC: Basic, Water, Natural,
10 Schooling
Chng Rm
Hacking
Livery Full, P/T, Break, School, Grass
Schooling General, Break, to Nov
Dress, to HT Nov
Accom S, Tw, SC
Exclusions No casual hire
Location Saintfield - Belfast road

MADDYBENNY STUD
Maddybenny Farm, Coleraine,
Co Londonderry, BT52 2PT
Tel 01265 823394/823603
Contact Mr & Mrs P G L White
Riding School Inst Riding & Jumping
Staff Chief Instructor Mr P G L White
(BHSAI, BHS Int Teach)
Plus 3 full time instructors
Ave No 4 Horses, 6 Ponies
inc 1 El Dress, 1 SJ Jun C, 1 SJ Jun A,
1 HT Int, 1 HT Adv
Courses WP, YT
Facilities
Covered School 20 x 40
Outdoor Manege 46 x 27
Outdoor Manege 23 x 23
SJ: Nov, Grade A, 1 Paddock
CC: Course, Int, Banks, Water, Natural,
Gallops
Lec Rm, Vis Aids, Chng Rm, Wait Rm
Hacking
Livery Full, P/T, DIY, Break, School,
Hunt, Grass
Schooling General, Break, to Nov
Dress, to SJ GR A, to HT Adv
Accom S, Tw, Db, Cottage, SC
Exclusions Wt Limit, 14st, Age Limit, 4

MILLBRIDGE RIDING CENTRE
Ballystockart, Comber,
Co Down, BT23 5QT
Tel 01247 872508
Contact Mr Lewis Lowry
Riding School, Training Centre,
Facility Centre Inst Riding & Jumping
1 full time instructor
Ave No 10 Horses, 10 Ponies
inc 1 Med Dress, 1 SJ GR A, 1 SJ Jun
A, 1 HT Adv
Courses YT, Short, Ev, P/T, Hol
Facilities

SJ: Nov, Grade A, 1 Paddock
CC: Int, Banks, Water, Natural,
50 Schooling
Lec Rm, Vis Aids, Chng Rm, Wait Rm
Hacking
Livery Full, P/T, DIY, Break, School,
Hunt, Grass
Schooling General, Break, to Med
Dress, to SJ GR A, to HT Adv
Exclusions Age Limit, 5, No casual hire

MONTALTO FARM & FORESTRY
Spa Road, Ballynahinch,
Co Down, BT24 8PX
Tel 01238 566110
Contact Mr G Wilson
Holiday accommodation for horses
& ponies
Specialities The establishment is run
solely for the livery of animals when
their owners are away on holiday
Facilities
Outdoor Manege 45 x 45 fl lt
Exclusions This establishment is
solely for horse holidays
Location Ballynahinch to Spa road

MOUNT PLEASANT
TREKKING CENTRE
15 Bannonstown Road, Castlewellan,
Co Down, BT31 9BG
Tel 01396 778651
Contact Mr P King
Facility Centre, Trekking Centre,
Livery
Staff Chief Instructor Mr V Bannon
Plus 1 full time instructor
Ave No 20 Horses, 10 Ponies
Facilities
CC: Water, Natural, Gallops
Chng Rm, Wait Rm
Hacking
Livery Full, Break, School, Hunt, Grass
Schooling Break
Accom Caravan, SC
Exclusions Wt Limit, 16st, Age Limit,
6, All rides escorted
Location 3/4 mile off A25 between
Castlewellan and Clough

MOY RIDING SCHOOL
131 Derry Caw Road, Moy,
Co Tyrone, BT71 6NA
Tel 01868 784440
Contact Mr & Mrs D Corr
Riding School, Training Centre Inst
Riding & Jumping
Staff Chief Instructor Mrs N Belford
(BHSAI, BHS Int Teach)
Plus 4 full time instructors

Ave No 15 Horses, 12 Ponies
inc 1 El Dress, 1 Med Dress, 2 SJ GR C,
1 SJ GR B, 1 SJ Jun C, 1 HT Int, Show
Horses
Courses WP, YT, Short, Ev, P/T, Hol
Facilities
Covered School 60 x 30
Outdoor Manege 61 x 30
SJ: Nov, Grade C, 1 Paddock
CC: Course, Basic, Nov, Int, Banks,
Natural, 25 Schooling
Lec Rm, Vis Aids, Wait Rm
Livery Full, P/T, DIY, Break, School,
Hunt, Grass
Schooling General, Break, to Nov
Dress, to Med Dress, to SJ GR B, to
HT Int
Exclusions Wt Limit, 16st, Age Limit, 5
Location Between Dungannon and
Moy

NECARNE CASTLE – THE ULSTER LAKELAND EQUESTRIAN PARK
Irvinestown, Co Fermanagh,
Tel 01365 621919
Contact Mr Eric Long
**Riding School, Training Centre,
Facility Centre** Inst Riding & Jumping
Specialities Top class facilities,
Excellent accomodation, very good
quality horses and instruction
11 full time instructors
Ave No 15 Horses, 4 Ponies
inc 1 El Dress, 1 Med Dress, 1 SJ GR C,
1 HT Int
Courses WP, YT, Short, Ev, P/T, Hol
Facilities
Covered School 58 x 24 gly
Outdoor Manege 62 x 36 fl lt
Outdoor Manege 90 x 85 fl lt
Outdoor Manege 70 x 40 fl lt
CC: Banks, Water, Natural, Gallops
Lec Rm, Vis Aids, Chng Rm, Showers,
Wait Rm
Hacking
Livery Full, P/T, Break, School
Schooling Break, to Nov Dress, to El
Dress, to Med Dress, to SJ GR C, to SJ
GR B, to HT Nov
Accom S, Tw, FB
Exclusions Wt Limit, 16st, Age Limit, 3
Location Irvinstown, 8 miles north of
Enniskillen

NEWCASTLE RIDING CENTRE
35 Carnacaville Road, Castlewellan,
Co Down, BT31 9HD
Tel 01396 722694
Contact Miss E S Martin
Riding School, Training Centre Inst
Riding & Jumping

Specialities Beach rides
Staff Chief Instructor Miss E S Martin
Ave No 16 Horses, 12 Ponies
inc 1 El Dress, 1 Med Dress, 1 Adv
Dress, 1 SJ GR C, 1 SJ Jun C, 1 HT Int
Courses WP, YT, Short, Ev, Hol
Facilities
SJ: Nov, Grade C, 1 Paddock
CC: Course, Nov, Banks, Water, Natural,
30 Schooling
Lec Rm, Vis Aids, Chng Rm, Wait Rm
Hacking
Livery Full, Break, School, Hunt
Schooling General, Break, to Nov
Dress, to El Dress, to Med Dress, to SJ
GR C, to HT Nov
Accom Dor, Cottage, SC
Exclusions Wt Limit, 14st, Age Limit, 5,
No unaccompanied hacking

PENINSULA EQUESTRIAN ACADEMY
4 Cardy Road, Grey Abbey,
Newtownards, County Down, BT22 2LI
Tel 01247 788681
Contact Mrs M J Dixon
**Riding School, Training Centre,
Facility Centre, Trekking Centre** Inst
Basic
Staff Chief Instructor Mrs M J Dixon
(BHSAI)
Plus 1 full time instructor
Ave No 10 Horses, 30 Ponies
Courses YT, Short, Ev, P/T, Hol
Facilities
Outdoor Manege 110 x 80 fl lt
Outdoor Manege 70 x 22 fl lt
SJ: Nov, Grade C, Grade B
CC: Course, Int, Banks, Water, Natural,
Gallops
Chng Rm, Showers, Wait Rm
Hacking
Livery Full, P/T, Break, School, Hunt,
Grass
Schooling General, Break, to Med
Dress, to SJ GR A, to HT Adv
Accom Db, F, Caravan

ROCKFIELD EQUESTRIAN CENTRE
18 Drumhirk Road, Comber,
Co Down, BT23 5LY
Tel 01247 872548
Contact Mrs D T Conroy
**Riding School, Training Centre,
Facility Centre** Inst Riding & Jumping
Specialities Small groups, very safe
friendly horses. Friendly atmosphere,
very active riding club. Pony club use.
Excellent scenic riding country
Staff Chief Instructor Mrs D T Conroy
(BHSAI)
Plus 2 full time instructors

Ave No 8 Horses, 9 Ponies
inc 4 El Dress, 3 SJ GR C, 4 SJ Jun C
Courses WP, YT, Short, Ev, P/T, Hol
Facilities
Covered School 40 x 20 gly
Outdoor Manege 40 x 20 fl lt
SJ: Nov, Grade C, 1 Paddock
CC: Basic, Banks, Water, Natural,
20 Schooling
Lec Rm, Vis Aids, Chng Rm, Showers,
Wait Rm, Tack Shop
Hacking
Livery Full, DIY, Break, School, Hunt
Schooling General, Break, to Nov
Dress, to SJ GR C, to HT Nov
Accom Caravan, FB
Exclusions Age Limit, 4
Location 1 1/2 miles from Comber
towards Killyleagh - Down Patrick road
turn right into Drumkirk Road

REPUBLIC OF IRELAND

**BALLINGALE FARM
RIDING SCHOOL**
Taghmon, Co Wexford,
Tel 00 353 53 34387
Contact Ms V Charlton
Riding School, Training Centre, Stud
Inst Riding & Jumping
Staff Chief Instructor Ms V Charlton
(BHSII)
Plus 3 full time instructors
Ave No 20 Horses, 10 Ponies
inc 1 El Dress, 1 SJ GR C,
Cross country horses
Courses WP, Short, P/T, Hol
Facilities
Covered School 34 x 21
Outdoor Manege 46 x 23
SJ: Nov, 1 Paddock
CC: Course, Nov, Banks, Water,
Natural, 50 Schooling
Lec Rm, Vis Aids, Wait Rm
Hacking
Livery Full, P/T, DIY, Break, School,
Hunt, Grass
Schooling General, Break, to SJ GR C
Accom S, Tw, Db, F, Caravan,
Cottage, FB
Exclusions Age Limit, 7,
Cater for accompanied and
unaccompanied children
Location Wexford - Waterford road,
9 miles Wexford

BANNER EQUESTRIAN
Toonagh / Fountain, Ennis,
Co Clare,
Tel 00 353 65 23487
Contact Noel & Simone Barry
**Riding School, Training Centre,
Facility Centre, Trekking Centre** Inst
Riding & Jumping
Specialities Showjumping is speciality.
Excellent hacking/trekking country is
adjacent to the school. Hunting is a
very strong pastime in this district
Staff Chief Instructor Mrs Simone Barry
(BHSAI)
Ave No 9 Horses, 7 Ponies
inc 3 Med Dress, 7 SJ GR C, 2 SJ GR
B, 4 SJ Jun C, 4 HT Int, 4 Hunting,
separate horses available
Facilities
Covered School 40 x 22 gly
Outdoor Manege 40 x 20 fl lt
Outdoor Manege 40 x 20 fl lt
SJ: Grade A, 1 Paddock
CC: Nov, Int, Banks, Water, 20
Schooling
Lec Rm, Vis Aids, Chng Rm, Showers,
Wait Rm
Hacking
Livery Full, Break, School, Hunt, Grass
Schooling General, Break, to Nov
Dress, to Med Dress, to SJ GR A, to
HT Nov
Accom S, Tw, FB
Location Ennis to Lahinch N85.
Right for Fountain to Corofin R476.
Four miles from Ennis

BRENNANSTOWN RIDING SCHOOL
Hollybrook, Kilmacanogue,
Co Wicklow,
Tel 00 353 1 2863778
Contact Ms J Kennedy
**Riding School, Training Centre,
Facility Centre, Trekking Centre,
RDA & Cross Country Rides** Inst to
BHSAI
Specialities General instruction,
student courses & career courses.
Producing Hunter and Show Ponies
6 full time instructors
Ave No 25 Horses, 25 Ponies
inc 2 El Dress, 2 Med Dress, 2 Adv
Dress, 2 SJ GR C, 2 HT Int, Show
ponies (Hunter)
Courses WP, Short, Ev, P/T, Hol
Facilities
Covered School 46 x 28 gly
Covered School 12 x 25 gly
Outdoor Manege 50 x 30 fl lt
Outdoor Manege 50 x 30 fl lt
Outdoor Manege 30 x 15 fl lt
SJ: Nov, Grade A, 1 Paddock

CC: Course, Nov, Banks, Water,
Natural, 20 Schooling
Lec Rm, Vis Aids, Chng Rm, Showers,
Wait Rm
Hacking
Livery Full, P/T, DIY, Break, School,
Hunt, Grass
Schooling General, Break, to Nov
Dress, to El Dress, to Med Dress, to
Adv Dress, to SJ GR B, to HT Int
Accom S, Tw, Cottage, SC
Exclusions Age Limit, 6
Location 15 miles south of Dublin on
the Dublin - Wicklow road (N11),
1 1/2 miles from Bray

CALLIAGHSTOWN RIDING CENTRE
Calliaghstown, Rathcoole, Co Dublin,
Dublin, Ireland
Tel 00 353 14589 236
Contact Miss G Sugars
Riding School, Training Centre,
Facility Centre Inst to BHSII
Specialities Career students, trail
rides, general instruction, shows and
events
Staff Chief Instructor Miss G Sugars
(BHSII, BHS SM)
Plus 5 full time instructors
Ave No 20 Horses, 10 Ponies
inc 3 El Dress, 3 SJ GR C, 3 HT Int
Courses WP, YT, Short, Ev, P/T, Hol
Facilities
Covered School 23 x 46
Outdoor Manege 23 x 46 fl lt
Outdoor Manege 40 x 30 fl lt
SJ: Nov, Grade C, 1 Paddock
CC: Course, Int, Banks, Water, Natural
Lec Rm, Vis Aids, Chng Rm, Showers,
Wait Rm
Hacking
Livery Full, P/T, Break, School, Hunt,
Grass
Schooling General, Break, to El Dress,
to SJ GR C, to HT Int
Exclusions Wt Limit, 16st, Age Limit, 4
Location Off the N7 (Dublin - Naas) to
Rathcoole. Turn behind Potin Still Pub
& the riding centre is 3 miles on the left

CASTLE HILL
EQUESTRIAN CENTRE
Briarlieas , Julianstown,
County Meath,
Tel 00 353 41 29430
Contact Ms A Stanley
Riding School, Training Centre Inst
Riding & Jumping
Specialities Sport Horse Sales
establishment used as viewing venue &
sales complex

9 full time instructors
Ave No 8 Horses, 7 Ponies
Courses WP, Short, Ev, Hol
Facilities
Covered School 55 x 25 gly
Outdoor Manege 60 x 30 fl lt
SJ: Nov, Grade C, Grade B, 1 Paddock
CC: Course, Basic, Water
Lec Rm, Vis Aids, Chng Rm, Showers,
Wait Rm
Hacking
Livery Full, P/T, DIY, Break, School,
Hunt
Schooling General, Break, to Nov
Dress, to SJ GR C, to HT Nov
Exclusions Age Limit, 5,
No casual hiring
Location 20 minutes from Dublin Airport

CASTLE HOWARD
EQUESTRIAN CENTRE
Avoca, Co Wicklow,
Tel 00 353 40235164
Contact Mr & Mrs I Fitzpatrick
Riding School, Training Centre,
Trekking Centre Inst Riding & Jumping
Specialities Cross country, scenery,
beach rides, hunting, trails & tracks. Golf,
fishing, historic sites and buildings
4 full time instructors
Ave No 13 Horses, 1 Ponies
inc 12 El Dress, 1 Med Dress,
4 SJ GR C
Courses WP, Ev, P/T, Hol
Facilities
Covered School 55 x 30 gly
SJ: Nov, Grade A, 30acr Paddock
CC: Course, Basic, Nov, Int, Banks,
Water, Natural
Lec Rm, Vis Aids, Chng Rm, Showers,
Wait Rm
Hacking
Livery Full, P/T, Break, School, Hunt,
Grass
Schooling General, Break, to Nov
Dress, to El Dress, to SJ GR A, to HT
Nov
Exclusions Wt Limit, 16st, Age Limit, 16,
No children under 16
Location Rathdrum - Avoca road.
Meeting of the Water

CLARE
EQUESTRIAN CENTRE
Deerpark, Doora, Ennis,
Co Clare,
Tel 00 353 65 40136
Contact Mr & Mrs J Burke
Riding School, Training Centre,
Trekking Centre Inst Riding & Jumping
Specialities Very suitable horses, large

175

indoor and outdoor school. Close to golf, sailing, walking, fishing and evening entertainments
Staff Chief Instructor Mrs Marie Burke Plus 1 full time instructor
Ave No 15 Horses, 12 Ponies inc 4 El Dress, 3 SJ GR C, 3 SJ GR B, 1 SJ GR A, 4 SJ Jun C, 2 SJ Jun A, 1 HT Int
Courses Short, Ev, P/T
Facilities
Covered School 60 x 26 gly
Outdoor Manege 76 x 40
SJ: Grade A, 2 Paddock
CC: Nov, Banks, Water, Natural, 12 Schooling
Lec Rm, Vis Aids, Chng Rm, Showers, Wait Rm
Hacking
Livery Full, Break, School, Hunt, Grass
Schooling General, Break, to El Dress, to SJ GR A, to HT Int
Exclusions Age Limit, 5
Location Ennis - Limerick road

CLONSHIRE EQUESTRIAN CENTRE
Adare, Co Limerick,
Tel 00 353 61 396770
Contact Mr D & Mrs S Foley
Riding School, Facility Centre, Trekking Centre Inst Riding & Jumping
Specialities All standards catered for. Adjacent to six hunts. Ideal for Hunting courses. Show jumping a speciality. Terrain for all disciplines
Staff Chief Instructor Mrs Susan Foley Plus 3 full time instructors
Ave No 25 Horses, 15 Ponies inc 6 Med Dress, 2 SJ GR C, 2 SJ GR B, 3 SJ GR A, 4 SJ Jun C, 1 SJ Jun A, 3 retired grade A
Courses WP, YT, Short, Ev, P/T, Hol
Facilities
Covered School 61 x 30 gly
Outdoor Manege 60 x 40 fl lt
SJ: Nov, Grade C, Grade B, Grade A, 2 Paddock
CC: Course, Int, Banks, Water, Natural, 12 Schooling
Lec Rm, Vis Aids, Chng Rm, Showers, Wait Rm, Tack Shop
Hacking
Livery Full, P/T, Break, School, Hunt, Grass
Schooling General, Break, to El Dress, to Med Dress, to SJ GR C, to HT Nov, to HT Int
Accom Tw, SC
Exclusions Age Limit, 4
Location 2 miles outside Adare on Limerick - Killarney road. 20 minutes Limerick, 40 minutes Shannon Airport

DEVILS GLEN HOLIDAY & EQUESTRIAN VILLAGE
Devils Glen, Ashford,
Co Wicklow,
Tel 00 353 404 40637
Contact Mr S O'Connell Miley & Ms M Ryan
Riding School, Training Centre, Facility Centre, Trekking Centre Inst Riding & Jumping
Specialities Schooling and breaking, cross country riding & jumping
2 full time instructors
Ave No 14 Horses, 10 Ponies
Courses WP, Hol
Facilities
SJ: Nov, Grade C, 30acr Paddock
CC: Course, Basic, Nov, Int, Banks, Water, Natural, Gallops, 40 Schooling
Wait Rm
Hacking
Livery Full, Break, School, Hunt, Grass
Schooling General, Break, to Nov Dress, to SJ GR C, to HT Nov
Accom Tw, Db, Cottage, SC
Exclusions Wt Limit, 16st, Age Limit, 8, No unaccompanied children
Location
Ashford N11 45 mins Dublin, in the foothills of the Wicklow Mountains

DUNFANAGHY STABLES
c/o Arnold's Hotel, Dunfanaghy,
Co Donegal,
Tel 00 353 74 36208
Contact Mrs Helen McDaid
Facility Centre, Trekking Centre, Specialising in Residential holidays Inst Riding & Jumping
Specialities Details on request on Trails (6 days - 7 nights) (a) Donegal from Saddle (b) Donegal by Sea. Adult Residential Programme (6 days - 7 nights). Unaccompanied Children (10 - 16yrs) 2 - 3 weeks
1 full time instructor
Ave No 11 Horses, 11 Ponies
Courses Hol
Facilities
Outdoor Manege 20 x 20
Wait Rm
Hacking
Livery Break, School, Grass
Schooling General, Break, to Nov Dress
Accom FB

FAMILY AND COUNTRY
Crossogue House, Ballycahill,
Thurles, Co Tipperary,
Tel 00 353 504 54123

Contact Mr Mark Molloy
Riding School, Facility Centre Inst
Riding & Jumping
Specialities Geared to the Pony Club
and foreign teenagers taken
unaccompanied by parents
Staff Chief Instructor Mr N Quinn
Ave No 12 Horses, 6 Ponies
inc 6 El Dress, 10 SJ GR C, 3 SJ GR B,
6 SJ Jun C, 7 HT Int
Courses Short, Ev, P/T, Hol
Facilities
Outdoor Manege 60 x 30
SJ: Nov, Grade C, Grade B,
1 Paddock
CC: Course, Int, Banks, Water, Natural,
60 Schooling
Lec Rm, Vis Aids, Chng Rm, Showers,
Wait Rm
Hacking
Livery Full, Break, School, Hunt
Schooling General, Break, to Nov
Dress, to El Dress, to SJ GR C, to SJ
GR B, to HT Nov, to HT Int
Accom Tw, F, FB
Exclusions Age Limit, 10,
Adults not taken April to October -
inquire about specials
Location Nenagh - Limerick road,
5 miles from Thurles

GRENNAN COLLEGE
EQUESTRIAN CENTRE
Newtown, Thomastown,
Co Kilkenny,
Tel 00 353 56 24112
Contact Mr Timothy O'Mahony
Riding School, Training Centre Inst
to BHSAI
Specialities Career students, general
instruction, college courses, riding club
and short courses
Staff Chief Instructor Miss B McCarthy
(BHSAI, BHS Int Teach)
Plus 2 full time instructors
Ave No 18 Horses, 7 Ponies
Courses YT, Short, Ev, P/T
Facilities
Covered School 30 x 20 gly
Outdoor Manege 40 x 30 fl lt
SJ: Nov
CC: Course, Basic, Nov
Lec Rm, Vis Aids, Chng Rm, Showers,
Wait Rm
Livery Full, Break, School
Schooling General, Break, to El Dress,
to SJ GR C, to HT Int
Exclusions Age Limit, 7,
No casual hire
Location Outskirts of town, off Kilkenny
road

GREYSTONES
EQUESTRIAN CENTRE
Castle Leslie, Glaslough, Monaghan,
Tel 00 353 47 88100
Contact Mr & Mrs J Bellew
Riding School Inst Riding & Jumping
Staff Chief Instructor Miss O Sheehan
(BHSII)
Plus 3 full time instructors
Ave No 25 Horses, 10 Ponies
inc 1 El Dress, 2 SJ GR C, 1 SJ Jun C
Courses WP, Short, Ev, P/T, Hol
Facilities
Covered School 20 x 45
Outdoor Manege 22 x 45 fl lt
SJ: Nov, 1 Paddock
CC: Course, Basic, Nov, Water, Natural,
Gallops, 200 Schooling
Lec Rm, Vis Aids, Chng Rm, Showers,
Wait Rm
Hacking
Livery Full, Break, School, Hunt
Schooling General, Break, to El Dress,
to SJ GR C, to HT Int
Accom Tw, Db, F, FB
Exclusions Wt Limit, 16st, Age Limit, 7,
No unaccompanied children under 14
Location Off L5 between Middletown
and Monaghan from Northern Ireland, off
the the N12 from Monaghan Town

KILCOOLEY ABBEY COUNTRY
& EQUESTRIAN CENTRE
Thurles, Co Tipperary,
Tel 00 353 56 34222
Contact Mrs Faith Ponsonby
Riding School, Training Centre,
Facility Centre, Trekking Centre, Side
Saddle Inst Riding & Jumping
Specialities Excellent cross country,
top class instruction, expert side saddle
instruction. Central all tourist attractions
Staff Chief Instructor Mrs Faith
Ponsonby (BHSII, BHS SM)
Ave No 10 Horses, 10 Ponies
inc 2 El Dress, 2 Med Dress, 3 SJ GR C,
3 SJ Jun C, 1 HT Int, All animals are
trained to side saddle
Courses WP, YT, Short, Ev, P/T, Hol
Facilities
Outdoor Manege 43 x 23 fl lt
SJ: Grade A, 2 Paddock
CC: Course, Int, Banks, Water, Natural,
Gallops
Lec Rm, Vis Aids, Chng Rm, Showers,
Wait Rm, Tack Shop
Hacking
Livery Full, P/T, Break, School, Hunt,
Grass
Schooling General, Break, to Nov
Dress, to Med Dress, to SJ GR B,
to HT Int

Accom S, Tw, Db, F, Cottage, FB, SC
Exclusions Age Limit, 5
Location 3 miles east of Urlingford N8
Portlaois - Cork road. Turn at end of
Urlingford town for Killenaule

KILL INTERNATIONAL
EQUESTRIAN CENTRE
Kill, County Kildare,
Tel 00 353 45 877208
Contact Mr F P Flannelly
Riding School Inst Riding & Jumping
Staff Chief Instructor Mr D Flannelly
(BHSII)
Plus 4 full time instructors
Ave No 32 Horses, 20 Ponies
inc 4 El Dress, 2 Med Dress, 6 SJ GR C,
2 HT Int, Horse Trials Novice 1
Courses WP, YT, Short, Ev, P/T, Hol
Facilities
Covered School 55 x 30 gly
Covered School 42 x 21
Outdoor Manege 60 x 60 fl lt
Outdoor Manege 40 x 20
SJ: Nov, Grade C, Grade B, Grade A,
1 Paddock
CC: Course, Basic, Nov, Banks, Water,
Natural, Gallops
Lec Rm, Vis Aids, Chng Rm, Showers,
Wait Rm, Tack Shop
Hacking
Livery Full, P/T, Break, School, Hunt,
Grass
Schooling General, Break, to Adv
Dress, to SJ GR A, to HT Adv
Accom S, Tw, Dor, FB
Exclusions Age Limit, 6,
No casual hiring
Location 15 miles from Dublin city
centre, off N7 at Kill village, fully
signposted from village

LENAMORE STABLES
Muff, Co Donegal,
Tel 00 353 77 84022
Contact Miss G L Graham
Riding School, Training Centre,
Specialise in Showjumping Inst
Riding & Jumping
Specialities Career training. Show
jumping
Production and sale of quality sport
horses
Staff Chief Instructor Miss G Graham
(BHS Int Teach)
Ave No 20 Horses, 10 Ponies
inc 1 SJ GR B, 1 SJ GR A, 1 HT Int
Courses WP, YT, Short, Ev, P/T, Hol
Facilities
Covered School 35 x 25 gly
Outdoor Manege 50 x 50

SJ: Nov, 1 Paddock
Lec Rm, Vis Aids, Chng Rm, Showers,
Wait Rm
Hacking
Livery Full, Break, Hunt, Grass
Schooling General, Break, to Nov
Dress, to Adv Dress, to SJ GR C
Accom Tw, Db, F, SC
Exclusions Age Limit, 7,
No casual hire
Location Between Muff and Bridgend

MULLINGAR
EQUESTRIAN CENTRE
Athlone Road, Mullingar,
Co Westmeath, Ireland
Tel 00 353 44 48331
Contact Mr & Mrs E Fagan
Riding School, Training Centre Inst
Riding & Jumping
Specialities General instruction,
shows, riding and hunting holidays.
Excellent hacking and trekking
1 full time instructor
Ave No 8 Horses, 8 Ponies
inc 3 El Dress, 2 Med Dress, 6 SJ GR
C, 2 SJ GR B, 3 SJ GR A, 4 SJ Jun C,
3 HT Int
Courses WP, YT, Short, Ev, P/T, Hol
Facilities
Covered School 55 x 24
Outdoor Manege 46 x 23 fl lt
SJ: Nov, Grade A, 1 Paddock
CC: Course, Nov, Int, Banks, Water,
Natural, 20 Schooling
Lec Rm, Vis Aids, Chng Rm, Showers,
Wait Rm
Hacking
Livery Full, P/T, DIY, Break, School,
Hunt
Schooling General, Break, to El Dress,
to SJ GR A, to HT Int
Accom S, Tw, Db, F, Caravan, FB
Exclusions All rides escorted
Location 2 miles from Mullingar on
main Athlone road, 1 1/4 hours from
Dublin

THE OLD MILL RIDING CENTRE
Kill, Co Kildare,
Tel 00 353 45 877053
Contact Mr & Mrs Creighton
Riding School, Training Centre,
Trekking Centre Inst Riding & Jumping
Specialities All aspects equestrianism
catered for. Training is main interest.
Prime school for producing competitive
riders for showjumping and eventing
Staff Chief Instructor Mrs Patricia
Creighton
Plus 2 full time instructors

Ave No 10 Horses, 14 Ponies
inc 2 Med Dress, 2 SJ GR C, 1 SJ GR B,
3 SJ Jun C, 2 SJ Jun A
Courses WP, YT, Short, Ev, P/T, Hol
Facilities
Covered School 42 x 22
Outdoor Manege 60 x 50 fl lt
SJ: Grade A, 2 Paddock
CC: Course
Lec Rm, Vis Aids, Chng Rm, Showers,
Wait Rm
Hacking
Livery Full, Break, School, Hunt, Grass
Schooling General, Break, to Nov
Dress, to Med Dress, to SJ GR A, to
HT Adv
Accom Caravan, FB
Location 15 miles Dublin, 4 miles
beyond Rathcoole on left, sign posted
for Old Mill, Kilteel. Three minutes off
dual carriageway

THE PADDOCKS RIDING CENTRE
Woodside Road, Sandyfords,
Co Dublin,
Tel 00 3531295 4278
Contact Teresa & Denise Cribben
Riding School Inst Riding & Jumping
Specialities There are outstanding
views from the hills and mountains. The
routes for hack and trek are safe, away
from roads, a very relaxing area to ride
in. Trails are well defined, this is a very
safe area to ride in
Staff Chief Instructor Mr James Mernin
Ave No 10 Horses, 6 Ponies
inc 3 El Dress, 1 Med Dress, 5 SJ GR
C, 2 SJ GR B, 6 SJ Jun C, 1 HT Int,
Horse Trials Novice x3
Courses WP, Short, Ev, P/T, Hol
Facilities
Outdoor Manege 60 x 30 fl lt
SJ: Grade C, Grade B, 3 Paddock
CC: Banks, Natural, 8 Schooling
Lec Rm, Vis Aids, Chng Rm, Showers,
Wait Rm
Hacking
Livery Full, Break, School, Hunt, Grass
Schooling General, Break, to El Dress,
to SJ GR B, to HT Int
Accom S, Tw
Location Turn off Enniskerry road at
the Mountain View Bar in Stepaside,
signposted up the hill

PORTLAOISE
EQUESTRIAN CENTRE
Timahoe Road, Portlaoise,
Co Laois,
Tel 00 353 502 60880
Contact Mr E E Sheehan
Riding School, Training Centre,

**Facility Centre, Riding & Road Safety
Centre** Inst to BHSAI
Specialities Show jumping
competitions
Staff Chief Instructor Miss A M Dunphy
(BHSAI)
Plus 2 full time instructors
Ave No 15 Horses, 8 Ponies
inc 2 El Dress, 1 Med Dress, 5 SJ GR C,
1 SJ GR B, 1 SJ GR A, 1 SJ Jun A
Courses WP, YT, Short, Ev, P/T, Hol
Facilities
Covered School 60 x 25 gly
Outdoor Manege 80 x 60 fl lt
SJ: Nov, Grade C, Grade B, Grade A,
1.5ac Paddock
CC: Course, Basic, Banks, Water,
Natural, 17 Schooling
Lec Rm, Vis Aids, Chng Rm, Showers,
Wait Rm, Tack Shop
Hacking
Livery Full, P/T, Break, School, Hunt,
Grass
Schooling General, Break, to Nov
Dress, to El Dress, to Med Dress, to SJ
GR C, to SJ GR B, to SJ GR A, to HT
Nov
Accom Tw, F, SC
Exclusions Wt Limit, 15st, Age Limit, 4

STAFFORD LODGE STUD
Glendalough Estate, Annamoe,
Roundwood, Co Wicklow
Tel 00 353 1 298 4897
Contact Jennifer & Elizabeth O'Brien
Livery, Stud
Ave No 10 Horses, 1 Ponies
Facilities
Outdoor Manege 25 x 45
SJ: Nov, 2 Paddock
CC: Banks, Water, Natural, 12 Schooling
Chng Rm, Wait Rm
Livery Full, Break, School, Hunt, Grass
Schooling to Nov Dress, to SJ GR C, to
HT Nov
Location 15km main Dublin - Wexford
road, Kilmancanogue turn off

THORNTON PARK
EQUESTRIAN CENTRE
Thornton, Kilsallaghan, Sword,
Co Dublin,
Tel 00 353 1 8351164
Contact Ms Suzanne Archer-Murphy
Riding School, Training Centre Inst
Riding & Jumping
Staff Chief Instructor Miss Jennifer
Breslin (BHS Int Teach, BHS Int.SM)
Plus 1 full time instructor
Ave No 32 Horses, 10 Ponies
inc 3 El Dress, 2 Med Dress, 6 SJ GR C,

1 SJ GR B, 2 SJ Jun C, 2 SJ Jun A,
1 Side Saddle
Courses WP, YT, Short, Ev, P/T, Hol
Facilities
Covered School 68 x 24 gly
Outdoor Manege 45 x 25 fl lt
Outdoor Manege 40 x 20 fl lt
Outdoor Manege 48 x 28 fl lt
SJ: Grade A, 3 Paddock
Lec Rm, Vis Aids, Chng Rm, Showers,

Wait Rm, Tack Shop
Livery Full, DIY, School, Hunt, Grass
Schooling General, Break, to Med
Dress, to SJ GR A, to HT Int
Accom Tw, SC
Exclusions Age Limit, 5,
No hacking or trekking
Location On N2 Slane - Derry road,
10 mins from Dublin Airport, 20 mins
from City Centre

Riding in the Channel Islands

**LA HAIE FLEURIE
LIVERY & RIDING**
La Haie Fleurie, St Martin,
Jersey,
Channel Islands, JE3 6BN
Tel 01534 857748
Contact Miss C F Binet
Riding School Inst Riding & Jumping
Specialities General instruction -
Courses - Livery - Breaking & schooling
- Shows
Staff Chief Instructor Miss C F Binet
Plus 2 full time instructors
Ave No 4 Horses, 9 Ponies
Courses YT, Short
Facilities
Outdoor Manege 80 x 20
Outdoor Manege 40 x 20
CC: Course, Nov, Banks, Water,
Natural
Lec Rm, Vis Aids, Chng Rm, Wait Rm,
Tack Shop
Hacking
Livery Full, P/T
Schooling General, to Nov Dress,
to SJ GR B

MULTINA RIDING SCHOOL
Ville au Neveu, St Ouen,
Jersey,
Channel Islands
Tel 01534 481843
Contact Mr & Mrs J Phillips
Riding School Inst Basic
Specialities Basic instruction - Hacking
3 full time instructors
Ave No 4 Horses, 8 Ponies
inc 1 SJ Jun C
Courses YT
Facilities
Outdoor Manege 60 x 40
SJ: 1 Paddock
CC: Basic
Hacking
Livery Full, P/T, DIY, Break, School,
Grass

Riding Overseas

The BHS Overseas Approval Scheme is growing steadily and additional establishments may have been approved since publication.
Please check with the BHS Training and Examinatons Office for the most up-to-date information.

BELGIUM

THE LORD NEWCASTLE STABLES BVBA
BrusselsesTeenweg 195, 1560
Hoeilaart, Belgium
Tel 00 3226573089
Contact Mr D Soyer BHSI
Riding School Inst to BHSII
Specialities Dressage, Sidesaddle, Vaulting
Staff Chief Instructor Mr D Soyer (BHSI)
Plus 1 full time instructor
Ave No 6 Horses, 2 Ponies
inc 6 El Dress, 6 Med Dress
Courses WP, Short, Ev, P/T, Hol
Facilities
Covered School 22 x 44 gly
Outdoor Manege 70 x 25
Lec Rm, Vis Aids, Chng Rm, Showers, Wait Rm
Hacking
Livery Full
Schooling General, Break, to Adv Dress, to HT Nov
Exclusions No unescorted riding

DUBAI

DUBAI EQUESTRIAN CENTRE
P.O. Box 292, Dubai,
United Arab Emirates
Tel 00 9714 361394
Contact Miss Joanne Ivimey
Riding School, Training Centre, Facility Centre Inst to BHSAI
Staff Chief Instructor Miss Joanne Ivimey (BHSII, BHS SM)
Plus 3 full time instructors
Ave No 90 Horses, 30 Ponies
inc 6 El Dress, 3 Med Dress, 10 SJ GR C, 2 SJ GR B, 10 SJ GR A, 1 vaulting pony
Courses Short, P/T, Hol
Facilities
Outdoor Manege 140 x 90 fl lt
Outdoor Manege 80 x 80 fl lt
Outdoor Manege 30 x 60 fl lt
SJ: Nov, Grade C, Grade B, Grade A
CC: Basic, Water, Natural, Gallops,

7 Schooling
Lec Rm, Vis Aids, Chng Rm, Showers, Wait Rm, Tack Shop
Hacking
Livery Full, Break, School
Schooling General, Break, to Nov Dress, to El Dress, to Med Dress, to SJ GR C, to SJ GR B, to SJ GR A
Accom Db, FB, SC
Exclusions Wt Limit, 14st, Age Limit, 7, No unaccompanied hacking
Location 15 kilometers from airport in the 'Nad al shiba' area

GREECE

THE EQUESTRIAN FARM OF CRETE
Karteros 71500, Karteros,
Iraklion, Crete, Greece
Tel 00 30 81 380244
Contact Mr & Mrs V Grammatikakis
Training Centre
Specialities Riding holidays, Horse & Wagon tours
Staff Chief Instructor Mr Grammatikakis
Plus 1 full time instructor
Ave No 39 Horses, 5 Ponies
Facilities
Outdoor Manege 60 x 40
Wait Rm
Accom Tw, F, Cottage, FB
Exclusions Escorted riding only
Location 5 minutes from Heraklion Airport

HONG KONG

THE HONG KONG JOCKEY CLUB
Beas River Riding School,
Sheung Shui, New Territories,
Hong Kong
Tel 00 852 2966 1980
Contact Mr M S Tibbatts
Riding School, Training Centre, Facility Centre Inst to BHSAI
Specialities Career training
Staff Chief Instructor Mr Nick Rodgers (BHSI)
Plus 9 full time instructors

Ave No 175 Horses, 22 Ponies
inc 15 El Dress, 9 Med Dress, 22 SJ
GR C, 18 SJ GR B, 22 SJ GR A,
21 HT Int
Courses Short, P/T, Hol
Facilities
Covered School 30 x 50
Outdoor Manege 20 x 40
Outdoor Manege 20 x 40
Outdoor Manege 59 x 130
Outdoor Manege 60 x 120
SJ: Grade A, 2 Paddock
CC: Course, Nov, Banks, Water,
Natural, Gallops
Lec Rm, Vis Aids, Chng Rm, Showers,
Wait Rm, Tack Shop
Hacking
Livery Full, P/T
Schooling General, to Med Dress,
to SJ GR B, to HT Int
Accom S, F, Dor, Cottage, FB, SC
Exclusions Wt Limit, 12st7 / 180lbs,
Age Limit, 7, No DIY livery, No trekking

LEI YUE MUN
PUBLIC RIDING SCHOOL
1 Chaiwan Road, Hong Kong
Tel 00 852 2568 9776
Contact Mr M S Tibbatts
Riding School Inst Riding & Jumping
Specialities All round instruction in
equitation
Staff Chief Instructor Miss G Porter
(BHSAI, BHS Int.SM)
Plus 3 full time instructors
Ave No 23 Horses, 10 Ponies
Facilities
Outdoor Manege 50 x 25
Outdoor Manege 30 x 20
SJ: Nov
Lec Rm, Vis Aids, Chng Rm, Showers,
Wait Rm
Hacking
Schooling General, to Nov Dress,
to SJ GR C
Exclusions Wt Limit, 12st, Age Limit, 7,
No unescorted hacking
Location Chaiwan Road, Hong Kong

POKFULAM
PUBLIC RIDING SCHOOL
75 Pokfulam Reservoir Road,
Pokfulam, Hong Kong
Tel 00 852 2550 1359
Contact Mr M S Tibbatts
Riding School, Training Centre Inst
Riding & Jumping
Specialities RDA and Vaulting
Staff Chief Instructor Miss G Porter
(BHSAI, BHS Int.SM)
Plus 2 full time instructors

Ave No 22 Horses, 14 Ponies
inc 2 El Dress, 2 SJ GR C
Courses WP, Short, P/T, Hol
Facilities
Outdoor Manege 40 x 18 fl lt
Lec Rm, Vis Aids, Chng Rm, Showers,
Wait Rm
Hacking
Schooling General, to Nov Dress
Accom Db, Dor, SC
Exclusions Age Limit, 7
Location On Hong Kong Island -
Pokfulam Reservoir Road

TUEN MUN
PUBLIC RIDING SCHOOL
Lot 45 Lung Mun Road, Tuen Mun,
New Territories, Hong Kong
Tel 00 852 24613338
Contact Mr M S Tibbatts
Riding School, Training Centre Inst to
BHSAI
Staff Chief Instructor Miss G Porter
(BHSAI, BHS Int.SM)
Plus 3 full time instructors
Ave No 40 Horses, 20 Ponies
inc 4 El Dress, 10 SJ GR C
Courses Short, Hol
Facilities
Outdoor Manege 90 x 45 fl lt
Outdoor Manege 60 x 40 fl lt
Outdoor Manege 40 x 20 fl lt
SJ: Grade C
Lec Rm, Vis Aids, Chng Rm, Showers,
Wait Rm
Hacking
Schooling to El Dress, to SJ GR C
Exclusions Wt Limit, 12st, Age Limit, 7,
No children under 7
Location North west corner of New
Territories in Tuen Mun City

MALAYSIA

BUKIT KIARA RESORT BERHAD
Jalan Bukit Kiara, Off Jalan Damansara,
60000 Kuala Lumpur, Malaysia
Tel 00 603 254 1222
Contact Dato Kamaruddin Bin Abdul
Ghani
Riding School, Country Club Inst
Riding & Jumping
Staff Chief Instructor Mr Syamri
Santaroena
Plus 3 full time instructors
Ave No 114 Horses, 18 Ponies
inc 1 El Dress, 1 SJ GR C
Facilities
Covered School 91 x 46
Outdoor Manege 90 x 50

Outdoor Manege 87 x 158
Outdoor Manege 15 x 30
SJ: Nov
Lec Rm, Vis Aids, Chng Rm, Showers,
Wait Rm, Tack Shop
Hacking
Livery Full, P/T, Break, School
Schooling General, Break, to El Dress,
to SJ GR C
Exclusions Only open to Bukit Kiara
Resort Berhad Members

SPAIN

CENTRO ECUESTRE EPONA
Apartado De Correos No 86,
Carmona 41410,
Sevilla, Spain
Tel 00 34 9 08 155359
Contact Senor & Senora F A Garcia
Carvajal
Riding School, Training Centre Inst
Riding & Jumping
Specialities Intensive riding and stable
managent training courses, childrens'
summer camps & riding holidays
3 full time instructors
Ave No 30 Horses, 20 Ponies
inc 1 Med Dress, 2 Adv Dress,
2 SJ GR C
Courses WP, YT, Short, Ev, P/T, Hol
Facilities
Covered School 40 x 20 gly
Outdoor Manege 18 x 36 fl lt
Outdoor Manege 15 x 30 fl lt
Outdoor Manege 20 x 60
SJ: Grade A, 1 Paddock
CC: Nov, Banks, Natural, 12 Schoollng
Lec Rm, Vis Aids, Chng Rm, Showers,
Wait Rm, Tack Shop
Hacking
Livery Full
Schooling General, to Med Dress,
to SJ GR C
Accom Tw, FB
Exclusions No unescorted hacking
Location Carmona - five minutes drive
from Sevilla Airport

ESCUELA DE ARTE ECUESTRE
'Costa del Sol'
(Acuazahara, S.A.), C/N 340 Km. 159.
Rio Padron Alto s/n, P.O.B 266, 29680
Estepona, Malaga, Spain
Tel 00 34 952 808077
Contact Mr T I Schmutzer
Riding School, Training Centre Inst
Riding & Jumping
Specialities Recreational and leisure
activities. Training for professional
qualifications
Ave No 25 Horses, 40 Ponies
Courses WP, YT, Short, Ev, P/T, Hol
Facilities
Covered School 64 x 24 gly
Outdoor Manege 7 x 7 fl lt
SJ: Nov, Grade C
Lec Rm, Vis Aids, Chng Rm, Showers,
Wait Rm, Tack Shop
Hacking
Livery Full, Break, School
Schooling General, Break, to Adv
Dress, to SJ GR C

HIPICA INTERNACIONAL
Escuela de Equitacion,
Camino de la Sierra 75, Churriana,
Malaga 29140, Spain
Tel 00 34 9 52 435549
Contact Ms Sally Harrison
Riding School Inst Riding & Jumping
Specialities Courses in riding and
stable management for children and
adults
Staff Chief Instructor Mrs Sally
Harrison-McLaren (BHSAI, BHS Int
Teach)
Ave No 10 Horses, 13 Ponies
Courses WP, Short, Ev, P/T, Hol
Facilities
Outdoor Manege 55 x 30 fl lt
Outdoor Manege 20 x 30
SJ: Nov
Chng Rm, Showers, Wait Rm
Livery Full, DIY, School
Schooling General
Accom S, Tw, Dor, FB
Exclusions No private hire
Location Malaga, Costa del Sol

MANAS DE LA HOZ
Escuela de Formacion Ecuestre,
39776 Liendo, Cantabria, Spain
Tel 00 34 9 42 643014
Contact Mariangeles Bravo de
Delclaux
Riding School, Training Centre Inst
Riding & Jumping
Specialities Student training, childrens'
riding holidays and recreational riding
3 full time instructors
Ave No 60 Horses, 16 Ponies
inc 5 Adv Dress, 3 SJ GR C, 1 x
Olympic
Courses WP, YT, Short, Ev, P/T, Hol
Facilities
Covered School 20 x 40
Outdoor Manege 80 x 60
SJ: Nov, 1 Paddock
CC: Course, Basic
Lec Rm, Vis Aids, Chng Rm, Showers,

Wait Rm
Hacking
Livery Full, P/T, Break, School
Schooling General, Break, to Adv
Dress, to SJ GR C
Accom S, Tw, Dor, FB
Exclusions Age Limit, 6,
No unescorted hacking
Location Approx 48 kms south of
Bilbao

USA

AVERETT COLLEGE
EQUESTRIAN CENTER
420 West Main Street, Danville,
VA 24541, USA
Tel 910 388 5950 barn
Contact Ms Mary Harcourt
Riding School, Training Centre,
Facility Centre, Stud (Reg. Stallion -
D W Oldenburg) Inst Riding & Jumping
Specialities Combined training
1 full time instructor
Ave No 40 Horses, 5 Ponies
inc 8 El Dress, 3 Med Dress,
5 SJ GR C
Courses WP, Short, Ev, P/T
Facilities
Covered School 30 x 60 gly
Outdoor Manege 30 x 60
Outdoor Manege 45 x 70
SJ: Nov, Grade C
CC: Course, Basic, Banks, Water,
Natural, Gallops, 15 Schooling
Lec Rm, Vis Aids, Chng Rm
Livery Break, School
Schooling General, Break, to El Dress,
to SJ GR C, to HT Nov
Exclusions No casual clients
Location Border of Virginia & North
Carolina, Route 29 near Danville

BITTERROOT RANCH
1480 East Fork Road, Dubois,
Wyoming 82513, USA
Tel 00 1 307 455 2778
Contact Bayard & Mel Fox
Specialities Western Riding
Ave No 100 Horses
inc Western Riding
Facilities
Outdoor Manege 60 x 30
SJ: Nov
Chng Rm, Showers
Accom Cottage, FB
Location Head of remote valley in the
Absaroka Mountains of north-west
Wyoming

CURRAGH EQUESTRIAN CENTRE
5595 Ben Day Murrin Road,
Fort Worth, Texas 76126, USA
Tel 001 817 443 3777
Contact Ms Noreen Corlett
Riding School, Training Centre Inst to
BHSAI
Specialities Training for Competition
(CT, Stadium Jumping, Dressage).
Summer camps for children, Adult short
courses, Breaking & Training young
horses
Ave No 10 Horses, 7 Ponies
inc 3 El Dress, 5 SJ GR C
Courses WP, Short, Hol
Facilities
Covered School 24 x 66 gly
Outdoor Manege 30 x 61
SJ: Grade B, 2 Paddock
CC: Course, Nov, Banks, Water, Natural,
40 Schooling
Lec Rm, Vis Aids, Chng Rm
Livery Full, P/T, Break, School
Schooling General, Break, to Adv
Dress, to SJ GR B, to HT Int
Accom Tw, Dor, Caravan, FB, SC
Exclusions Wt Limit, 16st, Age Limit, 6,
No hirelings
Location 5 miles South of Benbrook on
FM 1187 East of 377

DELAWARE VALLEY COLLEGE
700 E Butler Avenue, Doylestown,
PA 18901, USA
Tel 00 1 215 345 1500
Contact Ms Karin Glassman
Training Centre, Livery Inst Riding &
Jumping
Specialities General flat and jumping to
BHS Stage II level. Stable management
skills. Driving & Vaulting
Staff Chief Instructor Miss Karin
Glassman
Plus 1 full time instructor
Ave No 41 Horses, 1 Ponies
inc 8 El Dress, 6 Med Dress,
12 SJ GR C, 2 SJ GR B,
5 Driving Horses & 2 Vaulting horses
Courses Short, Ev, P/T, Hol
Facilities
Covered School 26 x 73 gly
Outdoor Manege 30 x 61
SJ: Nov, Grade C, 1 Paddock
CC: Basic, Nov, Banks, Water, Natural
Lec Rm, Vis Aids, Chng Rm, Wait Rm
Livery Full
Accom Tw, Db, F, FB, SC
Exclusions Age Limit, 17,
No casual clients
Location Main entrance off Route 202,
approximately 15 minutes Penn Turnpike

**GRAND CYPRESS
EQUESTRIAN CENTER**
Grand Cypress Resort,
One Equestrian Drive,
Orlando, Florida 32836, USA
Tel 00 1 407 239 1938
Contact Ms Elizabeth Trellue
**Riding School, Training Centre,
Facility Centre, Trekking Centre** Inst
Riding & Jumping
Specialities Training & teaching facility
as part of top class resort. Vocational
training for clients and apprentice
grooms and instructors.
Top competition venue for stadium
jumping & hunter jumper shows.
Dressage competitions to FEI level.
Childrens' programmes linked to
progressive riding tests
5 full time instructors
Ave No 28 Horses, 6 Ponies
inc 5 El Dress, 1 Adv Dress, 2 SJ GR C
Courses WP, Short, Ev, P/T, Hol
Facilities
Covered School 30 x 60 gly
Outdoor Manege 40 x 60 fl lt
Outdoor Manege 45 x 75 fl lt
SJ: Grade A, 1 Paddock
CC: Course, Nov, Banks, Natural,
Gallops, 20 Schooling
Lec Rm, Vis Aids, Chng Rm, Showers,
Wait Rm, Tack Shop
Hacking
Livery Full, Break, School
Schooling General, Break, to Med
Dress, to SJ GR B, to HT Nov
Accom S, Tw, Db, F, Dor, FB, SC
Exclusions Wt Limit, 15.7st / 225lbs,
No grazing due to climate
Location Orlando, Florlda

**THE MILLBROOK
EQUESTRIAN CENTRE**
Bangall-Amenia Road, RDI,
Box 120, Millbrook, NY12545, USA
Tel (914) 373 9626
Contact Mr P Lindsay BHSII
**Riding School, Training Centre,
Facility Centre** Inst to BHSII
Specialities Comprehensive range of
equestrian training in all disciplines, inc
field hunting. Advanced CT competition
facility. Training courses for professional
levels. BHS exam centre, extensive trail
riding (off road) through beautiful New
England countryside
Staff Chief Instructor Mrs J Armour
(BHS SM, BHS T)
Plus 5 full time instructors
Ave No 11 Horses, 3 Ponies
inc 9 El Dress
Courses WP, Short, Ev, P/T, Hol

Facilities
Covered School 26 x 67 gly gly
Outdoor Manege 25 x 62 fl lt
Outdoor Manege 25 x 62 fl lt
Outdoor Manege 25 x 62 fl lt
Outdoor Manege 70 x 70 fl lt
SJ: Grade B, 1 Paddock
CC: Course, Basic, Nov, Int, Adv,
Banks, Water, Natural, 40 Schooling
Lec Rm, Vis Aids, Chng Rm, Showers,
Wait Rm, Tack Shop
Hacking
Livery Full, Break, School, Hunt, Grass
Schooling General, Break, to Adv
Dress, to SJ GR A, to HT Adv
Accom S, Tw, SC
Exclusions Age Limit, 5,
No unaccompanied trail riding
Location 2 hours north of New York
City, USA

NORTHWIND STABLES
303 CR 179,
Leander, TX 78641, USA
Tel 00 1 512 259 3009
Contact Ms Kathy Guertin
Riding School, Training Centre Inst
to BHSAI
Specialities Beginner/nervous riders.
Training young horses and re-schooling
problem horses. Horse conditioning
Staff Chief Instructor Miss Kathy
Guertin
Plus 1 full time instructor
Ave No 28 Horses, 6 Ponies
inc 1 Med Dress, 1 SJ GR C
Facilities
Covered School 24 x 46
Outdoor Manege 30 x 61 fl lt
SJ: Nov
Chng Rm, Wait Rm
Livery Full, Break, School, Grass
Schooling General, Break, to Adv
Dress, to SJ GR C, to HT Nov
Exclusions Age Limit, 7,
No horse rentals,
No unaccompanied children
Location 1/2 hour drive north of Austin

RINGWOOD MANOR FARM
5016 Hyde Road, Cumming,
Atlanta, Georgia 30130, USA
Tel 00 1 770 667 1379
Contact Ms Linda Allen
Riding School, Training Centre Inst
to BHSAI
Specialities Training horse and rider
for stadium jumping, junior equitation
classes, show hunters & nervous adult
amateurs
Ave No 5 Horses, 2 Ponies

inc 2 SJ Jun C, Show Hunters
Courses WP, Short, Ev, P/T, Hol
Facilities
SJ: Grade B
Lec Rm, Vis Aids, Wait Rm
Livery Full, Break, School, Hunt
Schooling General, Break, to SJ GR B
Accom S, Tw, SC
Exclusions Age Limit, 8No horse
rentals
Location 30 minutes north of Atlanta.
7 1/2 miles off Georgis 400 on borders
of Alpharetta horse community

SALEM-TEIKYO UNIVERSITY
Equine Careers & Industry Management,
223 West Main Street,
PO Box 500, Salem WV 26426, USA
Tel 304 782 5322/4528
Contact Mrs Cecile K Hetzel Dunn
Inst Riding & Jumping
Specialities saddle seat/stock seat
2 full time instructors
Ave No 25 Horses, 25 Ponies
inc 4 El Dress, Western and saddleseat
Facilities
Covered School 60 x 40 gly
SJ: Nov
Lec Rm, Vis Aids, Chng Rm, Showers,
Wait Rm
Hacking
Livery Full
Schooling General, Break, to Nov
Dress
Accom S, Db, Dor, SC
Exclusions Age Limit, 7O,
Only students from university,
No casual clients

TEX-OVER FARMS
13217 Kidd Road, Conroe,
Texas, USA
Tel 00 1 409 273 2416
Contact Mr Paul Kathen
Riding School, Training Centre Inst
to BHSAI
Specialities Competition training for
horse & rider across CT, Dressage &
stadium jumping to top levels for horse
owners
Staff Chief Instructor Mr Paul Kathen
Plus 3 full time instructors

Ave No 3 Horses, 1 Ponies
inc 1 El Dress, 2 SJ GR C
Courses WP, Short, Ev, P/T, Hol
Facilities
Covered School 35 x 70
Covered School 15 x 15
Outdoor Manege 20 x 60 fl lt
Outdoor Manege 40 x 85
Outdoor Manege 20 x 20
Lec Rm, Vis Aids, Chng Rm, Showers,
Wait Rm
Livery Full, Break, School, Hunt
Schooling General, Break, to Adv
Dress, to SJ GR A, to HT Adv
Exclusions Wt Limit, 240lbs,
Age Limit, 6,
No horse rentals,
No racing, no driving
Location 20 miles north of Houston

WOODCOCK HILL
RIDING ACADEMY
17 Marsh Road, Willington,
Connecticut, 06279, USA
Tel 00 1 860 487 1686
Contact Ms M G Tenney
Riding School, Training Centre,
Facility Centre Inst to BHSAI
Staff Chief Instructor Ms M G Tenney
(BHSAI)
Plus 2 full time instructors
Ave No 30 Horses, 4 Ponies
inc 7 El Dress, 5 Med Dress, 4 Adv
Dress, 2 Spec Horse Trials Novice,
2 FEI Dressage
Courses WP, Short, Ev, P/T, Hol
Facilities
Covered School 26 x 65 gly
Outdoor Manege 50 x 100
SJ: Nov
CC: Basic, Banks, Water, Natural,
3 Schooling
Lec Rm, Vis Aids, Chng Rm
Livery Full, Break, School
Schooling General, Break, to Nov
Dress, to El Dress, to Med Dress,
to Adv Dress
Accom Tw, Cottage, SC
Exclusions Wt Limit, 12st, Age Limit, 5
Location 60 miles east of Boston,
5 miles off Interstate 84 at (exit 68),
Willington, Connecticut

Index
of BHS-Approved
Establishments